JUN

D0426711

A Difficult Woman

A Difficult Woman

*The Challenging Life and Times of
Lillian Hellman*

ALICE KESSLER-HARRIS

BLOOMSBURY PRESS

New York · Berlin · London · Sydney

Published by Bloomsbury Press, New York

All papers used by Bloomsbury Press are natural, recyclable products made from wood grown in well-managed forests. The manufacturing processes conform to the environmental regulations of the country of origin.

LIBRARY OF CONGRESS CATALOGING-IN-PUBLICATION DATA

Kessler-Harris, Alice.
A difficult woman : the challenging life and times of
Lillian Hellman / Alice Kessler-Harris.
p.   cm.
Includes bibliographical references and index.
ISBN 978-1-59691-363-9 (hardback)
1. Hellman, Lillian, 1905–1984. 2. Dramatists, American—20th century—
Biography. 3. Hellman, Lillian, 1905–1984—Political and social views. I. Title.
PS3515.E343Z74 2012
812'.52—dc22
[B]
2011028065

First U.S. edition 2012

1 3 5 7 9 10 8 6 4 2

Typeset by Westchester Book Group
Printed in the U.S.A. by Quad/Graphics, Fairfield, Pennsylvania

For Emma and Molly and Jake

and

For Daniel and Eddie and Callie

With hope and joy and love

Contents

Introduction

If a man could say nothing against a character but what he can prove, history could not be written; for a great deal is known of men of which proof cannot be brought.
—*John Boswell,* The Life of Samuel Johnson

In 1976, aged seventy-one, playwright and memoirist Lillian Hellman posed in a mink coat for a resonant advertisement. Cigarette in hand, gazing insouciantly at the camera, Hellman claimed the legendary status she craved. Her flirtatious stance, self-confident amid the wrinkled features, her posture at once brazen and enticing, Hellman gazed directly at the viewer. The advertisement did not reveal the name of its model. It did not have to. Everyone who read *Vogue* and the *New Yorker* and the other magazines in which the advertisement appeared would know that this was Lillian Hellman. She was at the peak of celebrity. In addition to a fistful of plays whose names were well known, she was a heroine to young women who adored her two bestselling memoirs. A star-studded celebration of her seventieth birthday had recently been covered in all the society pages. Just months before the advertisement appeared, Hellman published her third volume of nonfiction, *Scoundrel Time.* So controversial was that volume, and so divisive, that when the mink coat advertisements hit the stands, Hellman had already begun her long decline from the pinnacle of fame to the depths of notoriety.

1976: Everyone would know that this was Lillian Hellman. (Image courtesy of The Advertising Archives)

What was it, I wondered as I started on this book, that made Hellman's life matter so much to so many? To be sure, it traversed most of what historian Eric Hobsbawm has labeled the short twentieth century, the period that saw the rise and demise of the communist Soviet Union. Her life reveals the multiple tensions within which every politically engaged American juggled options and choices during that challenging period. Hellman was born in 1905, came to maturity with the flapper generation of the 1920s, learned her politics in the Depression-era thirties, became a celebrity playwright and movie scriptwriter during World War II, when America needed heroes, and earned her stripes in the struggle against McCarthyism in the early fifties. She survived blacklisting to become an idol of the New Left and the second wave of the women's movement, only to succumb to red-baiting and character assassination at the end of her days. She was, and is still, dragged from the grave to serve as an example of the perils of mendacity. But her words are still quoted, her plays are regularly revived, and her example still inspires.

It was hard to believe that this complicated and forthright woman had come to such a bad end in the popular imagination. Like many of my contemporaries, I read—devoured would be more accurate—Lillian Hellman's autobiographical work as it appeared in the late sixties and early seventies: *An Unfinished Woman* in 1969, *Pentimento* in 1973, and then *Scoundrel Time* in 1976. These memoirs, which deeply moved me at the time, drifted into obscurity in the wake of continuing accusations that they reflected more fiction than fact. More than a quarter century after her death her name still evokes bitter feelings. How had it happened, I wondered, that Lillian Hellman, once so honored and famous, admired for her blunt and plainspoken style, had become the archetype of hypocrisy, the quintessential liar, the embodiment of ugliness? How was it that she was so widely remembered as a rigid Stalinist, an angry woman, a greedy, self-aggrandizing individual in a world where so many others had committed many of the same sins? Why had these characterizations, this negative reputation and the controversy that swirled around her, so long survived her death in 1984? This book tries to answer these questions not by reassessing her character but by thinking through her relationship to the twentieth century. The questions that trouble me are not so much about her psychic dimensions—the traditional subject of the literary biographer—or even about the soil from which she grew, the question most often raised by the historical biographer. Rather, I wonder about what is to be learned from the surviving images of Lillian Hellman, from the sharp disjuncture between the glamorous and celebrated playwright and the "ugly" woman of popular memory.

The answers to these questions seem to me to lie in the historical drama within which Hellman acted her part: in the multifaceted and politically splintered America in which she spent her days. In Hellman's lifetime, America fought several wars for democracy and freedom abroad, yet engaged in extended episodes of political repression at home. Her life engaged a century during which women strode toward economic and political equality, yet remained constrained by popular images of beauty and models of traditional family relationships. This was a century when celebrity conferred fame, money, and standing, of which Hellman had her full share, yet it placed its recipients in the glare of constant publicity, turning them into public property. At the century's start, the nation challenged immigrants to assimilate by eliminating differences of language and culture; by its end, it encouraged pride in multiculturalism and unique qualities of ethnicity and identity. During the twentieth century, efforts to achieve the good life for every citizen yielded remarkable success, but they also produced an arrogant stance in the world. The twentieth century pitted two competing ideological systems against each other, fostering intense conflicts about the meaning of loyalty and the definition of virtue.

Lillian Hellman, as a historical figure who faced difficult choices, lived in a century sharply divided by ideology and morality. Repeatedly she made decisions about where to locate her political allegiance; how to construct her life as a woman in a world that limited women's aspirations; what it meant to live as a Jew, a southerner, a writer at a time when these identities all carried gender, economic, and political connotations that she only half understood and sometimes explicitly rejected. These issues could not be neatly separated. Her identity, her friendships, her sexuality, her writing, and her politics sustained and infected each other, producing an amalgam that was at once idiosyncratic and complicated and very American.

My task has been to see how the life of a single woman can help us to understand some of the salient contradictions of a challenging century by highlighting the thorny situations that Hellman faced. Fortunately, my job has been made easier by the spate of more traditional biographies that have already appeared. These (especially two very good ones by Carl Rollyson and Deborah Martinson) offer thoroughly researched accounts of Hellman's daily life.[1] I gratefully refer readers who wish to follow Hellman "cradle to grave" to them. Here I choose another path, one to which the historian is perhaps particularly attuned. I seek not only to explore how the world in which Hellman lived shaped the choices she made, but to ask how the life she lived illuminates the world she confronted. There is yet a third layer. Because Hellman's life seems to me to so deeply encapsulate many of the twentieth century's challenges, I ask as well how a changing political environment influences popular perceptions of her life. Hellman's actions alone, I argue, cannot account for the transformation in her reputation. Rather, over time, critics, reviewers, political friends and enemies collectively formulated a life that reshaped Lillian Hellman, turning her into something of a Rorschach test. Critics and friends alike viewed her through their own eyes and their own ideological biases. They helped to construct the Lillian Hellman whose work and reputation persists. That Lillian Hellman is an amalgam of the person and of our image of the person; of the good and the bad that she did and was thought to have done. This then is a book (a biography if you will) about a woman, about the idea of a woman, and about the world that formed and shaped her.

Hellman, living and dead, is a most uncooperative source. She was committed to controlling her own legacy and savvy enough to try to do so. In 1961, Hellman contracted to sell her early manuscripts to the Harry Ransom Center at the University of Texas at Austin, which also owns the papers of Hemingway, Faulkner, Fitzgerald, and many other major writers.[2] She was pleased that they wanted the manuscripts, and she settled for a generous initial purchase price along with an arrangement that would allow the library to accession some of the manuscripts immediately and to release others annually. As was then general practice, the library evaluated the additional accessions as it opened them to public use, recording them as gifts for which Hellman would receive tax deductions. Thereafter, she carefully adhered to her obligation to send future drafts of plays and published material to the library. But she rigorously excluded personal papers from the collection. In the seventies, she included provisions to donate her remaining manuscripts to the Harry Ransom Center in the several versions of her will. All of them instructed that personal papers be withheld as they "could be of no possible interest to anyone."

Because she wanted to remain the subject of her own imagination, Hellman tried, sometimes deliberately, to shape her image to her liking. In the diaries and appointment books that she kept sporadically all of her life, she often disguised the identities of lovers and friends. Recognizing herself as the butt of anger and misunderstanding, she frequently made up stories about herself, her childhood, and her family that illustrated who she wanted to be. With her friend Hannah Weinstein, she invented a fictional Mr. Schwartz who might or might not appear to marry her.[3] She narrated her stories in letters to friends, dinner-table conversations, and in four books of memoir and reminiscence that presented herself as she wished to be remembered. She destroyed, insofar as she could, anything that might allow another judgment or correction of the record. She asked her friends to return her letters to them. With a few exceptions (her first husband, Arthur Kober, didn't return her letters, nor did John Melby), they complied. Hellman then destroyed many of these and other letters.

At first, Hellman insisted that she wanted no biography written about her. "I am not sure that anybody's life shows us much about their work," she wrote, as she refused to cooperate with those who wanted to write about Dorothy Parker or Dashiell Hammett or herself. An early effort by

Stephen Marcus to undertake a biography of Hammett, her longtime lover, ended in discord and the threat of lawsuits. When she finally acquiesced to Diane Johnson's biography of Hammett, she monitored the sources and tried to control their interpretation, telling Johnson that she did not believe in "fictionalized biography" and hoped she would not write one.[4] When it became clear that biographers would write about her with or without her permission, she wrote to her friends asking them not to talk to them. The result, of course, was that, as William Wright confessed, he interviewed her enemies and produced a biography bent toward their derisive interpretations. At the end of her life, she appointed her friend and editor William Abrahams as her official biographer. She requested that the archive close all her papers to other researchers for an unspecified period of time. The archive complied. Abrahams gamely started the project, only to be interrupted by death.

Under these circumstances it would be folly to try to capture the "real" Lillian, whoever that is. Her story has emerged in bifurcated form. There is, first of all, the story as she remembered and wanted it. This perhaps was not deliberate manipulation so much as an artifact of the effort at self-representation. The writer Carol Kolmerten once noted that only when Kolmerten reread letters to her mother written during her first marriage did she notice that she had "constructed a fictional narrative of my life that I perceived my female relatives wanted to hear."[5] Hellman would have been sympathetic. She described *An Unfinished Woman* as a memory book. She never said that *Pentimento* was a memoir; indeed she begged the editor of *Esquire* (which republished a piece of the book) to "not use the words 'memoir' or 'autobiography' in connection with the pieces."[6] She did not want these pieces, she wrote, to be thought of as a sequel to *An Unfinished Woman*. These were her stories. She was the heroine of her own play.

Because we cannot take at face value anything she says about herself, we are led to ask about the meaning of her self-representation. Hellman wrote extensively about issues of honesty, decency, and integrity. All her life she worried about the meaning of memory, sharply distinguishing the truth of memory from other forms of truth. She tells us in a dozen different ways that she does not believe there is any absolute standard of truth, that her memory is poor and that she writes "as she remembers" rather than what is true, that she despises those who live by pretense and sham. As if to confirm her self-evaluation, she clearly tells large and small lies, expands and contracts the truth, mixes up the events, misremembers years, times, and dates, and omits salient details about her life. None of this should surprise us. In the larger frame of history, questions of truth and lies permeate the past. And the historian, as the great Russianist E. H. Carr once said, is no hanging judge. He or she asks what the writer reveals about the dialogue between the individual and history rather than whether it is factual. The genre of memoir, where low standards of veracity prevail, is a particularly useful vehicle for understanding what a subject wants us to know. Freud tells us we all remember things that never happened and mis-remember things that did. That is an invitation to the historian to fit together the jigsaw puzzle in order to place what is forgotten or misremembered into a pattern of explanation.

Hellman's memoirs, published between 1969 and 1980, situated her in the midst of the twentieth century's great conflicts. Filled with invention, written with verve and style, her books described a risky and exciting life and turned her into a bestselling author. But they also led readers to probe her image of herself as a reliable reporter, to produce their own stories about Lillian Hellman. Hellman's deliberate fudging of detail provoked these examinations. She shortened the number of weeks she spent in Finland on her way home from the Soviet Union in 1937 to make it appear that she had time for another (probably fictional) excursion that she wanted to re-late. She sometimes stretched the number of months she spent in Moscow during the war from two to four and even six in order to make a point about her familiarity with the scene. And she routinely adopted writing tics like "most certainly" and "absolutely" that signaled what was least certain, least reliable.

At first these misrepresentations served Hellman well, dramatizing her perceptions, place, and politics even as they rode roughshod over literal truth. Exaggeration and elision are the prerogatives of the memoirist, who, unlike the autobiographer, does not promise to write with unvarnished fidelity. And Hellman is very good at telling stories that extract her read-ers' sympathies. Did bombs really fall in Valencia while she was there? Was she shoved under a bench by a policeman? Did Hemingway give her the manuscript of *To Have and Have Not* to read and critique in Paris or anywhere else? The stories effectively display Hellman's memories of panic, her self-doubt, her need for courage, and, finally, they speak to one woman's capacity to overcome terror and prevail. They are not the first or only oc-casions when she tells us how fear immobilized her but that she did the right thing in the end. Some stories seem to stretch credibility and to back-fire. In *Pentimento*, Hellman tells us that she delivered $50,000 to a friend in the Austrian resistance, Julia. This story was made into a film starring

Jane Fonda and Vanessa Redgrave. At first "Julia" served Lillian's purposes well. It positioned Hellman as a courageous anti-fascist, a person of princi-ple. But when a woman whose story resembled that of Julia came forward, Hellman was accused not merely of enhancement, exaggeration, and self-aggrandizement, but of theft: of appropriating someone else's life. That cast a light on Hellman's character that ultimately reflected on everything she touched.

Lillian Hellman was, if nothing else, a controversial figure. During her life and after, she was the object of adulation and anger, love and hate. When I started work on this book my friends and colleagues told me that this was a subject that had no rewards. They attached adjectives such as *evil, cruel*, and *vindictive* to Hellman's name. She was, I was told, a Stalinist, a liar, a self-hating Jew, at best a second-rate playwright, already forgotten. She was said to be a polarizing and dishonest person. There would be nothing but misery in tackling the life of this hateful person. Besides, there were already several accounts of her life, most of them negative.[7] Why write another? I took all of these comments seriously, thinking at first to avoid this python's nest and to go on to another, less controversial, project. But I am one of that generation of 1970s historians who have taken it upon them-selves to examine gender as an ideological force, and Hellman appealed too strongly.

By the time I started to work on this project in 2001 Hellman had be-come deeply embedded in negative mythology. Those who had already come to damaging conclusions about her had done so less out of knowl-edge about the woman than from commitment to particular ideologies. Their own sense of themselves as liberals, Zionists, or feminists infused what they "knew." Several biographies about her reinforced the negative images, each slipping into, and confirming, the already-existing descrip-tions of a wicked and evil woman. If the biographer dared to provide a more empathetic view of Hellman and her politics, she was taken to task by reviewers whose imaginations could not transcend an accepted public picture. Minds were made up. And yet this too tells us something about a century in which what was remembered was often conditioned by which side you were on.

I discovered this early on when I began to speak publicly about this book. The events routinely attracted large and lively audiences and pro-duced open and helpful discussions. But their aftermath provided unex-pected insights. On one occasion, after I addressed a forum of academics, a participant went home to tell her partner about the talk. An e-mail message the next day described to me how "he laced into Hellman attacking her for being an apologist for Stalin and never repenting, for her self-righteousness, for her lies and self-aggrandizements." On another, I gave a talk to a small seminar of women biographers in which I averred that part of what I wanted to do was to examine the meaning of calling Hellman a liar, of labeling her as "ugly." Hearing of my effort, a young person—not present at the seminar—protested that I was being too kind to Hellman. In a message to a colleague, he asked, "Did anyone say, at any point, in these agreeable proceedings, 'hold on, Hellman WAS a liar? . . . Whether or not (as a good friend once observed) she had a face that looked as if a mouse had died on it, she lied about her Party membership, she lied about Communist infiltration in the Wallace campaign, and she lied about anticommunist liberals and the magazines *Partisan Review* and *Commentary*, saying that they never attacked McCarthy."

The palpable anger embedded in these assertions emerges in the distortions they reaffirm. Hellman did, several times before 1976 and three times in *Scoundrel Time*, oppose the actions of Soviet dictators and admit that she had been wrong about Stalin; she was criticized for not saying so apologetically enough and with sufficient force. She did lie about her party membership, a necessary maneuver in the fifties when the economic consequences of admitting party membership could be dire. She continued to deny that she'd ever been in the party, as did many others who only after the fall of the Soviet Union admitted membership.[8] She informed Wallace that communists were involved in his campaign: that wasn't illegal in 1948, just unpalatable. She did not accuse those magazines of failing to attack McCarthy: she accused them of not standing by the victims. In words infused with a passionate abhorrence of a long-dead woman, the critics repeated crude gossip, introduced irrelevant connections between Hellman's appearance and her politics, and repeated charges no more accurate than Hellman's defenses.

I puzzled over whether these rifts could have been due to fallout surrounding the Communist Party, of which she, like many of her peers, was briefly a part. But others had long been forgiven party membership and honored to boot. Paul Robeson, Langston Hughes, and Pete Seeger come immediately to mind. And, as this book demonstrates, neither in the period of her membership from 1939 to late 1941 nor afterward did she follow the party line. Robert Newman, who has studied the subject more carefully than anyone else, counts her as, at best, a bit player.[9] She was and remained what has come to be called a "fellow traveler." She never gave up her vision of a society with a greater measure of social and racial justice, and she clung longer and more naïvely than many to the hope that the Soviet Union might mend itself and prove to be a reasonable model. Many of her friends, including Arthur Miller, Aaron Copland, and Marc Blitzstein, did as much.

To what, then, was Hellman's capacity to elicit vituperation and anger due? Certainly her self-righteous stance, her continuing moral certainty, and her willingness to fight back played a role. Her continuing belief that she had "done no harm" irked many. To those who recognized the horrors of Soviet Communism early on, she and others who continued to believe in the possibilities of socialism in any form seemed willfully blind or complicit. Hellman's publicly acclaimed refusal to cooperate with the House Committee on Un-American Activities in 1952 fueled the anger of anticommunists who seethed at her unwillingness to acknowledge her sins and her escape from the punishments others experienced. Coming from a woman, the finger-pointing proved especially galling. But her greatest offense, and the one that called forth the most scathing denunciation, was her insistence on holding to account those who had failed to defend the victims of McCarthyism. Then and afterward she became, to anticommunists on the right and left, a kind of lightning rod, attracting public disapproval and criticism not because of her failures but because of her strengths. She had, after all, positioned herself as a truth teller, as a patriot acting in defense of American values.

Hellman's moralism (her insistence that she stood for truth, loyalty, antagonism to corruption, commitment to social justice, and racial egalitarianism) may have been her undoing, placing her, as it did, at the fulcrum of ideological disagreement. That she could not live up to her moral claims makes her merely human. But that she insisted on pointing fingers at those who did not live up to theirs turned her into a pariah. Her refusal to bend, her insistence on claiming the moral high ground, reignited a battle that some might have thought over. In *Scoundrel Time*, published in 1976, a quarter century after the events they described, Hellman argued that during the McCarthy period she and others had acted in the best traditions of American dissent. Others had flunked the moral test, failed to stand up to the bullies. In turn, accusations of Stalinism—rigid adherence to a particular line and intolerance for any who rejected it; unquestioning commitment to the politics of the Soviet Union—surfaced once again. The accusations came to implicate both her ideas and her personality. She was dismissed as strident and rude, her persona identified with cruelty and evil. Once a minor player on the political stage, she became the epitome of factionalization on the left. Long after the specific meaning of Stalinism has been lost to most American adults, when the word itself evokes a naïve commitment to brutal totalitarianism, Lillian Hellman remains a symbol of heightened ideological dispute, of malevolent and unreasoning thought and behavior.

"Would any of this have happened in the same way," sociologist Cynthia Epstein asked me, "if Hellman were not a woman?" I tend to think not. Hellman's life as a woman contains, as Patricia Meyer Spacks has pointed out, a crucial contradiction around the issue of freedom. Hellman sought freedom not only in the world but for herself. That search, as Spacks notes, is illusory, perhaps in general, but certainly for women.[10] And yet, Hellman was a spirited and independent soul who never gave up her search for love even as her anger and frustration worked against ever achieving it. Smart and straightforward, filled with wit and humor, she was by turns generous and judgmental. And she was breathtakingly courageous in her defense of civil liberties at a time when to stand up for what was right could exact a tremendous personal price. She wrote about herself with both pride and self-mockery, worrying about her sexual attractiveness and her looks even as she articulated an idealistic political morality.

Hellman's position as a woman among men confuses the situation further. And here, once again, she illuminates the tensions embedded in the twentieth-century transformation of women's lives and gendered power relationships. Arguably, she became the economically successful playwright and celebrity she was by blurring gender boundaries. In her role as a playwright in the 1930s and '40s, she ignored her place "as a woman," behaving "like a man" in the sense that she simply did as she pleased without apparent attention to prevailing gender norms. She did not, in her plays, turn romance and domesticity into plot lines. Feminine as she certainly was in her private life and private moments, Hellman never made any effort to craft a public feminine self, putting forward instead a transgressive persona. She insisted on writing serious plays about serious subjects and on presenting them in first-class venues. She was ambitious, quick to anger, and often rude and dismissive. She smoked like a chimney and used offensive language.

Her willingness to transgress drew fire while she was alive and continues to do so. Critics still compare her unfavorably to tough, sexy women of the thirties like Joan Crawford and Greta Garbo.[11] Of this insistence on placing her among women, Hellman is not the only victim. Poet and novelist Muriel Spark, a recent reviewer noted, behaved "like any number of male writers, including ones much less talented than she, but as a woman, so ruthlessly and coldheartedly in pursuit of her art she was a little ahead of her time."[12] Small wonder, then, that Hellman quickly earned an unenviable reputation for being demanding, greedy, ambitious, loud, and bad-tempered. The evidence suggests that she was, at times, all of these things. Yet her quick and angry style, her sexual energy, might have drawn less critical attention in a similarly situated male.

Hellman positioned herself as a southerner, a Jew, and a playwright before she ever identified herself as a woman. Yet she could not escape the pigeonhole of what a woman was supposed to be. In the eyes of many, she remained a woman first, forever assessed as a woman playwright, a daughter of the South, a renegade Jewish woman. So it was with her sexuality. Hellman's autonomous and vigorous pursuit of sexual satisfaction reflected the risky goals of young women of her class in the 1920s. Nor did Hellman change these behaviors as she matured. Unlike other women of her generation (Edna St. Vincent Millay, Dorothy Parker, and Mary McCarthy come to mind), she did not atone for her past promiscuity by settling down with a partner. On the contrary, she walked away from an early marriage with no hard feelings and the recognition that marriage was not for her. Critics in the 1930s sometimes described Hellman as a "she Hammett."

One suspects that her lack of conventional beauty multiplied the offense given by Hellman's want of decorous behavior. Still, she continued to be sexually active throughout her life and sexually attractive into her old age, when her magnetism drew comment. Look at her in that mink coat, sexy, knowing, ironic, plainly the picture of a woman thoroughly enjoying herself into her seventy-second year. Late in life, her sometimes salacious pursuit of young men attracted sneers and jokes that increased as she became sick and feeble. It was then that she became known to her enemies as a "sexual predator." The combination of wrinkled and leathery skin and sexual aggressiveness drew bitter comments like "she had a face that looked as if a mouse died on it."

Once again Hellman illuminates the historical moment. The twentieth century was, after all, a time of volatile gender relationships. Modernity, Depression, war, and suburbanization all challenged traditional gender norms; new habits of consumption and political protest led women in particular to seek new paths. The young Lillian who in the twenties enjoyed the sexual and lifestyle freedom of the flapper generation lived through the more traditional, family-oriented fifties, insistently committed to her own brand of independent womanliness. When the second wave of feminism came along, she dismissed the young women who participated in the new movement as lacking in seriousness. She refused to call herself a feminist, denied that she experienced obstacles to success as a woman, was reportedly fiercely combative with female subordinates. Small wonder, then, that a new generation of young women who adored her also felt a touch of ambivalence. They admired her explicit acknowledgment of sexual desire and appreciated her iteration of a free and self-made life. But they were disappointed at the lack of emotional autonomy it demonstrated—at the failure of women like Hellman to refuse dependence on men, or to identify with women.

In her search for economic independence, too, Hellman transgressed the idea of a woman's place. Unlike the lives of many early-twentieth-century women, whose stories rotate around courtship, marriage, and family even when their achievements are substantial, Hellman's tale is better captured by following a typically male trajectory. Her life tells a story of mounting attainment. At one level, she exemplifies the Horatio Alger myth that promises success to those who (with the aid of luck and pluck) pull themselves up by their bootstraps. At another, it manifests the courage and assertion it took for a woman to pursue a course generally closed to her sex. For a woman to achieve the economic resources that allowed her to function independently at a time when such independence was largely seen as the prerogative of men defied nature. Characteristically, an achieving woman, instead of accruing admiration, became known as greedy and self-serving. She met a more hostile world, fended off challenges with a sharp tongue and prickly temper, built a potent set of defenses. Being a self-made woman was not at all like being a self-made man.

The transgressive woman typically provides a troubling subject. To write about her empathetically is to display her temper, her anger, her rudeness. To explain these away does her an injustice; it denies the difficulties she faced in achieving her goals. Observers frequently describe Hellman as simply unliked and unlikeable by many, especially many women. I see another side of her, one much loved and cared for by a succession of friends who accepted or ignored the difficult parts of her persona because they so enjoyed the benefits of her warmth and wit and friendship. Her legendary anger and bad temper constituted part of a personality that was also generous, caring, hospitable, and womanly. The tension between the two parts tells us something about how twentieth-century women coped, how they repeatedly compromised their private lives and reframed their public personas as necessity demanded and opportunity allowed. Hellman's dual stance, simultaneously furious and nurturing, loving and dismissive, insecure and insistent, may well illuminate elements of gender that women have often feared to show.

Lillian Hellman is a juicy character: her life is filled with sex and scandal, with spirited advocacy and victimhood. She might be the subject of one of the melodramas she wrote so well. If we delve into the context in which she lived we might discover something more. For Hellman illuminates the interplay between the historical moment and individual responses. She earned her laurels and she brought her troubles on herself. But she did so within a shifting and changing political, social, and cultural environment that constituted the century's challenge. The persona and her reactions took on different colors as Hellman enacted them in changing contexts. Her capacity to contain (and to reveal) so many contradictory elements turned her into the perfect lightning rod, and thus the perfect subject for the historian.

Literary scholar Rachel Brownstein points out that literary biography poses the problem of finding out how the character imagined herself. It allows great play for the biographer's imagination—allowing the biographer to make the subject what she wants her to be. Political or historical biography shifts the emphasis to ask how the character related to the world around her—how she faced the world. In searching for the relational self, the historical biographer uses the individual as a window into a moment, a lens, a mirror. Inevitably that lens is clouded. But peering through Hellman, trying to experience the world in which she made political and personal choices and searched for a place, promises to provide a sense of how myriad ordinary folk made difficult choices under circumstances not of their own choosing. What can Hellman tell us, I ask, about the hope and anxiety that infused the war-torn and Stalinist worlds of fear in which she lived? What can she teach us about how any of us might react if we were faced with a choice between giving up a utopian dream and clinging to a false god? How would we behave if to achieve our goals we needed to abandon the rewards of constraint and appear rebellious? Would we, given the option, betray a friend or betray ourselves? These questions lead me to worry whether I do Hellman a disservice by using her life to access not only particular events but the larger cultural and social and even political processes of a moment in time. I do not know whether Lillian Hellman would approve of that, but I like to think she might find it more useful than the biographies she never wanted written about her.

And here, of course, I face my own motives. The distinguished British historian E. P. Thompson once justified a biographical study of William Blake by remarking that while many microstudies of Blake had appeared, and each had added significant particulars to the sum of knowledge about him, it would take a historian to put the parts together, to reveal the sum total. Yet the historian's is a flawed lens, pretending to an unachievable objectivity. He or she chooses which pieces to use and which to leave aside. Too much has been written about Lillian Hellman to pretend that all the parts can be neatly fitted together. Too much has been shaved and shaded and refigured to know what answers will emerge when the pieces are re-configured. For the challenge of Lillian Hellman is to see how the female, southern, Jewish, heterosexual playwright—the communist celebrity who modeled mink coats—lived in one body. Our challenge is to understand the relationship between the flesh-and-blood Lillian and the templates made of her. How else to account for her persistent hold on the American imagination?

In recent years Lillian Hellman has become a Rorschach test for a generation of women and men who lived through some of the most challenging days of America's history, a lightning rod for the anger, fear, and passion that divided American intellectuals and activists from each other. Perhaps, just perhaps, a new look will enable us to make sense of the obsession with her that will, I suspect, last until the issues she touched have disappeared into historical memory. Let us, then, follow Lillian Hellman through the minefields of the twentieth century. Let us explore how one woman survived its challenges.

CHAPTER 1

Old-Fashioned American Traditions

> I was raised in an old fashioned American tradition, and there were certain homely things that were taught to me: to try to tell the truth, not to bear false witness, not to harm my neighbor, to be loyal to my country...
> —*Lillian Hellman,* Scoundrel Time

Beautiful Julia Newhouse, daughter of a wealthy southern family, married Max Hellman—who had nothing to recommend him but charm—in 1904. A year later, Julia gave birth to a child they called Lillian Florence Hellman. Baby Lillian grew up to be a precocious and rebellious child. She spent her early years in New Orleans before the family moved north to New York City. But she returned to New Orleans and the South for months at a time throughout her youth. Geography, class, and gender all added up to life on the fringes.

Lillian belonged to no traditional world, but she lived on the outskirts of several. She was born and nurtured in southern soil although she grew up mostly in New York City; she lived in the shadow of her mother's wealthy family, reacting to it with both envy and contempt; she was Jewish by birth, embraced African-American lore and love as a child, and attended Catholic and Baptist churches as the spirit moved her. In the 1930s she wanted to change the world and to live in harmony with the great love of her life, Dashiell Hammett. She became a famous playwright and memoirist, a

Baby Lillian grew up to be a precocious and rebellious child. (Times-Picayune photo)

winner of many awards and honors, yet she never escaped the taint of communism nor suspicions that she lied about her past. She died cherished by a few good friends, despised and misunderstood by many.

That's the short story. There are many longer versions, each of them different, and each carrying a range of meanings. In some of them, she is not a southerner at all but a child of the New York City streets; in others she is a rebellious teenager whose spoiled and overindulged youth crystallizes into a narcissistic womanhood. Yet again she might be a bookish daughter with precocious reading habits and an overactive imagination. All of the stories begin in New Orleans.

Lillian's maternal great-grandparents, Marx and Newhouse, came to the United States from Germany in the mid-nineteenth century, part of a stream of migrants who left their homeland when arbitrary rules restricted the mobility of Jews and hampered their capacity to earn a living at home. Like many such immigrants, they started life peddling goods in

small communities in the Midwest and the South. The Marx family settled in Demopolis, Alabama, where they opened a small store that grew
into a large establishment and eventually fostered a banking business.
Sophie Marx, Lillian's grandmother, was born there. The Newhouse family set itself down in Cincinnati, Ohio, using the city as a base for trading
all over the South. Their son, Leonard, met Sophie Marx on one of his
trips and married her soon after. Sophie gave birth to four children: Gilbert, the only son, was born in 1877, then Julia in 1880, followed by two
sisters, Florence and Miriam. Grandfather Leonard died shortly after the
youngest daughter, Miriam, was born in 1891. Julia, destined to become
Lillian's mother, was eleven at the time of her father's death.

Left a widow with four young children, Sophie Marx Newhouse committed herself to expanding the fortunes of the Marx-Newhouse clan.
This would not have been unusual for a southern white woman in the
post–Civil War generation, for the war produced a plethora of genteel
middle-class widows bereft of husbands and income. Many such women
found ways to become self-reliant that would have been unimaginable in
an older South. They sought professional training and semiprofessional
jobs as nurses and teachers, opened small businesses and managed family properties. Sophie Marx benefited from their example. To expand her
resources, she relied heavily on family trading networks and especially
on her brother Jake, the ruthless great-uncle whom Lillian later claimed
to fear and on whom she modeled the critique of the South that infused
several of her plays. By 1900, Sophie could respond with one unequivocal
word to a census question about her occupation. She described herself as
a "capitalist."[1]

Sophie appears to have moved with her children from Cincinnati,
where she lived at the turn of the century, to New Orleans. The extended
family prospered. Lillian's great-uncles and -aunts, many of them from
the increasingly powerful Marx clan, settled into trading and banking.
Julia, her older brother, Gilbert, and her two sisters grew up in comfort. To
finish her education, Julia spent two years at Sophie Newcomb College—
the women's college of Tulane University. Though it could not be compared
with intellectually challenging northern schools like Wellesley and Mount
Holyoke, Newcomb was by no means a finishing school at the time. Julia's
presence there suggests that her mother might have been worried about
her future. Julia was already in her early twenties, with no prospect of marriage looming. But Julia had her own plans. She left school when she met
Max Hellman.

Max's family, though also of German-Jewish stock, had not done as well as Julia's. His father, Bartaute (or Bernhard), probably arrived in the United States in 1866, about a year after the Civil War ended. Family lore, sometimes repeated by Lillian, described the family as coming from older stock and the grandfather as a veteran of the Civil War. Lillian doubted that this was the case. Ship records confirm her suspicions. They show thirty-two-year-old Bernhard Hellman arriving in Baltimore from Bremen on the *Humboldt* in October 1866. He may already have been married to twenty-eight-year-old Babbette Kaschland, who arrived from Germany a year later. The couple moved to New Orleans, where he worked as a bookkeeper. They had two daughters (Jenny and Johanna, commonly called Hannah) before bringing baby brother Max into the world in 1874. Despite his immigrant origins, Grandfather Bernhard lived a middle-class lifestyle. He purchased a home in the Lower Garden District of New Orleans, not one of the city's most expensive areas but certainly respectable. The household kept a live-in servant. In a period when fewer than 10 percent of girls graduated from high school, both daughters did so, as did Max. The girls also had some sort of secretarial or office training.

Max Hellman, like his father, started life as a bookkeeper. Handsome, funny, and outgoing, he won the hand of shy Julia Newhouse over the objections of her family, who then and later thought him unworthy of their beautiful and rich daughter. But their daughter was already twenty-three years old. They reconciled themselves to the marriage, providing Julia with a handsome dowry. The couple married on Tuesday evening, September 27, 1904, at the home of the bride's mother. Max's mother attended, as did his and Julia's sisters. Brother Gilbert did not come but sent the couple a generous one-hundred-dollar check.[2] The young couple first moved into her mother's home at 10 Rosa Park, just north of Charles Street. Rosa Park was, at the time, one of New Orleans's most elegant neighborhoods. They brought baby Lillian Florence, born on June 20, 1905, home there.

Not unusually for the time, Julia hired a wet nurse for the baby. We might think of this as an explanation for Lillian's never-ending fears of rejection, the source of her anger at the human race and especially toward women.[3] Then again, we might not.

When Lillian was less than a year old, the family decamped to Prytania Street, just a few blocks from where Max grew up. Their new neighborhood included several boardinghouses with rooms occupied by teachers, clerks, salesmen, and a few professionals. This must have been a step down

The family decamped from the comforts of Rosa Park to Prytania Street. (Uri and Michal Alon)

for Julia. Still, her dowry enabled Max to start his own business manufacturing and distributing shoes, and the family, including the nurse, Sophronia McMahon, lived comfortably. When the business failed a few years later, the wealthy clan pretty much left the young family to its own devices. Thereafter, Max made a decent living as an itinerant shoe salesman.

The New Orleans where Lillian was born in 1905, a year into the marriage, was then a thriving port city, hub of an active financial and trading center. The twelfth-largest city in the United States, it boasted a diverse population of more than three hundred thousand souls. One quarter were African-American, many the descendants of former slaves and others the children and grandchildren of a large free black and Creole population that predated the Civil War. Italians, Germans, Irish, and French together constituted the bulk of the immigrant population. Like all southern cities and most northern towns as well, New Orleans was residentially segregated. Contiguous communities of racially mixed people sometimes overlapped to produce a rich cultural and social mix that gave the city a freewheeling character. In a decade noted for southern white terror toward African-Americans, New Orleans developed a reputation for cosmopolitanism and liberalism. In a South that rigidly prohibited social intercourse between blacks and whites, New Orleans, alone among southern states, did not prohibit intermarriage across the races.

The city's diversity produced a rich culture that included the parading of brass bands, a strong tradition of minstrel players, and, by the time Lillian arrived, the birth of jazz. Originated by black musicians, played and enjoyed by blacks and whites, jazz became the aural symbol of cultural syncretism. But there were other arenas of inclusion as well. The city's Storyville neighborhood boasted the famous New Orleans cribs where black and white women sold their sexual services to all comers for small fees. Finance and trade produced a prosperous middle and upper-middle class, whose members patronized dance, music, and theater. Here the new South grew apace, offering seemingly limitless opportunity to make money out of the area's natural resources.

As fate would have it, Lillian would be an only child. Cared for until she was five by Sophronia, she remembered her nurse with enormous affection as the great influence on her life. "If we'd been able to afford Sophronia until you were sixteen or eighteen," she recalled her father repeating mournfully, "everything would have been different. We'd have all been happy and you'd have been a different child."[4] By Lillian's account, it was Sophronia whose advice and direction turned Lillian into the southerner she remained and who inspired the egalitarian values from which she never strayed. Sophronia taught her to respect the beliefs of others, no matter how alien or uncomfortable to her. She instilled in Lillian a simple moral code: to mind her own business, to defer to her parents and their positions, to be loyal to friends and family. From Sophronia, Lillian absorbed a respect for tradition and an antagonism to racism that would remain with her forever. And from Sophronia, too, Lillian learned that she might appease her conscience by expressing empathy and solidarity but that real change required an active commitment.

If Hellman declared herself to be a southerner at heart, she was a particular kind of southerner, a Jewish southerner whose religion was held in abeyance. Neither her parents nor their families were religiously observant. Lillian had no formal religious training in her youth; had she been sent to synagogue, it would likely have been to a Reform congregation, typical in the New Orleans community of her childhood. Jewish lack of religiosity echoed among the Catholics and Protestants of the area, whose religious practice tended to be open and eclectic as well.[5] Among the Jews who surrounded her, Lillian would have learned lessons quite different from those imbibed by the Eastern European immigrants who peopled northern cities. Reform Jews explicitly rejected Jewish law as interpreted by the rabbis of old, and they turned away as well from the notion that Jews constituted a nation of their own. They subscribed instead to a code of justice and morality common to the Judeo-Christian tradition, holding their national identity to be located in the place where they lived. Reform Judaism constituted, in short, a way for Jews to become Americans.

As a child, Lillian learned to say prayers after the Christian fashion—asking God to protect her parents, her nurse, her aunts. When her father discovered this odd behavior, he teased her about becoming the first Jewish nun on Prytania Street—a memory that Hellman cherished. Her mother conveyed her own form of spirituality manifested by attending services at whatever church or occasional synagogue moved her. In the New Orleans of Lillian's childhood these visits would not have been unusual: at least one historian of the Jewish community remarks on its sociability, on a continuing "exchange of church visiting, where members of both the Jewish as well as the Christian community take one another to hear the new ministers, or partake of church suppers."[6] With Julia and with Sophronia, the small Lillian enjoyed an array of such visits.

In that respect, New Orleans was an oasis of a kind. It contained a rather small population of seven thousand Jews (less than two thousand families) who together constituted a little more than 1 percent of the population of the city at the time.[7] Jews had lived in New Orleans for two hundred years: about half of the Jewish families dated back at least three generations. The city contained no solidly Jewish neighborhoods, no self-created ghettos, no orthodox Jewish community. Julian Feibelman, writing in 1941, called it a place where "families have mingled socially for generations, and the tradition is continued today."[8] Jews, he continued, found themselves "in almost every nook and cranny of social, political and cultural life."[9] This was an area reasonably free of anti-Semitism. As one of her contemporaries put it, "I was Jewish and that was that, but nobody seemed to care very much and nobody so far as I could see was very exercised about it."[10] Hellman echoed these feelings, noting of Jews in New Orleans that "they had a pleasant community of their own and in turn the community allowed them to have it."[11] Such casual integration of Jews did not go unnoticed among the growing numbers of their co-religionists. Historian Leonard Reissman remarks on its problematic consequences. "More so than in most other American-Jewish communities, New Orleans appears to give substance to the fears of benign assimilation that have always dominated Jewish history."[12]

Elsewhere in the South, apparent assimilation hid more negative feelings that sometimes manifested themselves in violent outbursts. Lillian grew up in a South where Jews clustered in small groups in small towns and cities, where, to quote one scholar, they "played poker with the sheriff, fished with the county judge, hunted with the planters, and became leaders of the local Chamber of Commerce."[13] In the memory of Eli Evans, whose father was once mayor of Durham, North Carolina, Jews were "blood and bones part of the South itself: Jewish Southerners."[14] And yet Lillian was ten and still spending long summers in the South when a Marietta, Georgia, mob stormed the jail where Leo Frank, a twenty-nine-year-old Jewish factory superintendent, was being held under suspicion of murdering a young white woman. Could she have been unaware of the anti-Semitism that fueled the lynching that followed? She was probably in her twenties when the novelist Ronald Bern experienced the daily playground beatings and active anti-Semitism that characterized his school years in the South.[15]

The differential experience suggests that Lillian may well have suffered from what the historian W. J. Cash has called the paradox of "the eternal alien," never quite belonging. "In the general withdrawal upon the old heritage," notes Cash, Jews inevitably stood out. "It was perfectly natural that . . . he should come in for renewed denunciations; should . . . stand in the eyes of the people as a sort of evil harbinger and incarnation of all the menaces they feared and hated—external and internal, real and imaginary."[16] Among New Orleans Jews, that alienation was experienced in one important arena: Jews had never been invited to the Mardi Gras carnival balls, and this despite the fact that a Jew had originated the carnival in 1872 and been its first Rex.[17] As a child, Lillian did not feel deprived of this experience, and when she might have felt excluded she had already left the South. And yet years later she ridiculed the notion of exclusion with a suspicious vehemence. "May God bless them and keep them," she wrote of Jews who wanted to participate in the ceremonies, "and some day allow them to ride on those hideous Mardi Gras floats and become Kings and Queens, ermine bedecked, at the grand balls and as silly as their dancing partners."[18]

Hellman's deep commitment to racial egalitarianism seems to have emerged from both her eclectic exposure to religion and her southern roots. Unlike their poor white counterparts, Jews who lived in the South experienced few "turf" conflicts over jobs. Unlike New York's first- and second-generation immigrants, who frequently identified themselves as refugees from the pogroms of Eastern Europe and Tsarist Russia, the comparatively deep roots and relative economic prosperity of many southern Jews placed them in more secure positions. Still, the position of southern Jews was not without ambiguity. Their small numbers and dispersed presence, historian Paula Hyman notes, pushed Jews in the South and other small communities into a private commitment to their faith that substituted for the public exhibitions of Jewish culture more prevalent in larger Jewish communities. They were white people in a world where race mattered more than religion. As white people eager to achieve economic success and security for their families, they adapted to prevailing racial hierarchies and discriminations. But that did not mean that religion and ethnic tradition did not matter at all. As outsiders within, they tended to identify with the persecuted rather than with the persecutors. Even as they adopted southern white standards of segregation and place, southern Jews generally took liberal positions on the "Negro problem." Somewhat cynically, Hellman attributed this stance to self-interest—to respect for African-Americans as customers and as employees.[19] In this sense their Jewish identity differed from that of their northern counterparts even as their southern origins separated them from the rest of America.

Lillian's parents echoed the anti-racist lessons learned from Sophronia and were, if anything, more inclined to take matters into their own hands. She often told a story that she later reproduced in her memoirs of how her father got involved in a brawl in defense of a young black girl who was traveling by train alone in the deep South. Lillian (about ten at the time) and her parents were sitting one night on a deserted southern train platform when they noticed the young woman running from two white men, who caught up with her and grabbed her, knocking the girl's suitcase out of her hands and scattering her possessions. Max stepped up immediately—an unexpected act in the days before World War I— insisting they put the girl down. The men responded by taking a swing at him. He fended them off and hurriedly escorted the girl to the just-arriving train, telling Lillian to jump aboard. Only when the train began to pull out did father and daughter realize they had left Lillian's mother behind "on the ground carefully picking up and repacking the girl's valise." She headed for the train as it jerked to a stop, walking through the two men and smiling as she said, in a deep southern accent, "Excuse me, boys, excuse me. Mah husband wants us to get aboard the train."[20] Lillian later thought the accent might have saved her mother's life.

Hellman later ascribed the incident to her parents' commitment to individual liberty. It was, she thought, about "two people who believed in the right to go unmolested." Max Hellman, she later claimed, had a "genuine feeling for Negroes, and real pity." To her parents' example, she attributed her deeply rooted commitment to civil liberties and individual freedom. But the image of two perhaps drunken white men harassing an innocent black girl also illuminated the changes going on around her. For the benign images of paternalism that constituted her child's view of the South, she substituted the brutality of a new South focused on personal gratification and the accumulation of wealth rather than on mutual responsibility. She never reconciled her childhood memories of a safe and comfortable New Orleans with the abused and exploited population of the new South.

Lillian moved with her parents to New York in 1910, at the age of five. For the next eight or nine years, the family seems to have spent several months of every year in New Orleans. We know about these years mainly from Lillian, who clung to an image of herself as a child of the South despite the fact that most of her schooling occurred in New York. Hellman tells us that as a child she went to school both in New York and in New Orleans and experienced discomfort in both places. In the North, she could not keep up with her smart urban classmates; in the South, she found herself bored to tears and frequently playing hooky. She probably moved about until she was eleven. After that, southern summers spent in

New Orleans and in her mother's family compound in Mississippi mingled with school years in New York City. In all that time, Hellman maintained a distant though still loving relationship with her old nurse Sophronia, who continued to exercise moral authority in a world in which her parents proved more capricious and less predictable.

In New Orleans, the family generally lived in a boardinghouse run by her father's two older sisters, Jenny and Hannah. Set on the shabby, genteel end of Prytania Street for a while and then relocated to a somewhat seedier neighborhood, the boardinghouse provided Lillian with endless entertainment and immersion in the eccentricities of New Orleans family life.

There she learned to prepare crayfish, to make turtle soup, and to command such domestic arts as knitting, sewing, and embroidery. She admired her aunts' strong sense of themselves as independent women, acknowledged their love for her and her father, and noted the way they cherished and protected her mother. Warm, funny, and kind, Jenny and Hannah introduced Lillian to a tradition of generous hospitality that she would practice all of her life. Perhaps inadvertently, they also fostered Lillian's strong need to construct around herself a "family" of people who cared for her and looked after her needs. Coming from a South where she was pampered by aunts and where a tradition of service prevailed, she readily equated deference with love. This characteristic lasted all of her life, perhaps accounting for much of the bad temper and irritability that her associates observed when she failed to get the help she needed and wanted, or when her friends let her down.

The South too is the location of the fig tree where Lillian satisfied her "stubborn, relentless driving desire to be alone as it came into conflict with the desire not to be alone when I wanted not to be."[21] She hid herself in its branches to read and to educate herself, later recalling the delicious sense of freedom to read as widely as she liked. There, she shed her school clothes and her temper as she allowed the environment to comfort her and hold her safe, "nobody there to tell you what to read, or give advice, or interpret; no interest in whether the book is good or bad . . . You are just there reading anything you can put your hands on, all hot and sticky with excitement, and maybe fudge . . ."[22] The fig tree appears in several locations in Hellman's later work, and undoubtedly in her mind, providing a haven and a hiding place for a restless young girl. Generally, Hellman locates it in the front yard of her aunts' boardinghouse on Prytania Street, though occasionally it appears at "Pass Christian," the Mississippi resort frequented by the Marx-Newhouse clan, where she and her family spent a week or two every summer of her early teenage years.

An Unfinished Woman proudly recalls childhood moments when Hellman demonstrated courage and spirit, often flouting advice in favor of making her own decisions. Some of these seem, in retrospect, to have been trivial incidents, more reflective of her efforts to define her character than important as anecdote. She tells us that she often chose to skip school in order to spend time in the fig tree. She describes efforts to defy her mother's wealthy family by trading an expensive ring given her by Uncle Jake for books. Instead of punishment, she was rewarded by being told that she had spirit after all.

Lillian retreated to the branches of the fig tree to lick her wounds over her first great disillusionment. She had witnessed her father meeting another woman outside a restaurant, then getting into a taxi with her. Lillian tells us that in a blind rage she threw herself from the fig tree, breaking her nose. When she ran, for comfort, to Sophronia and told her the story, that wise woman instructed her to remain silent about her father's affairs, giving her the message that would resonate down the years: "Don't go through life making trouble for people."[23] The broken nose accompanied her for the rest of her life, unmended, despite Hellman's vanity about her clothes and her looks, and marking her exit from the safety of the South, the security of her parental home, and an implausible vision of herself as a curly-headed beauty. Zoe Caldwell, who played Lillian onstage shortly after her death, thought of the broken nose as a mark of courage, a reminder of the need for discretion.[24]

In the aftermath of the fall, Hellman ran repeatedly to Sophronia and the black community for help and solace. In one episode, she tells us that at fourteen she ran away from home after an argument with her parents and stayed away for two nights, making her way, finally, to what she calls the Negro part of town. She knew this area because it housed her family's dressmaker and she had often been brought there by Sophronia. She remembered it as peopled by cheerful souls and remarkable houses with welcoming doors. There, after invoking Sophronia's name, she was taken in by a suspicious black family that nevertheless protected her and arranged for her to be collected by her father. Did Lillian really run away from home at fourteen and manage to stay away for two nights, discovering that she had her first menses just as her father came to fetch her? That's doubtful. Yet whether this story recalls an event that happened or one that she constructed to capture her feelings of despair at the time, it reflects a sense of what racial relations meant to her, revealing something about Lillian's sense of the New Orleans black community as a place of comfort rather than one of terror.

Much that Hellman tells us about her experience of southern child-hood is clearly romanticized, the exaggerated and wishful memories of a child who recalls moments of pain and joy in the light of lessons learned and rewards received. Her identity as a southerner remained, all her life, firmly rooted in a mythical South where paternalism, gentility, culture, and self-respect trumped the quest for money in the battle for survival. The grown-up Lillian's reflections on these southern roots reveal a surprising nostalgia for the gentle past of her imagination, producing a bitter rage against those who threatened to destroy sweet memories. Her mother's family, especially her great-uncle Jake, is among those against whom her venom is directed.

Hellman held the uncontrolled search for wealth represented by Jake responsible for exacerbating the poverty and racial tension that would become characteristic of a new South. In the unnamed small southern town in which her most famous play, *The Little Foxes*, is set in 1900, Hell-man locates a predatory family intent upon becoming rich by learning "new ways" and learning "how to make them pay." The family echoes that of her mother. As brother Ben says, the plantation built on fine crops and Negro labor "now belongs to us . . . twenty years ago, we took over their land, their cotton and their daughter."[25] But the unhappy daughter whose marriage into the family provided it with the land and credibility to de-stroy the life she loved wants only to retreat into drink where she can shut out the present to revel in the beautiful past of memory. Her mother, she recalls, sold off everything out of need, never letting go of her anger at a "people who killed animals they couldn't use and who made their money charging awful interest to ignorant niggers and cheating them on what they bought."[26] The price of greed, Hellman tells us, is the loss of culture, civility, and humane values, especially toward poor people.

Lillian eventually learned to emulate the warmth and grace of the old South, but she would not, in any event, have been positioned to take ad-vantage of the new. There she was merely an ugly duckling, lacking tradi-tional good looks and without the kind of family wealth that might have compensated for them. She could not expect to marry into the world of romance and charm, nor could she have brought resources to a marriage or a business partnership. To be sure, she dreamed of being a beauty, but after her first boyfriend told her she looked like "a prow head on a whaling ship," she gave up on that dream.[27] Eventually, she created the head of blonde curls that she wished for, and she earned enough to live the life-style of her grandmother. But she never stopped envying good-looking women, nor did she transcend the feeling that she was a poor relative in an extended family where wealth not only mattered but was what chiefly counted.

New York City proved to be something of a haven for such a young girl. The family settled into a comfortable apartment at 330 West 95th Street. Lillian used the phrase "shabby-genteel" to describe the apartment; census records reveal it to have been solidly middle-class. The neighbors included a dermatologist, an interior designer, a musical director, and an art dealer, occupations that measured well against that of Lillian's father, who earned his living as a traveling salesman with a line of clothing. The family employed a daily housekeeper and, often, a cook. Both parents had a lively interest in all things literary and especially in the theater. They attended regularly, and afterward revisited the plays and actors' performances in the presence of their daughter. Though Lillian attended public schools, she took dancing and music lessons, and, as a teenager, had more freedom to explore the city than most of her peers.

Lillian adored her father, a genial host, a great entertainer, a man of quick wit and charming style. She admired his vitality and resolution, and she forgave him, perhaps even came to admire, his persistent attractions to other women. For Max was a philanderer who did not hide his affairs from his wife and family. True to southern tradition, Lillian's mother ignored her husband's long absences and his unfaithful ways. The small Lillian adapted to this behavior reluctantly, following the precepts of her beloved nurse Sophronia not to go through life making trouble for people.[28] Hellman remembers her mother as "small, delicately made, and charming" but also as flighty, timid, and impractical.[29] As the child turned into a young woman, she grew to despise her mother's acquiescence, only later coming to see it as a courageous and brave response to her father's misbehavior.

The models presented by her relatives offered a different perspective on life. Lillian's Newhouse grandmother had moved to New York around 1907, settling into a life of ostentatious wealth in a Park Avenue apartment where she lived with two unmarried daughters and a large staff of servants. Lillian remembered the "lovely oval rooms filled with the upper middle-class trappings that never managed to be truly stylish."[30] She recalled the glamorous parties that she watched as a peeping child from the servants' hall. Lillian and her mother visited often, but she experienced these visits in sharp contrast to her own life, which seemed shabby by comparison. From the discomfort she felt in the presence of her forceful grandmother and from the extended family's never-ending discussions of money and finances, she perceived her own family as economically marginal. The dissonance produced in her an unquenchable anger and at the same time "a wild extravagance mixed with respect for money and those who have it."[31]

Did consciousness of class enter her picture of the world as a result of the family dynamics? By her own account, Lillian claims to have learned in her teenage years to despise those who sought only wealth and power. She tells us that she did not want either money, or the lack of it, to control her own life. And yet her sense of injury is palpable: she felt cheated of the wealth that was her mother's due and that she always believed was rightfully hers. The perceived injustice of it all fed a sense of entitlement that led her then and after to claim (even aggressively demand) what she believed to be hers, inside and outside the family. Unwittingly she inherited the pattern her grandmother modeled. She expected and wanted the creature comforts of wealth. One day she might inherit some of them. Until then, she would carve out her own path, earn economic success by her own efforts, or gravitate toward the rich, benefiting from their largesse. Insecure about her place in the world, the teenaged Lillian became impatient, bad-tempered, sharp-tongued, and rebellious. Forever after, even when she became well off, she imagined herself as poor, feared losing her money, and insisted on the comforts that wealth could bring.

Marks of identity mattered in perverse ways in the New York City to which Lillian moved as a child, for once again she was outside. Hers was not the culture of recently arrived Yiddish-speaking immigrants. She experienced neither the poverty of the Lower East Side nor the community spirit of the working-class neighborhoods of Brooklyn and the Bronx. She did not belong to the immigrant community of legend where parents sacrificed to provide education for children who expected to climb the ladder of social mobility. But neither did she belong among the wealthy German Jews whom the East Siders contemptuously labeled "Jeckes"—for jacketed, prosperous Jews.

At thirteen, she entered Wadleigh High School for Girls. Founded in

1903, Wadleigh was the first college-preparatory public high school for girls in a city where there were already several elite public boys' schools meant to train the children of immigrants for college. By the time Lillian enrolled in 1918, Wadleigh boasted nearly three thousand smart female students from all over the city. Lillian was an indifferent scholar in a rather large class of bright schoolmates, and she remembered these years as unhappy. Still, when she graduated in 1922 at the age of seventeen, she had already begun her career as a writer: she wrote a weekly gossip column for the school newspaper entitled "It Seems to Me, Jr.," and served as an editor of the senior yearbook. In her last year of school she kept a diary that at first she thought of as private, but which she then allowed her boyfriend to read. She recognized, as she did so, that the meaning of what she wrote would change when her words became public.[32] This early effort to grapple with whether "truth" would flow from her pen would remain with her for the rest of her life.

A seventeen-year-old bright female high school graduate from a middle-class family in 1922 might reasonably expect to choose college as an option. Fewer than 10 percent of the young women in her age cohort would make this choice, but Lillian had little doubt about it. She wanted to go to Smith College—a destination favored by bright northern young women. Her mother proposed her own alma mater, Sophie Newcomb, which didn't suit Lillian's taste for clever and well-read schoolmates. They compromised on Goucher College in Baltimore. Goucher was southern enough for her mother and committed to serious education for women. Lillian applied and was accepted. In the end she enrolled in none of these, telling everyone that her mother was ill and would need her at home. The likelihood is that financial constraints, rather than loyalty to her mother, determined the choice. At any rate, when the fall came, she registered at Washington Square College of New York University.

The college was then a small affair, less than a decade old, and housing a few hundred undergraduate students. Though it was located in the heart of Greenwich Village, its students mingled neither with the literati who frequented the neighborhood nor with the local Italian families. There she encountered some great minds whose efforts to discipline her reading she resisted. College seemed to her to serve no useful purpose. Restless and bored, she quit after two years. An extended trip with her mother through the Midwest and the South followed. In the fall of 1924, just nineteen, she took a job in the publishing industry as a manuscript reader.

This time she chose well. Boni and Liveright, the firm for which she went to work, was a vibrant and exciting young publishing house that avidly represented itself as the perfect outlet for a city of speakeasies, automobiles, and creative intellectual ferment. Its head, Horace Liveright, founder of the Modern Library—which had introduced Americans to inexpensive editions of great European authors—remained committed to publishing new fiction in uncensored form. Liveright attracted to his lists such authors as Hemingway, Dreiser, E. E. Cummings, and T. S. Eliot. And he published the first novels of William Faulkner, Hart Crane, Bertrand Russell, and S. J. Perelman. If Lillian did not work directly with these authors or on their manuscripts, she found herself in a world exactly suited to her ambitions and her tastes and surrounded by creative and talented writers and cultural pundits, young and old. There she encountered Eastern European Jews who aspired to take their places in the thriving cultural communities of the twenties. This was a world where talent and intellect mattered more than money or religion or family background.

The job introduced Lillian to a world that she would thereafter make her home. At Boni and Liveright, she revealed the sharp critical skills honed by many years of reading in the fig tree, making good use of her quick wit and acerbic tongue. Her employers appreciated the speed with which she read and judged manuscripts and deplored the sloppiness and lack of discipline with which she approached her work. By Lillian's account at least, they valued most her standing as a representative of a younger, freer generation of women—the flapper generation—whose personal style they desperately tried to understand. Among the perquisites of the job were endless parties and gatherings to honor one book and one writer or another. Shy though she was at the time, Lillian did well at these, drinking in a time of prohibition, dressing in the short skirts and clinging fabrics that signified greater personal freedom for women, dancing and flirting in ways that violated contemporary rules about exhibiting sexual availability. No longer isolated, she found a community of people like her, eager to express themselves as consumers, happily declaring their creative ambition, and unafraid to live by their own standards. Disillusionment might follow, but in the middle of the prosperous and free-spirited 1920s, surrounded by the cultural ferment of New York, Lillian found a niche.

Just a year into the job at Boni and Liveright, Lillian met Arthur Kober, whom she married a few months later. Five years older than Lillian and the son of Austro-Hungarian immigrants, Kober grew up in the working-class Bronx where he spent his youth fending off the blows of Italian and Irish immigrant children and developing the sardonic humor of the New York Jew. His family background, so different in class and culture from Lillian's, must have been one source of his appeal to her. Marrying into New York's Jewish immigrant community would provide her the insider place that she lacked. And Kober had the advantage as well of being part of the creative cultural community in which she continued to see herself.

By 1925, working as a theatrical press agent and the author of several *New Yorker* short stories, Kober already knew he wanted to be a playwright. He worked in a heavy Yiddish idiom, using Jewish life in the Bronx as his vehicle for an affectionate humor. And he palled around with a young group of creative entertainers who were yet to make their names. Among them were Lee and Ira Gershwin, Laura and S. J Perelman, Herman Shumlin, Nathanael West, and Louis Kronenberger. These would become Lillian's lifelong friends. Along with them and her husband, she moved into the heart of the entertainment community, adopting the raucous and argumentative style that would come to characterize New York Jews. As she melded into the smart, creative, and culturally ambitious circles that now surrounded her, Lillian found an exciting new world of literary and theatrical arts.

She also found an identity. If she grew up on the edges, on the borders of north and south, of Jew and non-Jew, of rich and not so rich, of love

Just a year into the job, Lillian met Arthur Kober. (Photofest)

and anger, she found a place that transcended all these borders. Entering adulthood in the twenties, she could celebrate her generation, indulge her sexual passions, associate with a community of creative artists, and strive for her own economic independence in ways unthinkable to her mother's generation. Her sense of what it meant to be an American reflected values gathered from her childhood and interpreted in the light of the experiences of her young womanhood. Nurtured in Sophronia's lessons of honesty, integrity, justice, and decency, she would shape these concepts to her own experience, reacting with anger and frustration when they failed to resonate with others. To her, these concepts remained the heart and soul of American culture and of the life she would construct for herself.

CHAPTER 2

A Tough Broad

It's a question of what dignity is about.
—*Lillian Hellman, American Scholar Forum,*
"Women on Women"

You are above all entirely and impressively a lady; yet also a great gentleman, honorable to a fault, truthful and courageous, immensely and movingly straight.
—*Literary agent Robby Lantz to Lillian Hellman*

In her late forties, Lillian Hellman constructed an anecdote about her first party dress. "I was sixteen, too thin, too awkward and I had a long, sad face," she wrote. "I was not the girl for the pale orange tulle with appliquéd rosebuds and ribbons that my mother thought so right for me. I knew that day what my mother had wanted in a daughter and I felt sad." As if to affirm her desire to become a different kind of woman, Lillian concluded the anecdote with the dramatic flair that would become her signature. "A week later, at the party," she wrote, "somebody dropped a match and the tulle dress burned slowly and surely and it seemed to me proper that my mother's dream of a daughter went with it."[1]

But if Lillian could not live her mother's dream, neither could she entirely abandon it. She could not be the "beautiful, gentle, efficient woman" who

"I was sixteen, too thin, too awkward and I had a long, sad face." (Lillian Hellman Estate)

participates in southern legend. Nor could she "accept without question the doctrine of male superiority and authority."[2] Born to be a charming, solicitous, and nurturing southern belle, as her husband Arthur Kober once put it, she reached beyond southern tradition and turned into a misfit, becoming in the eyes of all around her a difficult woman. As a child, she escaped from her family's expectations to read in the fig tree of her memories, to run away to the arms of her nurse Sophronia when things got difficult. She was, in that sense, always defiant, in rebellion against emulating her mother's place as an obedient and submissive creature bred for a lifestyle that her father could not afford. We learn something about how hard it must have been for a woman of the twenties and thirties to be serious about her work and at the same time to hang on to whatever womanliness meant to her when we watch Hellman maneuver through the obstacles. She became outspoken and direct, some would even say rude. To protect herself, she developed a quick wit and a biting sense of humor. These qualities placed her at the cutting edge of changing twentieth-century gender norms, a leading symbol of the new independent woman. Yet even as she challenged traditionally appropriate roles for women, she cultivated deeply feminine qualities of warmth and generosity.

In *Pentimento*, Hellman provides us with a clue to the tension between her desire and her destiny. There, she draws a portrait of her distant cousin Bethe, who remained ever after a symbol of the teenager's wish to be able to act on one's feelings without shame. Hellman described her first (clearly invented) view of Bethe hanging clothes from a line. "She was naked and I stopped to admire the proportions of the figure: the large hips, the great breasts, the tumbled auburn hair that came from the beautiful side of my father's family."[3] As in so much of Hellman's writing, we can't tell what part of Bethe reflects the life of a living cousin and what part Lillian's own sense of how she imagined her own life. The Bethe remembered by Lillian emigrated from Germany as a young woman, briefly lived with aunts Jenny and Hannah, and then fulfilled the terms of a prearranged but bad marriage. She left it after a few years to live, unmarried, with an Italian mobster. That act led her kin to cut off their relations with her. The teenage Lillian describes herself as deliberately tracking down her cousin and trying to bring Bethe back to the bosom of the family. But in Lillian's story, Bethe would have none of it. She had willingly paid the price demanded of a woman who followed her heart and knowingly offended her relatives. She remained, in Lillian's fantasy life, the courageous young woman who had chosen her own path.

Lillian matured into a generation blessed or cursed with such choices, an "in-between" generation. Twelve-year-old Lillian watched women win the right to vote in New York State in 1917. She was fifteen when the ratification of the nineteenth amendment enabled women nationwide to cast ballots. But the young Lillian was not inspired by the social reform movements that transformed the political environment of her youth. She was too late for the activist feminism of the early 1900s that had won the vote for women, achieved a measure of property rights, and acquired legal access to divorce and custody of their children. Nor did she identify with the generation of college-educated women that continued, after suffrage, to carve out paths toward social justice as well as political participation. The well-off and the married belonged to one or more of the burgeoning women's clubs that by 1920 boasted some five million members united under the banner of the General Federation of Women's Clubs. These groups committed themselves to a variety of social causes that stretched beyond political campaigns for women's equality to a quest for freedom in other spheres. They wanted to assure justice for the poor, to reform corrupt municipal politics, and especially to guarantee the health of mothers and their children. But for Lillian's generation, as historian Susan Ware has pointed out, women's rights were not so much at issue.[4]

Instead, Lillian joined a cohort of young women who sought to achieve personal freedom by taking advantage of the rights won for them by "the shock troops," as she later called them, of the earlier generation. Before the First World War, working-class and poor women, black and white, married and single, generally earned their own livings or contributed to family support by doing domestic work, going off to factories, or taking in boarders, doing laundry, or sewing at home. But in the early 1920s, increasing numbers of young single women who, like Lillian, came from respectable families aspired to enter the world of work. Moving into new office jobs or training as semiprofessionals in teaching, nursing, and the new field of social work, they carved out permanent places for themselves outside the home. They were the women who grasped modernity and rode it full throttle into the twentieth century. "By their widely publicized accomplishments and non-traditional lifestyles," Ware notes, "such popular heroines suggested that women could be autonomous human beings, could live life on their own terms and could overcome conventional barriers."[5]

In popular parlance, they were the flappers: a cohort of young women who lived for pleasure, disdaining ideals of self-sacrifice and service held by the Victorian generations of women. Flappers disdained the authority of parents and social custom, danced the night away in jazz clubs, consumed alcohol in speakeasies in the face of legal prohibition, smoked, acted brashly, and followed their sexual inclinations. Among many young women of this generation, including Lillian, the powerful drive to transcend the limits of their mothers' generation pushed them beyond the search for pleasure to make something of themselves, to be their own persons, to earn their way in the world.

Sex played an important role for this group of women, signaling not merely a flouting of convention but the desire to live on their own terms, to be free. In Europe, before the war, men and women avidly read Otto Weininger, whose *Sex and Character* proposed that only male character (active, productive, logical, and moral) could produce genius and posited that the passive and amoral female would destroy male creativity.[6] Weininger's dire warnings about female sexuality took second place in the United States to those of Havelock Ellis, the originator of the science of sexology. His work stimulated public discussions of previously forbidden subjects like homosexuality, then called "sexual inversion" or deviance. At the same time, Margaret Mead began to publicize her studies of Pacific islands where men and women seemed to reverse roles, the men caring for children even as the women exercised clout within the commu-

1935: A powerful drive pushed her to be her own person. (Ransom Center)

nity. Popular culture, including films, stimulated sexual appetites; the growing use of automobiles created new possibilities for unchaperoned interaction between the sexes.

But it was Sigmund Freud whose ideas inspired the generation of the twenties in the United States to seek sexual liberation. Freud's notions about sexuality in infancy freed women to accept sexual expression as a normal part of human behavior and to acknowledge sexual desire. Lillian paid no attention to the flip side of Freudian theory, which equated female maturity with the quest for motherhood, ultimately reinforcing ideals of female submission. Like other women of her generation, she eagerly rejected old notions of chastity and sexual purity, convinced that the practice of free love provided healthier alternatives for women. Hellman's diaries from the early 1920s describe something of how a young woman then might have fantasized about sex and male relationships as well as how torn she might have felt. Self-consciously, with a sense of audience in mind, the seventeen-year-old Hellman records her feelings about boys and young men who court her and whom she views largely without interest. Slowly she begins to accept the possibility that a physical relationship might be satisfying—even without mental challenge. Sex, she finally concludes— still at the tender age of seventeen—"is like eating a meal. I try to make it like eating a banquet. But I am rather glad. This entails no heartaches or hurts—it leaves you satisfied if not breathing."[7]

The idea that girls and women, like men, derived pleasure from sex as part of normal daily life appears in some of Hellman's early short stories. In what is perhaps quintessential wish fulfillment, "Perberty in Los Angeles"—written in 1933 and featuring a fourteen-year-old protagonist— describes a mother, aunt, and uncle who try to encourage the teenager to welcome sex into her life. "Have you felt no yearnings to embrace the boys in the field . . . and to lie in the dells and crannies," asks her fictional aunt Minnie. The teenager, more interested in ancient Greek grammar than in sexual experience, responds by trying to change the subject, leading her mother to beg and plead with her to think about sex because "it is normal . . . and of course we will forgive you and assist you."[8] "I Call her Mama," published just a few months earlier, also features a fourteen-year-old female protagonist whose mother had prematurely pressed sexual freedom on her. Resisting sex instruction, the teenager tells her mother not to make such a fuss about sex. "It's not good to make my attitude toward sex any more beautiful," she tells her, and then concludes a long tirade against her mother's reification of sexual freedom with the simple assertion that "I want an old fashioned home."[9]

New understandings of relationships that involved sexual satisfaction and multiple partners for women as well as men produced a range of controversial but widely tolerated lifestyle options. This was especially true for bright urban young women like Lillian who were of undistinguished education and no great wealth. Their choices included careers without marriage, "Boston" (same-sex) marriages, companionate marriages without benefit of license until the couple decided whether they were compatible, and "marriage under two roofs" for those who, though legally joined, desired to live apart and could afford to do so. For the educated middle-class, unmarried, white woman, a loss of virginity or a discreet sexual relationship outside marriage no longer consigned her to shame. Rather, it marked access to freedom.

Hellman took advantage of these options as she became aware of them. The summer she turned nineteen, she engaged in a full-scale sexual affair, parts of which she recorded in her diaries. When her first love ends and

Jerry (the name she gives to her lover) disappears, leaving her in pain, she concludes that it is a "terrible and unwise thing . . . to become so engrossed with one being" in a way that shuts off all else.[10] The young Lillian, her diaries suggest, does not dismiss love lightly—but she does wonder how often it will come to her, how often she will attract it. As if anticipating the future by trying to control it, she places her first real love affair into the category of something perhaps deeply felt and genuine, but not worth continuing anguish. Later, she recalls it with distaste as a loveless encounter that lasted only a few months: "I suppose that the cool currency of the time carried me past the pain of finding nastiness in what I had hoped would be a moving adventure," she wrote.[11]

At Boni and Liveright, Lillian met and partied with a range of people who were no strangers to sex. Invitations came to the parties with great frequency, partly, she thought, because she was "young and unjudging" and partly for "reasons not so good."[12] Though she describes herself as shy in this period, to the company she appeared as an icon of flaming youth. Occasionally, Hellman recalled, Horace Liveright asked her and some of her young colleagues to explain the flapper phenomenon to clueless older male guests who seemed dumbfounded by the claims of young women to sexual freedom. Not particularly adept at her job, Lillian believed that Horace Liveright continued to employ her out of admiration for her youthful verve and audacity. To her colleagues, she represented a phenomenon they did not understand.

Lillian invited utter incomprehension when she returned to work one afternoon after having taken the morning off to have an abortion. She had already agreed to marry Arthur Kober but became pregnant by him a few months before the marriage was scheduled to take place on December 31, 1925. Not wanting her friends to assume that the pregnancy had fostered ideas of marriage, she decided on abortion. She returned to the office later in the day, dry-eyed, a bit wobbly, but ready to go to work. She remained there through the rest of the working day, resisting every effort to take care of her and refusing to entertain a word of sympathy. She did not, she said, want to become the "house pet." Her strength drew admiration from some but alienated others who could not understand her apparently casual attitude toward a difficult act.[13]

For all her rebellious spirit and her desire to act on her own instincts, Hellman quit her job and married Arthur Kober on New Year's Eve, 1925. She was just twenty. Arthur, then an aspiring writer who worked as a playwright, satisfied her desire to nurture—to create a loving relationship—that remained one part of her complicated persona. Together the newlyweds went to Paris, where she floated on the fringes of the American expatriate community, wrote a few short stories, traveled a bit in Europe—usually without Kober—and described herself as generally restless. She returned to New York alone and supported herself by writing book reviews for the *New York Herald Tribune* and reading manuscripts for some of her publishing friends. During the months they spent apart from each other, with Arthur's knowledge, she occasionally saw, and slept with, other men. Such behavior was not entirely unusual among the educated and arty young people with whom she traveled. Muriel Gardiner (whom Hellman did not then know but who would later play a significant role in her life) describes her experience in Greenwich Village in those years in language Lillian would have recognized: "There was an attitude of general camaraderie among us all, men and women. Many of the married couples seemed rather independent of each other, wives and husbands often dating someone of the opposite sex in accord with the mores of the 'roaring twenties.'"[14]

After Kober returned to the States, Lillian took a job as a publicity agent in Rochester, New York. She left after four months to accompany Kober to Hollywood, where he had received a munificent job offer as a screenwriter. In Hollywood, Kober, desperate to find Lillian something to do, arranged for her to work as a reader for Metro-Goldwyn-Mayer. Sometime in this period, Lillian stopped using birth control, became pregnant, and had an early miscarriage. She had returned to New York from the West Coast and was staying in the St. Moritz hotel when she discovered the loss. "I cried like hell for almost two solid hours," she wrote to Arthur. In a rare moment of visible vulnerability, she added, "Please don't feel bad—we can try again . . . Write me that you don't mind very much and cheer me up. It alters no promises I made you and I hope you understand that—if you don't and are still entertaining the idea of a divorce, now is your time to get it on the record. But please console me a little—I'm ashamed really—I always thought I was a super-creator of babies . . . Please write more often and please love me. I miss you an awful lot."[15] By then the marriage was all but over. Returning to Hollywood, Lillian Hellman Kober met Dashiell Samuel Hammett, with whom she was to begin a legendary thirty-year relationship.

By the standards of the literati in the late twenties and early thirties, Hellman's marriage to Kober was unorthodox but not terribly unusual.

Yet it did not entirely free her from the constraints of parental values. Even after she separated from Kober and returned to New York without a partner, she took care that her rebellious lifestyle did not offend her mother's sensibilities. On the eve of her twenty-ninth birthday, she wrote to Kober to complain that "my movements—particularly in the matter of visiting unmarried gentleman [sic]—have all to be accounted for to Mama, so that I am never quite free to move around the way I might want to."[16] If she feared parental disapproval, it did not stop her from behaving as she wished. "I have to account to mama for the details of my life," she wrote to Kober. "I guess someday she's going to find out I am not a virgin, and that's bound to be the end of our beautiful friendship."[17] Her generation, as she repeatedly proclaimed, "did not often deal with the idea of love . . ." When her aunts Jenny and Hannah challenged her for being part of a generation that "goes about naked all the time," she made it clear that her value system and theirs differed. "We sleep with everybody," she admitted, "and drink and dope all night and don't have your fine feelings." But, she added, recalling her aunts' ostracism of Bethe, her standards "did not involve spitting on people because they live with lowdown Wops and get into trouble."[18] Living in Hollywood surely legitimized these feelings. In Hollywood, where physical beauty reigned, Hellman had honed her sensual sense of self. She had also found an environment that encouraged sexual adventurousness.

Dashiell Hammett not only gave Lillian the space to develop her sexual persona but, in his sometimes brutal way, insisted on it. Married when he met her to a wife with whom he did not live but to whom he continued to remain loyal, the father of two small daughters, he had constructed a life that included sex with whatever woman was within arm's reach. In addition to being an attractive man in his late thirties, tall and thin, he was then a minor celebrity, the author of a series of bestselling detective stories that had been sold to the movies. Money was no problem: Hammett squandered it on expensive hotels and gifts; he drank excessively, gambled at the race track and at cards, and engaged in endless, meaningless, sometimes costly sexual encounters.

Hellman was not quite twenty-six when she met Hammett, and she struggled to reshape her life. She fled the West Coast, running from two men, both in love with her and eager for her full attention. One was a sweet and loving husband, a talented but unexciting friend. The other

He was a minor celebrity. Hammett in the late 1930s. (Photofest)

was a famous writer of detective novels, a flamboyant alcoholic, profligate around women and money and married to someone else. While she tried to sort out what she would do, she settled herself into the St. Moritz—a residential hotel—and wrote profuse letters to both of them. She also produced short stories for the *New Yorker*, which routinely rejected them. Hammett visited her in New York for a couple of weeks in the late spring and then returned to Hollywood. Conflicted and lonely, she sought solace in the company of old friends and sometime lovers, Jed Harris and Louis Kronenberger among them. Occasionally she would hole up with Kronenberger for a night or a weekend. She partied with Ira and Lee

1935: Back and forth to the coast she went. (Photofest)

Gershwin, Chester Erskine, and Herman and Rose Shumlin when they
were on the East Coast. By the fall, she had made her decision; she agreed
to divorce Kober and then went, nervously, to New Orleans to tell her aunts
about her divorce and her relationship with Hammett. There is no record
of how she told her parents, who were still living on West 95th Street.

Back and forth to the coast she went, each time leaving after an angry tiff. Occasionally Hammett came east, taking separate quarters in one residential hotel or another. Finally, late in 1932, Hammett moved to New York, living at first in the Hotel Pierre (one of New York's most expensive hotels) and then with Lillian in a three-room suite at the Sutton Club Hotel.

The Sutton, managed by their friend the writer Nathanael "Pep" West, housed a community of writers that included James T. Farrell and Edmund Wilson. There, they lived a life of cheerful dissipation, working, drinking, and partying. Together Hellman and Hammett developed a series of friendships that were filled with mischief and fun. Lillian probably had a short liaison with Pep West, and she grew fond of his sister Laura Perelman and her husband Sid (S. J.) Perelman. According to Edmund Wilson, Lillian "used to help West steam open the letters of the guests by means of a kettle which he kept in his rooms."[19] Hammett had a week-long fling with Laura. Subsidized by his publisher, Knopf, he finished what was to be his last novel, *The Thin Man*, which he dedicated to Lillian. She continued to write short stories that continued to be rejected. In the winter of 1933–34, she and Hammett moved together into a small apartment in the Florida Keys, and together they completed her first produced play: *The Children's Hour*.

Their behavior flew in the face of the Depression-produced economic misery all around. Amid unemployment and widespread suffering, a growing national concern with social responsibility and traditional family life had replaced the individualism of the twenties. Opposition rose to wage work for women, particularly for women with male partners to support them. Hellman's image of independent womanhood seemed callow in the face of such attitudes. But the depression that devastated the economic fortunes of many and threw a quarter of the work force out of jobs had a more salutary effect on Lillian. As she became a well-known playwright and developed her talents as a skilled movie scriptwriter, she benefited from a Hollywood industry that flourished by creating fantasies for a nation in despair. The laurels—and the income—Hellman earned in this decade enabled a celebrity lifestyle and encouraged her to continue to flout conventional family relationships.

When Lillian's mother died in 1935, Lillian felt free to follow Hammett's style more fully. The masculine pose she adopted then included an outspoken and brash persona, complete with a foul vocabulary, which she used indiscriminately. Like Hammett (and such other 1930s figures as Hemingway and Faulkner), she drank, smoked, and partied nonstop. She was, wrote one observer, a "tough broad . . . the kind of girl who can take the tops off bottles with her teeth."[20] Not infrequently she indulged her passion for gambling and managed to make money playing both poker and chemin de fer. Nor did she make a secret of her sexual liaisons: she approached men she desired aggressively and slept with them at will. Quickly she earned a reputation as a "she-Hammett." But she wanted to be manly in another way, too, by exhibiting qualities of courage and force-fulness, by refusing to back down from a fight. These qualities contributed to her reputation as a stubborn woman, a difficult woman, a fighter.

To be sure, the tough outer shell hid a core of self-doubt that remained close to the surface. As a child, she believed she was not pretty. Later in her life, when she was asked to draw a self-portrait, she drew a stick-figure that she labeled "What I wanted to look like and don't." The drawing presented a figure that Lillian identified as having "blond curls, natural" and "deep blue eyes, natural."[21] She was always, she said, "jealous of great beauties."[22] The absence of conventional good looks, the prominent nose and irregular features, would shape Hellman's persona in many ways. She was a woman who needed men yet could not wear the pale orange tulle she thought would attract them. So she adapted. From early on she dyed her mousy brown hair a strawberry blonde that sometimes took on a reddish tinge. She showed off appealing qualities like her slim ankles and expressive eyes. She exhibited pride in her slender and sensuous body, which she dressed with an exquisite sense of style. She cultivated a flirta-tious charm reminiscent of her mother's South.

Interviewers routinely found themselves confounded by the contrast between the "tough broad" of record and the woman who appeared before them. "It was teatime," wrote one, "and Miss Hellman was sipping a pale sherry. She wore a gray dress fastened up the front with a zipper but open at the throat, with a black silk scarf crisscrossed in front like a soldier's and secured with a crystal clasp. She had a slender gold wrist watch and black pumps."[23] Such responses were routine. Hellman's warmth and affa-bility in person belied the public image and the masculine writing. "She is genuinely feminine to a degree that borders engagingly on the wacky," wrote Margaret Chase Harriman in a *New Yorker* profile.[24] This appraisal remained consistent throughout Hellman's lifetime. "In her own drawing room," one interviewer commented, "Miss Hellman, less a woman play-wright than a woman and a playwright was gentle, thoughtful, courteous, her manner affable . . . The ferocity she so relentlessly anatomizes in the

1938: She cultivated a flirtatious charm. (Photofest)

theater . . . nowhere in evidence."[25] A decade later, a British reporter affirmed the judgment, declaring that "although she has the kind of forthrightness and directness usually called masculine" she was in fact extremely feminine."[26]

Still, Hellman was consumed with doubt about her own lovability, full of fear of both success and failure, and prone to feeling lonely and isolated even when she was surrounded by people. She ran away when she anticipated a negative response to one of her plays or when she saw successful love on the horizon. Furiously jealous of Hammett's dalliances and angry with him for his continuing attractions to women of all sorts, she responded, characteristically, by soliciting affection and sex from other men, as well as with displays of bad temper and bouts of anger that she readily acknowledged but could not control. When Hammett hit bottom, she invariably came to his rescue, grudgingly forgiving him his faults and remaining attached to him nonetheless. Fearful of loneliness, she arranged to have company and then complained that she was with "all people I deeply like but people I wanted to run from."[27] After a while, she began to recognize her behavior as what she later called "an old pattern."[28] Fearing abandonment, she courted rejection; fearing loneliness, she surrounded herself with people she then wished away.

But Hammett was often a generous partner, and there were good weeks and months. During their frequent separations, Hammett wrote Lillian loving letters, begged her to join him, and sometimes rearranged his life so he could be with her. But he did not stop sleeping with other women. The stories about Lillian's reaction to this behavior are legendary. Hellman once traveled cross-country to be with him, only to find him drunk and in bed with a prostitute. In a rage, she smashed up his furniture and returned immediately to New York. There were times when his friends Albert and Frances Hackett would call from the West Coast, pleading with her to come and rescue him from a hotel in which he was trapped because he could not pay the bill.

Hellman, in turn, engaged in a series of sexual relationships, each of them more meaningful than Hammett's one-night stands but none as powerful as her pull toward him. In the half dozen years after she met Hammett, she remained involved with Kober, from whom she never separated emotionally. Nor, apparently did Arthur seek such a separation. Long after their divorce, she continued to express concern for his well-being. "Please, please do not go into the swimming pool," she begged him when she feared infection from crippling polio disease. She concluded her plea with an admonition to "pay attention to mama and take care of yourself."[29] Once, she advised him to change his living quarters. "I do think you would be more comfortable with a beach house, a servant and someone to look after the dogs," she wrote. In the same letter, she urged him to suspend decisions about what he wanted to do after his current contract ended. She signed this letter, "You got Mother Lillian behind you if that means anything."[30] In 1934, Kober sent Lillian a new typewriter and she responded with delight: "It's a grand present and you don't know how much I needed it . . . you're a lovely, generous man. You always send me such fine presents and I'm so grateful. Maybe next year I can give you something very good too. It's about time. Maybe I can earn some money with this new one . . . It was a wonderful gift to me and I love you very much."[31]

Through the 1930s, during the first decade with Hammett, Hellman maintained her on-and-off-again relationships with several friends and former lovers. She saw much of fellow playwright Louis Kronenberger. She had an ongoing affair with up-and-coming producer-director Jed Harris. She maintained a decade-long intermittent sexual relationship with Herman Shumlin, who produced three of her plays. She probably got involved with Otto Katz, a communist double agent, when she went to Spain in 1937. Her relationships with these men, and with others, began as (or included) sexual liaisons and grew into committed work-related friendships. In 1936, she fell passionately in love with Ralph Ingersoll, who was then editor in chief of *Fortune* magazine. She met Ingersoll when they were both stranded by bad weather in a New Mexico airport lounge. The two fell quickly into an intense romance that ultimately foundered on Ingersoll's unfulfilled promises to leave his wife. Still, the liaison seeded a three-way friendship with Hammett and inspired the creation of *PM* magazine. There were more, many more, sexual encounters, but these are the most important ones.

Hammett disliked these involvements, but never, according to Lillian, expressed jealousy or did anything to resist them. He called them "juggling oranges" and distinguished them from his own behavior, which he characterized as simply having fun. Eventually the Hammett-Hellman relationship became asexual. As Lillian told the story, this was a result of Hammett's addiction to drink. One summer evening, probably in 1941, she rejected his drunken advances, and he vowed never to sleep with her again. According to Lillian, he never again did so.[32] There are, of course, other possible explanations for Dash's withdrawal from a sexual relationship with Lillian. She had just then begun a relationship with *New Yorker* writer St. Clair McKelway. Perhaps Dash was following through on his threat to leave her if she continued to juggle oranges, or perhaps she had revealed a weakness—her comment demonstrated that she was not as tough as he wanted her to be. Lillian never quite got over the humiliation of the rejection. She spoke about it when she was in her seventies to Hammett's biographer, Diane Johnson, who concluded that she remained attached to him even after his death because she never stopped struggling to "possess and command at last the elusive ghost of a man about whom she was insecure in life."[33]

But Hellman had, by all accounts, a far more complicated relationship with men. In the eyes of most observers, she seemed genuinely to love being around them and to cherish an enormous affection, especially for Dash. A strong-willed and highly sexual woman, not unlike such figures as Joan Crawford and Katharine Hepburn, she needed men in her life.[34] The actress Zoe Caldwell, who played Lillian onstage and studied her closely, thought Hellman must have adored men, that she loved to be around them and enjoyed making love with them.[35] Caldwell attributes Hellman's special appreciation of men to an absence of mothering that came from Julia's too-early rejection of her child. But vanity contributed to Hellman's persistent insecurity as well: she needed constant reassurance about her desirability and her attractiveness. Attached to a man around whom she was often insecure, she exhibited in public all the outward qualities of strength demanded of the free woman of the interwar decades. In private, she allowed her feminine self to slip out. The cost of women's freedom, as literary critic Patricia Meyer Spacks has noted, is "emotional impoverishment and restriction."[36]

We catch a glimpse of how closely Lillian guarded her feelings around Hammett when she tells us that occasionally she and Hammett talked of marriage, most seriously when Hellman became pregnant for the third time in 1937. On his own, Hammett urged his wife, Josie, to file for a Mexican divorce, which was granted on August 31, 1937. By the time he wrote Lillian the news a week later, Lillian had already had an abortion. This was the third time she had lost a child, and yet she did not comment. The moment passed and marriage did not come up again.[37] "I don't know why we didn't marry," Hellman told an interviewer some years later. "We thought of it but then after a while it became silly even to discuss it."[38] Somewhat later, in 1942, Lillian visited Arthur and Maggie Kober's newborn baby. She was caught staring at it for a long while with tears in her eyes. She readily agreed to be godmother.

Despite the gloom cast by the continuing Depression and an impending war, the period from the late thirties through the forties must have been among the most gratifying of Lillian's life. In May 1939, with money earned from *The Little Foxes*, she indulged in the then decidedly male prerogative of purchasing a home of her own. The house, which she called Hardscrabble Farm, and its 130 acres of woods and meadows were located in Pleasantville, New York, an hour or so north of the city. The property contained a large restored colonial house with four and a half baths, five fireplaces, and a four-car garage.

It boasted as well a six-room caretaker's cottage, two guest houses, barns, and an eight-acre, spring-fed lake. Together, she and Hammett, along with farmer Fred Hermann, who occupied the caretaker's cottage, set themselves to reclaiming some of the neglected land, raising poultry and poodles as well as pigs and cattle, immersing themselves in other farm chores. At Hardscrabble, Hellman participated in slaughtering animals, helped to make sausage and head cheese, and learned how to hunt, trap turtles, and to fish. She delighted in her dogs and especially in the new puppies that came regularly.

In some ways the years at Hardscrabble allowed her to open up her many-sided persona. She was in her mid-thirties, with two successful plays and several movie scripts behind her. She had achieved fame as well as fortune, and she had a satisfying male companion at hand. At the farm, she began the pattern of nurturing and entertaining that provided continuing fulfillment. She surrounded herself with guests of all sorts, including her father, who often showed up for weekends, and Hammett's children, who came for summer holidays. On weekends she invited the cast of whatever play of hers was then running on Broadway. The house was so often filled with people that Hellman sometimes remembered it as a sort of boardinghouse where "people came and stayed."[39] Still she found time to sequester herself in the study, where she wrote four great plays (*Watch on the Rhine, The Searching Wind, Another Part of the Forest,* and *Autumn Garden*) that solidified her reputation as a playwright of the first rank. To the study door, she taped a notice:

> This room is used for Work
> Do not enter without knocking
> After you knock wait for an answer
> If you get no answer, go away and
> Don't come back
> This means everybody
> This means you
> This means Night and Day
> By Order of the Hellman-Military-Commission-for-
> Playwrights. Court Martialling will Take Place in the Barn,
> and your Trial Will Not be a Fair One.[40]

The thirteen years Lillian spent at Hardscrabble, most commentators would agree, were surely the happiest years with Hammett, and probably the happiest of Lillian's being. By the 1940s, Hellman's relationships with men and women had taken the shape that would persist for the rest of her life. The heavy drinking over, more secure in her craft and capable of earning her own way, she cultivated the love and loyalty of good friends and colleagues without dependence on a single partner. In addition to her ex-husband and his new wife, Maggie, her close friendships included Lee and Ira Gershwin, lifelong friends, who persuaded producer Herman Shumlin to read and produce *The Children's Hour*; Talli Wyler and her husband, William, who directed her screenplays for *These Three* and *Dead End*; and Dorothy Parker. Lillian first met Parker in 1930, in Hollywood. The two became good friends when they shared scriptwriting and union-organizing experiences in Hollywood. They later traveled to Spain together and spent time supporting anti-fascist causes. Their friendship survived Hammett's fierce dislike of Dottie and Lillian's contempt for Dottie's husband, Alan Campbell. It foundered only at the end of Parker's life when Parker could no longer control her addiction to alcohol. In her lifetime, Lillian achieved a goodly measure of deep and reciprocated love. And with those she loved, she created long-term relationships that sometimes included sex and often did not. She may never have had a sexual relationship with a woman (there is no evidence that she did), but with women, as with men, she created long-term loving relationships and lifelong loyalties.

In 1940, Hellman entered analysis with Gregory Zilboorg. She was thirty-six and had just seen her third blockbuster success mounted on the Broadway stage. She could not, she thought, handle the success. "Somewhere by instinct I had sense enough to know that I was going to have a crack-up," she told interviewer Christine Doudna.[41] Success and the drinking, she would later say, were her main reasons for starting treatment. But she knew these were not the only catalysts. Hammett, still drinking heavily, began, around this point, to withdraw from a sexual relationship with her. A year or so after she began analysis, the birth of Arthur and Maggie's daughter shook her deeply. Perhaps she had finally decided to come to terms with her fear of abandonment, her deeply rooted sense that she could not be loved? Or perhaps Hardscrabble released some newly reborn sense of her nurturing self.

Whatever the immediate impulses that led her to the couch, Hellman committed herself to the process, worked hard at it, and discovered much about herself. She wrote about the "hidden nastiness and resentment" that she found in her unconscious and about the temper and the anger that she could not control.[42] And, repeatedly, she referred to the treatment as intimately related to the painful depressions she suffered. "It is very sad to watch a neurosis work," she commented to her then lover, John Melby, "especially when it belongs to you."[43] The analysis would last eighteen years and develop into a deep friendship with the analyst and his wife, Peggy. The Zilboorgs visited her at Hardscrabble; she traveled with them to Paris and Italy; she sent her friends to Gregory Zilboorg for therapy and analysis. And in his hands, Lillian seemed able to give scope to her nurturing qualities.

She had always maintained a warm relationship with her ex-husband, Arthur Kober, but the relationship deepened and strengthened after Kober's remarriage and, not incidentally, after she began psychoanalysis. Arthur married Maggie Frohnknecht in 1941; Lillian served as witness at their wedding. She helped the family find an apartment in New York, managed their move from one apartment to another, supervised the storage of their things when they went abroad, and advised them about servants and real estate transactions. From Hardscrabble Farm, she wrote them loving and sometimes playful letters that began "Darling Arthur, darling Maggie," and ended with salutations of love and affection. Sometimes she signed these letters "Lillikins"; often she invited them all to "come home." These letters expressed a genuine longing, hard to fathom. Maggie became ill in 1946, and Lillian visited and comforted her in the hospital. A year later, she was writing to her: "Above all I wish I could see you again. I can't tell you how much I miss you or how often I think about you. You have left a large, vacant place in my life, and I hope to God you will come back some day soon and fill it again."[44] Sometimes she started her letters with "Dearest Maggie and husband dear to us both," or concluded them with affectionate salutations such as "my love to you, our husband, and child" and instructions to Maggie to take care of "our husband."[45] Occasionally, she and Dash took care of Catherine at Hardscrabble. Catherine remembers these times as joyous moments when Dash paid special attention to her.[46]

This relationship, like so many others in Lillian's life, was anchored by a frequent exchange of gifts that continued for all of their days and that served as concrete manifestations of reciprocal affection. Arthur and Maggie sent Lillian Christmas and birthday presents regularly. Lillian reciprocated, and when she could not think of what to send, she simply asked. "What do you want for your birthday and how much should it cost?" she wired Kober in August 1941.[47] When he sent her the bill for the six hand-sewn shirts he requested, she promptly sent him "57 smackers for 6 beautiful shirts, which is my birthday present to you."[48] To the Kobers' equivalent question in May of 1943, Lillian telegraphed back, "Girl

*She enjoyed the love and loyalty of good friends. Here with Arthur Kober,
Mrs. Shumlin, Esther Keene, and Herman Shumlin at the Shumlin home on
Fire Island. (Ransom Center)*

of my fine type would love towels. It's a wonderful present and I am very
grateful. Much Love to both of you and will write next week."[49] The decision to buy presents themselves and send off the bills seems to have become routine. In response to one query from Arthur about a Christmas
present, Lillian replied that she would like a negligee and asked him if he
"would like me to buy it and charge it to you in order to save you trouble."[50] Later, Lillian asked whether Maggie had yet bought her birthday
present in the same letter in which she told Kober that she had bought
herself "a beautiful chair for the lawn . . . it cost $36.45 and I am very grate-
ful to both of you and pleased with it. Thank you darling, and thank
Maggie for me."[51]

For Arthur she reserved a special place marked by her affectionate
salutations to him: "Arthur baby darling," she might write to him. Occasionally she warned him, "If Maggie ever divorces you . . ."[52] And it was
not unusual for Lillian to remind Arthur of their own marriage, as when
she telegraphed to wish him "A happy New Year, Darling and with truly

loving memories of 22 years ago."[53] After Maggie died in 1951, Lillian briefly harbored hopes of resurrecting their earlier love affair, signing one letter to him, "your first bride." These hopes came to naught but left her with no residue of ill feeling. She continued to see Arthur and to share confidences with him until he died in 1975. Her last act of friendship was a tribute at his funeral where she claimed for him "an affection without any of the misery that so often comes with broken arrangements." It was, she thought, "a friendship that had no pause and never ended."[54]

Hammett, who joined the army in 1942 and was stationed in the Aleutian Islands, received a full measure of her warm affection. At the beginning of their separation, Hellman (whose letters are missing) complained of his being cold, to which he responded with a humorous comment about taking his temperature and seeming "warm enough to the thermometer."[55] But from Alaska, Hammett suggests that Hellman proved a very satisfactory correspondent. "You, if I may say so, Madam," he told her, "write very nice and warming letters."[56]

From Hammett's letters to Hellman, we learn about the loving relationship they shared, even after he had foresworn sexual intimacy, and perhaps in anticipation of a reunion when he returned. Addressed to "Dear Lilishka" or "Dearest Lily" or Lilibet, the letters sometimes expressed concern for her health; at others they commented on her work or his, as when he proudly noted the release of the movie version of *Watch on the Rhine* (whose script he had written), appreciated her work on *North Star*, or boosted her spirits when she despaired over a difficult new play (*The Searching Wind*). The letters are often sentimental, as when he noted the thirteenth anniversary of their first meeting and added, "They have been fine grand years and you are a fine grand woman and for all I know I must have been a fine grand man to have deserved them and you. And with such a start, think of not only the next thirteen, but the ones after that!"[57] They are also filled with the kinds of intimate details that recall a life together. When the army stopped censoring the letters of enlisted men in Alaska, for example, Hammett rejoiced that he would now be able to write to her "without feeling that I'm telling whichever officer in my unit happens to be unit censor about you in bed." He wouldn't want those officers to know, he wrote to her playfully, "that in cold weather you sleep with your buttocks sticking out from under the covers."[58] As the war drew to a close and Hellman took her lengthy trip to Moscow, Hammett longed for her return, telling her he would postpone a thirty-day furlough until he knew when she would be back, and closing his letters with "Now I'm off to bed, sweetheart, but not without sending you much love and many, many kisses."[59]

In every way, Lillian acted like the wife she might have been. While he was away, she held a power of attorney for him and she and her secretary, Nancy Bragdon, monitored his spending and managed his financial affairs. Lillian sent cookies to Fort Monmouth for him and his barracks mates and responded to his requests with alacrity. Once he was settled in Alaska, he asked for books—"books are something I've been missing a good deal lately"—and from Abercrombies: a "hood to thwart the elements; you know something to pull over my face when the weather's bad, with eyeholes or something to look through. I don't know—Abercrombies will know . . . Tell them," he wrote, "It's for winter—WINTER—tell 'em, in Alaska—ALASKA."[60] Unasked, she sent food of all kinds: rumcakes, maple sugar, chocolates, and grapefruit peel, but also caviar, goose liver pâté, and smoked turkey from an East Side gourmet shop called Martin's. To Alaska also went socks from Brooks Brothers and Saks Fifth Avenue, pipes and pipe tobacco from Dunhill, and, in the fall of 1943 (just preceding their second Christmas apart), a gold chain and a ring to which he avowed his instant attachment.[61]

After Hammett had been in Alaska for about a year, Lillian flew off on her Moscow adventure. There, she fell deeply in love with a State Department officer named John Melby. Hammett, who did not worry when he received no letters from Moscow, began to wonder why she did not write once she had arrived in England on her way back to the States. "Charitably," as he put it, he blamed her silence on the mail service, but he also remarked in a hurt note to Maggie Kober, "I guess I'll never understand women."[62] More seriously he wrote to Lillian, in March of 1945, that he would "expect some kind of explanation why you didn't write me all the time you were in England."[63] Lillian did not explain—and when Hammett returned to the United States in the summer of 1945, he found Melby at Hardscrabble. Hammett obligingly moved his belongings out. But Melby left for China within months, and Hammett resumed his on-again, off-again place in Lillian Hellman's life—sometimes living at Hardscrabble, at others in an apartment he took on West 10th Street in New York City, and, after 1952, in a cottage in Katonah, New York, owned by friends who gave it to him at nominal rent. Lillian, as she wrote to Melby, remained "very devoted to Dash, deeply devoted, and I wish I could see him happy and settled and sure of some kind of future. He is a wonderful human being, and it is heartbreaking to see it go to waste."[64] Dash, for his part, continued to read Lillian's work, and the two drew closer together in the difficult McCarthy years. Lillian tried to raise bail money for him when he was arrested for refusing to divulge the names of contributors to a civil liberties bail fund, supported him when he went to prison, and paid his bills when Hammett's income fell victim to charges of income tax delinquency. In 1958, ill and broke, he moved somewhat reluctantly into Hellman's townhouse on East 82nd Street. He was living there when he died on January 10, 1961.

With John Melby, as with so many of her lovers, Lillian retained an important relationship that survived their sexual attraction for each other. She met and fell in love with Melby in the winter of 1944–45, when she visited the wartime Soviet Union. Melby was then a cultural affairs officer at the Moscow embassy of the United States, and for a while both of them lived at the American compound in Moscow, known as Spaso House. It

She met John Melby in the winter of 1944. (University of Pennsylvania Archives)

was here that she met Ambassador Averell Harriman and his wife, Marie, who would remain her friends long afterward. When Melby returned to the United States on leave in the summer and fall of 1945, the two talked of marrying as soon as Melby could secure a divorce from his estranged wife. But the relationship foundered when Melby was posted to China, where, despite his continuing professions of love and commitment, he stayed for more than four years. Hellman treated the separation as temporary at first, writing long love letters to him and begging him to return. Slowly the requests turned to demands, and as Melby's replies demonstrated an increasing reluctance to return, a very sad Lillian slowly put the relationship aside. When Melby returned from China in 1950, he was involved with another woman. Still, he and Hellman, ever fond of each other, met intermittently.

Eventually, Melby found himself called before a government investigating committee questioning his loyalty. The charges against him included his relationship with Lillian (a "known Communist"). Hellman enlisted Joe Rauh, the lawyer who helped to defend her before HUAC, to represent him, and did what she could to stay quiet and not complicate his life; she shared his anger and distress when he ultimately lost his job and his career in the State Department. Briefly they resumed their affair, but in the end, Melby married another woman and reappeared in Hellman's life only intermittently.[65]

While Melby was in China, Hellman dealt with the illness and death of her father, and here, too, a sense of family feeling is palpable. Her father began to develop symptoms of dementia in 1948. Hellman tried first to provide nursing care for him at home and then, reluctantly and on the advice of his doctors, placed him in an expensive private nursing home. From there he wrote long anguished letters to his family and friends, begging to be released and venting his frustration on Lillian. His sisters, Hannah and Jenny, pleaded with Lillian to return him to his home, convinced that she was restraining him against his will and accusing her of being hard-hearted. Lillian responded angrily at first. She was hurt at their mistrust and invited them to come and visit their brother to see for themselves. For more than a year letters flew back and forth, each of them demonstrating Lillian's misery at having to incarcerate her father and her outrage at having to explain herself to her two beloved aunts. Not until they came to visit did they desist. The episode suggests something of Lillian's sense of herself as a daughter. Though she never felt close to anyone in her mother's family, she cherished her relationship with her

father and his sisters until they died, and their memories long
afterward.[66]

Family relationships did not come easily to Hellman, and in the fifties
she seemed to become needier and more emotionally dependent as well
as more fearful about her standing and status. Surely this is linked to the
devastating betrayals of the McCarthy period and the dissolution of
many friendships under the stress of government investigation. But the
fifties must have challenged Hellman in other ways as well. This was the
decade in which ideas about traditional marriage and heterosexual fidelity were linked to patriotism, when maintaining a home and family sustained American prosperity and the American way of life. In the parlance
of the time, a happily married suburban housewife represented security
and stability, the promise of capitalism in an age of potential nuclear
conflict.[67] Hellman's position as an unmarried and independent woman
now seemed anomalous rather than admirable, vaguely subversive of
American values rather than celebrated. A woman of her age and generation should, it was thought, have settled down with a husband as so
many of Hellman's female friends had done. Hellman, in contrast, continued to relish both her independence and her sexuality, attributes
some thought of as symptoms of communism. Yet Lillian seemed entirely comfortable in her double role. With Dash she acted, as actress and
friend Patricia Neal recalls, "like a little girl," solicitous and flirtatious.[68]

After 1952, while Hammett occupied the cottage in Katonah, he briefly
maintained his apartment on 10th Street. Hellman apparently visited
him in Katonah "often, not so very often, but often," as Helen Rosen, the
cottage's owner, put it; and he spent infrequent weekends in New York
with her.[69] In the context of the decade, the absence of a shared residence
struck many as odd. After Dash became ill in the mid-fifties, he no longer had the resources to live alone. Reluctantly he moved into her New
York City townhouse. But for all that she provided for him until he died
in January 1961, she never felt confident in his affection, never secure in
his love for her. "With other people there was warmth and need and maybe
even the last weeks a sexual need," she wrote in her diary two months
after he died, "but not with me."[70] Dash didn't want to be in her house,
didn't want to be dependent, but had little choice. Without him, she conducted an active social life, traveling at whim and dining out frequently.
When she entertained at home he often disappeared; when she went out

it was generally to see her friends alone. Her loneliness was certainly exacerbated by the death of Gregory Zilboorg just a year and a half before Dash died.

It took Hellman a while after Hammett died to come to terms with what their relationship had been. With uncharacteristic honesty, she confided to her diary, "sometimes, now, I think he wanted to be good friends, but more often I know that he didn't."[71] When she wasn't angry with Hammett, she blamed herself. "I did my best," she divulged to the diary, "and I know now and am sad about it, that it wasn't a very good best." Hellman buried her sorrow and her loneliness in her memories of Dash, turning him, in death, into the romantic and idealized soul that the living Hammett was not.[72] The memory of Hammett, and the stories she made up about him, became a crutch as she entered into her late fifties and sixties—a reminder of joy and physical vitality, of sensuality and happiness. She kept photographs of him everywhere, managed his estate and his image, recalled anecdotes about him, and quoted remarks he might have made.

Self-reliant now, and without Dash as an emotional backup, she re-situated herself both with relation to the men she loved and in her social relationships. She met and fell for Arthur Cowan, a wealthy Philadelphia lawyer, in the late 1950s and remained close to him until he died in 1964. Cowan's wealth, not his politics, created the glue that drew them together; her cynicism and anger about old political allies still got in the way of re-creating some of her old relationships. And though she denies wanting to marry him, her denials have a bit of the quality of protesting too much. She was willing to settle, she tells us in *Pentimento*, for the continuing, dependable, and generous male companionship he offered along with financial and legal counsel when she needed it. And yet when Cowan became involved with another woman, she suspected he would renege on his promise to take care of her forever. After his sudden death, Lillian insisted that he must have left something for her and set her lawyers to hunting for the will. It could not be found, and Hellman, feeling cheated and abandoned, was convinced that the family had destroyed it.

Her dependence on another friend, Blair Clark, was more emotional than financial. Clark was an executive at CBS and had been the college friend of Robert Lowell, who with his wife, Elizabeth Hardwick, was then Lillian's frequent companion. He became close to Lillian shortly after Dash died.[73] There is something of pathos in this relationship. Blair Clark befriended Lillian in 1962 with notes and phone calls and expensive dinners. Lillian believed and hoped that their friendship would develop into an ongoing intimacy and perhaps something closer. Clark claimed to have been unaware of Hellman's sexual attraction toward him and to have feared her neediness. Perhaps we must believe him, for Hellman's diaries of the period are filled with longing for him that include waiting for his calls, noting his silences, commenting on whether she called him. They record when they went out to dinner together, when he visited, how long he stayed, and whether the visit was good or not. Through the lines appears a kind of lovesick longing that suggests the wish for, if not the reality of, a more permanent relationship. To stir Clark's feelings and assuage her own desires, Hellman created an elaborate and fantastic fable about a fictional Yugoslav diplomat with whom she claimed to be engaged in a long-running affair. She had, she said, had a son with this man, and then she spun a complicated tale about the boy's youth and education, his career, his marriage, and his children.

The tale, clearly made of whole cloth, prefigures some of the later stories Hellman would tell to capture the self that she wanted to be. This style—critic Richard Locke calls it "inventing all the time"—endeared her to many people. It was, says Locke, "part of who she was"; Locke's partner, Wendy Nicholson, adds that it was "part of her gift." Friendship, in Locke's view, "involved play, a fantasy self-presentation, a different kind of exaggeration, a good story."[74] Certainly this seemed to be the case with Blair Clark. He remained fond of Lillian and affectionate toward her into the 1970s and after he remarried. Until she died, he took her out for dinner several times a year, acted as confidant when she needed a shoulder, and played a major role in the influential Committee for Public Justice that she founded in 1970. But, he claimed after she died, "we were never lovers, which may come as a surprise to some and which was surely a disappointment, and more, to her."[75]

The relationship suggests Lillian's continuing capacity to create emotional intimacy even as her physical attractiveness waned. As she moved into her sixties, she became increasingly close to young men who were attracted by the force of her personality and tempted into her orbit by the wacky sense of humor, the charming directness, and the confrontational stance. "Playfulness," as Blair Clark put it, "was very much part of her nature."[76] And she loved to pick an argument, to fight. Her continuing zest and energy compensated for the now leathery skin and the wrinkled, smoke-scarred face. In person, remembers Wendy Nicholson, "she had this incredible electrical charge about her . . . She really had a tremendous sort of personal force."[77] Many men, particularly younger men, found her both attractive and seductive. Her sometime lover and close friend Peter Feibleman, twenty-five years younger than she, called her the sexiest woman he had ever known.[78]

And yet her loneliness and her desire for male companionship some-times led her down hurtful paths. Stanley Hart claims to have been tempted into Hellman's sexual service in the mid-sixties. Hart, then an editor at Little, Brown who had encountered Lillian several times when they were both on Martha's Vineyard, proposed to his boss Arthur Thornhill that she be invited to write a memoir. Hart claims that he learned from Lillian's agent (then Robby Lantz) that the deal would carry a proviso. "If I slept with Lillian Hellman," concluded the then-thirty-six-year-old Hart after discussions with Hellman's agent, "I could get her signature on a contract."[79] Hart was not averse to the exchange. She was, after all, a star. Sleeping with her, he frankly admits, "offered the promise of a friendship that I thought would elevate me into an echelon in which writers, and artists and actors and the very rich tended to socialize."[80] Lillian, in his memory, was "game, sexy and flirtatious." She was also robust and energetic. Hart recounts how he made a date with Lillian and ended up in bed with her, beginning a reluctant romance that lasted for the better part of two years until he had her signature on the contract and she began to treat him with the disdain she reserved for those who served her. Then, in his eyes, she turned into an irritable, "self-centered, aging and ungainly" woman into whose "cruel, contentious" face he could no longer look.[81] Hart pub-lished the story thirty years later and fifteen years after Lillian's death. If it is true, it suggests some sense of Hellman's vulnerability to the existen-tial loneliness from which she suffered and provides a clue to her unre-quited need for physical affection.

Lillian generally satisfied her needs for companionship in an exciting social life in which she became involved after Dash's death in early 1961. At Har-vard, where she taught in the spring of 1961, she met Richard Poirier, then a young lecturer who would become a close friend and one of her literary executors. She also got to know Harvard instructor and playwright Wil-liam Alfred. There too she met Martin Peretz, who would become editor of the New Republic, and Fred Gardner, the young student who introduced her to the world of the student left. To these young men and to many others who recalled her defiance toward the House Committee on Un-American

Activities, she was still a heroine. "She was thought of as gutsy, brilliant, witty, noble, socially desirable, and sexually liberated," Stanley Hart tells us.[82] Her new contacts melded with her New York life to provide a place on the edges of the intellectual world of the sixties. She did not belong in the quasi-political group that became known as the New York intellectuals or in the literary circle that surrounded the *New York Review of Books,* but many of its members became her friends. They included Philip Rahv of *Partisan Review,* Lionel and Diana Trilling, Barbara and Jason Epstein, Robert Lowell and Elizabeth Hardwick. To this mix, and to her dinners, she added many others, among them conservative columnist Joseph Alsop, Norman Podhoretz (who became editor of *Commentary* in 1960), and McGeorge Bundy.

Celebrity provided access to broader and broader circles and simultaneously affirmed her status, a position she assiduously cultivated. Putting politics into the backseat, she constructed relationships with the rich and the powerful. She dined at the Princeton Club with Edmund Wilson and partied with Arthur Schlesinger Jr., Jackie Kennedy, Richard Goodwin, and Norman Mailer. She was recognized and offered a table at the most elegant restaurants; she attended and held court at the season's fashionable parties. An avid hostess, Hellman became, in Edmund Wilson's choice phrase, the Queen of the Cocktail Belt.[83] "No writer I had ever met before . . . or would ever meet again," recalled Norman Podhoretz of his younger days, "lived in as opulent a style as she did." When he went to one of her lavish dinner parties, he met "famous theatrical personalities—producers, directors, actors, and actresses—with the women all richly begowned and bejeweled and the men radiating the special air of self-assurance that seems always to accompany the making of a lot of money."[84] The numbers of these friendships, and the amount of time Hellman invested in them, suggests the plausibility of John Hersey's claim that he knew "no living human being whom so many people consider to be their one best friend."[85]

Others recalled Hellman's dinners for their warmth and energy: "She wanted everybody to be having a good time," remembers Peter Feibleman, so she moved people around to make sure that they were not bored.[86] Her dinners consisted of a mix of carefully selected people. "She knew who to ask, who to seat them next to. It was like choreographing."[87] At the dinners she was, in one attendee's words, "very attentive, very generous. The food was always wonderful."[88] Adds Morris Dickstein, "Whether she was throwing a small dinner party or a large party, she treated it like a kind of art. The amount of energy that went into the seating, the meal, the cooking, the mix of people was the kind of effort that a really good writer would expend on a sentence. She worked to get it exactly right."[89] Lillian did not, at these events, control her tongue. She could disrupt her own parties and those of others by fighting with her guests, verbally slugging at them for their likes and dislikes. And yet she had a quick sense of humor and a raucous laugh that concluded a debate and put everyone at ease. Lillian's parties were so wonderful and such fun that her friends coveted invitations to them. The writer Shirley Hazzard wrote to her friend William Abrahams of one dinner party she knew Hellman was planning: "If we are excluded we will just come round and moan beneath the windows."[90]

After the harrowing and unsettling fifties, in which she had been marginal in many worlds, the renewed celebrity demonstrated Hellman's importance. She enjoyed the attention thoroughly. "Whenever Lillian would walk into one of those New York parties where there were bankers and pretty girls and famous people there," remembers Peter Feibleman, "Lillian would walk in and the other ladies would all kind of disappear into the woodwork." Nor was Hellman above broadcasting her victories. She told all and sundry that "Lord" Sidney Bernstein invited her to dinner in London. And, when Britain's Lord Snowdon asked if he could take her photograph, she gloried in teasing her agent about it, insisting that he now display the respect properly due her.[91] Hellman might have started the decade of the sixties as a star chaser, but by its end she had become a star worthy of chasing.

The social nature of many of Hellman's contacts—often efforts to take advantage of celebrity—should not obscure the deep and long-lasting friendships she developed. These drew on her nurturing qualities. On the Vineyard, where she continued to spend her summers and soon built herself a smaller house to replace the large one she had occupied with Hammett, she became close to Jerome Wiesner (later to become president of MIT), his wife, Peggy, and to the poet Robert Lowell (known to his friends as Cal), though not to his wife, Elizabeth Hardwick. She fished with John Hersey almost daily and sometimes with William Styron too. She gossiped with screenwriter Jay Presson Allen, picnicked with John and Sue Marquand, quarreled with Robert Brustein, played Scrabble with Rose Styron, and planned dinners and parties with Barbara Hersey. She met Leonard Bernstein and his wife, Felicia, in the early fifties. That friendship survived an unsuccessful collaboration on the operetta *Candide*

(produced in 1955) to become a robust, complicated, and loving association. Lillian addressed him as "Lennie Pie"; he called her Dear Lillllly or
Dear Lilliana. In the seventies, Mike and Annabel Nichols often joined a
Vineyard crowd that not only summered together but occasionally spent
several winter weeks on an island in the Bahamas. Annabel Nichols would
become a loving and attentive companion as Hellman grew older and
more irascible.

These were Lillian's friends. Irritating, demanding, and bad-tempered
as she often was with them, stubborn and willful as she might be, they
took her flaws in stride and reveled in the warmth she exuded and the
practical jokes and high jinks in which she excelled. To her Vineyard
friends, she was simply part of the community: they supported her and
listened to endless complaints even as she enlivened their days with her
wit and inventiveness. Stories abounded about her swimming nude off
her boat or at the Vineyard beach. Brooke Allen, whose family summered
in that community, recalls her penchant for practical jokes. Lillian once
forged a letter to Bill Styron, signing it with the name of an attractive
woman he had long wished to meet. Styron read the letter, imagined that
it expressed genuine admiration, and immediately set out to find the supposed correspondent. The joke backfired when Styron briefly took up with
the young woman. Hellman's New York friends cherished the wicked
sense of humor that led her to let fly at friends and foes alike and then slyly
apologize for what she called "the snake in my mouth."[92]

It wasn't easy to be Lillian's friend as she grew older. Her forceful and
direct style, her penchant for saying what was on her mind without censorship, her quick temper and occasional tantrums, offended many. When
these qualities were not relieved by humor and warmth, they could be
destructive. This happened more and more after 1974, when, while in
Europe, she apparently suffered the first of a series of strokes. Peter Feibleman tells us that the strokes increased her level of irrational anger astro-
nomically and often led her into erratic emotional behavior. If she quarreled
with her Park Avenue neighbor over what kind of table should go under
a vase in their shared hallway, the two never spoke again. If she lost a
watch on the beach in Gay Head, she complained that the beach was insufficiently patrolled. Her capacity to make both men and women, but especially women, appear invisible was legendary. Anne Navasky tells a story
about how, having sat next to her all night at a dinner, she offered Lillian
a ride home. Lillian accepted, and Anne went out to get the car. Escorted

out of the house by Richard de Combray and Victor Navasky, Lillian noted the woman at the wheel and turned to Navasky to compliment him for having hired a female chauffeur.[93]

Even to those she loved, before and especially after the strokes, she could be, and often was, overbearing, arrogant, and just plain rude. She demanded much in terms of responsiveness and loyalty, and she was thin-skinned and sensitive to slights. But she was also remarkably giving, willing to focus on her companions and to be "interested in your life and what you were."[94] Not surprisingly, her friendships were volatile, marked by arguments that led to days and weeks of anger before reconciliation. She could pick an argument over a recipe, as she did with Bill Styron, and the two stubborn individuals would part company for weeks. If she disliked a question at someone else's dinner table or perceived an insult, she might pick up her handbag and leave. Or she could silence a conversation by shouting across a table to tell someone that he was wrong about something she had barely overheard.[95] Her friends tolerated or accepted these behaviors, in return for the genuine affection that Lillian so often displayed.

Her sexual energy directed toward men, Hellman often simply ignored the women in their presence. She often referred to wives as "Madam" as if she could not bother to remember their names. Insecure about her own looks and vain of her own appearance, she abhorred vanity in other women. She referred to those she disliked as "Mrs. Gigglewitz" out of aversion for their conceit, their mindlessness, or their careless display of wealth. John Hersey wrote, after her death, "she had a habit of liking husbands and very expressively not liking wives."[96] True, she made no special effort to appeal to the wives of men she cared about, sometimes maintaining strong relationships with men despite, not because of, their wives. Elizabeth Hardwick falls into that category. Lillian was extremely close to Hardwick's husband, Robert Lowell, in the late fifties and early sixties but maintained a coolly civil social relationship with Lizzie, as she was called. But Lizzie, who reciprocated the cool feelings, turned her back on Lillian once the marriage was over and publicly disparaged her and her work.[97] Still, her close woman friends included the wives of William Wyler, Leonard Bernstein, Richard Wilbur, Jerome Wiesner, and Arthur Kober, as well as those of V. S. Pritchett, John Hersey, and Mike Nichols. And many of the friends she made in the sixties and seventies, including Anne Peretz, Lore Dickstein, and Wendy Nicholson, testify to the attention she paid them, the notes of appreciation she wrote, and the small gifts she sent. These were friendships Hellman perceived as with equals—with women who had position or accomplishment of their own.

Perhaps Lillian's closest woman friend was Hannah Weinstein, who would become Lillian's touchstone. A loyal friend and companion through the political troubles of the 1950s and a confidante until she died in 1982, Weinstein returned from a self-imposed exile in Europe to found a successful Hollywood production company. In later years she lived around the corner from Lillian's Park Avenue home. The two were almost daily companions, often dining together at local restaurants. By some accounts, Hannah played second fiddle to the much tougher Lillian, but Hannah also seemed to have exercised some control over Lillian, insisting, for example, that she say thank you when appropriate.[98] Shirley Hazzard, Frances Hackett, and later Ruth Field and Maureen Stapleton were among the women who shared their thoughts with Lillian over the years and with whom she shared her deepest feelings.

Lillian's large heart and enormous capacity for warmth and generosity drew people to her even as her irascibility repelled them. She responded promptly to friends in need, though not always in the ways they wanted. She lent money—generally accompanied by advice and instruction. Hellman worked closely with the poet Richard Wilbur when he was called in to provide lyrics for some of the songs in her 1955 musical operetta *Candide*. She and Wilbur's wife, Charlee, had become good friends, a friendship perhaps best exemplified by the Wilburs' decision to ask Lillian to be godmother to their son and Lillian's decision, after Hammett died in January 1961, to send all of Hammett's clothes to Richard (who, like Hammett, was tall and thin). Lillian regularly exchanged Christmas presents with the Wilburs and sometimes lent them her Martha's Vineyard home. Charlee addressed her letters to "Dearest Pie" and signed them with affectionate remarks like "so much love, dear, from us all." Early in February 1961, the Wilburs ran into financial trouble and Charlee, without Richard's knowledge, wrote to Lillian to ask her for a loan. Their son had been ill, she wrote; she had given their only bit of available cash to a cousin without her husband's knowledge; she did not want to trouble Richard because it would cause him anxiety. Lillian responded immediately. She would loan the money—but only if Charlee told her husband everything. Charlee agreed, at first stipulating that the loan be made in her name alone. Once again Lillian balked. Finally, with Richard's full knowledge and consent, Lillian made the Wilburs the loan. Like every loan she made, she kept careful records of the amount and the repayment record.[99]

Hellman adopted a similar, sometimes unwelcome, but always well-intentioned interventionist strategy at other times. When she learned that Robert Lowell was searching for a producer for his five-hour drama *The Old Glory,* she insisted that only she had the skill and contacts necessary to find someone good. In the end she failed, but she did help to raise money for the production.[100] When her goddaughter Dina Weinstein asked her for help in setting up a catering business in France, Hellman replied with a counterproposal to support her for five months while Dina wrote a French cookbook. Characteristically, Lillian imposed a condition. She asked Dina to "turn over your research upon your return, to me and together, or perhaps I alone, will use the research for a cookbook." Dina turned down the offer but Lillian sent her money anyway, offering her advice about menus, holiday meals, and which customers to entice.[101] These examples suggest a desire to control that others experienced as problematic. In the mid-seventies, Catherine Kober, the daughter of Arthur and one of Lillian's four godchildren, inherited $10,000 that Lillian's mother had meant to leave to Arthur decades before. The money passed through Lillian to Catherine, by now an adult, and Catherine contributed it to her favorite charity. Lillian, incensed that Catherine had not solicited her advice, promptly and painfully broke off relations with Catherine.[102]

On the other side, Hellman's life was punctuated with routinely munificent gestures. Old friends often drew on her for support, and she gave generously but only to causes in which she deeply believed. Routinely she invested small sums in plays written, produced, or directed by her friends. She provided her producer, Kermit Bloomgarden, with several loans, the first of them in 1946. He did not finish repaying them until 1956. After Bloomgarden's leg was amputated in 1972, she asked her agent to restructure some of the conditions of the contract for *The Lark,* on which they had worked together, in order to give him a larger share of the royalties.[103] Later, she guaranteed a $5,000 loan to the ailing Bloomgarden from Bankers' Trust, paying it off when he could not. She willingly lent her 82nd Street house to whomever needed it. At one point, when she was abroad for several months, she instructed her secretary to ask the housekeeper to close down all the rooms except for her bedroom and study, which guests might want to use.[104] She lent her Park Avenue apartment to Edmund Wilson when her old friend, and very briefly her lover, became ill with what was apparently a tropical parasite. He and his wife, Elena, spent ten days there before he was admitted to Doctor's Hospital for a throat condition. Wilson's biographer, Lewis Dabney, counts Lillian "among the loyal friends of his later years" and remarks on what he calls the unjustified bitterness with which Mary McCarthy (Wilson's third wife) "would later attack Hellman for not telling the truth about her Stalinist past."[105]

Recommendation letters and introductions flew from Hellman's desk with great regularity. One after another, she referred *New Yorker* critic Penelope Gilliatt, theater director Robert Lewis, and photographer Richard de Combray to William Abrahams, her editor at Little, Brown.[106] She offered Renata Adler an introduction to Arthur Thornhill, Little, Brown's publisher, and asked Thornhill to look at the manuscript of psychologist George Gero, who was her therapist at the time. She recommended "a brilliant young woman called Alice Wexler" to her literary agent, Don Congdon, and nominated photographer Berenice Abbott as well as Australian novelist Christina Stead to membership in the prestigious American Academy of Arts and Letters.[107] Maureen Howard's memoir, *Facts of Life*, earned a blurb that described it as one of a handful of good books that "could only have been written by women."[108] These responses suggest a person devoted to friendship and committed to the actions that would keep it alive. For Morris and Lore Dickstein, who had purchased a summer home in Sag Harbor, Hellman contacted old friends. "It was like she had alerted people to be ready for us," reported Lore Dickstein.[109]

Perhaps to affirm friendship and to participate in an exchange that would make her feel loved, Lillian always placed great stock in the giving and receiving of gifts. The value of the gifts exchanged served as a measure of reciprocal affection. All her life she desired, even expected, gifts from the women and men who were her friends and lovers, chastising them when they failed to come through and teasing them with her own promises of generosity. Hammett won her heart with a mink coat and expensive jewelry; her friends brought back luxurious laces from Europe. John Melby sent her silk cloth and unusual items from China. Ruth and Marshall Field filled her house with flowers on the occasion of her HUAC hearing. Gifts tested as well as buttressed friendship, producing in some friends enormous anxiety as to what and how much to give. Leonard and Felicia Bernstein, for example, were said, annually, to have racked their brains to come up with a suitable Christmas gift for her.[110]

Lillian in turn went to Europe with lists of gifts she would bring back and distribute on her return. On one occasion she sought ties, scarves, a cigar cutter for Dash; lace collars for her friend Ruth and Ruth's daughter, Judy; leather gloves and crosses for some of the women in her life; a blouse for her secretary, Edith. Sometimes she made lists of things that she had bought, such as "7 extra ties, slip, blouse, Silver Hat pins, scarves (2), Lace front"—and then a second list that revealed to whom she would give them. On other occasions, she was more specific—reminding herself to buy a Swiss watch for John, pearl earrings for Helen, her cook, a perfume bottle for Mary Warburg, handkerchiefs from London for her aunt Florence Newhouse. Then again, she might jot down the sizes and colors of items of clothing she would bring back, as when she noted that John Hersey wore a size large or extra large and that he did not like red, gold, or green, while Barbara wanted a white slipover.[111] Gifts could take varied forms: Lillian expected and got invitations to dine at expensive restaurants, the use of her friends' homes in the Caribbean and warm climates, and, once, an invitation to travel by private yacht to Egypt. Sometimes they involved services: Felicia Bernstein would return to the United States from Rome through Paris, husband Leonard wrote, "so that she can pick up the dresses for you."[112] And sometimes they were prized possessions. Charlee Wilbur gave her a necklace that belonged to her grandmother and that was so precious to her that she hoped Lillian would leave it to the Wilburs' daughter in her will in order that it might remain in the family.[113]

To be sure, the demands of friends and acquaintances could become irritating, increasingly so as she grew more famous in the sixties. She ducked an invitation to support Tennessee Williams's candidacy for membership in the American Academy of Arts and Letters, scribbling a note to her secretary on the bottom of the letter, "Call and say I am somewhere—on a boat—Maine, maybe—and you won't be hearing from me for a few weeks."[114] To Arthur Schlesinger Jr., who asked her to support the candidacy of someone she hardly knew to the Academy, she wrote that she had already supported enough people and would do no more. And yet there were always more, and she always did.

Lillian Hellman never lost the edge of toughness she acquired in the 1920s and with which she conquered the 1930s. She never lost the feisty willingness to speak her mind, or the tough veneer that coded her as manly or masculine. Nor did she ever stop being the sexual creature of the 1920s. She remained always, as her friend Morris Dickstein described her, "at once a perfect lady and at the same time . . . obscene."[115] Jane Fonda, who played Lillian in the film *Julia,* experienced difficulty capturing her: "Lillian is a homely woman," she told an interviewer, "and yet she moves as if she were Marilyn Monroe. She sits with her legs apart, with her satin underwear partly showing—she's a very sexual, sensual woman."[116] Reading the interview, Lillian took umbrage not at Fonda's characterization of her sexuality but at the description of her as homely. Hellman's friend Richard Stern perhaps captured her best in these years. She was, he thought, "comfortable and expensive," as well as "cozy, warm, flirtatious, yet a powerhouse."[117]

We learn from Hellman how complicated it must have been for a woman in the deepest part of the twentieth century to stay true to her desires even as she juggled the pressures of the world around her. She never let go her mother's dream, cultivating the warmth and generosity that earned her loyal and loving friends. But she also wanted to be her own person, so she stubbornly insisted on having things her own way and could not curb the fierce temper and the foul tongue that created chasms. The gap between the two personas was mediated by talent, celebrity, and the earthy humor that kept friends and enemies alike in awe. Her agent, Robby Lantz, responding to an introduction she wrote in the mid-sixties to an anthology of Hammett's work, elegantly summarized the contradictions: "You are all heart, yet also all brain; all vulnerability, yet incredibly strong; all emotion, yet completely unsentimental; possessor of a rare sense of the tragic, yet full of pure, clear humor."[118] Even put together, these qualities could not disguise Hellman's existential solitude. She never overcame it, perhaps because it emerged from a century in which many women tried to be not one thing or another but to be all things at once. To Billy Abrahams, the editor of her memoirs, she described the resulting tension: "I asked almost nobody this summer, but the house has been too full. This week is good—nobody—and I sulk and make myself delicious things to eat, and tell myself nobody loves me and why should they?"[119]

CHAPTER 3

A Serious Playwright

I say again that the presentation of something besides mere entertainment and spectacle is the great function of the legitimate theater of the world today.

—Lillian Hellman, 1936

Everything that I had heard or seen or imagined had formed a giant, tangled time—a jungle in which I could find no space to walk without tripping over old roots, hearing old voices speak about histories made long before my day.

—Lillian Hellman, 1973

Before she became the Lillian Hellman famous for writing her memoirs, Lillian Hellman was a playwright. Between 1934 and 1964, she wrote eight plays of her own and adapted four others to the theater. She did not want to be just a good playwright, nor to be identified as a woman playwright. She wanted to be a great playwright. And she almost made it. For many years she was counted among the most important twentieth-century American dramatists, her manner reminiscent of Ibsen and Chekhov, her work placed in a category with that of Eugene O'Neill, Tennessee Williams, and Arthur Miller. Harvard professor of drama William Alfred introduced her to a university gathering in 1961 as "the conscience of the American theater," someone who reminded her audience "of the hunger for justice

which makes every play and adaptation of hers . . . a moving incitement
to seek out the home truths of life, and live in obedience to them."[1]

As a writer, Hellman attempted to speak to the issues of a traumatic
century: she thought of herself as a serious playwright, as part of an intellectual community that could influence the shape of ideas at a time
when ideas mattered. She aimed, in her plays, to illuminate moral questions that informed the everyday lives of her audiences, questions such
as how the pursuit of wealth distorted human relationships in and outside the family. She advocated a vigorous defense of liberty and freedom
in the face of internal political disagreements and international bullying; she explored the pernicious consequences of a culture of fear on the
capacity of any individual to speak truth and retain integrity. She promoted these ideas on the largest stages she could find, first in the Broadway
theater and then on the Hollywood movie screen. Aligning the message
with the medium would prove no easy task: appealing to a broad audience,
it was thought, required pandering to the public taste for lust and violence.
Serious ideas did not belong on Broadway. And yet it was Hellman's
genius to be able to write serious plays that enthralled audiences and

She wanted to be a great playwright. (Photofest)

kept them coming back for more. For this she was sometimes accused of appealing to middlebrow tastes; she would later find herself mocked and disparaged by those who represented highbrow intellectual culture.

The sharp-tongued and quick-witted voice that spoke plainly to a broad public offended those who heard in it a judgmental tone and a forceful advocacy of increasingly controversial ideas. By the 1940s, some thought of her as a political writer. Her reputation dimmed; she fell out of fashion. Critics referred to her as a "minor master," an architect of the "well-made play." They described her as an overemotional playwright who resorted to melodrama to resolve her plots and accused her of writing propaganda. Though she remained a celebrity, she self-consciously abandoned the theater and turned to writing short essays before she tackled the bestselling memoirs that would bring her fortune and notoriety. The tension between Hellman's dramatic writing style and her insistence on speaking to the critical issues of the day marks her engagement with moral and ethical issues. But it also teaches us something about the dilemmas faced by writers of her generation—the first to confront a media-driven environment—who sacrificed nuance and subtlety in order to obtain breadth and influence. From Hellman, we learn how difficult it could be for a writer, especially one who was a woman, to explore serious subjects and to attract audiences steeped in the popular culture of movies and the radio.

Hellman knew she wanted to be a writer early on. She recognized her calling when, as a girl, she curled up to read in the limbs of the perhaps metaphorical fig tree that she recalled with such pleasure. This experience, she told a Harvard audience shortly after Dash died in January 1961, stayed with her. "Somewhere I recognized the world was open . . . Somewhere in those years, I knew that I wanted to be a writer and I knew it so hard that I was amazed that other children didn't want to be writers."[2] The issues she wanted to write about came from those years, too. Her parents had a lively interest in all things literary and especially in the theater. They attended regularly and afterward revisited the plays and actors' performances in the presence of their daughter. They also exercised a powerful shaping force on her moral sensibilities. From their "fierce belief in personal liberty," Hellman claimed to derive her love of freedom and liberty and her passionate commitment to justice.[3] This "world of the half-remembered, the half-observed, the half-understood," she thought, was what had moved her to begin to write.[4]

Writing did not come easily to her. Hellman started out as a manuscript reader whose task was to select submissions worthy of being published. She did this first at Boni and Liveright, where she worked for almost two years, and then she screened scripts worthy of production for Broadway producers and for Hollywood companies. She proudly took credit for identifying Vicki Baum's *The Grand Hotel*, a 1930 blockbuster play and later an Academy Award–winning film that she encountered while reading for Herman Shumlin.[5] At the same time, she wrote spicy reviews for the *New York Herald Tribune*'s Sunday Book Review, for which she earned $7.50 apiece. Damning and praising with equal verve, these reveal something of the direct and assertive character that would soon emerge. She might call something "plain trash" one week, and then the next discuss a book's "exotic strength, fine directness and complete sincerity." Or she might characterize something she didn't like as "plain sensational bunk of the more powerful sort."[6] Of William Faulkner's *Mosquitoes*, a book published by her old employer Boni and Liveright, she wrote that she particularly admired "the humor, the delight of Mr. Faulkner's writing" and commented on the "brilliance that you can rightfully expect only in the writing of a few men." Ignoring the New Orleans origins of most of Faulkner's protagonists, she focused only briefly on the lively and sympathetic characters he had created. It was his craft that captured her, his capacity to produce "the fine kind of swift and lusty writing that comes from a healthy, fresh pen."[7] Hellman's choices capture her own lifelong concerns with the art of writing—with trying to get dialogue just right.

In this period, too, Hellman produced a few rather undistinguished short stories, several of which she published in a small magazine called the *Comet* that her then-husband, Arthur Kober, briefly edited. Despite her desire to succeed, she quickly discovered, according to her friend Peter Feibleman, that her talent lay in writing "ladies' magazine" stories, for which she had only contempt.[8] She tried her hand, then, at writing a play with Louis Kronenberger. *Dear Queen*, a never-to-be-produced comedy, was, in Hellman's words, "about a royal family who wanted to be middle class people."[9] While she and her friends participated in the 1932 election of Franklin Roosevelt and then celebrated the achievements of the first one hundred days, Hellman agonized about how she would become a writer. In that spring and summer of 1933, while the country survived a banking crisis, adopted the National Industrial Recovery Act, and flew the blue eagle, there is little evidence that she was either engaged politically or that she and her friends ever talked about the political issues of the day.

She was at loose ends, already living with Dashiell Hammett, when he gave her the idea for the plot of the play that became *The Children's Hour*. Lillian took that plot, the story of an early-nineteenth-century Scottish court case about two female schoolteachers accused by a disgruntled young pupil of "unnatural affection" for each other and turned it into the play that would spark her career. In Lillian's hands, the villain of the story becomes the child's grandmother, who, without ascertaining its veracity, broadcasts the accusation to the pupils' parents and leads them to withdraw their children from the school. The teachers, Karen and Martha, fight the accusation in court and lose their case. Their school and their relationship destroyed, Karen concludes that she has indeed been guilty of loving Martha. In despair Karen commits suicide. Shortly after, the grandmother returns to say that the child has admitted to lying. Too late: the dream of a school is over; Karen is dead; Martha no longer trusts the fiancé who doubted her. The tragedy is complete.

Adapting the play, Hellman kept the theme of the court case intact, focusing on the impact of what she called the big lie. But she omitted one crucial part of the original case. The child in question was the daughter of an Indian mother and an English civil servant, a child whose mean-spirited accusation made sense in the context of the daily racism that she faced. Hellman wanted to emphasize the dramatic effect of an unmediated "big lie," so she chose to focus not on the racism that led the child to act out but on the content of the accusation. She might easily have taken another path. Racial tension embroiled the country in the decade of the thirties and would certainly have been on Lillian's mind in 1934. That year, Congress once again debated a divisive anti-lynching bill against which southerners repeatedly filibustered; nine black teenagers, the Scottsboro boys, arrested in Alabama in 1931 for allegedly raping two white women, still sat in jail awaiting trial. The Communist Party had come to their defense, turning the issue of justice for African-Americans into a national cause. Labor strikes, unemployment councils, and the inefficient and uneven distribution of hurriedly enacted relief benefits stirred discontent and conflict among competing groups. Under the circumstances, a popular audience in the thirties might choose to empathize with the turmoil of a mixed-race child, drawing attention away from the destruction wrought by the lie. Hellman, the playwright, chose to simplify her story: she wanted to demonstrate how destructive a big lie could be.

For that, she needed a lie awful enough to undermine a school, several lives, and the trust of a community. A lie that focused on the issue of sexuality made sense. After a decade of unprecedented sexual indulgence, the Depression mentality encouraged more traditional family life and fostered widespread efforts to reestablish a sexual order rooted in the male-breadwinner family. Hellman might have turned her plot on a child's accusation of heterosexual misconduct (as she would do in the film that followed the play). But her own flagrant sexuality, her divorce from a good man, her unorthodox relationship with Hammett, made that risky. The sexual desire of two women for each other, on the other hand, fed into the widespread and Depression-fostered mistrust of sexual unorthodoxy without calling attention to her own sexual behavior. Imagining a potential lesbian relationship created the perfect opportunity for a child to reveal a secret that flouted conventional morality. In Hellman's hands, it effectively demonstrated the power of rumor to send the innocent into a whirling chasm of destruction.

Crafting the play was painstakingly hard work. For a while, she and Dash rented a cottage on tiny Tavern Island off the coast of Connecticut, where Hammett finished what was to be his last novel, *The Thin Man*, and she endlessly rewrote her play. Many versions later, all of them "condemned, praised, edited, cut, and fathered, in general, by Dashiell Hammett," she took the play to Shumlin.[10] Still it required the intervention of good friends to get him to pay attention. When he did, he immediately agreed to produce and direct it. He would go on to produce and direct three more of her plays.

The Children's Hour opened in 1934 to laudatory reviews. It was, commented one critic, "a genuine contribution to the American theatre. It is that wise, that interesting, that significant. It is that all-fired good."[11] Critics particularly identified Hellman's talents as a playwright in her capacity to tell a riveting story "with its own distinct brand of thrills and sympathies, coils and recoils."[12] This was, they agreed, "a fine brave play," one so cleanly and tightly written that "up until the last quarter . . . there is not one second when you can let your attention wander, even if you wanted to."[13] They noted Hellman's flair for plot, her capacity for rapidly delineating the persona of each character in precise language and with lifelike dialogue. She had a special talent, they noted, for capturing children without condescension and with full attention to the complexity of their problems. And her story, despite its unpredictable end and its grim theme, simultaneously entertained and uplifted audiences. Here was a theme, critic George Jean Nathan commented, that merited devoted attention to "the ruin and tragedy that befall two young women teachers in a girls' school following a whispered accusation—on the part of a maleficent little pupil—that they are lesbians."[14]

Only the last part of the final act drew objections. There Hellman's attention turned from the malicious child—who, along with her grandmother, had dominated the first two acts—to the unhappy love triangle. She focused on Martha and Karen, the two women whose lives devolved into mistrust of each other, ultimately producing the tragic suicide of one and the abandonment of the second by a fiancé who is convinced that they will never escape the rumors that overshadow their lives.[15] *New York Times* reviewer Brooks Atkinson admonished her for the melodramatic effect. "Please Miss Hellman," he wrote in one of several efforts to evaluate the play, "conclude the play before the pistol shot and before the long arm of coincidence starts wobbling in its socket."[16] But others would come to a different conclusion. Even with its melodramatic ending, wrote a *New York Herald Tribune* commentator, "*The Children's Hour* will still be the rightest thing in the recent American theatre."[17]

Hellman may have had a hit on her hands, but she also had a controversy. Mindful of the fact that Arthur Hornblow's *The Captive,* a play about lesbian lovers, had been attacked and closed down in 1926, critics repeatedly raised (if only to dismiss) the charge of sensationalism. Had Hellman, they asked, introduced the subject of "unnatural affection" only for its box-office effect? Most agreed that what one critic called her "honesty of purpose" should overcome audience skepticism. "Certainly there can be no offense to the adult mind," he wrote. "On the contrary, the effect should be highly salutary in the horror aroused at the enormity of irresponsible slander in such matters."[18] But the refusal of many to name lesbianism, their insistence on substituting euphemisms like "unnatural behavior" or "abnormal attachment," drew persistent attention. Some described lesbianism as "a forbidden theme . . . which is not discussed openly in respectable society."[19] Others criticized the title (which Hellman had fought to keep) on the grounds that it falsely advertised the play as suitable for the young.

Hellman bitterly resented the charge that she had chosen the title for *The Children's Hour* for its scandalous appeal or that the notoriety of the play stemmed from its attention to a subject that "has been forbidden in the theater as unfit for public illustration."[20] When a negative review in *Town and Country* magazine opined that she had chosen the title for the sake of its "smug sensationalism," she angrily demanded a retraction from the magazine's editor. She deserved it, she wrote, not because the reviewer was "malicious and vulgar"—that was his right—but because he had cast aspersions on her honesty and insinuated that she merely sought publicity for herself. "It is not his privilege to interpret my motives or my character," she concluded.[21] The reviewer lost his job.

The scenario in which Lillian protested that she was a victim of misguided reviewers and critics would become increasingly familiar. Like so much else that Hellman would write, *The Children's Hour* appealed to audiences for reasons quite different from those she imagined. Hellman had intended *The Children's Hour* as a morality play about good and evil; she had wanted to question the impact of rumor, the failure of justice in the face of crowd action. Hellman had never imagined Mary Tilford, the child liar, as the "miniature genius of wickedness," who appeared to audiences and critics as diabolical, fiendish, sadistic, and vicious. Rather, she would later tell an interviewer, she imagined the thirteen-year-old child as "neurotic, sly, but not the utterly malignant creature which playgoers see in her."[22] To her the real villain was the destructive and judgmental grandmother, who had willingly absorbed and spread the lie. *The Children's Hour* was "really not a play about lesbianism," she repeated more than once, "but about a lie. The bigger the lie the better, as always."[23]

Yet the harder Hellman fought, the more obscure became her intended theme, and the more visible the question of lesbianism. Believing that her integrity and her reputation for honesty were at stake, resenting what she believed to be an unwarranted debate over her motives, she tried endlessly to get people to pay attention to the consequences of the "big lie" as opposed to the subject matter of the accusation. She deplored the publicity generated when the producers encountered resistance from potential female leads who did not want to be associated with lesbianism. She encouraged her producer to fight a ban imposed by Boston because, said the mayor, *The Children's Hour* was "identified with a theme that would automatically bring it to the attention of the Board of Censors."[24] And she publicly denounced the decision by London's Lord Chamberlain that the play could be offered only under a limited private subscription basis. It was not to be fully produced there for twenty years.[25]

Lillian and her producer, Herman Shumlin, fought each act of censorship, fearing that the accusations would obscure the themes she wanted to emphasize. Yet a year after *The Children's Hour* opened, when Sam Goldwyn offered to turn it into a film, she changed her tune. As if to demonstrate how little the lesbian theme mattered as compared to the big lie, she altered the film script, turning the "inappropriate acts" witnessed by Mary Tilford into scenes from a heterosexual love triangle. Her new script featured a sly and more appropriately neurotic child claiming to have observed the fiancé leaving the bedroom of the other woman. It retained only the tiniest reference to a possible attraction between the two women, eliminated Martha's suicide, and sent the reconciled heterosexual couple off to Australia to live happily ever after. To distance the film still further from its Broadway provenance, Hellman reluctantly agreed to give up the title for which she had originally fought. The adapted film emerged as *These Three*.

For all the publicity, perhaps because of it, *The Children's Hour* ran on Broadway for two years to enthusiastic audiences. Hellman did not appreciate her good fortune. Right after the play's November 20, 1934, opening, she fled to Hollywood, unclear about how to handle her newfound success. She describes herself as puzzled "about why people wanted to interview me," confused about "what to do with the money that poured in every week." She felt herself, she later wrote, "too young for my years: high spirited enough to question the value of such fame and low spirited enough to refuse the natural pleasures it should have brought."[26] Newfound celebrity turned into despair as she realized that a successful first play would impose on her the heavy burden of public expectations of future success.

Her second play, *Days to Come*, turned out to be a critical and box-office disaster whose failure Hellman never fully understood. She started work on *Days to Come* in 1935. Nominally, the play focuses on labor strife in a small Midwestern town. Andrew Rodman, a paternalistic and well-intentioned Midwestern factory owner, has, along with his family, developed a reputation as a caring and generous employer. Hit hard by the Depression and by his wife, Julie's, excessive spending, Rodman is forced to cut wages and to lay off some workers in order to save the factory. The workers turn to an outside union organizer to protect their jobs. Rodman, in turn, brings in strike breakers who turn out to be gangsters. Class issues divide community members against each other with predictably tragic results. Layered into the play is a second tale about Rodman's unhappy wife, Julie, whose affair with Rodman's best friend and lawyer places her in a position to witness the crimes of the gangsters and to save the life of the organizer. A third thread follows the machinations of Rodman's sister, who, anxious about her fortune, fosters much of the conflict between the two sides. The resulting violence not only turns his former workers and the community against Rodman but splits his family asunder. Good and evil are pitted directly against each other: the humane and virtuous workers responsible for the prosperity of the factory owner's family are trampled by the forces of industry and the thuggish hand of greed.

Hellman thought she had written a more complicated play, one about a financially and emotionally troubled family unable to resolve problems not of their own making. As she put it, "they lived in a place and time where old convictions, a way of life, clashed sharply with unexpected new problems."[27] The Depression, source of these problems, serves as a background that allows Hellman to sympathize with the weak-willed and good-hearted Rodman and with workers who rely on a rising trade unionism to protect their jobs. The only true measure of evil lies in the strike breakers, whose appearance signals the victory of the sister and the lawyer, both more interested in profits than in the well-being of the workers. But the play's message was too obscure for its audience. Hellman's sharp arrows directed against the selfish search for individual wealth missed their target. Instead of wounding the greedy sister and manipulative lawyer, they pierced an unfaithful wife and a labor-organizer lover whose passion for love and justice compete with each other. The play, which opened on December 15, 1936, closed after only seven performances.

The failure of Days to Come tells us something about the tormented choices of the 1930s. On its face, as the critic Joseph Wood Krutch noted, Days to Come promoted "a definite Marxian moral—namely, that men are sundered from one another by a difference in class interests between which no personal good-will can adjudicate."[28] But Hellman described the play as something else altogether. "It's the family I'm interested in principally," she told an interviewer just a few days before the play opened, "the strike and social manifestations are just backgrounds. It's a story of innocent people on both sides who are drawn into conflict and events far beyond their comprehension."[29] The outcome of Days to Come rested, after all, on the twists and turns of a plot in which a dependent wife drives her husband into debt; a greedy sister persuades her brother to disappoint desperate workers rather than risk her own profits; a lawyer's affair with a factory owner's wife leads him to place self-interest above duty to his client. More than forty years later, when the play was revived for the first time, critic Terry Curtis Fox commented on its complex amalgamation of moral and political subjects. To him, *Days to Come* seemed to open up Hellman's "great continuing theme . . . that there is no line between private morality and public policy, that political choices are moral choices."[30] In the thirties, Hellman chose to see in the play a different dimension: she focused on the willingness of individuals to put their own interests before those of community. To her, its moral lay in its condemnation of the ease with which one person could betray another to protect himself.

Years later, when her celebrity was assured, she would remember the pain that failure caused her, calling "the failure of a second work . . . more damaging than failure ever will be again" because it made the success of the first seem like an accident.[31] "Failure in the theater," she wrote to Arthur Kober after the play closed, "is more dramatic and uglier than in any other form of writing. It costs so much, you feel so guilty."[32] It was to be two years "before I could write another play, *The Little Foxes*," she later commented, "and when I did get to it I was so scared that I wrote it nine times."[33] Yet for all her agony, Hellman never gave up on *Days to Come.* To her it seemed "a good report of rich liberals in the 1930's, of a labor leader who saw through them, of a modern lost lady, and has in it a correct prediction of how conservative the American labor movement was to become."[34] Four decades after its debut the play was, for the first time, revived for a twelve-day limited run in a small theater. Hellman took the opportunity to explain it once again to an interviewer: for her, the divisions incited by class may have been present, but they were not central. Rather, the idea that some people remain simple and undemanding while others pursue self-gratification, that the honorable may become victims of injustice while justice eludes the principled, that one's own integrity is, in the end, all there is constituted the fundamental values and themes that would underline her life's work in the theater and beyond. "Justice and injustice, integrity and dishonor, principle and self-gratification," to paraphrase one critic, were the themes around which both her life and her work evolved.[35]

Emerging as a playwright in the depths of the deepest economic depression the United States had ever known, Hellman might have taken a different route. She had, after all, first thought of herself as a writer of fiction, and particularly of short stories. But with little recognition for her stories, the theater seemed a logical choice. Hellman found there "a place for the expression and exchange of ideas," a location where she could "present an idea for the consideration of intelligent audiences."[36]

And yet Hellman was not drawn to the lively ferment of the off-Broadway theater of the late twenties and early thirties. Her desire to develop and articulate ideas rather than to investigate form led her rather to follow the social realism of Henrik Ibsen and George Bernard Shaw. She was not attracted to theater companies like the Provincetown Players, which turned to direct social criticism in the late 1920s. Nor did she follow in the footsteps of the new experimental theater that emerged in the early years of the Depression and whose quintessential expression is in the Group Theatre. Founded in New York in 1931 by Harold Clurman, Cheryl Crawford (both of whom Lillian admired), and Lee Strasberg, the Group Theatre created a community of actors, playwrights, and directors who pioneered ensemble acting and freely responded to play scripts by turning the production of a play into a collaborative project. Some of Lillian's soon-to-be-well-known contemporaries, including friends John Howard Lawson and Marc Blitzstein as well as Elmer Rice and Clifford Odets, found inspiration in the Group Theatre's effort to join political statements with acting methods that drew on real-life issues and characters. Just a year after *The Children's Hour* opened, New York's Group Theatre offered to the public two plays by Clifford Odets: *Waiting for Lefty* and *Awake and Sing*, which did not merely critique the American experience but called for political action. They suggested a newly assertive theatrical experience in which plays and playwrights called upon audiences to raise their voices, often in alignment with the dogma of a rising Communist Party.

Hellman took no part in this theater of protest, nor did she express much interest in the New Playwrights Theater or the WPA Theater project in which many famous playwrights and theater figures like Blitzstein and the young Carson McCullers made their names. Her work, Arthur Miller would later recall, was not angry enough. And yet the critics of the day had little doubt about her anger. "She is a specialist in hate and frustration, a student of helpless rage, an articulator of inarticulate loathings," wrote one commentator after seeing *Days to Come*.[37] The anger, in Miller's judgment, didn't seem to take political form. It didn't seem to him "to belong to these impassioned, challenging plays."[38] There was, remembered Miller, "a certain eloquence in her dialogue that set her apart from the theatre of protest which was so brash and exciting then."[39] Hellman, in Miller's view, was "preeminently Broadway."

The artist of Hellman's mind's eye needed to involve herself not with immediate political questions but with the larger concerns of her generation. Her job was to make the world a better place to live by engaging with moral issues rather than problems of the day. With some exceptions, Hellman chose subjects engaged with everyday life: the tension between human feeling and the pursuit of wealth, the corruption of money, the perversity of extended family relationships, the unforeseen costs of human apathy. She wanted to underscore the behavior of bullies, to condemn racism, and to portray people who could resist both. She sought to illuminate pretense and vanity, and above all to focus attention on questions of justice.[40] She did this by drawing lively portraits of individuals confronting the conundrums posed by these issues in their daily lives. Like Ibsen, she placed her characters in what the critic Jacob Adler has described as "clear and firm dramatic structures."[41] And like Ibsen, she produced problem plays—plays that assumed, perhaps too optimistically, that "to reveal a problem is a step toward correcting it." Adler called her "the single most important American Ibsenian outside of Arthur Miller."[42]

To Hellman, a good society included one without poverty or racism, one built on principles of social justice. But she did not advocate for these by calling her audiences to arms or urging political action; nor did she turn to abstract questions about the human condition as her successors in the theater were apt to do. It was not, she told one interviewer, that "all literature must have social or economic implications." And yet, she continued, "unless you are a pathological escapist there must be some sort of propaganda in everything you write." For her, propaganda meant explicit advocacy of some cause. "The truth must be the main objective of any one who seeks a form of literary expression . . . If a person doesn't want to involve himself with the truth he has no business trying to write at all."[43]

Hellman attributed her moral positions not to any particular event, such as the New Deal, but to her moment in time. She belonged to a particular generation, she told an audience of Harvard students in 1961, a "little bracket . . . too old to be depression children, too young to have known the fun and brilliance of the 1920s." As a writer, she was part of this "between-times group." Unlike her literary predecessors who had emerged in "the hurricane winds of the early 1920s . . . who were ten or fifteen years older than my generation . . . more brilliant and frequently more talented than mine," she saw herself as having missed out. "We were born later than Faulkner, or Fitzgerald or Hart Crane or Hemingway or O'Neill," she ruminated, "and by the time we might have been ready the depression had appeared and the world, and literature took a sharp turn."[44] Her group was "bright and lively, but not as good." They represented "a bracket of ten years between the wonderful fresh wind that blew so good between the First World War and the days when what we called a depression . . . turned later into a world storm, the ugliest war of history."[45] Hers was a generation tasked with sorting out the meaning of social justice, racism, and fascism, of good and evil in a dangerous and insecure world.

This sense of herself as a creature of her time permeated her work and obligated her to speak to the moment. Neither she nor any writer could accurately account for the influences on her work, she would say, but like the best playwrights of her moment, she found herself caught in the "combination of economic fear and spiritual uplift" of the Depression years, admiring of "the new and daring and remarkable things that were happening in the country."[46] A good play, she thought, must be based on real life; writers could write only about the "world that was made for them . . . they reflect their origins." She would not identify her own location in space and time as "influence." Most writers, she would say when asked, invented influences for interviewers: clarity about a work's origins in "influences, people, events, comes much later, and sounds good, but very often hasn't much to do with the facts."[47]

The best writers, of whom she hoped she was one, would "bring new light" to the world from which they had come. In that respect, she thought of the theater as "the clearest mirror of its time."[48] For her, the issue of why a writer wrote was less important than the product. The writer, she thought, had to have something to say: her job was to "use it right. Right? Right for what? Right to have something to say and to say it well."[49] But there was no point in speaking if nobody listened. To achieve her goal of addressing broad questions that extended beyond the political-economic crisis of the 1930s, Hellman would have to find larger audiences than the relatively narrow world of experimental theater allowed. Her ambition was to write "serious plays for the commercial theater." To this end, she sought "first class" productions in good theaters whenever possible. She wanted the attention of major reviewers in the leading media. And she wanted the monetary rewards of successful Broadway production.

The theater proved to be a curious choice for Hellman, exacting compromises from her that she did not enjoy and to which she sometimes could not acquiesce. To attract the audiences she wanted, she chose to resort to plot devices and melodrama that often drew criticism; these earned her the reputation of a middlebrow rather than a highbrow writer. To acquire first-class productions for her plays—equity actors and a professional stage to show off her work—she would need to cultivate the acquaintance of producers and actors whom she claimed to despise. She denied that she craved the glamour of the theater, insisting that to her it was mostly hard work, but she found that she relished center stage and enjoyed consorting with leading actors, actresses, producers, directors, and eventually the movie moguls who would employ her in Hollywood. She dropped their names in conversation until, eventually, her name became one of those that others dropped.

Hellman worked hard at her writing, disciplining herself to put in long hours and to work to deadlines. In her plays, as in her short essays and later in her memoirs, she relied on careful research and thoughtful prep-aration, keeping notebooks for each of her projects and recording in them ideas as well as incidents. Sometimes research involved, as it did for *Days to Come*, visits to unfamiliar sites; other times her subjects demanded investigations of particular personas, like that of the labor militant. She wanted to get every detail right. For *Watch on the Rhine*, she claimed to have made digests of more than twenty-five books, to have read widely in the memoirs and the history of the period, and to have kept notebooks that ran to a thousand pages or more.[50] All her life she explored, or had as-sistants explore, such things as the appropriateness of particular locations, the dates of key events, the attributes of period garments. Her concern for accuracy persisted throughout her life—a particular irony in light of accu-sations of lying that hounded her at the end of her life.

To write well she claimed the need for calm, "for long days, months of fiddling."[51] Not infrequently, she complained, as she did to Arthur Kober at one point, about the interruptions that got in the way. "It is becoming increasingly obvious," she wrote Kober from New York, "that I cannot work here: the telephone, the cause, the thousand nuisances who want me to speak or breathe or donate, the friends and half-friends who see no reason why you can't stop working and come to dinner and run right back and work after dinner."[52] Playwriting was, like any other form of writing, not glamorous, she told a Wellesley College audience.[53] Hellman thought writing for the theater a magical thing—a gift that you either had or didn't and that could not be taught. Yet she credited Hammett with teaching her how to write. "Patiently and persistently he hammered away. He began

About 1942: She credited Hammett with teaching her how to write. (© Time & Life Pictures/Getty Images)

by attacking most of what I had written, teaching me along the way that writers must go to school at writing, and learn and read and think and study."[54] But she was a good student and learned quickly to use dialogue to evoke character. Under Hammett's tutelage, she became expert at drawing sharply delineated characters and providing them with succinct and often raffish voices. In a few lines, she could capture the essence of a personality as well as its major flaws.[55]

Hellman counted on Hammett for critical readings of one draft after another: "Over and over again he would tell me how bad was the first draft, the second, the fifth, the sixth; over and over again I would bring the next drafts, giving them to him with what I thought was the truthful notice that if this wasn't any good I would never write again and might kill myself."[56] *The Little Foxes* went through nine drafts, each of them worked on by Hammett, perhaps, thought Hellman, because after *Days to Come* he was as scared for her future as she was. *Watch on the Rhine* was "the only play that came out in one piece," she recalled.[57] Hammett never shirked. In one instance—the last speech of *Autumn Garden*—when she could not get it right, he rewrote the speech for her. Repeatedly and gratefully, she acknowledged his role as a critic. "He was generous with anybody who asked for help," she told an interviewer after his death. "He felt that you didn't lie about writing and anybody who couldn't take hard words was about to be shrugged off, anyway. He was a dedicated man about writing. Tough and generous."[58]

Her biggest difficulty, she would often say, was plotting. "I'm scared of plotting," she confided to Arthur Kober. "The few things I've ever done well were plots laid out for me beforehand."[59] Unsurprisingly, Hellman leaned heavily on Dashiell Hammett for many of her plot ideas. The idea for *The Children's Hour* came from him, as did the framework of her last original play, *Toys in the Attic*. But her plot structures tended to be contrived: in the manner of the "well-made" play, they relied on surprising revelations and twists. To bring her plays to their conclusions, Hellman introduced such devices as a letter found in a Bible, an overheard telephone conversation, or a revelation that there was no keyhole in the door through which sexual contact was said to have been observed. These fed the popular audience's desire for drama but did little to enhance the literary quality of the work.

Wanting her plays to be read as well as acted, Hellman made sure that the literary and dramatic forms "come together."[60] When she did not have time to ensure that she had got things right in a script prepared for rehearsal, she edited it for the published version, recasting a sentence, changing the place of a verb, or revising punctuation to meet the standards of readers. She was finicky about every word, seeking, as the drafts of her plays show, the right adjective and the pithy phrase, attempting in a sentence to capture a character's personality or a complicated motive. And she was sensitive about efforts to change anything: "It is not getting an idea for a play that drives playwrights mad so much as the business of having the idea still recognizable, even to its author, at the completion of the script," she explained to an interviewer.[61]

As her plays entered production, Hellman became more possessive of her work and reluctant to cede even an iota of control. The writer, she insisted, was the heart of the process of producing plays. She had seen the Russian theater, she said more than once, and appreciated its sometimes wonderful "production, directing and acting," but Russia was no longer producing good new writers and so, she judged, it could have only "dead end theatre. Fine to see, but it ain't going nowhere."[62] As a writer, she took full responsibility for failure: "I do not believe actors break plays or make them either," she asserted.[63] For these reasons she wanted to maintain control over her work and found collaboration of any kind difficult. She wielded a heavy hand with regard to casting her plays, attended rehearsals regularly, and accompanied plays when they first went out on the road. She believed in the importance of every word she had written, refusing to allow actors or director any input at all. She would, and did, fight in defense of her positions, insisting that this was a way to work out differences and often revealing her legendary temper if opponents continued to disagree. "I didn't know about my nature," she wrote in the early forties, "which turned out to be angry at the suggestion of any change, even the most innocent and foolish."[64] But she chided those who took her anger seriously, dismissing her explosions as "a comic waste" and attributing them to nerves "in a time when people believed too much in the civil rights of something called temperament."[65]

Hellman claims to have discovered these qualities when *The Children's Hour* went into production. In one of her first stands, she fought successfully for the child, Mary Tilford, to retain a lisp that everyone including her producer-director, Herman Shumlin, thought overdone. As she explained, "I learned early that in the theater, good or bad, you'd better stand on what you did."[66] She learned her lesson well. "I took a stand on the first play and now I have a reputation for stubbornness," she told an interviewer.[67] The quality earned her a reputation as "difficult"—a label she acknowledged with some humor. Being difficult, she told a group of Swarthmore college students, "means refusing to alter a line, protecting your own work, arguing for salary," and then she described the qualities of the difficult woman as "pig-like stubbornness" and "rigidity."[68] Harold Clurman, who directed Hellman's 1951 production of *The Autumn Garden*, agreed with Hellman's assessment of her persona. "There's a certain rigidity about her, a certain self-protective element," he told an interviewer.[69]

To be fair, Hellman's refusal to budge seemed to be as much a principled decision for her as one based on ego. Much later in life, she exercised the same kind of control over the work of Dorothy Parker (of whose estate she was executor) when she refused permission to adapt her work to film. Nor would she allow Hammett's unpublished stories to see the light of day, claiming that he had not thought them ready. Of her own work she was equally protective. Even when she saw the need for changes, she could not easily make them, and never at a moment's notice. It threw her off when she tried to do otherwise—as she did, for example, when she worked with Leonard Bernstein and several lyricists including, finally,

Richard Wilbur on the 1956 production of the musical *Candide*. She had adapted the book and designed the characters, but as the musical went into rehearsal she found herself overwhelmed by demands to alter one element after another to fit the needs of a musical production. The musical that finally appeared was far too long and something of what she called a "mish mash." She defended herself later from accusations about its messiness: "I was working with people who knew more about the musical theatre than I did, I took suggestions and made changes that I didn't believe in, tried making them with speed I cannot manage."[70]

But in the end she put down the weaknesses of *Candide* to her own failure at the art of collaboration. "I am not a good collaborator because I am unable to do the kind of pressure work that goes with other people's understandable demands. I am unable to take other people's opinions about writing. I work best on my own for good or bad."[71] She generalized this into a commentary about herself. Noting about *Candide* that she "had become, with time, too anxious to stay out of fights," she remarked that "everything I had learned about the theater, all my instinct went out the window." Finally she concluded that collaboration "was truly not my nature, that I must never go through it again."[72] Hellman's ready acknowledgment of her weakness at collaboration did not prevent her from defending her original book and attributing the musical's failures to repeated efforts to tinker with her original conception. Finally, when Bernstein wanted to adapt the original music to a new treatment of the subject, she agreed, provided that her name be removed from its revivals.

At the root of Hellman's neurotic behavior lay anxiety about the end product. The production process overwhelmed her—perhaps because, much as she tried, she could not control it. Though she insisted on a heavy hand in selecting or approving casts, in attending rehearsals, in faithful adherence to her words, she found, as the critic Walter Kerr noted, "the simple act of entering the production process so fundamentally distasteful, such an invasion of creative privacy, that she can rarely bring herself to write about it; one senses that she does not wish to remember it."[73] She once recalled that she "complained and fussed a good deal" during rehearsals for *The Little Foxes* and then added that she only knew that "because I have continued to do so through the years." Others testify to her irascibility. Harold Clurman remembered her whispering audibly during rehearsals. "It's disturbing to me and disturbing the actors," he told her. "She didn't understand that the actor is also a sensitive being just as she is."[74] Austin Pendleton, who acted in a 1967 revival of *The Little Foxes*, remembers her sitting in the back row of the orchestra section during rehearsals loudly dictating notes about the actors' performances to her assistant. Once she walked around the theater to check sight lines and called out to director Mike Nichols all the mistakes she thought he was making. This incident, according to Pendleton, drove Nichols to ask her to stay away from rehearsals until the first public preview.[75]

As her plays came closer to opening night, she became increasingly nervous—pacing through rehearsals, drinking, and unable to sit still. "I have never felt anything but fear and resentment that what was private is now to become public, what was mine is no longer mine alone," she told a Harvard audience. "More than anything else the commitment takes place on that day, and final commitments, a final having to stand up, stand beside, take responsibility for, open yourself to, is for me an act of such proportion that I have never on all the many first days that came, ceased to be my kind of sick."[76] Pendleton, who directed the 1981 production of *The Little Foxes* that starred Elizabeth Taylor as Regina, provides a vivid picture of her behavior on such occasions. There wasn't "one scene that could make it to opening night without her saying she hated it," he affirms. Toward the end of the New York previews, Hellman, still unhappy with how things were going, stormed out of the theater at the second intermission and, in full view of the preview audience, pounded her cane on the ground to emphasize how much she hated the performance. Pendleton says of himself: "I just lost it, and I started yelling—the lobby's jammed, people are ordering drinks in line—and I started yelling, 'This is the worst fucking night of my life.' To which Hellman yelled back, 'Every night I see this fucking production is the worst fucking night of my life.'" This incident so upset Pendleton that he left the theater, unable to watch Act 3. He walked around the block several times, threatening to quit the show, until the curtain came down, and then he retreated with some close friends to an obscure bar where he thought nobody could find him. Just a few minutes into their first drinks, Hellman, who had tracked him down, called. "You still angry?" Pendleton recalls her asking in a way that he found enchanting. "We laughed for a few minutes about our blow-up," he remembers, "and I had a wonderful hour or so of drinking with my friends." The relationship mended; the revival turned out to be a critical success.[77]

Hellman's neurotic misbehavior was in such full play on opening nights that Hammett, whenever he could, avoided them. Time and again she recalled the scene of William Randolph Hearst and a large party walking out during the middle of the first act of *Days to Come*, making loud

Her neurotic behavior in full play. With the 1981 cast of The Little Foxes, *Anthony Zerbe, Maureen Stapleton, and Elizabeth Taylor. (© Bettmann/CORBIS)*

negative comments as they did so. "I vomited in the back aisle . . . I had to go home and change my clothes. I was drunk," she tells us in one version of the story.[78] In another she describes herself getting sick in a back alley. She offered her lecture audiences vivid descriptions of herself able to watch a first night only from the wings, or of herself vomiting, getting drunk, or simply leaving the theater. And she admitted that she "jump[ed] up and down through most performances."[79] Almost always, after the opening of a play, successful or not, she fled the scene—for the West Coast (after *The Children's Hour* and *Days to Come*), to Cuba (after *The Little Foxes*). Nor did success alleviate the pain. She "snarled at it," she wrote. "It took me years to find out that I was frightened of what it did to people and instinctively I did not trust myself to handle it."[80]

Embedded in Hellman's persona—her lack of faith in the theater, her fear of failure, her commitment to the craft of writing, her continuing need for adulation and money—are some of the reasons that she took jobs as a Hollywood screenwriter. There were other reasons, of course. In the 1930s, talking films were still quite new and Hollywood was very much in need of the words that would turn actors into mouthpieces. Many of her close friends—Dorothy Parker, the Perelmans, Arthur Kober, and Hammett himself—worked there off and on, transforming plays, novels, and plot lines into movie scripts. Most significant artists, including more distant friends of Hellman's like John Dos Passos and F. Scott Fitzgerald, did it for the money. Moving peripatetically from coast to coast, they reaped the lavish rewards and then freely spent their earnings. Many of Hellman's friends thought of this work as "whoring," selling their souls at the cost of artistic fulfillment. Hollywood, thought playwright Arthur Miller, was "the heart of decadence." If Lillian were indeed "a genuine lightbearer," he and others speculated, she would not be "spending so much of her life writing for Samuel Goldwyn and the other merchants."[81]

Hellman claimed to be "one of the few people who liked writing for pictures" when most of her generation made fun of them.[82] Screenwriting allowed (indeed required) Hellman to relinquish control of the production process and to trust the cameras to do their work.[83] It enabled her to do what she did best: namely to craft believable scenes out of her own, or someone else's, plot and characters. She took the craft seriously, separating the writing from the shooting of the film in a way that she could never separate the writing of her plays from their production. In Hollywood to revise the script of *The Children's Hour* for the film *These Three*, she wrote to Arthur Kober, "it should be finished some time this week, and then I figure two weeks work, and home." Director Wyler, she added, wanted her to stay for at least part of the shooting. She would not, she wrote Kober, because "Goldwyn wouldn't pay me for that, and I wouldn't do it."[84] Writing for Hollywood had its drawbacks, of course: it offered none of the intellectual challenge of live theater where, she told an interviewer, "you can present an idea for the consideration of intelligent audiences, which of course is completely outside the gaudiest opium dreams of possibility in Hollywood."[85] But it not only paid very well and regularly, it also allowed her to draw characters quickly and precisely through dialogue—a skill at which she excelled.

Hellman more or less redeemed the failure of *Days to Come* when she returned to Hollywood to work on the script for *Dead End*—a Broadway production contracted to Sam Goldwyn as a film. There she made the moral point that had fallen so flat in her failed play. She focused on social injustice and inequality in the context of the Depression, pursuing what one critic called her "single minded devotion to her own idea of what is important today." *Dead End*'s author, Sidney Kingsley, had acted with the Group Theatre and written one piece for them before he wrote the Broadway play that Hellman turned into a movie. In it, a working-class heroine, on strike from her job, seeks to salvage the lives of the slum kids in her neighborhood who are courted by the same gangster who is courting her. The kids, whose lives of mischief and petty crime are threatened by luxury housing that is slowly displacing them, are tempted by the apparently glamorous life of crime that the gangster represents. He is countered by an idealistic young architect who rejects the wealth of real estate interests to design housing for the poor and who thus wins the heart of the heroine.

Hellman's voice permeates the film. The action is melodramatic, but class conflict holds center stage. The gangster, who is wholly bad, comes to a tragic end; the heroine, wholly good, is saved from a moll's life. But the dead-end kids are good and bad: they could go either way. The film ends with the dream of a hopeful future still only a glimmer in the eye of the idealistic young architect. As in most of her work, Hellman cannot restrain herself from a final summing up. She wants social justice for the poor; she admires not the abstractly idealistic but those who willingly risk their own lives and fortunes to act on their beliefs.

Hellman came closest to hitting her twin goals of attaining artistic success and scoring commercially with *The Little Foxes* (1939), one of the important plays of the American twentieth century. Set in the South in 1900, it explores some of her conflicted feelings about her wealthy grandmother and uncles, whose rise paralleled what one critic called "the ruthless rise of industrialism" in America. But it also contains hints of nostalgia for the mythical past of a South governed by family values rather than competition for position.

The plot revolves around the efforts of Regina Giddens and her brothers, Ben Hubbard and Oscar Hubbard, to capitalize on a proposed new cotton mill that will make them all rich by paying low wages to the displaced black workers who will become its labor force. The proposal requires each of the three Hubbard siblings to invest one third of the necessary capital. When Regina fails to persuade her sickly husband, Horace, to cooperate in the scheme, her brothers steal his bonds from a bank vault and plan to cut her out of the deal. Horace discovers the theft and decides not to prosecute. Regina, furious, withholds his medicine and watches him die as he struggles to retrieve it. Now in a position to blackmail her brothers, Regina bargains for a larger share of the pie and succeeds. Avarice, manipulation, and murder triumph; the romanticized South is destroyed.

In the context of the Great Depression and its ongoing misery, in the face of the apparent failure of capitalism to restore prosperity, *The Little*

Foxes seemed to many to be a more political play than her earlier efforts. Like her fellow intellectuals of the period, Hellman seemed to have lost faith in the free enterprise system. In contrast to those who hoped that recovery would restore economic progress, Hellman foregrounded the moral crisis posed by the process of industrialization, especially as it would affect the value system of an old South that, whatever its sins, had preserved a graceful old culture. In this context, *The Little Foxes* appeared not only cynical of capitalism but perhaps a bit too unwilling to face the racial indignities of the old South. "Plainly," wrote Joseph Wood Krutch, a professor of theater at Columbia University, a regular reviewer for the *Nation* magazine, and among the most severe of her critics, "the play is directed against contemporary society."[86]

Hellman would have none of this. She denied the political implications of the play, claiming that *The Little Foxes* was designed as "a drama of morality first and last and that anyone who reads too much cynicism into [the Hubbards] is being misled."[87] She told one interviewer, "I just wrote what I thought I'd write. It turned out to be an attack. I suppose somebody had to tell me about it afterwards, because I really didn't know it."[88] For her the key questions of the play revolved around such questions as whether humane values would survive the materialism of capitalist demands; or whether the daughter, Alexandra, representing the next generation, would have courage enough to reject the values of her mother and search for a brighter world. Hellman located these questions in the moral sphere—as issues not of politics but of good and evil.[89] *The Little Foxes* participated in the broader themes she cared about, including issues of justice and injustice, right and wrong, power and its victims. The play's keystone line, placed in the mouth of the household's loyal black servant, Addie, supports both contentions. Addie notes of the Hubbards, "There are people who eat the earth and eat all the people on it like in the bible with the locusts. And other people who stand around and watch them eat it." And then Addie follows with the quiet observation that could almost be a call to action: "Sometimes I think it ain't right to stand and watch them do it."[90]

If critics assessed *The Little Foxes* as a more political statement than Hellman had meant to make—as propaganda against industrialism—they explained the play's audience appeal and power as a product of its flaws. *The Little Foxes* marked Hellman as the author of "well-made" plays. Critics had applied this label to her first plays, as when the *New York Times*'s Brooks Atkinson commended *The Children's Hour* for its "hard, clean economy of word and action" and praised the play as "vigorously planned and written."[91] But the designation of the "well-made" play took on a more negative connotation when reviewers assessed *The Little Foxes*. While they continued to approve her tightly knit plot structures, they questioned whether her plays relied too heavily on surprising revelations and plot twists designed to maximize their theatrical appeal. "It is not only a play that is well made. It is a play that is too well made," wrote one reviewer of *The Little Foxes*. "It suffers from being far too well contrived for its own enduring health. Much of its writing is much too expert in the worst manner of Ibsen."[92] Looking backward from 1939, others wondered whether this had not always been characteristic of her work. Had she not always tailored her plots to fit the needs of the play's message? How was it that *The Children's Hour* turned on the testimony of the only child left in the school over the holidays?

In the eyes of the critics, Hellman was too clever by half. In their view, *The Little Foxes* not only successfully melded the tightly structured and plot-driven play with melodrama; it did so too successfully. Brooks Atkinson led the chorus, declaring that while Hellman had provided "a knowing job of construction, deliberate and self-contained," "she writes with melodramatic abandon, plotting torture, death and thievery like the author of an old-time thriller."[93] Joseph Wood Krutch chimed in, claiming that only Hellman's extraordinary gift for characterization rescued her play from the "righteous uncontrollable anger" that overwhelmed "Hellman's carefully contrived plots."[94] Richard Watts, though he described the play admiringly as honest, pointed, and "more brilliant than even her triumphant previous work," thought it a "grim, bitter, merciless study . . . a psychological horror story."[95] Hellman never again outlived the verdict of melodrama: "Essentially a melodrama," wrote one influential critic of her next play, *Watch on the Rhine* (1941). "The sense of artificial contrivance, also, is more conspicuous."[96]

In her 1942 introduction to *Four Plays*, Hellman defended herself against the attacks. To her mind, critics simply did not understand that the theater imposed its own limits, providing a "tight, unbending, unfluid, meager form in which to write."[97] Surrounded by three walls, with the audience making up the fourth, Hellman argued that the playwright had little choice but to pretend or, in other words, to "trick up the scene." She thought the well-made play was one "whose effects are contrived, whose threads are knit tighter than the threads in life and so do not convince." But she believed her plays did convince, contradicting the notion that her plots were too tightly knit. "I've never understood this charge because it seems to me that then one would say, 'well-madeness, if that's what it is, too much technique, is bad because it's bad work, because the writing is bad.'"[98] But nobody ever accused her of bad writing, and so the puzzle remained.

Nor did Hellman concede that her plays were melodramatic in any negative sense. Accusations of melodrama, raised with respect to her early plays, reemerged as well in the context of *The Little Foxes*, whose characters seemed so rigidly demarcated as either good or evil. She believed the meaning of the word had been corrupted by the modern world, and she defended her own plays as melodrama of the good sort. "By definition," she wrote, melodrama is "a violent dramatic piece, with a happy ending," where good triumphs over evil. She objected to its current usage to refer to plays that deployed "violence for no purpose, to point no moral, to say nothing," and appealed to critics to consider that "when violence is actually the needed stuff of the work and comes toward a large enough end, it has been and always will be in the good writer's field."[99]

The question, then, was whether the ends were large enough to carry the violence—and here Hellman claimed innocence. She did not see her characters as quite as greedy or as mendacious as her critics insisted. Nor did she see them as good or bad: "Such words have nothing to do with the people you write about."[100] In her eyes, *The Little Foxes* was a family saga—a tale of the greed and hatred that infuse a family eager to make its profit from a changing world. Hellman sometimes described it as a satire and other times as a morality play. She had meant, she wrote in *Pentimento*, "to half-mock my own youthful high-class innocence in Alexandra, the young girl in the play; I had meant people to smile, and to sympathize with, the sad, weak Birdie, certainly I had not meant them to cry; I had meant the audience to recognize some part of themselves in the money-dominated Hubbards; I had not meant people to think of them as villains to whom they had no connection."[101]

Whether it went through the nine drafts she claimed to have written or not, *The Little Foxes* was the play that Hellman described as the most difficult to write and the one with which Hammett was most involved. The play—once again produced and directed by Herman Shumlin and with Tallulah Bankhead in the leading role—was a huge financial success. It would also become her most enduring claim to artistic fame. It ran for 410 performances and was immediately bought for the movies by Sam Goldwyn, who asked Lillian to write the movie script. The film, starring Bette Davis, still appears regularly on late-night television. The play has had several first-class revivals, with great stars vying to play the role of Regina. And it has become a staple of American repertory theater.[102]

After *The Little Foxes*, no one could doubt that Hellman was a serious playwright. But the dual sin of well-madeness and melodrama continued to vex her. John Gassner, sympathetic to her accomplishments and one of those who continued to count her among the great American playwrights, wrote in 1949: "We have had our reservations; we have felt she plotted too much or calculated her effects for theatrical purposes, if not indeed for propaganda."[103] And twenty years after its opening, Jacob Adler had not resolved his critical ambivalence toward *The Little Foxes*. He thought its carefully tailored plot was subverted by "the total depravity of the Hubbards . . . their murdering, blackmailing, scheming and stealing sensationalize the play, ultimately making it unbelievable."[104] Critics continued to ask whether Hellman was not too good at what she did: too effective, too careful, too measured. They accused her of writing in a vein that was too vituperative, too direct, and too real. They asked if she was not too angry for a southern playwright, for a moral playwright, for the times in which she wrote, and especially for a woman playwright. They wondered about her political agenda. Such comments would haunt Hellman for the rest of her playwriting career, leading her ultimately to dismiss criticism and to claim that she never read it.

Hellman's considerable successes with audiences did little to diffuse critical judgments of her plays by criteria that seem, in retrospect, to be narrowly tailored to unexamined assumptions of how a woman should write. These assumptions were just one step removed from judgments about Hellman as an individual. *Herald Tribune* reviewer Richard Watts and other critics dismissively acknowledged Hellman's meticulous preparation and careful use of language as if these reflected qualities of womanhood rather than the skills of a playwright.[105] Her effort to draw moral lessons seemed to them typical of women writers. In that context, her penchant for melodrama seemed to cross gender lines. When *New York Times* critic Brooks Atkinson took her to task for writing sheer melodrama, Hellman challenged the designation. She thought his criticism an expression of discomfort with a woman who paid attention to the serious problems of evil that existed in the world. This she thought was a comment on his nature, not on hers.[106]

The commentaries would not be worth dwelling on had they not been a harbinger of what was to come. Whether used positively or negatively, the melodrama label would stick. Fifteen years later, Walter Kerr, a critic who admired Hellman's work, would note that the quality that lifted her above that of her playwriting contemporaries was "an almost masculine control of the more melodramatic emotions, a muscular arm that comes down on a situation as though it were a handy anvil. Her sound, if I may say so, is usually the sound of steel."[107] Conflating Hellman's persona with the content of her plays turned both into fair game. Moralist she may have been, and as moralist she deserved to be taken to task. As a *female* moralist she was not only fair game but also meddling in politics that were not her sphere. She would be judged not in light of the validity of her positions, but in the shadow of the difficult and opinionated woman that critics perceived.

Firmly and consistently, Hellman resisted the label of a "woman playwright." The idea, Margaret Chase Harriman discovered when she interviewed her for a *New Yorker* profile, simply made her angry.[108] Women playwrights, she pointed out in her defense (and with reference to peers who included Rachel Crothers, Susan Glaspell, and Clare Boothe Luce), tended to write sentimental plays. The label conjured up writers of comedies and romances rather than the tough-serious issues with which Hellman dealt. She dismissed such comparisons as "products of the facile imaginations of reviewers and reporters who will go to any length to achieve an easy and meaningless generality."[109] Protest as she might, Hellman could not escape the designation. "Even the best of our women playwrights," critic George Nathan wrote of her, "falls immeasurably short of the mark of our best masculine."[110] Hellman would not concede: "I am a playwright. I also happen to be a woman," she told Harriman, "but I am not a woman playwright."[111]

CHAPTER 4

Politics Without Fear

I don't understand personal salvation. It seems to me a vain idea. Conscience includes the fate of other people.
—*Lillian Hellman, 1977*

It was one thing to become a famous playwright; quite another to make one's way in the bracing political scene of the 1930s. When Hellman returned to New York from Hollywood in March of 1931, she found a city deep in the throes of the Depression. In that year, the city's unemployment rate doubled, reaching an astronomical 15 percent of the city's workforce. That figure would increase every month of her first year in the city until by March of 1932, one of every four workers was unemployed. Hellman seems at first to have been uninvolved in the political scene. Broke and unemployed herself, she did not identify with the men and women on the breadlines; she did not join the ranks of those demanding unemployment insurance or participate in the unemployment councils sponsored by the Communist Party. Nor did she march with any of the hundreds of political factions waving banners on the streets of the broken city. We have no evidence that she participated in any of the anti-eviction activities that tried to protect increasing numbers of families struggling to pay their rent. And Hellman does not seem to have been involved in the formal political proceedings of those years, as Governor Franklin Delano Roosevelt

set up a run for the presidency and clinched the nomination in the summer of 1932, or good-government groups clamored for an investigation into
the corruption of Mayor Jimmy Walker, who was forced out of office in
September 1932. In the summer and fall of 1931 and in the winter of 1932,
as the nation sank deeply into the Depression, the young Lillian Hellman
took no visible political position.

And yet we know that Hellman was not without social compassion or
sympathy for the working class. A resourceful and creative young woman
surrounded by writers and artists, most of them on the left and some of
them already beginning to choose sides, she must have been pulled in
many directions. Though she had matured into a 1920s culture that placed
a premium on individual expression and achievement and was personally ambitious, she harbored a streak of anger toward the rich and corrupt members of her own family that translated into visceral hatred of
power and wealth. She had long valued class equality and racial justice,
and she understood that achieving these goals would disturb cherished
individual rights, including those of property ownership. To this extent
she was a socialist.

Together these translated into what some later called naïve politics.
She wanted desperately to believe, in the jargon of the day, that "a better
world" was possible, wanted to believe in a world where democracy, individual liberty, and especially freedom of speech could thrive. No political
program captured these desires. Rather she invoked a desire for decency,
justice, and morality as though these were self-evident and easily definable
goals. As her friend Peter Feibleman puts it, she had the "sense of justice
of a very small child."[1] Hellman's commitment to an ethic of justice often
presented itself as a stubborn certainty about the righteousness of particular political positions and a persistent loyalty to those who shared her
beliefs. Hellman was not unusual in the 1930s, a decade riven by ideological arguments, each proposing the one right solution to the ills of the
economy and the discontents of the poor. But moral ideals are like blank
checks: real people confront real problems, full of paradoxes and contradictions. Like millions of others drawn into the complicated politics
of the thirties, Hellman found herself caught up in the currents of the
moment as she responded to the situation around her.

While she struggled to find her place within the maelstrom of ideas and
juggled with her personal life, Hellman became involved with organiz-

1938: She wanted desperately to believe that a better world was possible. (Photofest)

ing a union of writers among the drama and film communities on the East and West coasts. This would be her first leap into the political maelstrom of the thirties, and it would lead her straight into the larger political conflicts of the day.

East- and West-coast communities of writers were closely connected. Dramatists who wrote for the stage lived a precarious economic existence until and unless they achieved renown. Those who worked in Hollywood, on the other hand, tended to live much better. Since the advent of talking pictures, screenwriters had been highly valued by the Hollywood studios and relatively well paid. In 1933, a time in which a family of four could live comfortably in most parts of the country on $25 a week, run-of-the-mill screenwriters routinely drew $50 weekly salaries. This was Hellman's salary in her first years in Hollywood. The talented among them earned an exceedingly generous wage of between $200 and $1,000 a week. The best, including Hellman after the success of *The Children's Hour*, earned much more: $2,500 weekly, in Hellman's case. Such high wages attracted the nation's most talented writers, who, governed by their need for income, participated in a commuting culture between the East and West coasts. In this community Hellman's friends Laura and S. J. Perelman, Dorothy Parker, Arthur Kober, and Nathanael West joined the likes of John Dos Passos and F. Scott Fitzgerald. The large studios each kept a stable of writers, none of them larger or more respected than those who worked for the Metro-Goldwyn-Mayer studios headed by Louis B. Mayer.[2]

Already by 1933 there had been rumblings of discontent across the ranks of theater and studio employees. On the East Coast, some of the craft workers had organized themselves into guilds under the umbrella of the International Association of Theater and Stage Employees (IATSE). The Authors' League of America sponsored a special unit for dramatists, and some dramatists organized into a Dramatists Guild. These spread, along with the workers, to the West Coast studios. In self-defense, the producers created their own association, which they called the Academy of Motion Picture Arts and Sciences and which they described as intended to bring disputing parties together. A few writers, some of them members of the Writers Club of the Authors' League of America and others inspired by the example of playwrights who had formed the East Coast–centered Dramatists Guild, called a meeting in February 1933 to discuss the possibility of unionizing. They wanted a share in the royalties earned by movies on which they worked, and, crucially, they wanted screen credits for their scripts.

Then in March, under cover of the Depression and as other studios struggled to pay their bills, Louis Mayer announced that he was cutting the wages of MGM's employees by 50 percent. The moment seemed ripe: FDR had only just been sworn in as president; the unemployment and banking crises had reached catastrophic levels. Mayer and other producers saw an opportunity to cut costs, and they took it. But movies had flourished during the early years of the Depression, and the industry had prospered. Employees, among them the writers, were outraged, especially as it became clear that MGM could well afford to continue to pay its workforce. Albert Hackett, then writing for MGM, recalled that "when they found out what Mr. Mayer did, everybody started to organize. The screenwriters got together and they got into an organization."[3] To avoid the appearance of a union, still somewhat distasteful to professionals, they called their organization the Screen Writers Guild. The producers, in turn, felt betrayed by their relatively coddled writers. They had, they claimed disbelievingly, provided generous wages and extensive creative freedom. High wage scales led Irving Thalberg and other producers to believe that writers would never jeopardize their livelihoods by joining a union. As Thalberg put it, "These writers are living like kings. Why on earth would they want to join a union like coal miners or plumbers?"[4]

Hellman was then on the East Coast and only just beginning the challenging task of writing *The Children's Hour*, so she was not involved in the initial West Coast unionization effort. But she was a member of the Authors' League of America, under whose auspices the campaign initially emerged and which housed the stage playwrights' Dramatists Guild, to which she also belonged. Among the organizers of the Screen Writers Guild were old friends of Hellman's and especially of Hammett's, some of them either members of or sympathetic with the Communist Party. They included John Howard Lawson, and Albert Hackett and Frances Goodrich, the team that had written the screenplay for Hammett's *Thin Man*. Hellman's friend Dorothy Parker, who worked with Hellman in the organizing campaign, was probably already active in the party. The writers argued that their creativity had been purchased: they had sold their artistic freedom to the producers. They wanted either greater control over the content of their scripts or a share in the profits.

Lillian cut her teeth in the ensuing conflict as she firmly supported writers in their claims against producers. The struggle was painful: striking workers lost their jobs, those sympathetic to the Guild discovered their contracts would not be renewed, and some workers settled for smaller pay reductions. The writers took their case to the newly created National Recovery Administration, claiming a right to organize under section 7a, which mandated recognition of organizations of workers. The producers contended that writers were not employees at all but independent contractors. The writers won this first round, but it was a short victory. Within the year, the Supreme Court declared the National Industrial Recovery Act unconstitutional, leaving the producers free to try once again to control them.

By the summer of 1934, Lillian, like all her friends, was flirting with the Communist Party. That winter had witnessed a wave of strikes, some of the most successful led by communists of one stripe or another. To Kober she wrote that she had spent an evening arguing with Mani— Herman Shumlin. "Mani as you know is now an ardent Communist, and being more intelligent than most, sees things more clearly. However there are many things which he also gets confused and dogmatic about and we screamed at each other for several hours."[5] Midst the screaming, Hellman struggled to find a place within the turmoil on the left, moving at every step closer to the communism of the 1930s.

The 1935 decision of the American Communist Party (CPUSA) to embrace Popular Front tactics provided an opening. Since 1928, the CPUSA had followed a path dictated by Joseph Stalin's conviction that the Soviet Union would lead the way to a new worldwide revolutionary moment. The Communist International (Comintern) then ordered the Communist parties of the countries within its orbit to avoid all compromise with socialist, social-democratic, and labor parties that did not strictly follow the communist line. The CPUSA responded by policing its own ranks, expelling those like Jay Lovestone who would not accept Comintern leadership, and turning venomously on those who followed Leon Trotsky's faith in the possibilities of worldwide revolution. Instead of creating coalitions with former allies in the farmer-labor parties and the various socialist parties, the CPUSA declared all these groups to be enemies and labeled them "social fascists."[6] As the Depression deepened and the left grew in influence, factional struggles among left-wing groups grew sharp and deep. Leading American socialists like Norman Thomas and A. J. Muste strongly disagreed that a revolutionary path required adherence to a dogmatic line disseminated by an increasingly paranoid and Stalinist Soviet Union. Some New Deal liberals and reformers toyed with the ideals of communism without following the party line; others strongly believed that bigger government, stronger regulation of banking and industry, and a larger voice for labor would save capitalism. Decrying the sins of fascists and "social fascists" alike, the CPUSA demanded a defense of even the worst delusions of the Soviet Union.

In the summer of 1935, after nearly a decade of attacking anyone who did not fully and completely support Stalin's Soviet style of communism, the Seventh World Congress of Communist Parties adopted a new Popular Front policy. Convinced that the worst enemy of the Soviet Union was fascism, it called on Communist parties the world over to lead an attack on fascism in all of its forms. To this end, the Comintern called for a change from revolutionary strategies to cooperation and alliance with existing left-wing groups. In the United States, the Communist Party, encouraged by Chairman Earl Browder, led a campaign to reconfigure the image and practice of the CPUSA, turning from virulent antagonism against potential allies on the left to efforts to join with them in antifascist coalitions. From early opposition to Franklin Delano Roosevelt's New Deal, the party lent its support to New Deal programs. Instead of organizing alternative trade union structures, Communists embedded themselves in existing trade unions, particularly those organized under the banner of the new Congress of Industrial Organizations (CIO). At the same time, the CPUSA adopted the language of democracy, progressivism, and social justice—a language that Hellman had been employing for at least a decade. And it participated in a multifaceted array of coalitions of like-minded people, with or without membership in the party. The effort was captured in the party's new slogan, "Communism is Twentieth Century Americanism." The outcome was Popular Front politics, a term that aptly designates the millions of people then sympathetic to socialism.

The Communist Party's new appeal immediately manifested itself in dramatic growth. From a pre–Popular Front strength of perhaps 30,000, the party's membership climbed to close to 100,000 members by 1938. All kinds of people joined, including a large assortment of writers, public intellectuals, and theater figures. Their numbers were enhanced by the party's growing willingness to countenance dissent in a wide variety of front organizations that supported a range of popular causes and that did not make an issue of the participation of party members. Hellman joined several of these, including the League of Women Shoppers, the League of American Writers, the Anti Fascist League, and the Motion Picture Artists' Committee. What mattered now was not what party one belonged to or worked with, but how effectively one could join with others to pursue antiracist, antifascist, and trade union activities.[7]

Dashiell Hammett most likely found a home in communism before Hellman did. Flailing a bit after completing *The Thin Man*, which was to be his last novel, he became increasingly committed to left-wing positions. His letters to his daughter Mary, written in the early fall of 1936 in the midst of FDR's campaign for a second term as president and in the aftermath of the CPUSA's turn to Popular Front politics, have the ring of the insider. "There is no truth in the statement that the Communists are supporting Roosevelt," he wrote to her disingenuously on September 11, "that's just the old Hearst howl."[8]

For Hellman, the catalyst might well have been the war in Spain. Both Hellman and Hammett were horrified by the brutal fascist bombardment of what Hellman called "Little Spain." In 1936, the Spanish elected a Popular Front government that included communists and social democrats among its members. Hellman and her friends watched, paralyzed, as a group of generals led by Francisco Franco and supported by Hitler's Germany and Mussolini's Italy attacked a legally elected government. None of the Western democracies—not Britain, not France—would do anything about it. When Franco began his offensive on July 17, 1936, both refused the Spanish government's request for aid, and, to make matters worse, they, along with the United States, embargoed arms to Spain. Popular Front movements all over Europe came to the government's defense, as did the Soviet Union.

Both Hellman and Hammett strongly sympathized with Spain. To his daughter Mary, Hammett wrote that losing the war in Spain would be a

> great set-back for the cause of working people everywhere. Don't believe too much of what the papers say: they are largely on the side of the rebels, and so are such Fascist countries as Germany, Italy and Portugal. The truth is that the present Spanish government is far from perfect, but it at least tries to be on the side of the poor people . . . while its enemies are the sort of people that most of our ancestors came to this country to escape.[9]

Later that fall, he tried to enlist in the Abraham Lincoln Brigade of American soldiers who fought on the Loyalist side. If legend is to be believed, the Communist Party urged Hammett to remain in the States, where he could usefully serve as a fund-raiser and advocate.[10] He was then perhaps already a member of the Communist Party.

Hellman took longer to decide. Her indecision illuminates the tensions of many thoughtful people in the mid-1930s, sparked perhaps by the dramatic growth of the party itself. Large numbers of liberals, socialists, and communists became vaguely aware in the 1930s of Stalin's increasingly ruthless methods, of the thousands of people who had starved as a result of his economic policies, and of the thousands more subject to arrest and murder as a result of his growing paranoia. They objected to what seemed to be the growing subservience of the CPUSA to the Comintern in Moscow. In their eyes, the American wing of the party, financially supported by and consistently favorable to Soviet leadership, could not be trusted. These left-wing opponents accused party members of slavish adherence to an evil bureaucracy, of overlooking the antidemocratic methods of the dictatorial Stalinist regime.

Neither Hellman nor Hammett stood among these opponents. Their relationship to the left-wing activities of the thirties was as members of the entertainment community, rather than as intellectuals. Like many others, they believed themselves independent of Soviet influence and capable of thinking for themselves with regard to the direction of U.S. politics. Still, they held the Soviet effort as a model and accepted its leadership. Though they understood, vaguely perhaps, the imperfections of the Soviet Union, they strongly believed in its potential and trusted that communism with a small *c* could be harnessed to the purposes of democratic and progressive causes. If they heard rumors of purges and deaths, they remained skeptical. This was, after all, a period when rumors flew. In circles like Hellman's, solidarity in the interests of class politics and international harmony seemed an achievable goal, not to be undermined by factionalism and in-fighting.

Hope and belief in the future guided Hellman's vision of a nation that could solve problems of class injustice, racism, and poverty. In this she was not unusual. Betsy Blair, a blacklisted actress who was, perhaps ironically, denied membership in the Communist Party because she was married to the famous Gene Kelly, who did not wish to join up, recalled what her left-wing activity meant to her: "It's like the light that comes from heaven in paintings of saints. We felt such joy believing in the better world that communism would bring, feeling part of the great brotherhood of man. I guess it was a kind of religious ecstasy that we thought would embrace the most deprived and persecuted."[11] Many of Hollywood's entertainment community and certainly huge numbers of writers and intellectuals shared this hope. For Blair, as for Hellman, the central issue in this period was the search for social justice that the ideal of communism seemed to represent. Only the Soviet Union provided a living example of this ideal, even if it did not fully live up to its promise. And in any event, most believed that the dangers of an aggressive fascism posed a greater threat to democratic practice than the Soviet Union. Blacklisted screenwriter Alvah Bessie, responding to a question about why he joined the party, replied, "Why? I was intellectually convinced that it was the right thing to do, and I thought—as any number of people thought—this was the only organization that was actually fighting Fascism in the world, that was actually fighting unemployment, racial discrimination, national chauvinism."[12]

In February 1937, depressed by the failure of *Days to Come*, Hellman returned to Hollywood to work on a film script for *Dead End*. With one brilliant stage success and one flop behind her, she was not yet a name to be reckoned with, but she was certainly a known quantity. The film adaptation of *Children's Hour*, for which she had written the script, had opened to critical acclaim. Her liaison with Dashiell Hammett assured her entrée into all the celebrity circles. And with a lucrative contract in her pocket from Samuel Goldwyn, head of MGM studios, she had enough money to live well without relying on Hammett's erratic funds. Her timing could not have been better, for the Hollywood scene had taken on its own political furor.

In the aftermath of the unfavorable decisions around their efforts to organize, playwrights and screenwriters briefly called off their campaign. The producers created an alternative organization called the Screen Playwrights, which they insisted their writers join and whose members got preference for jobs. They went so far as to call all SWG leaders communists and to blacklist those who had been active in the SWG. Among those blacklisted was John Howard Lawson, the SWG's first president. Lawson, who was to be blacklisted again for political reasons in the late forties, called this the first blacklist.[13] The SWG struggled against the Screen Playwrights for a while, but it could not retain members who had no work. Reluctantly, it dissolved. To all appearances, the Screen Writers Guild had died.

Here was a cause after Hellman's heart—one in which principle overruled pecuniary interest. By 1936, she ranked among the best paid of Hollywood's well-compensated screenwriters. In January she had signed a contract with Samuel Goldwyn, committing herself to adapt five stories (to be selected by Goldwyn) for the screen. Each assignment was expected to take ten weeks, and she would be paid $2,500 a week.[14] Yet like her writer colleagues, she had little control, even over her own work. When it came to adapting the stage version of *The Children's Hour*, she grudgingly altered the plot into a heterosexual triangle to satisfy the demands of the movie code and to meet the requirements of the movie moguls who feared that a lesbian theme would not be commercially viable. And she agreed to rename the film *These Three* to distance it even further from the controversial play.

Hellman readily identified with the demands of the writers for a voice in how credit was distributed and attributed on the screen. The producers believed that, having hired writers for particular tasks, they also owned and controlled the work produced. Hellman and others agreed to a point, but insisted that as artists they deserved credit for their work, distributed according to the proportion of work they had contributed to a picture. Because producers had the authority to move writers around at will or to insist that they work in teams, they could deny any writer ownership of his or her work or attribute it to replacements whose names they wished to promote. This amounted to a kind of censorship because it gave producers complete control not only over words but over who got the credit for them. Like her fellow writers, Hellman wanted to constrain the power of movie producers—to retain at least a modicum of control over how her words were used. To her, the producers' acts resembled the bullying with which she already identified fascism and that she would soon deplore in the case of the Spanish Civil War. A member of the New York–based Dramatists Guild, the author of a failed play that empathetically depicted factory workers, she became a labor organizer.

Just a few months after the Supreme Court declared the National Industrial Recovery Act unconstitutional, Congress passed the Wagner Act, which created the National Labor Relations Board (NLRB). This board was charged with supervising union campaigns and monitoring fair elections, free from employer intervention. Now the Screen Writers Guild quietly regrouped.[15] When Hellman returned to Hollywood in the winter of 1937, the SWG had already begun a new organizational campaign. Lillian's friend Dorothy Parker (already a celebrity) and Parker's husband, Alan Campbell, immediately became involved. Lillian, who had come west to work on the script for *Dead End*, joined the cause. She seems to have been quite serious about her trade union commitments, belying accusations that she never took politics seriously. She lectured on "The Stage and Social Problems" for the International Ladies' Garment Workers' Union on January 21, 1937; along with Dorothy Parker and Hammett, as well as such early activists as Donald Ogden Stewart and John Howard Lawson, she held meetings in her home.[16] With them she handed out leaflets at studio gates, knocked on doors in Hollywood, and buttonholed writers at parties and events. And she was effective. According to Maurice Rapf, whom she recruited to membership in the guild and who had never previously met her, she "was working to sign everybody up for the Guild. She could have asked me to join the local fire-fighters; I would have joined. It didn't make any difference to me."[17]

Determinedly, this group began to gather the signatures necessary to conduct an NLRB-supervised election, finally coming out into the open in June 1937. Then it elected a new leadership that included communist and noncommunist left-wingers, staunch conservatives and writers who had grown wealthy working for the industry, and hacks who ground out B movies for a weekly wage.[18] Hellman, along with Hammett, was elected to a new board. With the board, she participated in a March 1938 meeting with NLRB executive secretary Nathan Witt to discuss the guild's capacity to represent the writers. A few months later—on June 7, 1938—the NLRB ruled that screenwriters were employees under the provisions of the Wagner Act and scheduled an election for just three weeks from that date. On June 28, 1938, the SWG roundly defeated the Screen Playwrights to become the screenwriters' legal representative.

The struggle wasn't over. Along with Philip Dunne, Charles Brackett, and Donald Ogden Stewart, Hellman became part of the negotiating team that first tried to bring in a contract. But though they had lost the election, the producers were not yet ready to settle. As Dunne recalled, "they pretended to negotiate with us" but they were "full of dirty tricks and evasions."[19] "The main thing we were interested in," remembered Dunne, "was that we wanted to determine the screen credit . . . it was the most important issue for writers . . . We didn't want control of the material, because we recognized ourselves as employees, but what we did want was control of credits, because credits meant hiring . . . so long as the producers could designate who got the credit they controlled the hiring hall."[20] The producers held out for almost three years, settling only after the United States entered World War II. By then Hellman was no longer on the negotiating team, which had shed its communist members. The final contract was a victory of sorts. It called for a minimum wage of $125 per week for all writers as well as minimum periods of employment, and put the guild in control of screen credit.[21] Hellman played only a bit part in this victory, her own political commitments less relevant to the successful establishment of a guild for screenwriters than her activities in the ensemble.

While the guild negotiated with producers over how to acknowledge the work of writers, it harbored a simmering internal dispute. The producers, eager to discredit the SWG, accused its leadership of communist sympathies. In the period of the Popular Front, when communists and noncommunists often worked together and when attachment to communism was often understood as a search for social justice rather than a commitment to Stalinism, the accusation did little more than roil the waters. To be sure, many who were involved in organizing the SWG were sympathetic to communist goals of racial equality and social justice and opposed to untrammeled capitalism. Some (including John Howard Lawson and Ring Lardner Jr.) were probably members of the CPUSA in 1936 and 1937. Hellman had not yet joined the party.

Increasingly the producers insisted that the issue was as much political as it was economic. Only the producers, they argued, could adequately police political content in order to diffuse the influence of communism that crept into the language of writers. This seemed farfetched to experienced writers like Albert Hackett (who early served on the SWG steering committee). "Mr. Mayer," he concluded after reflecting on the emergence of the left in the movie industry, "really is the cause of all the communism in Hollywood."[22] In his view, the source of the problem was Mayer's heavy-handed insistence on controlling both wages and credits for writers, denying them ownership of their work or any element of creativity. John Howard Lawson agreed. Himself a member of the Communist Party by the mid-1930s, he confirmed Hackett's sense that "nobody was ever suspicious about our slipping anything into the pictures."[23] Even later in the decade, most denizens of Hollywood still insisted on the distinction between party membership and Marxist convictions. When screenwriter Allen Boretz, a party member, glimpsed Dashiell Hammett at a meeting in 1937, he noted that he "stood in a corner and said very little . . . It was a Marxist study group," he emphasized. "These were not yet Communists, if they ever did become Communists."[24]

To the outside world, however, this was a distinction without a difference. Association with communists, such as existed in many trade union groups in the Popular Front period, seemed to be evidence of subjection to communist dogma. Fearful that communism and membership in the CPUSA amounted to the same thing, insistent that loyalty to the CPUSA involved taking orders from Moscow, and conceiving those orders to be mandatory and therefore an abrogation of the free will and free thought essential to a democratic society, those suspicious of the left, including the producers, accused writers of acting as foils of the Communist Party. Producers pointed to the League of American Writers (a front organization founded in 1935) and its creation of the School for American Writers in 1940, where some of the leading left-wing screenwriters (including Lawson and Stewart, Paul Jarrico, and Michael Blankfort, but not Hellman) taught. By hurling accusations of communism, producers hoped to divide the writers, to discourage uncommitted writers from joining the union, and perhaps to discredit the union altogether. Inadvertently, they created a political whirlwind of sorts when state and federal legislatures took a hand in the situation—setting up committees to explore communist influence in the entertainment industry.

On the very same day—June 7, 1938—that the National Labor Relations Board ruled that screenwriters could organize, the U.S. House of Representatives resolved to form a new committee—the House Committee on Un-American Activities—under the leadership of Texas congressman Martin Dies. Modeled after an already existing California committee headed by Jack Tenney that had weighed in on the side of the producers, the committee took it upon itself to "inquire into the realm of political thought, affiliation, and association" of everyone in the industry.[25] Tenaciously, the committee, better known as HUAC, called upon members of the many front groups that now appeared in Hollywood to testify as to whether they were or were not party members. Hellman was not called.

The producers now had an ally, and the writers a larger concern. The Dies Committee called on members of the SWG and its parent organization, the League of American Writers, to defend themselves against charges of communist leadership.[26] Their efforts were buttressed a year later by the passage of the Smith Act, which prohibited the dissemination of ideas and the distribution of literature that sought to overthrow the U.S. government. This, thought Hellman, marked the moment when the United States officially declared war against communist ideas inside and outside the Communist Party. And yet bitterly as Hellman felt about the act's prohibition against advocacy of communist ideas and its chilling effects on the ability of writers to speak their minds, she and other party members would cheer when, in 1943, the Smith Act was used to investigate Trotskyists.[27] Even when the Second World War came and the United States allied itself with the Soviet Union, both the SWG and the League of American Writers remained targets of suspicion. And when the two organizations joined forces to sponsor a fifth annual Writers Congress in 1943, the Dies Committee condemned the effort by the Congress to allow writers to say what they wanted as "a plot by communists to take over the industry."[28] Fearing destruction, the Screen Writers Guild began to purge its leadership of known communists. Hellman remained a member and staunch supporter of the organization but did not again assume a leadership position.

While the campaign to unionize screenwriters unfolded, Hellman found herself increasingly involved in the debate over the Spanish Civil War. Under the auspices of left-wing groups including the Communist Party, sympathetic individuals everywhere volunteered to fight on the government's side in an international brigade. By the fall of 1936, American volunteers, organized into what was called the Abraham Lincoln Brigade, were already on their way to Spain. Additional numbers of young men and women joined the cause of the Republican Loyalists as ambulance drivers and reporters. The war took a complicated turn in early 1937 when the Republican Loyalists turned to the Soviet Union for help, which was quickly granted. As Soviet money and influence escalated, government defenders found themselves helpless to resist a disastrous and divisive Soviet effort to exert leadership over all the Spanish Republican forces. Anarchist and socialist members faced off against the Soviet-led communists, leaving Republican Loyalist fighters in disarray. American and non-Soviet partisans found themselves not only fighting Franco but torn apart by Soviet attacks on those who resisted their leadership. What was an American to do?

In the early fall of 1936, while confusion reigned, antifascists of all stripes tried to provoke some sort of intervention by the United States. Hellman, her heart clearly with the Spanish Republican Loyalists but her head deeply involved with the production of *Days to Come*, stayed on the sidelines. Hammett wrote long letters to his teenage daughter Mary to try to explain why he supported the Republican cause. The Spanish Civil War had started, he told her, when a triumvirate of wealthy landowners persuaded the army to overthrow the elected government (only two of whose twelve members were communists). "They decided to buy a revolution," he wrote, and then followed this assertion with advice to "be in favor of what's good for the workers and against what isn't. Follow that and you may not be the most brilliant person in the world, but you'll at least be able to hold your head up when you look at yourself in the mirror."[29]

Then film producer Joris Ivens approached Hellman for money to make a documentary film about the war. This was to be the beginning of Hellman's lifetime commitment on behalf of the Republican Loyalists and wartime refugees. Hellman joined with Dorothy Parker, Herman Shumlin, John Dos Passos, Archibald MacLeish, and others to found a group called Contemporary Historians. Together they raised $3,000 to send Ivens to Spain, and they put together a script he could use to guide his filmmaking. But Ivens abandoned the script as soon as he arrived in Spain and followed his instincts and opportunities instead. The film that emerged that spring as *The Spanish Earth* had a narrative written by Ernest Hemingway (whom Ivens had met in Spain) with a little help from John Dos Passos. Marc Blitzstein (Hellman's friend and the acclaimed composer of *The Cradle Will Rock*) and Virgil Thomson compiled a score made up of indigenous Spanish music.

The film was never intended to be dispassionate. Joris Ivens viewed it as a fund-raising vehicle for the Republican Loyalist side, and when Hellman first saw it, on July 10, 1937, she was in Hollywood at such a fund-raiser. Hellman was uncomfortable: she had wanted more "facts," she said; she would have preferred a film more outspokenly condemnatory of fascism.[30] Other viewers responded more sympathetically. At its first showing, Hemingway made a pitch for money and raised $20,000 for ambulances in Spain. Legend has it that Hammett contributed the first $1,000. Later in the summer, President Roosevelt and Eleanor Roosevelt invited Hemingway, his partner, Martha Gellhorn, Joris Ivens, and others to a special showing at the White House. Eleanor wrote favorably about the film and the war in her column. And in surprising concord, after the film's release in August, the *New York Times*, the *New York Herald Tribune*, the *New Masses*, and the *Daily Worker* all reviewed it favorably.

On August 25, just six weeks after the viewing and only a day after the release of the successful film *Dead End* (on whose script she had worked during the spring), Hellman set off with Alan Campbell and Dottie Parker for an extended trip to Europe. Arriving first in Paris, she left after several weeks to travel through Berlin to attend a theater festival in Moscow. This was the trip on which she may or may not have encountered her old friend Julia (about which more later); it was also her first personal encounter with Soviet communism. She stayed in Moscow only a few days, then returned to Paris through Helsinki. Tired from several weeks of traveling, she was prepared to rest.

Otto Katz intervened. Katz (a man with twenty-one aliases, known to Hellman at the time as Rudolph Breda and later as Otto Simon) was a handsome and dashing Czech-born and German-educated journalist with a reputation for charming women. Some think that he and Hellman had a passionate affair when they met, first in Hollywood in early 1937 and again in Paris. A dedicated communist, loyal to the Comintern, Katz was then engaged in encouraging celebrities to speak out against fascism. He would later serve as a press attaché for the Spanish Republican government.[31] At dinner in Paris, he talked Lillian into going to Spain. He probably didn't have to try very hard. Jim Lardner also influenced her. He was the brother of her old Screen Writers Guild colleague Ring Lardner Jr., who would later be indicted for refusing to testify as to his communist connections. Dottie Parker and Alan Campbell, who had just returned from Spain, may have played a role as well. With so many people encouraging her, she could hardly refuse to go. "I had strong convictions about the Spanish war, about Fascism-Nazism, strong enough to push just below the surface my fear of the danger of war," she later wrote.[32]

The trip became an important turning point in her life. As was her style, she focused on the human side of the war, neglecting larger political meanings in deference to its poignant and destructive effects on ordinary people. In one trip across the country, she wrote, she encountered a kind farm family who fed her out of their meager stores. They had taken in a refugee from Madrid, a woman who recognized that Hellman's bleached-blonde hair would soon need color. In the midst of her misery, she recommended that Hellman go and look up her cousin when she arrived in Madrid: "She works good on the hair. Tell her I send you, tell her I didn't have the baby. Tell her to put soap in the bleach and do a good job."[33] The gesture touched Hellman's heart, as did the defenselessness of most ordinary people. She described a bombardment in Madrid that terrified the population the evening before she left. "In a kitchen back of my hotel, a blind woman was holding the bowl of soup that she came to get each night. She was killed eating the bowl of soup."[34] The episode confirmed her sense of fascism as the fountain of brutality and the refuge of bullies. "Finding the range on a blind woman eating a bowl of soup," she concluded sarcastically, "is a fine job for a man."[35]

Spanish Loyalists and their international-brigade allies, in contrast, were doing noble work. "I came to Spain because I was puzzled," Hellman insisted. "I had been taught in school that it was the right of every man to decide the form of his own life, and the form of the government that was to rule that life. I believed that. I believed that hard."[36] Hellman expressed similar feelings in a piece she wrote on her return. Intended for national distribution, it was turned down by an important newspaper syndicate and published in the liberal weekly the *New Republic*. In it, she recalled a day of bombing in Valencia and the feelings evoked by the wounded members of the international brigades that had defended it. "They had come," she wrote after she returned home, "because they thought that if a man believed in democracy he ought to do something about it . . . I prayed, for the first time in many years, that they would get what they wanted."[37]

In a fury against the fascists, she neither saw nor registered the dangers of the divisive Soviet policy. Did this make her a dupe—an ideological fellow traveler with no mind of her own? Why didn't she, unlike George Orwell or John Dos Passos, see the danger at hand? Did the wish to defeat the fascists blind her, as it did many noncommunists as well as communist partisans of the Spanish Republic? Neither Hemingway nor Dorothy Parker nor hundreds of survivors of the international brigades condemned a destructive Comintern policy that turned weapons against its own allies. Left-wing journalist Isadore Feinstein—also known as I. F. Stone—faced the same dilemma and remembered the confusion. Even as he knew that socialist, anarchist, and dissident communist soldiers were being attacked and killed by the pro-Soviet side, he remarked, "We knew there were anguished choices . . . we didn't know what to do."[38]

Whatever her initial motives for going to Spain, Hellman invested herself in the morality of the Republican cause. She recalled the courage of the Spanish under bombardment with deference and respect. She remembered the wartime privation with horror. After she returned to Paris, she could no longer tolerate what seemed to her a meaningless social round. She escaped to London, where, she tells us, she spent weeks, hobbled by a broken ankle, reading Marx, Engels, and other left-wing literature for the first time. Afterward she reflected on her experience in the simple language of the newly committed. "The Spanish are a gentle people and patient," she wrote a few months after her return.

> It had taken them a long time to declare . . . that there was something wrong with a world which allowed a king to have more racing cars than he could use, more pheasant to shoot at than he could eat, when their own children walked without shoes and ate without bread. They wanted, as all people of dignity will always want, a chance to work and to live and to be happy. That was the future they wanted, and that was the future they thought they were making.[39]

Within months after her return to the United States, Hellman and other single-minded antifascists found themselves embroiled in disputes with American communists deeply critical of Stalin's ruthless efforts to take control of opposition to Franco. The split ran deep, but despite evidence of vicious Soviet intervention, Hellman insisted on continuing to support the Republican cause as though it were still unified. She lauded the elemental courage of Spanish citizens and castigated the American press for its refusal to weigh in against the forces of fascism. An angry diatribe she wrote in the summer of 1938, published in the *New York Post*, captured the strength of her feelings. There, she attacked a *New York Times* correspondent who reported that American prisoners (probably largely communists) were "simply chronic bellyachers."[40] The *New York Times*, she suggested sardonically, chose to print dispatches of this "very naïve journalist" in preference to those of a "brilliant and daring" reporter already on the scene because it feared attention to its Jewish ownership. "Every Jew must be an anti-Fascist to be either a good Jew or a good American," she concluded.

The Spanish Civil War ended in 1939 in a victory for Franco. Hellman never forgot the international and American soldiers who had been maimed and wounded in Spain. She engaged in fund-raising for them and for the Spanish men, women, and children who fled after Franco proved triumphant. Already a supporter of the Veterans of the Abraham Lincoln Brigade and a member of the Hollywood Anti-Nazi League, which had been started by her friend Dorothy Parker in 1936, she helped to found the Motion Picture Artists Committee to Aid Republican Spain in the battle against fascism. In 1939, this group helped to launch the Hollywood section of the Joint Anti Fascist Refugee Committee, under whose auspices the Spanish Refugee Appeal was formed. Hellman was honored by this group early in 1945 for her tireless fund-raising efforts "in the name of the thousands of Spanish refugees throughout the world."[41] A few years later she agreed to publish a short piece in Alvah Bessie's collection about the war, *The Heart of Spain*. When the book appeared without a contribution from Ernest Hemingway, she excoriated Bessie for the omission. "If I had known of your censorship of Hemingway," she wrote, "I would not have allowed you to include me in the anthology." She continued by condemning "the self-righteous conviction that censorship is fine if one side practices it, and evil if another side plays the same game."[42]

1938: She never forgot the members of the international brigade who had been maimed and wounded in Spain. (New York University Tamiment Library)

Decades later, long after the Soviets had abandoned all interest in Spain, when the war had receded from memory and her own credibility was under attack, Hellman remained a staunch contributor to Spanish refugees. For most of this time she supported a group that favored refugees who had fought with and for the communist side. But after 1969, she agreed to let her name appear on the letterhead as a "sponsor" of Spanish Refugee Aid. That organization was founded by members of the non-communist left to provide help to "the displaced, disabled, hungry, sick, weary Spanish refugees" who had been chased out by Franco's government and abandoned even by the United Nations' Refugee Relief Association because the UN had recognized Franco. It helped everyone *except* those who had fought with the communists. In the spring of 1978, Hellman came under attack for her putative former and continuing Stalinism. In one of those illuminating footnotes to history, Mary McCarthy threatened to resign from the board if Hellman's name was not removed. In the end the board held fast. Despite other disagreements with Hell-

man's politics, most of its members never doubted Hellman's commitment to all those who fought for a free and democratic Spain.[43]

Whatever their political differences over the factional fights in Spain and
the centrality of the Soviet Union in their politics, whatever their party
affiliations, Hellman and her friends could unite over their hatred of fascism. We can watch that hatred build over the course of the 1930s, from
Hellman's political awakening during her 1929 stay in Bonn to her increasing use of the language of antifascism and democracy in the early
1930s. It emerges clearly in *Days to Come* as well as in the film script for
Dead End. We note her disappointed response to the weak antifascist
language of *The Spanish Earth*. Her extended European visit in the fall of
1937, and particularly the attacks on civilians in Spain, confirmed all her
worst suspicions.[44] Fascism relied on the mindless exercise of power.
Democracy, in contrast, counted on the individual's capacity to express
his or her own thoughts, to govern his or her own direction.

But it would be a mistake to see Hellman's commitment to the left,
and particularly her relationship to the Communist Party, as merely tran-
sitory exercises directed at defeating fascism. It would be equally misguided to imagine that she espoused antifascism to obscure her sympathy
for communism: as a vehicle aimed at change without the language of revolution. Rather, in the context of the moment, these commitments converged.
Antifascism was one of many reasons to join the Communist Party. In
1936 and 1937, the heyday of the Popular Front and the moment when the
New Deal seemed to be veering leftward, Hellman found in a broadly
defined socialism the value system she held dear. In the Communist
Party, to which Hammett probably already belonged, she saw the opportunity to oppose fascism and construct a political path for socialism. Her
friends Dorothy Parker and Alan Campbell, Marc Blitzstein, Herman
Shumlin, and many of her acquaintances were already members. The
question was not why did she join the party, but how could she not have
joined?

Her writing in this period, particularly *The Little Foxes*, embodies the
critique of capitalism that party membership implied. By some interpretations, that play, which opened in February 1939, spells out the power of
greed to corrupt even the most intimate relationships in the family. Capitalism, *The Little Foxes* seems to be saying, can destroy even the most intimate relationships. The play's success, the power of its message, and its

resonance with American audiences speak to the mood of a country still enmeshed in economic depression. And yet like many of her plays, *The Little Foxes* was consistent with some of the favorite themes of American communists without following them mindlessly or even closely. The *Daily Worker*, the organ of the Communist Party, admired the play on the whole, but critic Milton Meltzer objected to the film version for placing the character of the family ("they're terrible because it's in their nature") at the film's center. If only, he lamented, "*The Little Foxes* had been able to show more directly the necessity under a competitive economic system for the dog-eat-dog of people out to make good by this same society's standards. It would have reached even greater stature."[45] Perhaps ironically, *The Little Foxes* made Hellman rich, providing her not only with enough money to buy her beloved Hardscrabble Farm in Pleasantville, New York, but with the celebrity to make her a valuable asset to what can only be called "front" causes.

By some accounts Hellman was already in the party by 1937. Louis Budenz—a notoriously unreliable FBI informant—told the House Committee on Un-American Activities in 1950 that he had learned about her membership when he joined the party that year. He had, he wrote, been "officially advised" that she continued to be a member until 1945.[46] Martin Berkeley claims to have spotted her at a meeting in Hollywood in the summer of 1937. Perhaps so. She was, that summer, briefly in Hollywood for a screening and fund-raiser for *The Spanish Earth*, which had not yet been formally released. And her presence at a meeting suggests the kind of serious interest in the party that she often claimed. In November, after her trips to Moscow and to Spain, when she retreated to London to recover her stability she says she sat down to immerse herself in Marx and Engels. Perhaps the point is not worth debating. If she wasn't already in the party in 1937, she was certainly drawn to it by multiple strands. But then so was everyone else she knew.

By her own account, Hellman joined the party in 1938 "with little thought as to the serious step I was taking." In a statement she drew up in 1952, she tells us that she remained "a not very active" member until late in 1940 when she stopped attending meetings and "severed all connections with the party."[47] Despite her later protests, Hellman seems to have been a pretty loyal trooper during her two years of party membership. Her name appears often, in a variety of front organizations and in some that would have been unusual for her. For example, it doesn't surprise us to see it among the sponsors of the National Committee for

People's Rights, July 13, 1938. Nor do we blink when we see it among the sponsors of the Foster Parents' Plan for Children in Spain, October 31, 1938, or the signators of the Coordinating Committee to Lift the Embargo. But what is she doing in the League of Women Shoppers (of which she became a vice president in 1938 and in which she seems to have remained active until at least July 1941)? Why, for the first time, did she contribute an essay to the *New Masses*, in October 1938? And why, though she was by now immersed in the Screen Writers Guild unionizing campaign, did she agree to chair the Sponsors' Committee of the United Office and Professional Workers of America, Local 16, Fifth Annual Stenographers' Ball? That she was drawing closer to the Communist Party constitutes the best explanation for all these activities.

Hellman's increasing commitments to a variety of Popular Front groups suggest a significant incidence of involvement with the CPUSA during the heady late 1930s. They also tell us something about how, afterward, people like Hellman came to camouflage both the memory of their membership and its nature. Some say that she continued to be a "concealed" member well after 1941. Her celebrity status might have made her more valuable in that role. And yet Hellman's outspokenness in defense of Soviet causes during the war years suggests that concealment would have served little purpose. Hellman neither hid her support for the Soviet Union nor allowed herself to turn into a mindless follower.

If Hellman's dates are accurate, then she joined the CPUSA after the worst of the Moscow purge trials and in full awareness of them. Not only had she been in Moscow while they were going on, but she had returned to a United States where the press fully covered them. Consistent with the party line, Hellman remained silent during the trials; she did not (as some factions on the left did) question their validity nor query Stalin's motives for condemning hundreds of high-level officials and army officers to death. Instead, in April 1938, a few months after her return and around the time that she apparently joined the party, Hellman, along with 150 other artists, writers, and scientists, signed a letter declaring their faith in the guilt of the defendants and accepting the trials as necessary to preserve progressive democracy in the Soviet Union.[48] The act allied her with the Stalinist wing of the Communist Party and helps to explain why the label stuck to her until she died.

Did Hellman really believe that Stalin needed to summarily eliminate thousands of people whom he suddenly declared to be enemies of the state? Or—what is more likely—was her willingness to sign this letter,

circulated in the first flush of her party membership, an effort to demonstrate that she could be loyal to a party line? Was not the CPUSA the
most vociferous defender of racial equality and the most consistent supporter of her union, the Screen Writers Guild? Did she sign because
she wanted to stop the spread of fascism at all costs? Did she, like many
others, rationalize Stalin's efforts to cover up his crimes out of despair
over the continuing inroads of fascism? After all, she and many others
saw the Soviet Union as the most consistent opponent of fascism in Germany and Italy. Or could it be that, as she confessed to her goddaughter,
Catherine Kober Zeller, many years later, she simply had not seen the
full spectrum of Stalin's sins?[49] In the sharp glare of history, neither the
act of signing that letter nor her failure to repudiate the document thereafter is defensible. But by the dim light of the 1930s, both acts are understandable.[50]

The most plausible explanation for Hellman's defense of the Moscow
Trials at the time lies in her despair over the continuing inroads of fascism. The months before she signed that letter had been disastrous for
the antifascist cause. In March, Germany had incorporated Austria into
a province of the Nazi state. By April it had become clear that the Spanish Republican Loyalists (faced with the adamant refusal of European
and American democracies to ship arms to them) would go down to
defeat. Such pressures influenced many defenders of the Moscow Trials.
Nathaniel Weyl, who had joined the CPUSA in 1930, commented on his
own response: "My wife and I had read the official transcript of the
trials, and concluded that the accused men had been judicially murdered.
However, we thought that the communist movement was the most powerful world force against Nazism, and therefore, that we should not join
the public critics of Stalin."[51]

Even after the letter appeared, international events continued to go
downhill. On September 29, Britain's prime minister Neville Chamberlain signed the Munich Agreement, which turned over part of Czechoslovakia to Germany. And in November, the destruction of Jewish
property during Kristallnacht signaled a newly vicious phase of the
Reich's attack against Jews. Faced with an isolationist spirit in the United
States—Time magazine had just been accused by some members of its
own staff of espousing fascist sympathies—it made sense for people like
Hellman and Hammett to join with their friends to try to consolidate
their forces against fascism. On November 17, 1938, a group of thirty-six
prominent authors, including Dorothy Parker and Alan Campbell,

called on President Roosevelt to stop trading with Germany. Not long after, well-known communist and noncommunist figures like Richard Wright, Harold Clurman, Lester Cole, Jerome Davis, and Malcolm Cowley joined together with many others to call for a cessation of attacks against the Soviet Union.[52]

On the principle of "the enemy of my enemy is my friend" and because it promised to stem the fascist tide, the CPUSA grew apace. Indeed, the antifascist cause often flowed into that of communism. Sam Jaffe, Hollywood agent and producer and a great admirer of Lillian Hellman's, recalled attending a meeting of the Anti-Nazi League in the late 1930s. After he, his wife, and their friend Oscar Hammerstein left, they turned to each other and said, "'My God, this was a Communist meeting.' It was a cover-up. We were in a Communist meeting. But it was labeled Anti-Nazi League. Well, sure they were Anti-Nazi, but it was strictly a Communist meeting . . . It was Anti-Nazi, true, but it was Communist propaganda that they were propagating."[53]

The antifascist cause (like every good cause in this Popular Front period) attracted Jews, intellectuals, and champions of liberty of all kinds as well as Communists into its fold. But the coalitions often surprised even close friends, setting off bitter recriminations and factional fights. For all their hatred of Hitler, many on the left, including Trotskyists and other anti-Stalinist communists, rebelled against associating with members of the CPUSA who refused to acknowledge the horrors of the bloody purges of the 1930s. To these opponents of Stalin, whipping up a frenzy against fascism seemed merely a ploy to cover up the evils of Stalinist communism. Then and later they wanted Stalinism acknowledged for the evil it was. Still there were others to whom it made not a whit of difference who was energized in the fight against fascism as long as the fight was won. Hellman probably belongs in this group. The evidence suggests a trajectory that reflects the difficult moral choices that she and many other intellectuals and creative artists of her day faced. She had moved from a generic and unformed concern for democracy and liberty to a hatred of fascist bullies, and then to membership in the CPUSA. In the crucial years at the end of the thirties, she and many others believed that victory over fascism required loyalty to the party. Still, her decision to join and to remain in the party would haunt her for decades after.

The Soviet pact with Germany, signed in the summer of 1939, opened a chasm on the left. Two weeks after the pact was signed, Germany invaded Poland, setting off the Second World War. A wartime atmosphere enveloped the United States, posing for many the question of whether the United States should remain neutral or whether it should join the war to help its traditional allies—Britain, France, Holland, and Belgium—fend off the German assault. The war turned intellectuals and artists on the left, people who had been friends and allies, into instant enemies. Some argued that the Soviet Union signed the pact to buy time to build up its defenses. On these grounds, they abandoned their earlier support of action against Germany and advocated for peace. Others insisted that a neutral position meant giving up the fight against fascism. Particularly for Jews who were aware of the laws that isolated their coreligionists and deprived them of jobs, freedom, and food, choosing sides must have been torturous.

Hellman sided with the Soviets. Her long history of antifascist work notwithstanding, she did not withdraw from the Communist Party. In what perhaps constitutes the most persuasive evidence of her party loyalty, she did not condemn the Soviet Union's ruthless betrayal of its own principles and its callous division of Polish territory with the Germans. For her, the argument that the Soviets needed to buy time to build up their strength proved persuasive. A few weeks after the start of the war, in October 1939, the Soviets invaded Finland, accusing its leaders of harboring fascist sympathies. In solidarity with the Finns, much of the Broadway theater community turned its productions into benefit performances to raise money for Finnish resistance. Such benefits were not uncommon; Hellman had previously supported them for Spanish War Relief. Now, however, when Tallulah Bankhead, the star of *The Little Foxes*, pressed Hellman to do the same for Finland, Hellman refused. The story has often been used to demonstrate Hellman's adherence to the communist party line during this period. That interpretation is supported by a statement she made at the time. She feared, she told a reporter, that such a benefit "would give dangerous impetus to war spirit in this country."[54]

Later she told a different story, one that depicted the disagreement as based on personal animus. Bankhead had earlier refused to perform a benefit for Spanish Republican fighters who needed money to get out of a Spain then falling to Franco.[55] Hellman, who had passed through Helsinki in 1937 and noted the posters and rallies in support of Hitler, had little sympathy for the Finns. Along with her like-minded producer Herman Shumlin, she was not inclined to raise money for what she considered a country with fascist sympathies. Angry with Bankhead for denying her an opportunity to raise funds for Spain, she simply took her revenge. Hellman claimed that Bankhead turned "what had been no more than a theatre fight . . . into a political attack: it was made to seem that we agreed with the invasion of Finland, refused aid to true democrats, were, ourselves, dangerous Communists." She claimed to be a victim: "It was my first experience of such goings-on."[56]

It is difficult to believe that Hellman did not invent the second story to justify her behavior after the fact, and yet she did not mindlessly support the party line. She would later write of the German alliance with Russia: "While I believed that the Soviet Union's disillusionment with Munich in 1938 afforded some justification for the Nazi-Soviet Pact of 1939, I wholly disagreed with the position of the Communist Party in its glorification of Nazism."[57] Two projects in which she was then engaged illustrate this complicated position: *PM* magazine and her antifascist play *Watch on the Rhine*. Together, they reveal something of her unconventional intellectual stance.

Ralph Ingersoll, Lillian's old friend and sometime lover, planned to develop a new daily newspaper intended to serve truth "whether the truth takes us to the right or to the left." Ingersoll claimed to have been inspired to produce *PM* by Lillian herself and gave her credit for the name. As the story goes, Ingersoll, the distinguished editor of *Fortune* magazine and soon to become general manager of Time, Inc., fell into a passionate romance with Hellman that lasted through the summer and fall of 1935. When Lillian, in the presence of Dashiell Hammett, mocked him once too often for being under the thumb of the corporation's owner, Henry Luce, Ingersoll vowed to prove his manhood by creating a publication of his own.[58]

By the fall of 1939, Ingersoll was ready to start the newspaper, whose credo he succinctly described in one of many drafts of his "Proposition to Create a New Newspaper" as "against people who push other people around." Talented writers of all kinds would write for it, he believed, because "only here can they write honestly what they know and see."[59] This would be possible because *PM* would not be dependent on advertising. Rather it would be supported, at five cents a copy, by the "subway rider." He proved to be partially right. Launched with the help of funding from a large advisory board and particularly from the department store heir Marshall Field (whose wife, Ruth, was a good friend of Lillian's), Ingersoll produced an afternoon newspaper whose circulation reached nearly two hundred thousand daily.

To get *PM* going and to hire its staff, Ingersoll placed on its planning committee a range of intellectuals who included Hellman and Hammett, both of them by now understood to be members of the Communist Party. Together they hired a young staff, some of them communists. Others, like Ingersoll himself and the journalist I. F. Stone, were committed to noncommunist antifascist politics. The staff also included liberals who despised the Soviet Union. Among these, the news reporter James Wechsler stood out. Ingersoll deployed his talent effectively, insisting that everyone had to work together and that the paper would publish only independent thought. Communists were fine; single-minded followers of the party line would be rejected. Not everyone believed him.

For a while the paper worked beautifully. *PM* was apparently read in the White House. Avidly antifascist, President Roosevelt and Eleanor used the paper to create support for interventionist policies and to construct sympathy for the refugees of fascism. Both Hammett and Hellman devoted time and attention to it in 1940 and 1941. FDR invited Ingersoll to the White House to consult with him about policy and politics. Despite widespread accusations of sympathy with communism, Ingersoll successfully laughed off any taint of Communist Party influence.

Yet the several pieces that Hellman wrote for *PM* during its short eight-year life span reveal how awkwardly even the most talented writers responded to the injunction to independent thought. Hellman, still drawn to communism in the years of the Nazi-Soviet pact, would not defend either the Soviet Union or the Germans, and yet she demonstrated an unrelenting cynicism with regard to American democracy. Sent to Philadelphia to cover the Republican national convention of 1940, she soon left the convention hall, frustrated by the apparent deal-making that undergirded the process of selecting a president. On the street, she buttonholed "three white men and two black men" to ask them "whether they thought Mr. Roosevelt might run again, or who did they think the Republicans would pick for a candidate." Unconvincingly she reported that one after the other refused to speak to her. A taxi driver told her "he had been instructed not to talk about politics, the war, or the state of the nation." Another replied to her questions by telling her, "We don't think around here much. It's too hot to think." Yet a third replied that he "didn't have any ideas, sometimes it wasn't smart to have ideas." She concluded, in what can only be interpreted as an obvious projection, that they were "too suspicious and too tired and too frightened to exercise their primary right of free and easy speech."[60]

About this time, Lillian Hellman came to the attention of the Federal Bureau of Investigation. Their files on her, numbering close to a thousand pages, start in 1941 and, with sporadic breaks, follow her into the 1970s.[61] Hellman seems not to have been aware of the surveillance—and yet this too is part of the American twentieth century. The bureau searched its inventory and newspaper databases back to 1936 to compile evidence of her association with left-wing groups.

Hellman was growing impatient. The Nazi-Soviet pact had effectively, if only momentarily, curtailed the Communist Party's criticism of fascism. But Hellman was not to be silenced. She had always defended the right to speak freely, and, whatever the Soviet line, she would speak up now. Swiftly, she sat down to pen *Watch on the Rhine*, the only play she ever wrote, she tells us, that flowed from her pen in a single draft. The play eloquently celebrated "men willing to die for what they believed in."[62] In so doing, it implicitly condemned Soviet efforts to convince Americans to remain out of the war then spreading across Europe, and it appealed for engagement with a fascist enemy. Inaction, *Watch on the Rhine* seemed to warn, would stifle freedom everywhere. Hellman had no need to name Germans as the enemy in the play; a German villain who drew on the German embassy for support made its targets clear. She preferred, she would later say, to speak to the issue of sticking by one's convictions.

The communist press predictably attacked the play. As it had taken issue with *The Little Foxes* for being too easy on capitalists, now it condemned *Watch on the Rhine* for its "fabric of omissions." Why, wondered communist critics, did the play fail to illuminate the economic ills that provoked the rise of fascism? Alvah Bessie, writing in the *New Masses*, deplored the play's lack of sensitivity. Instead of "trying to whip or cajole us into imperialist war against the fascists," Bessie commented, "Hellman might have used her skills to promote the world-wide organization by the working people against their separate home-grown brands of fascism."[63]

Nine weeks after the play opened in April 1941, the Germans invaded the Soviet Union. The alliance of fascism and communism was over. The west joined with the communists to defeat fascism. Dashiell Hammett settled in at Hardscrabble Farm to write the screen version of *Watch on the Rhine*. Hellman became a darling of the communist press. Simultaneously, she earned a treasured invitation to both supper at the White House and a command performance of her play on January 25, 1942. There, as she remembers it, President Roosevelt inquired about the provenance of the play and, when she told him she had started it in the summer of 1940, asked her how she reconciled the play with rumors that she had supported communist pickets then opposed to U.S. entry into the war. Hellman denied that she had ever supported the pickets.[64]

By the time she dined at the White House in January 1942, Hellman had probably already withdrawn from the CPUSA. But before and after she withdrew, she joined an astonishing array of antifascist organizations. She remained active in the Spanish Refugee Relief Campaign and in the Hollywood Joint Anti-Fascist Refugee Committee. If the Friends of the Abraham Lincoln Brigade sponsored a fund drive to aid wounded volunteers, Hellman's name appeared on the invitation. If the American Friends of Spanish Democracy held a dinner, Hellman gave a talk. She joined the American League for Peace and Democracy—an organization of mixed provenance formed in August 1939 to sponsor refugee scholarships and to campaign for peace.[65] She helped to found the American Committee for Democracy and Intellectual Freedom, whose first act (on January 17, 1940) was to circulate a petition to discontinue the Dies Committee. To the FBI, Hellman's name on a group's membership list affirmed the presence of communists and earned the group the label of a "front" organization.

But Hellman seemed to care little about whether a particular group bore the communist imprimatur at any given time. After the United States entered the war, she raised money for Russian war relief; she lent her name to the Artists' Front to Win the War (sponsor, October 1942); she signed petitions circulated by the League of American Writers to open a second front (in September 1942); she sponsored a call for the Congress of American-Soviet Friendship, November 6 to 8, 1943. She cheered when the Dies Committee suspended its investigations and cooperated happily when the federal government asked Hollywood producers to make films that encouraged sympathy for a Soviet Union under fire. At a moment when the United States and the Soviet Union fought on the same side, Hellman's American patriotism and continuing admiration for the Soviet Union blended smoothly. Throughout the war years, she retained a warm sympathy for those who struggled for democratic rights, a high regard for the people of the Soviet Union, and a growing commitment to issues of world peace. If she became instrumental in Popular Front activities, she was never a party liner, never an ideologue.

While the United States and the Soviet Union were friends, Hellman could do what she could not bring herself to do when the party was under attack. She could comfortably withdraw from the party, though not from her deep antifascist and antiracist commitments, without feeling that she had somehow betrayed her friends. Perverse as this behavior may seem, it speaks to the code of loyalty that Hellman maintained consistently thereafter, and especially in the years of the Cold War. She could not hit a person, nor attack a friend, when he was down. True to form, as the war drew to a close and suspicions against the Soviet Union's postwar intentions mounted, she joined the National Council of American-Soviet Friendship and later served on its women's committee. But she did not care for the party, did not like being under its discipline, did not follow a line. She refused always to betray friends who remained within the Communist Party orbit, and she never wavered in her admiration for the Soviet people. Most of all she resisted the efforts of government "bullies" to deny her right to think about communism in any way that suited her. In what is perhaps the most backhanded of compliments, one of the FBI reports on her commented that its sources indicated that "Lillian Hellman is one of the few Communists or Communist sympathizers who will discuss Communism openly and honestly."[66]

At the same time she became deeply committed to exorcising racism within the United States in this time of war. When Paul Robeson, who was probably a member of the Communist Party at this point, persuaded a Council on African Affairs meeting on April 8, 1942, to adopt a resolution advocating the end of discrimination in the armed forces and government services, Hellman joined him on the podium. This turned out to be only one of many fund-raising affairs in which Robeson and Hellman were associated. And it turned out to be one of several issues championed by Eleanor Roosevelt as well as by the Communist Party.[67] At the end of that month, she and Hammett traveled to Hollywood, where Hellman wrote a short script for an armed-forces documentary called *The Negro Soldier*. Hellman aimed for a film that debated what were then called Negro rights. The forty-minute short that ultimately emerged in 1944 was not the ringing plea for white and black unity against discrimination that Hellman imagined. Rather, director Stuart Heister produced an upbeat documentary showing the contributions of African-Americans to the armed services over time. It had no relationship to the film Hellman wanted, and neither her name or Robeson's was later associated with it. September 25, 1943, found Hellman at Hunter College, leading a group discussion of

Jim Crow in the armed forces sponsored by the Citizens Emergency Conference for Inter-Racial Unity. Robeson, her ally and friend in these endeavors, in turn joined Hellman on the platform when she raised money for Spanish Loyalists.[68]

In July 1944, Hellman received a cablegram from the Russian Embassy in Washington with an invitation to visit the Soviet Union. Two of her plays, *The Little Foxes* and *Watch on the Rhine*, were to be performed there, and Hellman was invited to observe the rehearsals, expenses paid by the Soviets. She accepted the invitation with alacrity. There followed months of delay during which the FBI recommended refusing her a passport because, as one of their records puts it, "she is considered to be a Key Figure in Communist activities by the New York Field Division."[69] The FBI report on Hellman, sent to assistant secretary of state Adolf Berle, tarred Hellman with the brush of guilt by association, naming her as "a member of many organizations allegedly Communist dominated and that have followed the Communist Party line." The report also noted that she had been "closely associated with a number of individuals who have been identified as members of the Communist Political Association." The bureau report took particular umbrage at Hellman's efforts to protest the activities of the FBI, noting that an unnamed informant had reported in 1940 that "Lillian Hellman had been assigned by the Communist Party to 'smear the FBI' in the newspaper, *PM*."[70] If so, Hellman fell down on the job.

After Harry Hopkins intervened on Hellman's behalf, it took a while to arrange transportation, but at last in early October she set off. All the while, the FBI tracked her.[71] Arriving first in Los Angeles, she stayed for several days with her ex-husband, Arthur Kober, and his wife, Maggie. The FBI carefully noted that she was staying with her mother-in law, though agents must have known she was unmarried. It also noted that she spent most of her time conferring with Hal Wallis. She was then working with him on a film production of *The Searching Wind*. She took a train to Seattle, stopping overnight in San Francisco. In Seattle, the FBI held her luggage overnight while she flew on to Anchorage, Alaska. Agents duly reported that their search of her baggage "indicates Hellman has contract with Collier Magazine for short stories. No derogatory information developed."[72] Hellman stayed in Anchorage for two days while the Soviets cleared her visa, and finally, on October 19, embarked on an arduous two-week journey via Murmansk to Moscow, where she arrived in early November.

1944, In L.A. on the way to Moscow, she spent most of her time conferring with Hal Wallis. (Photofest)

For all the fuss that the passport office made about her trip, and for all that the FBI followed her travels with keen interest, Hellman herself seems to have treated the trip as an opportunity to get to know the Russian people, and even then her contacts were limited. If her diaries are to be trusted, Hellman judged the Soviet Union in terms of how well it observed her comfort and how tenderly she was cared for. At every stop we learn whether the room is clean or dirty, warm or cold, large or small; we find out about the inadequacy of toilets and read a litany of comments about the freezing outhouses; we know whether and if she had a "fine" dinner. Central in these diaries are comments about the people she met along the way. She writes about those who greeted her, escorted her, and entertained her; she offers generous judgments about the character of the men—most of them in uniform—she encountered. Day after day she comments that "Russian men are nice to women, very kind and tender," or writes, "They have all been so kind and so nice and so warm," and concludes, "These people have a real kind of Christianity."[73] These judgments mingle with her sense of herself, for, as always, she cares about what people think of her. "I do alright with these people," she comments after a few days of traveling. And then again, "I am a little pleased with myself because they like me and yesterday said so."[74]

Because she was ill and tired when she finally arrived in Moscow, Ambassador Averell Harriman invited her to stay in the American compound for the duration of her visit. There, comfortably housed and well fed, she wandered about Moscow with her interpreter, Raisa Orlova. Her diary records where she went and her impressions, almost all favorable, of those she met. Over and over again she repeats phrases such as "these are warm, strong men . . . They are men who know they are men and like all such act with simplicity and tenderness . . . I think maybe Russians have the best natural manners in the world . . . All Russians have a sense of humor."[75] She writes that "the Russian soldiers treated Poles courteously" and comments that she witnessed "the deep reverence and respect that even intellectuals have for Stalin."[76] Such remarks evoke the reader's skepticism about Hellman's judgment. And yet Orlova remembers a Lillian Hellman who had little admiration for the Soviet system as

1944: Moscow. "I do alright with these people." (Ransom Center)

a whole. When she tried to convince Hellman of the virtues of living under socialism, she writes, Hellman replied acerbically that she would "start listening to the victories of socialism after you've built the kind of toilets that don't make you want to retch at all the airports from Vladivostok to Moscow."[77]

A rare invitation to visit the front lines as the Russians moved west affirmed Hellman's positive impressions of Russian men and perhaps convinced her to characterize them favorably while ignoring issues of power and leadership. Forbidden to ask questions, Hellman absorbed the experience of war with her soul, noticing the devastating destruction, first in Leningrad and then in the villages and towns she encountered as she moved toward Warsaw. After she returned home, she wrote about the bravery and nobility of Russian soldiers in the line of fire, continuing the positive assessments her diary records. Her first article for *Collier's* magazine hardly mentions Stalin's name. Instead it romanticizes the soldiers she met on the way. They are, she writes, open and informed about "political issues at home and abroad."[78] They speak "without self consciousness and without fake toughness; they speak simply, like healthy people who have never, fortunately, learned to be ashamed of emotion." They engage with her in rituals of mutual admiration. Hellman does not forget to tell us that on leaving the front, she received a tribute from the veterans of Leningrad—an inscribed cigarette case given to her by the "men, officers and generals of the First White Russian Army on the Warsaw front."[79]

The story of Hellman's wartime visit to the Soviet Union ends with a flummoxed FBI. On January 2, 1945, while she was still at the front, the ever-watchful FBI noted that she was likely to return to the United States soon and asked its agents to make arrangements to have her baggage searched. Hellman didn't leave Russia until early February, and then she flew to London via an arduous route that took her through Iran, Egypt, and France. She stayed in London for several weeks and then flew to Baltimore on February 27, 1945. She seems not to have been aware of the Keystone Cops ritual that accompanied her return to the States. On February 9, the director of the St. Paul office sent a memo to "Director, FBI" indicating they did not know where she was.

> Inasmuch as an Agent of this office recently read in a Washington D.C. newspaper that Lillian Hellman had returned to this

country, the Bureau is being requested to check its files in order to ascertain whether Lillian Hellman has in fact recently re-entered the United States. The Bureau may wish to advise the St. Paul Office and other offices . . . of the whereabouts of Lillian Hellman.

On March 27, after Hellman had been back in the States for a month, J. Edgar Hoover's office sent out another memo inquiring whether anyone knew if Hellman had returned to the United States and asking whether her baggage had been examined. Not until mid-May did agent Fred Hallford inform his boss that "the subject had arrived at Baltimore 11 weeks earlier." "She was not interviewed at great length," he wrote. "She stated that during this trip she was a guest of the Soviet and British Governments. She described her tour as a cultural tour." Hallford noted that "no baggage or body search of the subject was conducted upon her entry at the Port of Baltimore." And then he added: "For your confidential information, Miss Hellman displayed at the time of the interview some indignation that a person of her prominence should be subjected to any questioning upon entrance into the United States."[80]

Perhaps Hellman was right to be indignant. On March 21, 1947, the New York Field Division of the FBI told Hoover's office that they were about to delete Hellman's name from their "key figure" list. Her name was in fact removed two years later. "No further investigation of this subject is contemplated at this time," the New York Bureau director wrote, "and the case is being placed in a closed status."[81] Little did he then suspect that Hellman's code of loyalty and her moral compass would soon face its severest test.

CHAPTER 5

An American Jew

I've asked myself many times what I would have liked to have been born and decided a long time ago that I was very glad I was born a Jew. Whether brought up as one or not, somewhere in the background there was a gift of being born a Jew.
—*Lillian Hellman, 1981*

As Hellman resisted being thought of as a *woman* playwright, so she resisted the idea that her Jewish birth and family origins shaped her view of the world. Jewish-born and southern-identified, she occupied complicated positions in both communities, but especially in the bifurcated world of twentieth-century Jews. She was not a Jew in the Yiddish-speaking, upwardly mobile, immigrant sense of the word. Nor was she a member of a close-knit southern community of Jews whose isolation lent itself to creating a public face of assimilation and cooperation. Rather, she imagined herself committed to a set of overarching values that included racial egalitarianism and political and social justice. These provided the framework within which she measured human dignity and judged what she called "decent" behavior.

But the twentieth century—notable for pogroms, migrations, the destruction of most Eastern European Jewry, and the creation of the state of Israel—placed enormous stress on the meaning of Jewish identity, twisting and shaping it in response to historical and personal circumstances.[1] For prominent cultural figures like Hellman, the times demanded more than a passive acquiescence to one's roots. As the political climate changed, she sometimes found herself at odds with a divided Jewish community, struggling to reconcile her commitment to larger values with her sense of herself as a Jew, often unable to see why they should be in disagreement. She was, in this sense, an American Jew, her identity woven into the fabric of political debate.

Hellman took her first journey abroad in 1929, when she went with her husband to Paris. Bored, she traveled alone to Germany that summer. There she watched brown-shirted Nazis march and experienced her first taste of outright anti-Semitism. For the first time she felt herself part of a larger, specifically Jewish, identity. After she returned home, she followed Kober to Hollywood, where he found her a job as a studio script reader. There, as she had in New York, Hellman found herself among Jews of Eastern European descent, many of whom had already risen to prominence in the movie industry. These were not the Jews of her southern heritage, eager to assimilate into southern soil. Rather, they were the transplanted Jews of her New York acquaintance, proudly spreading the cultures and traditions of their parents to the American west while they discarded the spiritual impetus of the old religion. Lillian found their relationship to religion all too familiar. To the Hollywood moguls, as to the writer friends she was coming to know in her bicoastal life, Jewishness did not then, as author and critic Irving Howe would later recall, "form part of a conscious commitment; it was not regarded as a major component of the culture . . . It was simply *there*."[2] Howe, in the thirties a young radical and later to become a chronicler of the Jewish tradition, did not imagine Jewishness as a religious impulse. It was "inherited, a given to be acknowledged, like being born white or male or poor," something that "could be regarded with affection since after all it had helped shape one's early years."

In these years of the 1930s, when Jewish identity seemed more a matter of culture and style than of religious practice, Hellman adopted the manners and politics of her peers. She adapted her voice and her persona to the fractious and argumentative mode of her East Coast friends, and she grew into the opinionated and self-dramatizing self that persisted for the rest of her life. Though she was a southern Jew, a German Jew, she reveled in the vibrancy of the Eastern European literary and entertainment worlds of which she formed a part, and she enjoyed the freedom provided by the rich cosmopolitan lifestyles in which her friends participated. In that world, the success of Jews in the competition for upward mobility could be readily tied to attaining the American dream, and Jewish commitment to social justice could take many political forms, including the adulation of Roosevelt and adherence to communist ideals. In Hellman's world of the 1930s and early '40s, Jews tended to gravitate toward the political left, expecting to bury religious differences in campaigns for justice and fairness for all. Though the friends with whom she argued about left-wing politics and whom she enlisted in social causes tended to be Jews, she donned, like them, a cloak of religious invisibility. For all of them, the freedom to argue, the liberty to choose one's political and social causes, seemed part and parcel of American life, as much a fulfillment of the dream as economic success.

The thirties was an odd decade in that respect, for if Jews were excluded from elite colleges and some professions, they found places in other arenas like teaching, medicine, and the new profession of social work. In Hellman's world of theater and film, being Jewish constituted no barrier at all. Hellman was not hurt by the continuing febrile anti-Semitism that persisted in many sectors of American society. She did not find herself excluded by the admissions quotas deployed by elite colleges and professional schools, or face the closed gates of the higher professions.

But if she found no doors locked to her creative ambitions, Hellman could hardly have avoided noticing what we can only call the latent or casual anti-Semitism that surrounded her. This often took the form of simply attending to what was and was not Jewish, a practice common among her friends and acquaintances. Edmund Wilson, for example, who befriended Dash Hammett and with whom Hellman later had a close relationship, carefully noted the Jewish ancestry of his acquaintances in his diaries of the thirties.[3] Mary McCarthy, who would marry Wilson at the end of the decade and later go on to play a major role in Hellman's life, recalls her "stunning surprise" as a young woman when she discovered that an early boyfriend was Jewish. It was, she says, "a disillusionment, like learning the real names of one's favorite movie stars."[4] She went on to conceal the existence of her Jewish grandmother from her Vassar college friends and to participate in marginalizing the only student in her circle who acknowledged her Jewish parentage.[5]

Dashiell Hammett, who became Hellman's lover and partner after 1931, participated in this culture of noticing, pointing out Hellman's Jewish affiliation and simultaneously distancing himself from it by denominating Jews as "your people." During the war years, from his remote posting in the Alaskan Aleutian Islands, he plied her with loving, upbeat, and humorous accounts of his life on an army base. Amid his appreciation for her talents, her generous gifts of tobacco and warm clothing, and her love, Hammett casually reminded Hellman of her origins. Sometimes this came in the form of a joke, as when he repeated a comment to her from "one of your people." A soldier by the name of Glick, he wrote, had remarked to him, "Thank God my people had sense enough to give me a good American first name, Irwin."[6] On another occasion, he wrote her that "one of your people just gave me the heel of a very fine hunk of salami."[7] Another time he told her that he'd just read a very good play written by "one of your people."[8] Once he asked her if in her "twisted oriental way, you look on Christmas as an extra day of atonement for your people."[9] None of this seemed to be tainted with malice, for as he told her once, "your people are sometimes remarkable."[10]

To her friends, and in letters to Arthur Kober, Hellman expressed a mixture of love and hate toward Jews, an acerbic irreverence that indicated both her identification with the talented core of literary and cosmopolitan people and an effort to distance herself from those Jews who did not share her values. She went to a bad concert, she wrote to Kober, where she was "sick and frightened at the homosexuals, rich Jews and refugees who were there."[11] Later she described the repulsive behavior of another Jewish writer (Irving Stone) by telling Kober, "If you were not a Jew, I would be anti-Semitic."[12] And yet she took comfort in claiming the bonds of family when it suited her. After one of her plays closed prematurely on Broadway, she sought solace with close friend Heywood Hale Broun, comforting herself by telling him: "We're just two old Jewish failures."[13] Notorious for her capacity to swear, she demonstrated her self-consciousness about what it meant to be Jewish by throwing around offensive words like *goy* and *kike*. She used these in the ways that African-Americans today sometimes use the n-word—as an affectionate and comradely attribution, a signal that she too was a member of the group. "I myself make very anti-Semitic remarks," she would later claim when challenged, "but I get very upset if anybody else does."[14]

Hellman's associations with the left seemed merely natural in the thirties. Like her, many of Hellman's creative and often Jewish friends entered the arena of politics through the twin gates of a search for social justice and a virulent opposition to fascism. At the same time, a new generation of men and women just a decade or so younger than Lillian dismissed their Jewish identities to find their places in the larger political world. Men such as Daniel Bell, Irving Howe, Irving Kristol, Sidney Hook, William Phillips, Philip Rahv, and Alfred Kazin who would go on to found magazines, write novels, and become influential critics began their careers in the halls of City College in the thirties, where their political differences guided affiliation into the many left-wing factions of the decade. Mary McCarthy boasted a particularly sensitive streak for the relationship between Jewish origins and political impulses. Herself a "Trotskyist," she recalled the guests at the little dinners she attended at the end of the decade as "mostly Stalinists, which is what smart successful people in that New York world were. And they were mostly Jewish; as was often pointed out to me with gentle amusement, I was the only non-Jewish person in the room." It was at such a dinner that McCarthy recalls first meeting Lillian Hellman.[15]

It mattered little that some up-and-coming young men (Phillips, Bell, Howe, and Rahv among them) would change their names to meld more smoothly into the larger culture. Liberal or left-wing, they abandoned Jewish ritual and tradition for the religion of politics. Later some of these men would coalesce into "the New York intellectuals" and become powerful cultural voices in the postwar years. They would reorganize themselves along political lines, and Jewish identity would become one of many factors in their appraisals of left-wing politics. But in the 1930s and for most of the 1940s, their secondary attachment to Jewish descent resembled Hellman's; she found herself firmly in the mainstream of the American Jewish intellectual and cultural tradition.

This remained the case even during the decade and a half when German Nazis and others invested their political capital in racializing those born or descended from Jews. Despite these campaigns, and even in the face of widespread rumors of extermination strategies, a 1944 survey of young Jewish literary figures found that few of them placed their Jewish identities at the forefront of their self-definitions. Lionel Trilling, soon to become the first Jewish professor of English at Columbia University, declared that he did not regard himself as a specifically Jewish writer.[16] He described himself, rather, as a minimalist Jew. "For me," wrote Trilling, "The point of honor consists in feeling that I would not, even if I could, deny or escape being Jewish."[17] Muriel Rukeyser preferred "more than anything else to be invisible."[18] Delmore Schwartz took a position closer to Hellman's, insisting that "the fact of Jewishness was a matter of naïve and innocent pride, untouched by any sense of fear."[19] In the aftermath of the Holocaust, in the wake of the creation of the state of Israel, and in the light of Cold War aspersions on "Commie Jews," all this changed. Then many Jews who had been part of the left in the thirties became associated with being pro-Israel. Those who criticized Israel in any respect risked identification as Soviet sympathizers. It was then that Hellman faced disparagement about her refusal to meld her politics with her Jewish identity.

Was Hellman then simply one of those Jews who preferred, in Muriel Rukeyser's memorable phrase, "more than anything else . . . to be invisible"?[20] Certainly her most famous work, *The Little Foxes*, supports this notion. Critics correctly identified the play (which opened in February 1939, at the height of anti-Semitic attacks in Germany) as a thinly disguised portrait of her mother's family. Hellman avoided describing the rapacious Hubbard family as specifically Jewish, preferring instead to speak to a more general concern about the corrupting effects of money. Yet the family's effort to profit from the industrializing new South could easily be interpreted as a depiction of the stereotypical money-grasping Jew. The Hubbards, two brothers and a sister, have since become symbols of how perverted ambition for money and power can ride roughshod over human feeling, discarding community and tradition along the way. At the time, Hellman insisted that the play was meant as satire, a lesson to illuminate the impact of greed on the lives of innocent people and their children. And surely its success is attributable to the way that message struck an America still struggling to get out of the Depression. Only later would she acknowledge its relationship to her own childhood—and even then it was class, not Jewish identity, to which she pointed. She had reacted to her grandmother's wealth and the abuse of her class position with anger and self-hatred, she wrote in one of her memoirs. She resolved this conflict only "after *The Little Foxes* was written and put away."[21]

But Hellman invoked her Jewish identity under other circumstances without a moment's hesitation. After she returned from Spain in the spring of 1938, she called the *New York Times* (which she described as owned by Jews) to task for not featuring antifascist articles about Spain on its front page. "It stands to reason," she wrote, that "every Jew must be an anti-Fascist to be either a good Jew or a good American."[22] As fascist regimes increasingly fastened on the salience of Jewish heritage as a cause of conflict, she wielded her identity like a weapon. "I am a writer, and I am also a Jew," she told an audience of twelve hundred at a 1940 book luncheon. "I want to be quite sure that I can continue to be a writer and that if I want to say that greed is bad or persecution is worse, I can do so . . . I also want to go on saying that I am a Jew without being afraid that I will be called names or end in a prison camp or be forbidden to walk down the street at night."[23]

As the fight against fascism escalated and the Second World War loomed closer, Hellman increasingly perceived anti-Semitism and racism as of a piece. Her position in those years paralleled that of the Communist Party, which, during the Popular Front period from the mid-thirties to the Nazi-Soviet pact of August 1939, promoted the values of brotherhood and recognized suffering as a universal condition engendered by capitalism. But the party also advocated acculturating "nationalities," including Jews, in order to create solidarity across group lines. It supported activities like mandolin orchestras, folk singing, and summer camps that encouraged young people to take pride in their Jewish identities not for their own sake but as vehicles for social change.

In the spring of 1939, Hammett became the editor of a new Communist Party–sponsored monthly journal called *Equality*, whose masthead proclaimed its mission "to defend democratic rights and combat anti-Semitism and racism." The bold purpose of the journal, on whose editorial board Lillian Hellman was listed along with Bennett Cerf, Moss Hart, Louis Kronenberger, Donald Ogden Stewart (of the SWG), and Dorothy Parker, was to "combat every expression of defeatism among the Jews, to expose all fascist conspiracies in the United States and to defend the rights of labor and all minorities in this country."[24] Inspired and funded by the Communist Party, the journal was nevertheless praised by leaders of the Jewish community, who normally kept their distance from communism in any form. With the U.S. entry into war, Hellman's efforts on behalf of racial justice escalated. Like other progressives, she sought "to use the outsider experience and the experience of discrimination to make common cause with other outsiders."[25] Hellman became particularly active in the struggle to end racial discrimination in the armed services, appearing on platforms with Paul Robeson to promote that cause and chairing luncheons to raise money for it. The FBI kept close track of her efforts on this score, deeming them subversive.[26]

Hellman's generalized condemnation of racism and anti-Semitism in all their forms got her into trouble when she wrote her only overtly antifascist play, *Watch on the Rhine*. Produced in 1941, the play focuses on the tensions generated in an American family when a German anti-Nazi fighter bringing his American-born wife and children to safety in the United States confronts a family guest who threatens to reveal his presence to German intelligence. The play forcefully advocated abandoning passivity to enter the war in order to defend the freedoms Americans valued. The argument ran counter to the policies of both the Soviet Union (which was still allied with Germany in a peace pact) and the United States (which was still formally neutral). Hellman chose not to comment on the specifically anti-Semitic activities of Germany at the time; she pleaded instead for people to join in resistance to anti-democratic regimes, for courage and bravery in the face of abusive power. Consistent with her resistance to racism wherever it appeared, she depicted the Nazis as bullies, their attack directed against freedom everywhere.

In the context of the moment, *Watch on the Rhine* resonated differently with different groups. The play appeared at a time when, fearing outbursts of anti-Semitism, influential American Jews made little public noise about Hitler's atrocities. Some Jewish critics distanced themselves from its message, wondering if it was a critique of their stance, while others attacked Hellman for neglecting to name Jews as pivotal targets in the fascist dream of an ethnically cleansed world. To Hellman, the larger morality involved in the brutal assertions of fascist power over many forms of human life seemed more important than identifying specific victims. It was wrong, she argued, to humiliate and beat up people in the streets, to take away their livelihoods and deport them—wrong no matter whether they were communists, gypsies, homosexuals, or Jews. In this sense, Hellman understood her identity as a Jew as deeply entwined with her commitment to human freedom and democracy. The White House recognized this sensibility when it scheduled the play for a command performance that the president and Mrs. Roosevelt both attended. The performance took place less than two months after the United States entered the war.

Hellman's decision to speak to the universal theme of human brutality rather than to name Jews as particular victims in *Watch on the Rhine* tells us something about the politics of the moment. To her, Jews certainly constituted victims of fascism, but they were not the only victims. She devoted many hours during the war to specifically Jewish causes, to be sure, but just as many to the victimization of others. Among her com-

1943: Hellman was thinking about what it meant to be a Jew. (Photofest)

mitments, she raised money for the Jewish Anti-Fascist Committee, a creature of the Soviet Communist Party intended to generate money and support for the Soviet Union when it went to war against Germany. In 1943, the JAFC sponsored the visits of Itzik Feffer (a beloved Yiddish poet well known in the American Jewish community) and Solomon Mikhoels (actor and director of Moscow's distinguished Yiddish-language theater). Hellman, along with notables like Albert Einstein, Marc Chagall, and Charlie Chaplin, served as part of a welcoming committee.

But other incidents suggest that Hellman was thinking about what it meant to be a Jew. As she moved between worlds, some of them rich, narrow-minded, and reactionary, others cosmopolitan, intellectual, and feisty, she developed a more specific concern for anti-Semitism. Hellman's script for *The North Star*—a prizewinning film about the brutal invasion of a peaceful Ukrainian village by German troops—includes an otherwise inexplicable exchange between two German military physicians that reveals the anti-Semite as the more brutal of the two. As the superior, Von Harden, is about to draw blood from helpless children, he is confronted by a subordinate who challenges his medical ethics. The superior defends himself, boasting that he was the most famous pupil of Dr. Freedenthal at the University of Leipzig.

DR. RICHTER: Freedenthal, the Jew?
VON HARDEN: Yes, Freedenthal the Jew.
DR. RICHTER: You did not mind his being a Jew?
VON HARDEN: Mind? I never thought about it in those days.[27]

This episode, along with Hellman's wartime diary documenting her trip to Russia toward the end of the war, suggests just how much the question of what it meant to be a Jew permeated her consciousness. Her diary notes the Jewish identities of those she encountered along the way and comments critically on their dress, behavior, and generosity. One of her dinner companions, she noticed just a week after her arrival on November 7, 1944, was an American she described as "vicious with anti-Semitism."[28] A short time later, she attributed the absence of engaged political conversation to the scarcity of Jews among her companions. She had spent the evening conversing with Russians who spoke about leading Western artists such as Sargeant, Titian, and DaVinci in the most abstract terms. The experience led her to ask not about the stifling of political curiosity but "is the Jewish Intellectual anywhere?"[29] On her way to the front on December 26, 1944, she reacted negatively to a New York Times reporter who accompanied her for part of the trip: "Mr. Lawrence scared me as all who aren't afraid and aren't Jews I guess, always do. Then I'm like the Jewish shopkeeper during a pogrom rumor."[30] When, toward the end of her trip, she met a sympathetic young man whose sister, an army doctor, was killed in Sevastopol, she added a parenthetical comment to her notes about the meeting: "Joseph was a Jew, I think."[31]

Once home, Hellman maintained her interest in Jewish causes supporting refugees, accepting honors from groups like the American Jewish Congress, Women's American ORT, the Jewish War Veterans, and the Hebrew Immigrant Aid Society. As late as 1950, she accepted a Woman of Achievement award from the Federation of Jewish Women's Organizations.[32] And yet Russian anti-Semitism remained invisible to Hellman long after she should have begun to notice it. She did not distance herself from the Soviet Union when, after supporting the creation of the state of Israel, the Soviets changed their line and refused to recognize the distinctive claims of Jews as special victims of genocide. Nor did she see

Stalin's increasing paranoia against Jews in his regime. To her everlasting shame, she did not comment when Jewish writers and artists, many of whom she met and admired, were singled out for persecution. She uttered no public word when the poet Itzik Feffer and the director of the Yiddish theater, Solomon Mikhoels—whom she had warmly welcomed to the United States in 1943—died in Soviet prisons.[33]

Hellman's blindness to Soviet anti-Semitism in the late forties and early fifties and her continued faith in the possibilities of a Soviet state in spite of its persecution of Jews contributed to the sense that she was a non-Jewish Jew, even an anti-Semitic Jew. If before the war to be a Jew had meant to be against fascism, and a claim to invisibility gone unremarked upon, the wartime extermination of millions of Jews, among others, brought issues of identity to the fore. Jews, especially intellectual Jews, in the words of Alfred Kazin, now lived "at the edge of the abyss," vulnerable because they had put their faith in the life of the mind, which had failed them.[34]

At the time, the latent anti-Semitism of the prewar period seemed to lift. New educational opportunities and home mortgages provided by the GI bill resulted in a dramatic expansion of the middle class, of which Jews took full advantage. They moved into the new suburbs, entered universities and the professions, and acquired respected political positions at a rapid pace. This did not mean an end to gentlemen's agreements that denied Jews admission to the best clubs or law firms. But it did mean an increasing willingness on their part to fight for access. Many Jews who had willingly shed religion and tradition before 1939 began to protest their exclusion, to question the meaning of being Jewish, and to identify once again with their Jewish roots. Magazines like *Partisan Review* and the new *Commentary* spoke for this group. Men like Philip Rahv and William Phillips turned from more left-wing positions to a Jewish-identified stance. Arthur Miller commented later that he had been surprised by the numbers of his generation who, after the war, "began to contribute to something called temple."[35]

The fight over the creation of the state of Israel in 1948 aided and abetted a new consciousness by producing a healthy debate over a Jewish homeland as Jews of all kinds began to wonder whether their identity did not ultimately reside in identification with the new and vulnerable state. Hellman, along with many on the left, supported the creation of the Jewish state, though she quickly lost interest in it. But now the Jewish left fragmented once more. A surge of Zionist enthusiasm led some to fight in Israel's war for independence: to them the new state represented both a home for persecuted Jews and a haven for restorative justice. To partisans of the left, Israel constituted hope for a social-democratic option. As Zionism attached itself to liberal and anticommunist Jewish opinion, those like Hellman who remained unconvinced of its centrality in creating a better world became suspect.[36]

By the early fifties, Israel had become something of a litmus test among Jews. Jewish nationalism required primary allegiance to the imperiled refuge of a beleaguered European Jewry. Hellman, never a Zionist, withheld enthusiastic support. Her stance diverged from that of the Eastern European intellectuals with whom she had allied herself on many issues before and during the war. Liberal, anticommunist, and pro-Israel: their Eastern European Jewish culture and origins worn proudly on their sleeves, New York intellectuals, in the postwar years, came to depart from their former stance as minimalist Jews to understand themselves as distinctively Jewish-Americans. New and sparklingly successful writers like Saul Bellow and Philip Roth soon came to root their work in refugee and immigrant cultures, drawing their heroes and their stories from the Bronx and Brooklyn and Newark, New Jersey, and from the children these cities produced. Their position with respect to Israel became a decisive factor for identification of a brutally destroyed minority. Hellman never passed the test. As Norman Podhoretz noted later, he broke relations with Hellman because he was violently offended by her "extreme hostility (or perhaps hatred would be a better word)" to Israel.[37]

The Cold War mentality, too, helped to highlight the particular role of Jews in politics—almost universally identifying their stance as communists, fellow travelers, or, in the jargon of the period, "pink." To be sure, in the thirties and forties Jews constituted a disproportionately large and visible segment of the country's small number of organized communists. Some thought the committee hearings and investigations of the McCarthy period sought not only to unmask secret communists but to test the patriotism of Jewish radicals as well.[38] The procedures of the McCarthy period did little to ameliorate suspicion. The House Un-American Activities Committee that subpoenaed its first victims in 1948 went after Hollywood, according to most accounts, because the movie industry was heavily staffed by Jews who were identified with left-wing causes.[39] Six of the famous Hollywood Ten who were blacklisted and sent to jail were Jews. One committee member, John Rankin, was an avowed anti-Semite who had once referred to Walter Winchell as "a little slime-mongering kike."[40] It didn't help that there were Jews on both sides. Martin Gang, the Hollywood lawyer who became the clearance agent for Hollywood celebrities, was also a Jew. Nor did it help that Jews were implicated in some of the famous spy cases of the period. Julius and Ethel Rosenberg constitute only the best-known examples.

Around the same time, word of the trials and subsequent executions of Jewish poets and artists in the Soviet Union reached the West, shattering what remained of the image of the Soviet Union as a tolerant nation. Jewish intellectuals who had once thought of themselves primarily as socialists of one kind or another turned a painful gaze onto the nature of authoritarian personalities and totalitarianism of the left as well as the right. We began to recognize, says Irving Howe, that "there was now a greater enemy by far—the totalitarian state, sometimes of the Right, sometimes of the Left."[41] But, as Howe notes, in 1952 a "totalitarianism of the left" seemed "the harder to cope with and, thereby, in a sense, more terrifying." Howe handled the dilemma by becoming a democratic socialist. But many others shed any hope for socialism and turned sharply toward what would become known as free-market democracy.

Hellman, not yet ready to make the break and not convinced that her Jewish identity should impinge on her politics, faced a set of difficult choices. During all this turmoil, Jewish community leaders feared an outburst of anti-Semitism. Leaders of national Jewish organizations such as the American Jewish Committee, the National Council of Jewish Women, the Anti-Defamation League, and many others responded to McCarthyism not by demanding that the hearings stop but by cleansing their own houses of communists and joining in the attack on communists in general. Leading Jewish intellectuals split, many of them not only recanting their former beliefs but branding those who could not or would not do so as Stalinists. A horrified Hellman, herself banned from the film industry, immediately labeled those who would not speak up "cowardly bastards." Just a few years later she would tell her friend Bill Alfred that she no longer cared "about those so-called friends who never lifted a finger to protest the ban."[42] But now she was an outlier. The lions among the intellectual Jews (people like Elliot Cohen, Midge Decter, and Barbara and Jason Epstein) founded or became active in magazines such as *Encounter* and *Commentary*. Some of these organs became vehicles of a new politics, unashamedly Jewish, pro-Israel, anticommunist, and moralistic.

In this context, whether or not one was a Jew mattered, and to be a Jew who did not denounce Stalin, whose murderous purges many now equated with Hitler's slaughter, immediately drew suspicions of being a self-hating Jew.[43] Hellman, who took a brave position for civil liberties and freedom of speech in 1952, took no public position in the debate over totalitarianism. She simply dropped out of it. Her silence as well as her hostility to Zionism fueled suspicions about a possible hostility to Judaism. In the context of the postwar turn toward Jewish identity, Hellman's brand of "international" antiracism seemed particularly suspicious. While the intellectuals around Partisan Review, Commentary, and other influential journals adapted to the postwar environment, Hellman appeared increasingly rigid. By the mid-1950s, whispers of Hellman's continuing Stalinism mingled with allegations about whether she too might be a self-hating Jew.

This was the background behind attacks on Hellman around the publication and stage adaptation of the diary of Anne Frank, a subject worth exploring because it enacts the alliance of heightened Jewish nationalism and anticommunism. Together they created a political vortex in which Hellman found herself spinning, turning what might have been a trivial conflict into one with a much larger significance. The enormously popular diary, written by the fourteen-year-old daughter of a Dutch Jewish family who had hidden in an Amsterdam loft, appeared in Dutch, German, and French before it was finally published in English in 1952. Journalist and author Meyer Levin read the diary in French and contacted Otto Frank (Anne's father and the only surviving member of the family) to see if he might play a role in its English-language publication. In the event the book was published by Doubleday, without Levin's intervention.[44]

Encouraged by Otto Frank and hoping to reach a larger audience, Levin then prepared a theatrical treatment of The Diary of a Young Girl. His purpose, he would later write, was to bring to the public "the voice from the mass grave."[45]

In Levin's mind, Anne Frank's diary spoke to the specifically Jewish suffering engendered by the Nazi policy of extermination. He and many others read the diary as a tribute to the six million Jews who had died and as a memorial to their brutal executions. In contrast, the diary was read by many, including Anne's father, as a more generic tribute to human suffering. The Soviet Union, still wounded by the loss of twenty million civilians and soldiers, took a similar line around the Jewish question. It acknowledged Jews as a symbol of universal suffering but did not focus on them alone. These differences led Levin to target Lillian Hellman as the architect of the rejections that would follow.

Levin's dramatic treatment got short shrift. Herman Shumlin, Hellman's now-estranged longtime producer, refused the play because he thought audiences wouldn't come to a play about "people they know to have ended up in the crematorium."[46] Cheryl Crawford, an equally distinguished producer, considered the play at length. She turned it down after she asked for the opinion of good friends, including Hellman. Asking Hellman's advice should have surprised no one. She was then a dominant figure in the literary world, her critical judgment highly valued. Writers as talented as Saul Bellow turned to her for criticism and advice, which she generously gave. Bellow commented at one point that he was reduced to misery by Hellman's judgment that what he had written was "admirable, but not a play."[47]

Hellman read the play and didn't like it, commenting only that it had little dramatic content. Crawford turned it down but suggested that Kermit Bloomgarden, producer of Hellman's most recent play, *The Autumn Garden*, might be willing to produce it; Bloomgarden, too, refused. In the face of all these rejections, Otto Frank backed out of his commitment to Levin. Grateful to Levin for resurrecting the diary in English and reluctant to offend him, he nevertheless turned to other avenues to ensure that a play based on the diary would finally see the light of day. Bloomgarden took a new option on the diary and asked his old friend Lillian Hellman to suggest new writers. Soon the newspapers announced that Albert and Frances Goodrich Hackett had been commissioned to write a new play.

Meyer Levin now began to wonder whether he had been somehow blacklisted. He was convinced that the diary should be produced as it existed, with Anne's consciousness of suffering as a Jew intact. He could not imagine any better interpreter of the diary than himself. Only an anti-Jewish conspiracy, he believed, could account for his dismissal; only a "merciless critical cabal" of communists was powerful enough to explain the play's rejection.[48] Now he began, publicly, to talk about "possible ideological intrusion in the handling of the Jewish content of the Diary."[49] The implication was clear. He blamed anti-Semitic communists for suppressing his version of the diary.

The Hacketts had been Lillian's companions during her early days in Hollywood. Well known in Hollywood circles, they had successfully brought Hammett's *Thin Man* stories to the screen and had since written a range of prizewinning films including *It's a Wonderful Life* (1946), *Easter Parade* (1948), and *Seven Brides for Seven Brothers* (1954), which was then in production. To Levin, however, they had two serious flaws: they were not Jews, and they were closely associated with Hammett and Hellman, in his mind two of Hollywood's leading communists. It did not help that the Soviet Union was, at this moment, persecuting and executing Jewish writers. Levin, putting together his own interpretation of events, accused Hellman of blindly following a communist party line that denigrated Jewish suffering in deference to the human tragedy that the Holocaust represented. Hellman, he insisted, had exercised undue influence over Bloomgarden: she was a communist and an anti-Semite.[50]

In desperation, Levin began what would become a lifelong campaign to produce his version of the diary. He wrote endless letters to Otto Frank begging for a chance to try his play out in Buffalo or other small venues; he took an advertisement in the *New York Times* claiming that he had been ousted by those who disliked his Jewish approach and accusing those who had suffered from McCarthyism of using innuendo to smear him and his reputation. He consulted distinguished lawyer Ephraim London (who reappears in our story later as Lillian's lawyer in her suit against Mary McCarthy), who told him he had no grounds for legal action and no rights to the diary.

The Hacketts' play, which reached Broadway in 1955 to rave reviews and an almost two-year run, presented Anne as a teenager who identified with all of suffering humanity rather than as an Anne whose Jewish God had allowed her people "to suffer so terribly up to now." Levin could not be controlled. Anne's words had been altered to omit any hint of her Jewish identity and consciousness, he argued; the family's commitment to Judaism had disappeared; one could hardly tell why they were in hiding. And the Hacketts were, in his view, guilty of plagiarism. They had quoted some of the same words from the diary that he had selected for his play. Small matter to him that by now Otto Frank wanted the play to provide a message that would embrace its audience, nor that the director Garson Kanin, agreed with the playwrights that removing most of the Jewish ritual, as well as references to Nazis and concentration camps, would yield a play whose audiences didn't have to be Jewish to identify with it. The play's heartfelt critical and popular reception suggests that it spoke effectively to its 1950s audience, affirming the accuracy of Hellman's commercial instinct. In a decade when few were ready to come to terms with the Holocaust—indeed the word did not yet exist in the common vocabulary—the play hit the right note. Whatever the morality of the Hackett's decision to de-emphasize the Jewish theme, it is plausible that any other interpretation would have failed to reach its mark.

Tortured by the successful production, Meyer Levin first sued the Hacketts for plagiarism, and when that proved unsuccessful, he launched attacks on Bloomgarden and Hellman. To explain his rejection, Levin settled on the notion that he had been victimized by nothing less than Stalinism, and that Hellman (whom he characterized as an assimilationist German Jew) was at the center of a conspiracy against him and all Jews of his ilk. From the start, he later wrote, he "had suspected that some doctrinaire formulation rather than pure dramatic judgment had caused Miss Hellman's attack on my play and after the substitute work was written, I became convinced that I had been banned because my work was in her political view 'too Jewish.' "[51] Neither the fact that others (including Otto Frank) shared Hellman's view nor that Hellman had been only marginally involved deterred Levin. And the commercial success of the Hackett play infuriated him. In his eyes, Hellman had simply followed a party line that obfuscated Jewish suffering in a shroud of more generic hatred that was also directed at gypsies, homosexuals, the mentally retarded, and communists.

Little evidence supports the notion that Hellman was central to the diary's transition to the stage and then to the screen.[52] At the height of the McCarthy period, Hellman could hardly have been a major player, even had she wanted to be one. Hellman did suggest the Hacketts as writers, and she read their script toward the end, offering some suggestions for staging. As was her habit, she invested a small sum (in this case $750) in the company that staged the play. The play, and the movie that emerged four years later, were so successful that over the years she managed to make a tidy amount from them. The total (about $25,000 over fourteen years) suggests the validity of her instincts about what made a good dramatic story.[53]

Despite Hellman's tangential association with the play, its producer, and its playwrights, Levin continued to attack Hellman both as a self-hating Jew and as a Stalinist. Over the course of two decades he brought one unsuccessful lawsuit after another and signed agreements to desist from accusations that he routinely violated. He accepted compensation not to seek productions of his play, then claimed exemptions; he agreed to stop talking publicly about the diary and continued to do so. The campaign drew many supporters in the Jewish community. Norman Podhoretz would say later that one reason he stopped speaking to Lillian Hellman was her "de-Judaization" of the stage version of *The Diary of Anne Frank*.

Hellman responded to these attacks wearily. She could not, she wrote to her friend Bill Alfred in 1959, sue Levin, because she lacked the money. And she did not know if she would, even if she had the resources. "Now I just think he's crazy and I take my beating."[54] Arguing that the damage had been done once Levin's accusations were printed, she would not accept invitations to respond to them in writing: "They all know full well the harm that has been done me on this and other grounds, and they can go fuck themselves before I defend myself from the Levins of the world."[55] As late as 1974, she complained to her lawyer that "Mr. Meyer Levin has begun the red baiting all over again."[56]

The Meyer Levin experience suggests something of the complexity of living as a secular Jew in the Cold War moment. As Hellman became caught in Levin's obsession with his particular view of Jewishness, so the idea of what it meant to be a Jew became the subject of larger conversations and debates. Hellman's reluctance to accede to the primacy of identification as a Jew, her recalcitrance in the face of the successful politics of the new Jewish nationalism, made her a perfect target. To her, a literature rooted in the Jewish immigrant tradition appeared to be only a momentary fad. Though she admired Arthur Miller and read Philip Roth, she did not see their work as great literature, nor believe that its use of Jews successfully captured the larger social meanings she thought important. When, in the early sixties, she tried to play in this ballpark by adapting Burt Blechman's novel *My Mother, My Father and Me* into a stage play, she failed miserably. The play, like the book, meant to satirize the purposeless new middle class, whose lives contained no trace of old-world values of caring and community. But the satire is rooted in a Jewish family, and when it turns into a multipronged attack on the aimlessness of children, on business practices, on old-age homes, Hellman exposes her own bitterness about the failure of family life in general and Jewish family life in particular. Lacking empathy for Eastern European immigrant communities and without patience for the self-centered aimlessness of young people, Hellman turned family relationships into a parody of racism and materialism. What she had intended as comedy emerged as vulgar parody.

The play she wrote featured a businessman husband who flirted daily with bankruptcy as he tried to control a spendthrift wife. Their twenty-six-year-old son lacks external or internal constraints. When the wife's elderly immigrant mother briefly joins the family, she exposes their inauthentic feelings about the importance of kin. As she treads on the toes of the African-American helper, she also challenges the shallow liberal ideals of those for whom status and comfort are final goals. Retreating to a nursing home, the grandmother cashes in her funeral policy to support the youth's effort to find himself. Hellman skewers his search in a final scene where, masquerading in Indian costume, he is shown selling doodads to tourists. Filled with black humor and rife with casual racism, the play offered such a barren and hopeless portrait of Jewish family life that it closed after only seventeen performances. Its lead player, Walter Matthau, himself a Jew, told Hellman the play was anti-Semitic.[57]

As American Jewish identity shaped itself around nostalgia for the Eastern European past and pinned its hopes on Israel, so it also encompassed a growing antagonism to the Soviet communism that now added anti-Semitism to its other sins. In the Cold War years, intellectuals rushed to join the ranks of anticommunism, claiming fervent opposition to the Soviet Union while insisting that they had not abandoned the humane values of their younger days. But the vortex of anticommunism allowed little space for maneuvering. Hellman, still committed to the larger values of social justice, egalitarianism, and antiracism, seemed to give comfort to Soviet-style communism, to aid and abet enemies of democracy and the free market. Hellman's decision to remain loyal to values that had seemed self-evident before the war negated the new Americanism of the postwar period. To be pro-American meant signing on to free-market democracy. For Jews, this meant a movement away from the goals of shared responsibility and economic security that characterized the Roosevelt period; it meant a pull toward the new liberalism of individualism, consumption, and philanthropy. The old values, so consistent with the Americanism of the 1930s, became, in the context of the fifties, outdated. Hellman was out of step, her claims to decency, honesty, and loyalty to friends now confronted by the animus of a newly influential group of Jewish intellectuals.

There was a repressed tension in this debate about what it meant to be a Jew. Martin Peretz, then still a graduate student at Harvard and soon to become editor of the *New Republic*, described himself as "Jewish Jewish" in the years when he and his wife befriended and remained close to Hellman. Commenting to her on his relief that blacklisted writers began writing again for the movies less than fifteen years after the blacklists, he noted to her, "It wasn't like the Soviet Yiddish writers who were all shot." He remembers Hellman replying, "Always, always the Jews, Marty."[58]

Years later, Norman Podhoretz confirmed the tension between himself and Hellman on the subject. Recalling their relationship in the sixties—when Podhoretz was the newly appointed editor of *Commentary* magazine—he declared himself to have been disturbed by "Lillian's attitude toward Jews in general and toward Israel in particular. She never denied being Jewish herself . . . But she also had a streak of Jewish anti-Semitism which came out . . . in cracks or sardonic comments about the vulgarity or the tastelessness of some 'kike' or other."[59] He attributed this to her German-Jewish background and to her "radicalism." In the end, he tells us, it was her "blind and blinding hatred of America" that led to the end of the relationship. What Podhoretz described as a blinding hatred of America seemed just the opposite to Hellman. When the students of the 1960s began to organize and become political, Hellman applauded their efforts. What she described as spunky, *Commentary* called "Anti-American." Hellman's strenuous objection to the use of this vocabulary—she said it reminded her of "un-American"—led to a final break. At the core of the tension between her and Podhoretz lay their very different perceptions of what it meant to be a Jew in America. Hellman's identity as a Jew melded into a larger cultural commitment to Americanism that most definitely included the capacity to dissent. Podhoretz placed a Jewish identity in the forefront of his value system.

The difference between Hellman and the group of Jewish intellectuals who lived in an uneasy truce with her came to a head in 1976 when Hellman published her account of her painful experience before the House Committee on Un-American Activities. The book attributed the silence of intellectuals at the time to nineteenth-century immigration. "The children of immigrants are often remarkable people: energetic, intelligent, hardworking; and often they make it so good that they are determined to keep it at any cost," she wrote in *Scoundrel Time*.[60] To make her meaning absolutely clear, she singled out the *Partisan Review*, *Commentary*, Lionel and Diana Trilling, Irving Kristol, and others for having "made no protest when people in this country were jailed or ruined."[61]

Hellman spoke out of a sense of betrayal that she could not shake. These were her people who had not spoken up, her people—as intellectuals and as Jews—who had abandoned her. "I had no right to think that

American intellectuals were people who would fight for anything if doing so would injure them," she wrote in *Scoundrel Time*. To the outside world this sounded like, and was, an attack on liberals writ large. But the now-disintegrated New York intellectuals heard in the words the recriminations of the German Jew. Children of immigrants, long uncomfortable with Hellman's outsider stance, they took her to task for many things, among them her effort to label them as the frightened children of immigrants. They accused her of snobbishness, of using her privileged German-Jewish background to obscure political differences. As Sidney Hook noted, caustically, her attack on "anti-Communist liberals . . . betrays the priggishness of the unconsciously would-be assimilated 100% American whose ancestors had reached American shores a few boatloads ahead of other immigrants."[62]

Hellman insisted that she "meant nothing snobbish" by the statement. "My family were immigrants once upon a time, too. We all were," she told an interviewer.[63] But her defenses made things worse. In the seventies, as in the thirties and the fifties, she found herself in a different camp from many of her fellow Jews. Then as earlier, the notion that "Jews" constituted a coherent political or identity group appalled her. She thought of them as neither particularly liberal nor radical. Southern Jews, in particular, had a wide variety of political opinions: "I find no solid liberal strain in the Southern Jew, East or German, or in the Southern goy, French, Scottish, or English," she wrote. And she added, "The South made for many good things—maybe the best writers of our time—but it made very few rebels or reformers, then or now, Jew or non-Jew."[64] Self-interest, she was convinced, played as great a role in the racially egalitarian commitments of Jews as did humane inclinations. She once described herself as a "toilet-trained Jew," and therefore acceptable to some who despised "just plain Jew."[65]

Sadly for Hellman, this stance turned out to fan the flames of a defensive and torn post–World War II American Jewry. In a period when claims to Jewish nationalism and particularism vied with assertions of the representative and universal nature of Jewish suffering, Hellman found herself on one side of a struggle whose meaning she never fully understood. Except under the threat of fascism, she had never flaunted or announced her Jewish identity. But the 1950s witnessed the emergence, as key players in the intellectual and political life of the nation, of Jews who identified strongly with a particular Jewish heritage and with Israel. When she maintained her prewar stance, insisting that her Jewish identity was merely part of a larger, more universal humanism, Hellman turned into the perfect lightning rod, attracting widespread criticism among Jews who believed that universalism was merely a cover for continuing loyalty to the Soviet Union. She was neither the first nor the only Jew to be accused of being an anti-Semitic and self-hating Jew. Influential art critic Clement Greenberg, novelist Philip Roth in the early sixties, and philosopher Hannah Arendt, a little later, all came under scrutiny.[66] But in Hellman's case, her continuing refusal to denounce the Soviet Union—the growing public sense that she remained a fellow traveler—lent fuel to the fire. From another perspective, Hellman's stance suggests that her world remained that of the southern Jew, for whom religion was a peripheral part of her life and her identity. Her live-and-let-live attitude—the attitude she had absorbed as a child in New Orleans—turned her into a vehicle for channeling the frustrations of those who demanded a different standard. It also affirmed a political stance that Hellman understood as quintessentially American.

CHAPTER 6

The Writer as Moralist

I am a moral writer, often too moral a writer, and I cannot avoid, it seems, that last summing up.
—*from the introduction to* Four Plays *by Lillian Hellman*

Like every other writer, I use myself and the time I live in.
—*Lillian Hellman, 1965*

Hellman's great plays of the thirties, *The Children's Hour* and *The Little Foxes*—with their broad-brush commentaries on malicious wrongdoing, on greed and immorality—stamped her not only as a playwright prone to melodrama but as an angry playwright. Hellman thought of them as fundamentally moral plays, as plays that flailed at injustice. In that sense they reflected the core of her being. She described herself as "bewildered by all injustice, at first certain that it cannot be, then shocked into rigidity, then obsessed, and finally as certain as a Grand Inquisitor that God wishes me to move ahead, correct and holy."[1] Nobody, she tells us in *Pentimento*, "has ever been able to control me when I feel that I have been treated unjustly."[2] More and more certain of what was right and wrong in the world and with human nature, she began in the early forties to point her material toward contemporary themes, producing work that she thought of as embodying moral lessons but that were, nevertheless, overtly political.

For most of the twentieth century, definitions of good and evil, though never as clear as Hellman would have liked, attached themselves to political ideologies. The world divided between fascists and communists, she could see only good in communism and in fascism only evil. The wartime plays—*Watch on the Rhine* (1941) and *The Searching Wind* (1944), along with the film script for the 1943 film *North Star*—shied away from explicitly naming Nazis and Soviet communists as the respective champions of the evil and the good. But her fierce anger against an unnamed fascism resonated with the beliefs of her audiences, infusing her plays with a political voice that contributed to her fame and honor. She was on the side of the angels. Yet Hellman did not imagine herself as a political writer. "I've never been interested in political messages so it is hard for me to believe I wrote them," she would say later.[3] After the war, the political scene shifted, and though Hellman's sense of right and wrong remained consistent and her voice strong and forceful, the politics embedded in her work seemed less relevant, even out of touch.

Watch on the Rhine took a theme dear to her heart—the defense of human liberty in the face of powerful forces (she called them bullies)—and translated it into an award-winning story rooted in the efforts of one family to speak and act against fascism. This was clearly an issue after her heart, but when she approached the subject as drama, she was at first stymied: "I wanted to say that we had little understanding of Europeans and little understanding of the conflicts among them."[4] Ultimately the play she wrote made a powerful appeal for ordinary people simply to pay attention.

Once again, she used the family—this time a well-informed and affluent family, loving and respectful of each other—as the vehicle through which to play out a larger struggle. On the eve of war, the American-born daughter of a former diplomat's family comes home from Europe with her three children and her German resistance-fighter husband in tow. Her large and graceful childhood home harbors a guest, a Romanian count sympathetic to the Nazis, who threatens to betray the resistance fighter to German officials. In order to return once again to Europe where he can continue the fight, the husband murders the guest and draws the entire family into active support for the antifascist cause. As he makes his escape from the scene, he tells his children, "In every town and every village and every mud hut in the world, there is a man who might fight to make a good world."[5] Silence in the face of evil, Hellman says, the cowardly refusal to act when inaction will promote injustice, is the real sin.

Watch on the Rhine opened on April 1, 1941, two months before Hitler broke his peace pact with the Soviet Union and at a time when American communists had committed themselves to silence about German aggressions. It drew its share of criticism for the awkwardness of some of the plot line and a somewhat contrived final scene. And it drew as well the predictable accusations. "The play as it stands is, of course, essentially a melodrama," wrote the *New Republic*'s critic, who followed with a comment that "artificial contrivance" in this play was more conspicuous than in some of her earlier plays.[6] But others confronted Hellman's message. "It is hard to say what our children will make of it," wrote *New Yorker* columnist Wolcott Gibbs, "this story of a political refugee who murders a guest in a peaceful American household with everybody's complete moral approbation and even their connivance."[7]

Widely understood as an indictment of Nazism (though the word *Nazi* was never mentioned), the play was received as an effort to rally good, but apathetic, citizens to the fight against tyranny. Calling it "infinitely better than the propaganda plays we are used to in the theatre," one critic noted that "it is the story and characters that really carry us along, however much or little the anti-Nazi connotations may stick in our minds."[8] *Watch on the Rhine*, wrote critic Brooks Atkinson, not always a fan of Hellman's work, translated "the death struggle between ideas in familiar terms we are bound to understand."[9] It did so, he added, without beating "the drum in favor of any cause."[10] Critic George Jean Nathan called it "the best anti-Nazi play we have so far had, whether from a man or a woman."[11] Hellman's plea for engagement did not go unheeded by ordinary folk. She saved one of the many fan letters she got—this one from an unknown man who wrote that he had seen the play many times and from it drew the lesson "that a man and wife must have an abiding faith and willingness to participate side by side in the same liberating struggle without any limitations."[12] This "moving and beautiful play, filled with eloquence and a heroic spirit," as one critic described it, won the New York Drama Critics Circle Award and ran for almost a year.[13]

On the left, Communist Party critics expressed more doubt. With Germany and the Soviet Union still tied together in a problematic peace pact, party loyalists wondered if Hellman had not undermined the Soviet cause. Artists, like all others—so went the party line—should subject

1941: Hellman with Joseph Wood Krutch receiving the Drama Critics Circle Award. (Ransom Center)

themselves to political constraints; good art could be measured by its political rather than aesthetic effect. In this instance, the *Daily Worker* grumbled, a "fabric of omissions" hung like a veil between the play and its audience. Hellman had failed to note "that a land of socialism has already established the permanent new life of peace and freedom, morality and comradeship and is the greatest guarantee that the ultimate struggle will be won."[14] Protagonist Kurt Müller described himself as an antifascist but would not reply when asked if he was a radical, and never admitted to being "a member of a Communist group fighting for German freedom." It was not, the *Daily Worker* reviewer hastened to add, that he believed "that a play stands or falls because it does or does not include a certain few lines. But, oh, how this play needs such added explanation."[15]

Two months later, in June 1941, Germany launched a direct attack on Soviet territory, breaking its pact with the Soviet Union. Two years after that, Warner Bros. released a film version of the play, its script partly written by Dashiell Hammett. The timing was right. The play attacked by the communist press in early 1941 became a critical favorite as a 1943 movie. The different receptions became something of an issue in the party, setting off a debate over the meaning of party loyalty. Albert Maltz, writing in the Communist Party publication the *New Masses*, asked why the change of heart and answered his own question. "Events had transpired in the two years calling for a different political program."[16] *Watch on the Rhine*, he argued, should be measured by aesthetic rather than political standards. Hellman could not have agreed more. Her integrity rested on her sense that art had its own voice. As she would put it later, "perhaps nothing in literature turns so quickly shoddy as those works which use the cloth of fashion to make the cloak of success."[17]

Hellman had a chance to stand by this principle when it came to the production of *North Star*, a 1943 film designed to familiarize American audiences with the Soviet war effort. She had not yet fulfilled a three-year contract, signed in 1936 with Sam Goldwyn, when Goldwyn proposed the film to her. The offer came as a relief. For more than three years theirs had been a tense relationship as Goldwyn offered her a series of books to adapt to the screen that Hellman routinely labeled "junk" or insulting. But in 1942 the Roosevelt administration called for film studios to provide a positive image of the Soviets "to counter the negative Soviet image that dominated mass media before the war."[18] Goldwyn saw a chance to make peace with Hellman. Her friend William Wyler agreed to direct the film, and everyone hoped that Hellman could persuade the Russians to give her a visa for Moscow, where she and Wyler might do some research. When Goldwyn balked at spending studio money on such a trip and Wyler accepted a commission in the air force, Hellman was left hanging.

Goldwyn and Hellman finally worked out an uneasy compromise. Hellman agreed to write the script for a film that Lewis Milestone would direct. Through the spring and summer of 1942, Hellman worked on *North Star*. Following her usual pattern, she read extensively, keeping thick notebooks of research notes on the nature of collective farm villages and typewritten summaries of stories from the *Moscow News*, Anna Louise Strong's recently published *The Soviets Expected It*, and Alvah Bessie's *The Soviet People at War*. She followed the progress of the war in Cyrus Sulzberger's August–September 1942 series in the *Herald Tribune*, and she kept track of German atrocities, noting especially German massacres of Jews in Kiev.[19] Most of what she read was uncritical—even of the collective farms that had drawn such antagonism from the Ukrainian and Russian peasantry. Still, she made note of the occasional cynical comment. Along with notes about the extensive legal rights accorded to women, she recorded the telling Russian proverb: "What are you doing? Nothing. And him? He's helping me!"

By December 1942, the script was complete. Hammett had enlisted in the army that fall and was doing his basic training in Fort Monmouth, New Jersey. Despite his occasional weekends at Hardscrabble, she was more or less on her own. The script she turned over to Goldwyn and Milestone was a hard-hitting story about a prosperous collective farm village in the Ukraine, peopled by brave young men and women committed to socialist ideals. The village comes under attack by Germans who commit such atrocities as draining the blood of children to transfuse into wounded soldiers, leaving the children at the point of death. The heroic peasants of the village rebel; the German officer who has ordered the bleeding is shot; the peasants burn their own village to the ground and flee, vowing to return as an armed resistance to fascism.

Hellman thought she had written a film that called attention to the courage of unarmed and peaceful people struggling against a fascist menace. Her script juxtaposed caring socialist values against fascist cruelty in a struggle for the human soul. Romantic though it was, the script did not satisfy either Goldwyn or director Milestone. Though it idealized the collective spirit and reified Soviet prosperity, Hellman had written a complex portrait of real people and their fight to defend themselves. Goldwyn and Milestone quickly moved to eliminate the ideological thread of the story, rewriting huge portions of the script and providing the film with a saccharine musical background that gave it an American idiom and flavor. "Mother dear, do not fear, we're the younger generation," sang the collective's bright young sparks. In an effort to turn the village into "anywhere," Milestone and Goldwyn removed everything distinctively Russian and socialist about the village, noting only once that this village was a collective and eliminating the words *socialism*, *communism*, and *comrade* wherever possible. In the process, they turned characters Hellman had drawn as angry and resistant peasants into a posse of cowboys intent on wiping the Germans out.

This was the first time that Hellman had experienced what she called a betrayal. She had written a script; Milestone rewrote first fifty pages, and then another fifty, removing its core points. She did not immediately walk away. Under contract to Goldwyn, she gamely tried to link the new parts of the film together. But she was incensed that the possibility of producing an honest film had been sabotaged and, even before its release, she gave a long interview to *New York Times* reporter Theodore

Strauss in which she deplored the diminishing power of writers in the face of an industry wedded to "a lovely dollar."[20] A few months later, Hellman once again reiterated her commitment to the struggles of the Screen Writers Guild to achieve some respect for writers and their craft. She vented to Strauss about the writers' helplessness in the face of the studios and averred that "an author's final security probably can come only in finding craftsmen with whom he can work harmoniously and, if need be, join in an independent unit as so many craftsmen in Hollywood are beginning to do."[21]

Goldwyn produced a picture admired by most of the critical reviewers, a box-office success that won six Oscar nominations—one of them for best original screenplay. Some critics noted the elements of political un-reality introduced by Milestone. Mary McCarthy wrote a particularly vituperative account of the film. In a survey of wartime films, she merci-lessly attacked *North Star* as "political indoctrination," noting that it rep-resented the Soviet Union as "a peace loving country; an idyllic hamlet" instead of depicting "the terror which held the country in domestic siege long before the first German company moved across the frontier." Mc-Carthy, then a young novelist who identified with the Trotskyist faction on the left, insisted that "the Soviet Union had never been innocent." "Here," she wrote, "was where liberals parted company with communists." She described the film, in language to which she would return more than thirty-five years later, as "a tissue of falsehoods woven of every variety of untruth."[22]

Hellman might, on this occasion, have agreed with McCarthy. She hated the film, describing it as an "extended opera bouffe peopled not by peasants, real and alive, but by musical comedy characters without a thought or care in the world." But while she complained bitterly about Milestone's version, she did not entirely abandon it. It had, she thought, "said some true things about fascism" and "had been useful in promot-ing the united front."[23] Of her own romanticization of the farm and its peasants she said nothing. She had, after all, chosen to ignore Ukrainians' massive resistance to collectivization and to depict them as a gentle and quiet people. When Goldwyn and Milestone turned peasants into actors in a musical comedy, she experienced their disagreements as artistic rather than political. She had lost a battle with Goldwyn that she had always previously won—the battle to retain the integrity of the writer's voice. She left her name on the film. But she dug deep into her pockets to buy back her contract with Goldwyn for $30,000. She vowed never to work with

Goldwyn again, and she never did. Ironically, perhaps, the screenplays of the film version of *Watch on the Rhine* (written by Hammett and revised by Hellman), and *North Star* were both nominated for Academy Awards in 1943. Both films lost to *Casablanca*. Still, *North Star* became the most commercially successful wartime propaganda film.

Though she consistently denied interest in "political messages," Hellman thought her next play, *The Searching Wind*, "the nearest thing to a political play" she had ever written. *The Searching Wind* opened on April 12, 1944, to mixed reviews—some of them praising Hellman's courage in confronting the problems of the day, others attacking the confusion that ensued from trying to follow the story of a love triangle through the complex interwar years. *The Searching Wind* condemns as cowardly the misguided attempts of the Western powers to appease Mussolini and Hitler before the war, creating a wounded hero to pay the price for the failures of that policy. As in her earlier dramas, the family serves as the pivot around which Hellman constructs two confrontations, one a love triangle and the second the refusal of a diplomat and his father-in-law to speak up against fascism. And as in her earlier plays, Hellman leaves room for ambiguity about her political stance.

The play is set in 1944 with the world engaged in a war Hellman thought "could have been avoided if Fascism had been recognized early enough."[24] Through flashbacks, the action recalls moments when Americans chose to overlook the potential dangers of fascism or to appease fascists. As a young diplomat stationed in Italy in 1923, Alex Hazen trivialized the rise of Mussolini. As a consul in Germany in the late 1920s, Hazen minimized the dangers of German inflation and ignored rising anti-Semitism. As an ambassador in 1938, he advised supporting the strategy of appeasement that led to Munich. Along the way he is challenged briefly by his father-in-law, a liberal newspaperman, who chooses to retire rather than to fight against the tide. Repeatedly his perceptive former sweetheart alerts him to the coming dangers, but he spurns her affections rather than heed her warnings. Refusing to see, Hazen buries himself in the arms of his rich and ignorant wife, who supports his diplomatic silences. The price of denial and cowardice is paid for by the next generation. Their son Sam enlists in the war that America enters in 1941, and at the time of the play is in danger of losing his leg to wounds suffered in Italy.

Hellman wrote *The Searching Wind* while Hammett, who at age forty-eight had enlisted in the army, was stationed in the Aleutian Islands in

Alaska. Writing for the first time completely on her own, she fussed over the play and wondered whether she could get a copy of it through the army censors to him. Hellman's letters to Hammett are lost, but Hammett's replies to her reveal that even from a distance, he provided a remarkable level of support for a relatively high level of anxiety. He asked her not to worry about writing to him while she was deeply engaged in the play and reassured her that her anxiety was appropriate. "I'm sorry you're going through one of those worry-worry spells about the play, but I guess that's part of writing," he wrote to her on February 9.[25] As the play came closer to production her level of anxiety must have increased, because Hammett wrote to her, "You're practically breaking my heart with your letters about the play. I think we're going to have to make a rule that you're not to tackle any work when I'm not around to spur, quiet, goad, pacify and ease you, according to what's needed at the moment. It is obvious that you're not capable of handling yourself."[26] And yet in the end he encouraged her to stand on her own feet: "What the hell," he wrote, "you did your best and you'll have to let it go at that no matter what you'd like to do."[27]

From Pleasantville, Hellman sent Hammett a finished draft of the play that arrived at his Alaskan outpost just a month before the play was to open in New York. His comments were reassuring but not uncritical. He wished, he wrote, that she had told her story in chronological order so that the love triangle could follow the historical trajectory. He wondered if catching the characters "now here, now there" would do justice to any of them, or leave in the audience's hands the task of rounding them out. And most of all, he argued that "the essential frivolity that fucked things up ... isn't *shown*. No answer is provided to the question, But what else could these people have done?"[28] He closed with the needed reassurance: this was "in ways the most interesting play you've done, and it's got swell stuff in it, and, as I said before, it's defter than any of the others, and you are a cutie." And then he added a final postscript that identified himself as one "who does not always know as much about everything as he acts like he does, and who hopes the play gets its points over in a manner that makes this letter sound like the work of a smart-aleck." When the play did in fact turn out to be a box-office success, Hammett expressed genuine delight: "Let this be a lesson to you, my fine buxom cutie. You are a big girl now and you write your own plays the way you want them and you do not necessarily give a damn for the opinions of Tom, Dick or Dashie unless they happen to coincide with your own. No matter how close to you T, D or D may be and no matter how hard they try to think in terms of your play, you must always bear in mind that what they're actually fooling around with is some slightly different idea of their own, which may be all right, but with which you have no business involving yourself."[29]

Given the weight of Hammett's comments, we are tempted to wonder if Hellman was being disingenuous when, later, she observed that she meant, in *The Searching Wind*, "only to write about nice, well born people who, with good intentions, helped to sell out a world."[30] There is something unsatisfying in her refusal to claim the play for what it was: a pointed condemnation of rich liberals whose refusals to "see," whose denials and silences around world-shaking historical events, finally led the world into war. Sam, the son whose leg will soon be sacrificed to the silence of his grandfather and the denials of his parents, makes the point directly. He recalls conversations with his fellow soldiers as they sat in the mud of the trenches fulminating against the "old tripe who just live in our country now and pretend they are on the right side." He repeats to his parents his desire to get away from the people who "believe they're all for everything good" despite the fact that they "made the shit we're sitting in."[31] The rage speaks for itself, forecasting feelings Hellman would express thirty years later in *Scoundrel Time* when she would direct her venom at the same liberals who, in her view, had continued to betray the world. In *The Searching Wind*, Sam asserts only shame at the behavior of his parents. He won't mind the loss of the leg, he tells them, "as long as it means a little something and helps to bring us out someplace."[32] The next generation, he seems to be saying, would speak up. Hellman soon learned that they would not.

Insofar as *The Searching Wind* called to account those who refused to stand up to Hitler and the fascists, the play affirmed Hellman's position as a moralist whose finger pointed blame. When Sam hurled at his parents and his grandfather a painful assessment of their responsibility, Hellman indicted an entire generation. History, Sam told the audience, was "made by the masses of people" not by "one man or ten men." But, he continued, that was no "excuse to just sit back and watch," to act as if "nothing anybody can do makes any difference, so why do it?"[33] This was the moral issue that Addie had posed in *The Little Foxes* when she deplored those who ate the vines just like locusts eating the earth, and then asked if it was right for others "to stand and watch them do it?"[34]

Many critics judged *The Searching Wind* as the best, the most impelling play of the season. Hellman was, wrote one admiring critic, "the least reluctant [of contemporary playwrights] to admit to being alive and thoughtful in a parlous time."[35] *The Searching Wind*, wrote another, "brought back a full measure of dignity, perception and beauty to the theater." He then went on to praise Hellman's "bitter and lucid" indictment "of supposed men of good will who brought us to this terrible moment of the present."[36] Hellman was at her best, thought a third, when she was dealing with the politics of the world. She left the audience "wishing for more politics and less emotional triangle." "To get an audience thinking in this day and age probably is a matter of the sheerest genius."[37]

Other critics found Hellman's effort to grapple with the politics of her time mystifying. The play, wrote one reviewer, might be "superb theater," but Hellman's political aim remained unclear to him. She had not, he mourned, solved the problem of how to keep Europe from going periodically to war . . . a problem that has defied solution for at least 2,000 years."[38] Others were even more critical. They appreciated her efforts to turn a mirror to her times but at the same time fulminated that Hellman had pretended to a social omniscience that nobody could have had in the twenties or even the late thirties; they accused her of exhibiting "a general impatience with, or contempt for, people less elaborately informed than herself."[39] Why, they asked, did *The Searching Wind* not include a fourth flashback that condemned the 1939 Soviet-German pact? Why not denounce Stalin's efforts to make peace with Hitler as no more than appeasement? Hellman, they argued, was preaching the lessons of collective security to a nation that doubted it could ever fully trust a communist regime. She was accused of being a political playwright.

But the most vehement protests came from those on the left who wondered why Hellman had failed "to link the appeasers of yesterday with the defeatists, the 'nationalists' and 'isolationists' of today."[40] The play, argued the *Daily Worker*'s Ralph Warner, was strongest when it recalled "the support democracy gave to its mortal enemy, fascism." But it fell short in many ways, most pointedly by refusing to acknowledge "the unwavering anti-fascist position taken by the Soviet Union" and failing to see "that many Americans worked and are still working to perpetuate the policies of appeasement" that continue to support fascism.[41] So pointed were these critiques that several nonparty publications commented that "the rich and famous Miss Hellman, hitherto one of the most ardent of the Communist fellow travelers," may well have fallen out of favor with the party.[42]

Inevitably, perhaps, Hellman's ambiguous political stance inserted it-self into judgments of the play itself and resulted in ad hominem attacks. Had her talent deserted her? As one skeptic wondered, could it be that this latest play was merely a "shallow meretricious piece of reactionary claptrap?"[43] With barely disguised irony, critics complained that the play reflected her status as an "advanced or indignant woman." In one re-markable assessment, the *New Republic*'s reviewer let loose a diatribe on Hellman's writing—the subject of almost universal admiration—calling it "pseudo-analytical-psychological, head-in-the-box-office-feet-in-the-clouds, feministic, novelistic rubbish."[44] Hellman, as she tended to do, publicly shrugged off the criticism, insisting that this was a play about well-intentioned people who had simply let their opportunities pass and attributing the personal attacks to narrow political disagreements. For all its relevance in 1944, when *The Searching Wind* appeared as a film two years later—Hellman adapted the script for the screen herself—it fell completely flat. By 1946, nobody was interested in analyzing whether American appeasement of fascists had brought on the war.

Hellman might have been perceived as a political playwright during the war, but she didn't like the label very much and she claimed never to have really liked *The Searching Wind*.[45] Before the film's June 1946 re-lease, she had already decided to shift gears and was working full tilt on the play that would become *Another Part of the Forest*. There she tried to deflect criticism by backing off current events and revisiting the themes of greed and human nature that had animated *The Little Foxes*. But the parallels between the southern world she created and the one in which she lived were unmistakable. World War II had now ended; America was busily retooling its industry to serve the needs of an expanding consumer culture. Setting the scene twenty years before *The Little Foxes*, Hellman placed the Hubbard siblings in small-town Alabama in 1880, just after the 1877 withdrawal of northern troops from the South. There, Hellman resurrected the two brothers, Ben and Oscar, and their sister, Regina, as they reached maturity and wrested control of their family's fortune from their father. The father, much despised in the small town where he was the wealthiest man, had made huge profits during the Civil War by run-ning salt through the southern blockade and then selling it at enormous prices. This was the kind of profiteering familiar to goods-deprived families in the Second World War. As if that were not enough, Marcus Hubbard betrayed a group of southern soldiers to the enemy, an event that towns-people suspected, but could not prove, and that led to the soldiers' massacre. When Ben discovers that his mother has secreted evidence of his father's guilt in the family Bible, he blackmails his father into giving up control of his wealth and, at the price of parental humiliation, starts on the path to capitalist success.

There was no way to miss Hellman's condemnation of the endless rapacity of capitalism, its ruthless destruction of everything that lay in its way, including the cherished traditions of family honor and southern solidarity. But postwar America had had enough of conflict with capitalism. It relied now on the entrepreneurial spirit to raise it from the despair of war, and Hellman had overstepped the limits. She had created, thought one reviewer, characters of sheer unredeemed wickedness, characters filled with "relentless hatred . . . cold hatred, Iago-hatred," characters utterly lacking in human decency.[46] These were characters so monstrous, so venal, so brimming with odium that they immediately raised the question of whether such evil had any relationship to real life.

In the view of critics, her malevolence backfired. As Brooks Atkinson put it in the *New York Times*, "this time her hatred for malefactors of great wealth in post-war Alabama has driven her play straight over the line into old fashioned melodrama." This play, he thought, was hokum.[47] By trying to turn a serious effort to expose predatory capitalists into popular entertainment, noted another critic, Hellman had "deprived it of validity," turned it into a play "as easy to enjoy as it was difficult to take seriously."[48] The new millionaires of the 1880s might have been villainous, argued another, but they were not unmitigated villains.[49] And yet the criticism was muted by awe at Hellman's accomplishment. Even as they disparaged her melodramatic style, even as they ridiculed it for its lack of verisimilitude, several critics praised the play as "expertly written, well acted, superbly directed."[50] As one wrote, "from a less practiced pen," the play "might have been so overwrought as to be funny." Only "a dramatist of extraordinary skill and strength," he added, "could have managed" to pull this off.[51]

Criticism of character and plot in *Another Part of the Forest* was balanced by admiration for the production, and this time Hellman could take credit for that too. Up until then, Herman Shumlin had produced and directed all of her original plays. He had also been her most enduring admirer, and often a lover as well. "Dear smart, gorgeous, lovely, darling Lillian," he wrote to her after the opening of *The Children's Hour*, and with unfailing loyalty continued for a decade to work with her on everything she wrote. For a long time Hellman appreciated the partnership, and shared with Shumlin the triumphs and hurts of his other successes and failures. "Herman would do just as well to stay away from comedy," she wrote to Arthur Kober after one of Shumlin's failures. "I feel very sorry about all the mess."[52] But in 1945 strains emerged in the relationship. Hellman's decision to direct *The Searching Wind* while Shumlin produced it may well have created tensions. And Hellman's deep involvement with John Melby surely exacerbated ill-feeling. In early 1946, she told Shumlin she could not work with him any longer. Lacking trust in any other partner, she asked Kermit Bloomgarden to produce the play and decided to direct *Another Part of the Forest* herself.

She was, by her own account, poor at the job: not adequately clear, impulsive, and often quick to change her mind. She thought she could simply "explain something and that was that." Her penchant for treating actors as "normal, logical people" backfired when she discovered that people in the theater were neither normal nor logical.[53] Remarkably, none of this showed onstage. She received universal accolades for her selection of actors (particularly the young Patricia Neal as the teenaged Regina, and Mildred Dunnock as the mother driven crazy by her husband's machinations), her staging, and the overall sense of the direction. The play, not a smash hit, nevertheless ran from late November to late April, a respectable five months.

Two themes run through the controversy about *Another Part of the Forest*, both worth our attention. The wickedness that permeated the play rubbed off on Hellman as a person. Richard Watts, who briefly compared Hellman to Ibsen in terms of plot structure and directness of language, chose on second thought to associate her with Clare Boothe. They shared, Watts thought, a "malice toward the human race . . . distaste for mankind . . . venom and their bitterness."[54] Joseph Wood Krutch concurred: "Miss Hellman's ability to imagine dirty tricks and nasty speeches is unrivaled in the contemporary theater," he opined. "There can be no question of the theatrical virtuosity which enables her to extract from each all the ugliness it can possibly yield."[55] To some, Hellman became the personification of the evil that she was describing. As Sam Sillen put it in the *Daily Worker*, a communist newspaper typically sympathetic to the broad outlines of her work, "In the sheer projection of wickedness in human beings, Miss Hellman has no competitors in the American theater." She had written a play so depraved and mean-spirited that it could not be taken seriously. John Chapman concurred. The theater, he argued, needed "a good stiff dose of pure hellishness. Miss Hellman . . . is just the girl to give it to us."[56] From then on, Hellman would be identified with the ugliness of her characters, her persona vested with their cruel and malevolent behaviors. The critic Jacob Adler would conclude his assessment of her work a few years later by suggesting that "what sustains her is a concentrated presentation of sheer, almost supernatural evil, to be matched in almost no other modern playwright anywhere."[57]

Then, too, *Another Part of the Forest* offered a view of history with which many (including some of her former friends) disagreed. Based in the South like *The Little Foxes*, *Another Part of the Forest* imagined its corrupt protagonists bent on the destruction of a pastoral and paternalistic land that had never existed. Hellman's South overlooked the legacy of slavery and racism to display a latent admiration for the cultured and gracious lives lived by its ruling elite. In defense of this oversimplified and idyllic South, Hellman took proponents of a new industrialism to task. One sympathetic critic concluded that "Miss Hellman is, among other things, becoming a social historian of provocative gifts."[58] But those less inclined to romanticize the old South could reasonably dissent. The portrait raised questions about Hellman's identification with the South and led some to wonder if her capacity to draw on a fund of negative materials about that changing region, and even to throw off southern ties in her work, might negate the label of a southern writer in her case.[59] Hellman was herself ambivalent on this point. Asked late in life if she considered herself southern, she replied, "Well, I have no right to, because the New York years now far outweigh the Southern years, but I suppose most Southerners, people who grew up in the South, still consider themselves Southern."[60]

In the context of the times, *Another Part of the Forest*, itself seemingly without a relevant politics, created something of a stir. Hellman had followed *The Searching Wind*—a play that blamed American isolationism for bringing on the Second World War and that advocated collective security in a period of deep suspicions against the Soviet Union—with one that offered yet another dose of criticism. Even as the nation turned to anticommunism and Hellman herself turned away from communist activities, *Another Part of the Forest* condemned capitalists as unmitigated villains and romanticized traditional community values. In turning the

Hubbards into an evil family, wrote a *Commonweal* reviewer who had also disliked Hellman's portrayal of the events leading up to World War II, Hellman had drawn a portrait that was "Americanly wrong."[61] Later, other critics would associate these two plays with the kind of simplistic social-realist writing characteristic of the 1930s left, and which Hellman disliked.[62]

There was the rub. In the postwar period, vast divisions emerged about what was "American" and what was not. As the country settled into the era and its leaders tried to sort out how to live with a Soviet Union perceived as increasingly threatening, Hellman's views diverged from those of an apprehensive mainstream America. During the Depression thirties, the idea of communism served as a beacon of light to radicals who sought to change the world. As long as the Americans and the Soviets were allied, the light lasted. Then it faded. The brave Soviet citizens who had resisted Hitler during the war years and driven him back remained confined and silenced in a nation desperate to spread Communist influence and ideas over the world. Revelations about Stalin's atrocities against anybody who threatened his power reached the West. The Soviets were known to be searching for the secret of the Atom bomb, and close to achieving it. A tense and fearful U.S. searched for spies in every nook and cranny. And an aggressive United States Congress attacked those it deemed guilty of spreading un-American ideas. Hellman resisted the onslaught of fear and hostility, clinging, as many did, to the hope that some mechanism for peaceful coexistence could be found, and insisting that the search for enemies within the United States would surely destroy the freedoms its citizens most valued. After *Another Part of the Forest*, her writing, long in tune with a wartime desire for cohesion, seemed flat and out of harmony, even perilously dangerous. She turned increasingly to contemporary issues and especially to the defense of artistic freedom.

In 1948, Hellman agreed to adapt Norman Mailer's bestselling novel *The Naked and the Dead* for the theater, drawn by its critique of conflict within the American military and its dissection of the inner lives of American soldiers. She interrupted her work on the script—as it happened never to resume it—to attend a premiere of *The Little Foxes* in Belgrade and to write some short pieces on Yugoslavia for the *New York Star*. Writing in early November 1948 as Henry Wallace was winding up a campaign for the presidency that Harry Truman would win, Hellman took time in these pieces to educate her readers about the recent expulsion of Yugoslavia from the Communist bloc of nations led by the Soviet Union. Tito, who did not believe that the Soviets had sufficiently aided Yugoslav partisans in their wartime struggle, chose to chart his own path toward communism, independent of Soviet influence. This was a conversation that Hellman could have stayed out of. But she chose to enter it on Tito's side—averring at every opportunity that, although she knew nothing about the quarrel, she was happy to learn that communists sometimes disagreed with each other and insisting that Tito's strength, candor, and charm would prevent a face-off between them.[63]

Before she returned to the United States, Hellman stopped in Paris, where she saw Emmanuel Robles's play *Montserrat*, a piece that appealed to her so much that she abandoned Mailer's *The Naked and the Dead* to adapt it to an American audience. Robles's play spoke powerfully to one of Hellman's favorite themes: the price of human liberty. Set in Venezuela in 1812, the plot revolved around the rebellion led by Simon Bolívar. To persuade one man, Montserrat, to speak the secret of Bolívar's hiding place, a Spanish officer rounds up six innocent Venezuelan villagers (men and women) and tells them they will be shot in an hour if they do not convince Montserrat to reveal the hiding place. Alone with the prisoners, Montserrat listens as each pleads a case. Wives and children will be without support, argue the captives; nursing babies will be motherless; young people at the threshold of life will never contribute their might. Montserrat counters by trying to persuade the six that their individual lives are worth nothing as against the millions for whom Bolívar's escape will bring liberty. Their sacrifice is for the larger human freedom that Bolívar represents. But the six are not convinced, and each dies pleading with Montserrat to speak. Finally, when the Spanish threaten to round up six more innocents, Montserrat relents. But by now Bolívar has escaped, and in retribution Montserrat is sent to his death.

As she worked at the adaptation—a much harder task than she had imagined—Hellman tinkered with the Robles play, in the process facing some of the moral problems confronting a tense world. She neither drew explicit political lessons nor preached revolt against oppression. And yet the historical moment enveloped the play. With Berlin under blockade for most of the spring and the Chinese communists racing through Beijing and then Nanking toward victory, the world seemed headed for an indefinite conflict. At home, the hunt to identify and curtail communist activity intensified. In March, the Cultural and Scientific Conference for

World Peace in which Hellman participated endured sharp protests for issuing invitations to "approved" Soviet writers. In June, the attack struck close to home when an FBI report named Hellman's close friend Dorothy Parker a communist. Could liberty prevail in the face of a large and spreading fear? The noose around communists and fear of them tightened that August when the Russians tested their first atomic weapon.

Kermit Bloomgarden agreed to produce *Montserrat*, but Hellman chose to direct it herself, her second effort at directing. This time she did not succeed so well. Though critics appreciated Hellman's usual "sharpness and bite" and praised "the fervor of her hatred for injustice and her belief in man's right to shape his own destiny," they missed her usual directness. The production, they agreed, lacked the verve and intensity of her earlier work.[64] Hellman stood by her play, though she later confessed that she directed it in "a fumbling, frightened way," intimidated by the powerful acting of Emlyn Williams.[65] It might not have mattered.

The timing of the production was all wrong, and to make matters worse, just a few days after *Montserrat* opened, Marc Blitzstein's *Regina*, an operatic adaptation of *The Little Foxes*, hit the boards. Except for insisting that the story line of the opera remain faithful to her original play, Hellman pretty much stayed out of the work on *Regina*. Blitzstein, an old friend, took the opportunity to blunt the edges of *The Little Foxes* by creating a chorus of black folk whose musical instruments and voices underlined the play's antiracist themes and suggested that a new day was coming. With Blitzstein already identified as a communist, critics took aim at both message and music. Inevitably, musical and play together opened up questions about just what political side Hellman was on.

As if to avoid the taint of writing political plays, and in the midst of the spreading attacks against communism, Hellman turned in the spring of 1951 to *The Autumn Garden*, a play she sometimes described as her favorite. Shunning the overtly political, she avoided the carefully constructed plots that had sustained her for many years. She turned, instead, to Chekhov, whose plays she much admired and whose letters she had begun to assemble in preparation for a book. For a setting, she provided a summer guest house on the Gulf Coast near New Orleans, run by a refined, down-on-her-fortune woman. There she brought together ten middle-aged people for their annual summer holidays. These were characters, as a *Commonweal* reviewer put it, trapped "in the half life they have been living while waiting for the full life" of a dream that would never be to be.[66] The play, Chekhovian in the sense that it portrays the illusion of hope and promise that fuels human activity—and records the ultimate futility of the human condition—ends in predictable stalemate. Neither particularly unpleasant nor evil, each character learns, in the weeks they are all together, just how little he or she has taken hold of life. All of them return to the separate locations from which they came neither better nor worse than when the summer began. As the play ends, we know that they will return home unable and unwilling to salvage meaningless lives.

The sense of despondency that infused *The Autumn Garden* captured Hellman's frustration with a nation caught in the vise of its own fear. One by one, she took to task each of her characters for their lack of courage, their aimlessness. Collectively the players created an allegory for America. Middle-aged, self-absorbed, and unable to see purpose in their lives, the summer visitors passed through their experiences unwilling to do more than acknowledge their gloomy circumstances. America, Hellman seemed to be saying, had abandoned faith in change and progress.

Critics tended to see something else. To them, the world of the fifties called for an aggressive commitment to secure the prosperity and might of a newly powerful United States. They responded to *The Autumn Garden* by rising to the defense of the America they loved. Hellman takes on "the South as her pet whipping boy," wrote one critic, who added, "We think Miss Hellman might do well to pay a visit to the new South which boasts a good many happy, prosperous and moral people."[67] Another dismissed the play as the work of "an undefeated and untied misanthrope."[68] Still a third took her to task for failing in her political loyalties. *The Autumn Garden*, wrote *Christian Science Monitor* reviewer John Beaufort, is "an unfairly slanted representation of American life." If produced abroad, he continued, "it may handily serve the Kremlin's determined campaign to convince Europe that life in the United States is preponderantly decadent."[69] Beaufort went on to lecture Hellman on her responsibilities as a citizen of a free democracy: "Aware that the drama can be a powerful weapon in the war of ideas, playwrights who enjoy the freedoms of a democracy may usefully reflect to what extent they intend contributing to Moscow's propaganda arsenal."

So off-target were the reviews that Harold Clurman, who directed it, intervened in the debate about it. Undoubtedly urged on by Hellman, he wrote a piece in which he defended *The Autumn Garden* as a quintessential moral statement. The play, he argued, expressed Hellman's critical feelings about "most of us of the educated near-upper class. We are earnest, we yearn, but we are not serious, we have no clear purpose. We have no binding commitments to ourselves or to others; we are attached to nothing. We allow ourselves to be deviated because we do not know exactly where we want to go."[70] To no avail: it was the political, not the moral, lessons of Hellman's work to which critics turned in the fifties.

Hellman, tuned in to the politics of the moment, understood the criticism of *The Autumn Garden* as part of a climate of fear intended to discipline artists. This was a period in which rhetoric against the communist threat reached fever pitch; anticommunist campaigns, fraught with accusations of disloyalty, filled with hyperbole and outright lies, carried the threat of job loss and perhaps even death. The resulting anxiety led individuals who had (and had not) been close to the Communist Party, or in it, to distance themselves from former friends and from causes associated with sympathy for the Soviet Union. An atmosphere of fear and apprehension effectively curtailed the civil liberties of Americans, constraining freedom of spirit and of mind. In this topsy-turvy world, dissent was unpatriotic, refusing to betray one's friends was tantamount to admission of communist affiliation, and calls for "peaceful coexistence" (which Hellman supported in *The Searching Wind* and again at the 1949 Cultural and Scientific Conference for World Peace) became declarations of Soviet sympathy. In a world painted in black and white, in which one form of government protected liberty while the other thrived on despotism, there was no room for compromise. If you were for liberty you must be an anticommunist; even mild criticism of capitalism signaled advocacy of communist slavery. Hellman, who never accepted this dichotomy, watched in horror as patterns of fear began to overwhelm the work of once-brave artists.

In the several lectures and talks that she delivered to young people during the early 1950s, as socialist ideas came to be perceived as unpatriotic and attacks against the Soviet Union escalated, she repeatedly noted that playwrights wrote in the light of "the social and economic forces of their day."[71] To hammer home her point, she returned to her own roots as a child and as a creature of a particular historical moment: "My generation," she would begin, and then go on to describe values inspired by FDR's humane efforts to deal with poverty, unemployment, and insecurity. She urged her students not to be silenced, and puzzled over how many musical comedies in contrast to serious dramas were produced in the early 1950s, when life was "hard and insecure and frightening." Surely, she thought, this was because "any play that comes along to show life as such makes people more uncomfortable and more unhappy."[72] Fear, she thought, was the real enemy of the writer. Addressing a group of students at Swarthmore College in April 1950, she told them that "because of the political and moral and ethical forces that surround us, we have entered an age in which it is becoming downright dangerous not to conform." She continued her warning, telling the students that "we are—or are being unnaturally made into—a fearful people, and fearful people will stand for very little deviation."[73] She repeated this theme in and around the time of her own 1952 HUAC testimony and the Hollywood blacklist, as she tried to alert students to the debilitating consequences of the silences induced by "fear of other countries, fear of ourselves and our neighbors, and the discomforts and shame that come with fears and the displacement of ordinary middle-class values."[74] This, she scrawled in a lecture note to herself, was "not first time fear has led to persecution and injustice." But now fear was "leading to thought control."[75]

We can watch Hellman squirm (along with many others of her generation) as her plays were increasingly viewed through anticommunist lenses and the shadow of Joe McCarthy hung ominously over the entertainment community and the intellectual world. She was caught now in a moral dilemma fostered by a political witch hunt. What seemed to Hellman to be issues of good and evil or right and wrong appeared to audiences and critics to be political rather than moral statements. Hellman understood the dilemma and chose her stance. If she ceased to be an outspoken advocate of communism, she would nevertheless continue to vigorously oppose the anticommunist crusade. She would acknowledge the temper of the times without succumbing to it. She continued to defend *The Little Foxes* as satire, for example, but she refused to revive it in the decade of the fifties for fear that the "warm acceptance" it received in 1939 would not be repeated. American society in the fifties, she told a group of students at the end of the decade, preferred a "gentle picture of itself, togetherness and goodness, normality or decency." This was not her picture of America at the time, but it influenced the acceptance of her work. She consoled herself by adding that even if the reception of a play changed, "the worth of a play is not altered by time."[76]

She chose, in that difficult historical moment, to focus on the theme of justice she had captured in *The Children's Hour*, hoping that in bringing it back to the stage, she could call attention to the larger consequences of unthinking acquiescence to an age of lies. With Kermit Bloomgarden's help, *The Children's Hour* opened once again on December 18, 1952, for a successful six-month run. Hellman cast Pat Neal in one of the starring roles and for the last time directed it. Audiences responded well, though, and once again critics chose to find in it a political message that they immediately skewered. The play, wrote Eric Bentley, "has nothing directly to do with communism, but it was written in the thirties, and is the product of the dubious idealism of that time."[77] Cleverly, Bentley turned the accusation of lesbianism leveled at the teachers into an allegory for communism. "Suppose it had been about teachers accused of communism," he wrote, "that for two acts we had been asked to boil with indignation at the wrongness of the accusation, only to find towards the close of act three that one of the pair *did* harbor communist sympathies?" In his view, Hellman could not escape the conclusion. "Is it not in politics rather than the theatre that we have witnessed this drama before?" he asked with a flourish.

Hellman would not be silenced. Between 1949 and the end of 1956, at the height of the Cold War and in the midst of the frenzy of McCarthyism, she mounted one original play (*The Autumn Garden*) and three stage adaptations (Emmanuel Robles's *Montserrat*, Jean Anouilh's *The Lark*, and Voltaire's *Candide*). Consistently she described her efforts as reaching for moral rather than political truths. Appreciative audiences certainly understood them that way. *Montserrat* asks about the value of human life in the context of a larger struggle for liberty; *The Autumn Garden* explores the futility of trying to change oneself or the world. *Candide* satirizes the assumption that we can ever imagine, much less create, a world without pain. *The Lark*, from 1955 and based on the life of Joan of Arc, suggests willingness to sacrifice the corporeal body in order to save the soul. Each speaks in the political-moral voice that had by now become her trademark. But in a world where moral debates seemed to harbor embedded political dangers, Hellman's voice remained suspect.

The Lark carried the additional weight of taking a position on women's issues. For Hellman, its appeal lay in a heroine whose martyrdom symbolically evoked women's fate. The United States, just out of a war in which it called on women to sacrifice for their country, asked them, at war's end, to leave their jobs and return to their homes. Hellman, who played a role in efforts to involve women in the war effort, ignored the injunction to women to return home. She saw Joan as "history's first modern career girl, wise, unattractive in what she knew about the handling of men, straight out of a woman's magazine."[78] The portrait she drew of Joan—which, as we shall see later, got her into some trouble with the original playwright, Jean Anouilh—centered on her womanly leadership. "It has remained for a woman dramatist to give us the first really tough minded Joan of Arc," wrote one critic. "I have a strong suspicion that a great deal of the biting briskness, the cleaver-sharp determination, the haughty and hard-headed candor of this Joan comes from the pen of the lady."[79]

Hellman turned to editing the letters of Russian playwright Anton Chekhov, perhaps because he most closely reflected her thinking at the time. She started to work on this volume as early as January 1950, and the notes in her files suggest that she saw in Chekhov both a reflection of herself and an allusion to her own time. She described him as a writer with whom she would not only have liked to share a dinner, but one with whose family she would have enjoyed spending a summer. She thought him "a pleasant man . . . witty and wise and tolerant and kind."[80] She admired his optimism, his warmth and gaiety; she appreciated his desire to surround himself with friends and to open his house to them. She wrote admiringly: "He was intelligent, he believed in intelligence, and intelligence for Chekhov meant that you called a spade a spade: laziness was simply not working; too much drink was drunkenness; whoring had nothing to do with love; health was when you felt good and brocaded words could not cover emptiness or pretensions or waste."[81]

More poignantly, Hellman seems to have imagined herself in a parallel moment in time: a moment when the demeanor and stance of intellectuals had become unclear. She describes Chekhov as living in a place where "the scenery had gone hog wild," where "men lay preaching gibberish to each other in the mud" or "screamed men down in Moscow and St. Petersburg with anti-Orthodox reason that sounded very like Orthodox prayers."[82] Under these circumstances, she admired his ability to keep his head, to act on principle. Despite the chaos, she thought of Chekhov as "a man of sense, of common sense," as someone who "tried to see things as they were and to deal with them as he saw them."[83]

The words capture an aching sense of how she wished intellectuals might behave in her own time. In her notes, she commented that Chekhov "was not a political man, or a radical," but he was "a social man, and a deeply responsible one."[84] Though his friends took more active revolutionary roles than he did, she cautioned that judgment "depends on where you're standing. For our conservative, frightened days, he did remarkable and daring things." He visited a prison camp in Siberia; sheltered Gorky, who was then under police surveillance; broke with his best friend over the Dreyfus affair; "and over and over again he gave money and shelter to men of revolutionary activity." And then the telltale identification: "One has a difficult time today trying to think of writers who would do any one of these dangerous deeds, and who would not be considered dangerous by doing so." Here was the pain at the betrayals, the anger at the weak-minded, the longing for support that she did not again articulate until she wrote about her Cold War experience in *Scoundrel Time*.

Hellman's struggles tell us something about the problem of continuing to write serious plays (or do serious art) in an ideologically divided world. Her 1956 stage adaptation of Voltaire's *Candide* is a case in point. Before she took on *Candide*, she toyed with the idea of adapting Emile Zola's *Germinal* to the stage. She was attracted by the story of a failed strike among coal miners in a small French village, and its horrendous consequences in terms of human life and family relationships. In some respects Zola's chronicling of the effects of capitalism on the family history of the Second French Empire is not dissimilar to Hellman's much narrower look at the South in the period of *Another Part of the Forest*. As one critic noted, for the 1950s, *Germinal* was perhaps too direct a statement about "the conflict between the forces of modern Capitalism and the interests of human beings necessary to its advance."[85]

Hellman dropped the idea of *Germinal* when the rising young composer and conductor Leonard Bernstein agreed to work with her on the more universally critical *Candide*. The project excited Lillian in a way that nothing had for a while, but ever after she regretted her involvement. A satire on efforts to construct an ideal world and a parody on the folly of optimism in the face of malevolent self-interest, *Candide* seemed especially germane at the height of the McCarthy period. Hellman at first imagined that Bernstein would do no more than compose incidental and transitional music. But Bernstein had other thoughts. He wanted to write the music for an operetta based on her adaptation, and Hellman wanted so much to please that, for one of the few times in her life, she gave way to every demand to add, reshape, and rewrite the story she had conceived. Unfamiliar with the genre of musical theater and awed by Bernstein's musical creativity, she responded with unusual alacrity to requests for changes in the script and in the direction of the plot. The process, and the final production, turned into a mess and confused audiences who sat through its three-and-a-half-hour duration.

Voltaire's bitter satire on optimism—his critique of the possibilities posed by imagining that one lived in the best of all possible worlds, and his insistence that greed and bigotry were part of human character— constituted a perfect foil in an America convinced that its particular view of freedom had no parallel, immersed in the contest to prove capitalism the best possible economic system. Hellman said as much just a few years later when she told an interviewer, "I think this is a great period of self-deception. We've wanted to think of ourselves as the best and kindest and most generous and most moral and most middle-class and most split-level and most wall-to-wall-carpeting people that ever existed, and anything that intruded on that tranquil self-regard was castigated or ignored."[86] Hellman's *Candide* is the story of a young man, ousted from a home that he imagines the best of all possible places, who sets off on a journey to find the perfect place to live. Alas, there are no perfect worlds, Hellman tells us, insisting that we must turn to our own soil, make the place we live as good as we can. Along the way, the play declared skepticism of faith in any form and repeatedly revealed her disillusionment with 1950s America. Her version revealed the seamy side behind every image of perfection, emphasizing the stupidity, corruption, venality, and ideological blinders that Candide encountered at every turn. In a memorable scene, removed from the final text, Hellman parodied the hearings in which Joseph McCarthy and others were then engaged. "Were you ever," asked inquisitors dressed like churchmen, "or have you ever been, or intend to be, or once were, or even thought of being a member, participant, or affiliate of any group, bund, klan, club or scout troop that advocated the violent overthrow of the earth's crust?"[87]

Though Hellman loved the possibility of enhancing *Candide*'s satirical thrust by framing it as an operetta from Bernstein's talented pen, she quickly learned that the music also defused the satire: the show lacked the power that she had written into her treatment. Working on *Candide* affirmed Hellman's skepticism about artistic collaboration. Indeed, she came to hold collaboration responsible for undermining the integrity of not only this play but of playwrights in general. Affirming her early convictions about the need to stick to her own instincts, she insisted that collaboration on *Candide* led to a weak plot structure. John La Touche, the original lyricist, died before he could finish the job. Hellman called on her friends, Dorothy Parker among others, to produce lyrics to accompany the still unfinished score. She herself wrote the lyrics to one tune. But the music, which Hellman had originally imagined as merely interstitial, drove the narrative.

Eager to find a lyricist who could convey her sensibilities, Hellman turned to the poet Richard Wilbur, with whom she worked closely through 1955 and into 1956. It was not enough. Wilbur entered the scene too late to do more than seal the disjunctures exposed by brilliant music that did not carry Hellman's meaning. Hellman, called on again and again to alter a line or a word in order to meet the musical demand, found herself desperately patching things up. In the end, she believed that "the deep collaboration being practiced today robs a play of individual force. Three or four people cannot collaboratively make a serious piece of writing. There's no such thing as art by democratic majority."[88] Much later she admitted the pain that she felt at the compromises she made. "It took me a year or two after the failure of *Candide* to understand that it was truly not my nature, that I must never go through it again."[89]

When the operetta opened on December 1, 1956, its satire seemed tame, the story without punch. Candide's search seemed silly, his optimism unquenchable, his decision to cultivate his own garden conveying defeat rather than the informed engagement that Voltaire advocated and Hellman hoped to capture. Mary McCarthy, then writing theater criticism for the *New Republic*, called the operetta a failure of nerve in which "anything in the original . . . that could give offense to anyone has been removed."[90] Hellman might have agreed. Overshadowed by the biting wit of the successful off-Broadway production of *The Threepenny Opera* that had opened just months before, *Candide* seemed no more than an evening's entertainment and not serious theater at all. When Bernstein's *West Side Story* opened just a few months later, *Candide* was eclipsed.

Hellman shifted gears with *Toys in the Attic*, which opened in February 1960, and to some extent she succeeded. The play returned her to a familiar setting in New Orleans around 1912; this time it echoed her father's family history. It features two sisters eager to maintain their attachment to a newly married, beloved younger brother who has long been dependent on them but is now on the verge of a shadowy success. Written in a Chekhovian style, it explores the relationships among the three siblings without attributing villainy to any of them. And it offers, unusually for Hellman, compassionate empathy toward those caught in the turmoil of change. Its most famous line has the ring of a universal truth: "I guess most of us make up things we want, don't get them, and get too old, or too lazy to make up new ones."[91] But in the end Hellman could not resist resolving the action with an act of violence that brought the drama to a head. The play judged by some to be her best—"her first

1960: Hellman with Kermit Bloomgarden and Arthur Penn, watching a re-hearsal of Toys in the Attic. *(Photofest)*

play to combine all her earlier virtues with compassion, truth, detach-ment, and tremendous dramatic power," said critic Jacob Adler—was seen by others as mediocre.[92] It felt imitative of O'Neill, whose ability to capture irrational family dynamics far exceeded hers. It did not capture the languid feel of the south as Tennessee Williams did, nor its subterra-nean and sporadic violence. And it was not innovative in the mode of the newly popular Beckett and Pinter. Critics accused her of returning to her melodramatic roots in order to appeal to audiences.

Hellman was now in her mid-fifties, talking repeatedly not about her own failures but about the failures of the theater to live up to its promise and her expectations. She turned to a novel by Burt Blechman, which focused on the transformations within the Eastern European Jewish family as it moved into middle-class America. Blechman, whose family had more or less followed this path, captured the movement with sar-donic humor and empathetic prose. But Hellman had little insight into that process. She turned her characters into caricatures, each of them a foil for her anger. The weak and distant father, the overconsuming and silly mother, the visionary grandmother, the teenage son who had no spark of purpose in his life—all of them became a mockery of a community striving to become American. The play fell far short of her other work. *My Mother, My Father and Me* opened on March 23, 1963; it closed after seventeen performances. Hellman blamed a New York newspaper strike and the consequent lack of publicity for its failure. But even sympathetic critics thought otherwise. "Every playwright earns the right to a lapse of the typewriter," wrote Walter Kerr, who thought the play failed "because she was trying something new."[93] Hellman put down her playwriting pen.

It was not fear but something else that drove Hellman out of the theater. Perhaps it was her slowly increasing sense of marginality as the fifties gave way to the sixties. In 1961, when she was asked to speak about her work or to lecture on theater, she was already saying that "the drama as such is not truly my subject."[94] She would repeat that refrain on many lecture platforms, sometimes expanding it to insist that she had always felt uncomfortable in the theater, or, "I don't think my nature ever fit too well with it." Occasionally she would respond to questions about drama with "That's not my subject but that won't stop me from speaking."[95] There was a wall between her and the theater, she told one interviewer, "which has always been there, which I cannot explain and which has widened with time." It's a nice world, "full of charming and gay and witty and generous people," she continued, "but like all small worlds, it's a very small one, and it's a vain one."[96] She had felt this for many years, aligning herself with Chekhov in that respect. She had, after all, written about him that he had no illusions about the theater, and "neither did Shaw or Ibsen—no sentimental stuff about its glamour."[97]

Then there was the question of money. She believed that the commercial theater had pushed writers to orient their work toward subjects that promised high earnings. The 1960s emphasis on "aloneness," was, she thought, "the surest buck of all."[98] After *Watch on the Rhine*, she would say, "the theatre, like the rest of the country, became expensive, earnest and conservative." She came to believe that to meet the needs of the commercial theater, the writer had to sacrifice too much. "It's a case of wanting, at the same time, a large sounding thing called integrity, and a large amount of money," she told an interviewer. "Sometimes they go together, thank God, but sometimes they don't."[99] She blamed the endemic problem of resources, not her own pen, for the final failure of *My*

Mother, My Father and Me. It was a good play, she thought, that ultimately might have found its audience had not a New York newspaper strike kept the play in Boston until the producers ran out of money. This was a line that she continued to tout: "I left the theatre," she told an interviewer, "because the fun ran out and the raw-money stuff came in."[100] The Broadway audience today, she added at another point, "is mainly an expense account audience for something somebody tells them is stylish. There's very little place for straight drama now, very few of them can succeed, and then it's make it fast or fail overnight."[101]

Hellman never attributed her success in the theater, or her withdrawal from it, to her position as a woman in a man's world. She refused to imagine that she had made it in the theater either because of or despite her sex. And yet her success, along with the negative commentary that followed her, depended in part on her willingness, as a woman, to express her anger, throw tantrums, use forceful language, eschew sentimentality. The sense that she was being treated as a woman—her work measured by its author's gender as much as her skill—could not have escaped Hellman, yet she would not acknowledge that she had ever been subject to discrimination. Nor did she concede that being a woman who wrote for the theater posed any particular structural difficulties. While other female playwrights, in the thirties and later, cited the demands of family and children as hindrances, and some spoke wistfully of needing to choose between love and writing, Hellman publicly proclaimed the theater to be fair to women.[102] Asked why there had been so few women playwrights, she replied, "I just don't know . . . I don't know since women make quite good writers in other fields and certainly write a great deal in other fields. There's certainly no barrier to women in the theater."[103]

But the principal source of Hellman's alienation from the theater surely arose from a change in the subject matter and staging of plays. Fifties audiences turned away from the sometimes painful realism of the first half of the century to embrace more abstract approaches that explored the human condition. By the sixties, she declared "a sense of sadness about my not understanding the theatre anymore." She could not shake the conviction that drama was no longer directed at saying what was "right." Rather, she thought that writers had turned toward two themes for which she had little but contempt: aloneness and love. "The great answer of our time," she said of these words dismissively. "The idiot word nobody bothers to define." She thought they came straight out of "ten-cent store Freud" and laughed that "the discovery that all of us are, finally, alone, must have been made by the first ape as he stood up to look over his shoulder."[104]

Hellman's style of playwriting, as she was the first to acknowledge, had passed by. "Ibsen goes and Ionesco comes. Ionesco goes and Ibsen returns," she wrote somewhat cynically, at the same time admiring the work of Brecht, Beckett, and Harold Pinter, who held the day with their disorderly social commentary, their refusal to plot.[105] She was, she tells us, "caught between a so-called realistic theater and a so-called new theater coming after the Second World War, the theater of the absurd, the theater of the imagination, whatever words one has for it."[106] After seeing Beckett's *Endgame*, she reported that "The play is too consciously odd for me." But then she added that it had qualities she admired: "it was sharp, and hard-hitting, and funny, and gay."[107] By comparison, Hellman's work, as critic Jacob Adler concluded, seemed "too limited in theme and attitude for general or permanent value."[108] She lacked Arthur Miller's capacity to place contemporary disagreements in a universal context, or to adapt the social-realist vocabulary to a looser and less didactic frame.

The well-made play had gone out of fashion, become a phrase of disparagement. If such plays had earlier attracted a modicum of respect, as Ibsen's did, for example, to describe a play as well-made in the sixties bordered on insult, implying the limited competence of its author, a lack of creativity. "In our new state of mind," wrote critic Walter Kerr, who admired Hellman enormously, "we distrust what is orderly because we are now sharply aware that in everything ordered there is something extremely arbitrary. To have an order of any kind—political, religious, social, domestic—some of the things embraced must be arbitrarily embraced, whether they quite suit us or not."[109] Kerr offered a laudatory assessment of a 1967 revival of *The Little Foxes*, arguing that it "reminded us very, very clearly of what it was like to have material fully organized for us. Miss Hellman had known exactly what she was doing every step of the way as she slipped into place just those character traits, just those lines, just those decisive gestures that would build a trim dramatic house." But even as Kerr wrote in 1968, he understood that those days were gone.

So did Hellman. At the invitation of the organizers, she went to Edinburgh in 1963 to participate in a four-day conference on the state of drama. One boring afternoon she encountered Mary McCarthy returning from a session, and, as if foreseeing the future, begged her agent to find a way "to relieve her from the stunning smile of Miss McCarthy." Returning to

New York, she wrote a piece for the *New York Review of Books* tellingly called "Scotch on the Rocks" in which she let out her feelings not only about the conference but about the state of the theater. The conference itself was "timid and dull," she wrote: "People who might have talked seriously among themselves" played to the cameras.[110] Others spent time explaining themselves—an exercise she thought pretty useless. Finally, she concluded with a stab at "that fashionable disease which caused the conference to come out in a rash—the need of the well established to be anti-established, the belief that to question the work of the avant garde is to be square . . . I think the same thing has become true of the theater as in painting—the avant garde has met and embraced the Establishment. Now it's all just fashions."[111]

But if Hellman recognized that something new was happening in the theater, she did not know how to address it. Instead, in the changing political climate of the 1960s, she found new audiences and new popularity among young people committed to challenging authority, supporting civil rights for African-Americans, and opposing an escalating war in Vietnam. In 1967, Mike Nichols undertook a major new production of *The Little Foxes* that burnished Hellman's reputation and revivified her image. But the production regenerated questions of art and politics. This time the attack came from some of Hellman's former friends in New York literary circles and signaled a reignited warfare between left-wing anticommunists and the remnants of the old left.

Elizabeth Hardwick, once close to Hellman and herself a southerner, led the charge, condemning Hellman for failing to do justice to the complicated questions of who might benefit from industrializing the South. This, wrote Hardwick, "is an idea of great interest, and in Lillian Hellman's failure to do justice to its complications so much about our theater and our left-wing popular writers of the Thirties is revealed." Hardwick then went on to damn Hellman's plays in general. They included lines reminiscent of popular movies written by leftists of the thirties and designed to articulate the author's political beliefs rather than illuminate difficult issues. They resorted to a "craftsmanship of climaxes and curtain lines and discoveries" designed to ensure commercial success rather than intellectual profit. In a ringing conclusion, Hardwick condemned Hellman for squeezing her characters to death between "the iron of an American version of Socialist Realism and the gold of a reigning commercialism."[112] A flurry of accusations and denials about the personal nature of the argument ensued. But Hardwick's dagger struck deep, damaging Hellman's reputation as a writer with something serious to say. In the world of the literati, a wounded Hellman appeared as merely middlebrow—a woman with a "torn spirit" who vacillated between "the bright stuffs of expensive productions and the hair-shirt of didacticism."[113]

CHAPTER 7

A Self-Made Woman

No man but a blockhead ever wrote, except for money.
—*James Boswell*, Life of Samuel Johnson

I do not believe in giving away the work by which one lives.
—*Lillian Hellman, 1946*

Work hard enough and you are bound to get rich.
—*Lillian Hellman, note to self*

Lillian Hellman was born not exactly poor, but poor enough to see herself as an outcast in her mother's wealthy family. She died with enough money to endow a trust fund for the benefit of persecuted writers and to contribute to the support of her good friend Peter Feibleman for the rest of his life. In between she mostly made her own way, earning her living as a writer for the theater and for the cinema and as an occasional journalist. She worked hard, invested well, and lived comfortably: an apartment in a fashionable section of New York City, a house in the country or on the island of Martha's Vineyard, where she could enjoy the sea she loved. She was well cared for by an array of servants who generally included caretakers for her homes, a cook, a housekeeper, and a secretary, as well as additional help when she needed it and as she aged. She traveled widely and well—sometimes on assignments of one sort or another, but often for the pleasure of the trip. She was famous—some might say infamous—for half of her life, a celebrity in every sense.

This picture might not be unusual were its subject male. But Lillian Hellman was a female who had neither inherited nor married into wealth. She was certainly not the first or only woman of her generation to rise by her own efforts. Actress and movie producer Mary Pickford, writer Fannie Hurst, and cosmetics entrepreneur Madam C. J. Walker all come immediately to mind. But Hellman's money and lifestyle generated more comment than most. Had she been a male, she would have been perceived as the archetype of the American dream. But she was a female who prospered because she adopted what was, in the mid-twentieth century, a decidedly transgressive gender role. As she aimed to live by her own standards of desire, so she sought to construct an economically self-sufficient life for herself. She paid attention to how much she earned, managed her resources carefully, counted and kept track of her assets. These qualities fit public expectations of an upwardly mobile male. But the casual onlooker, observing these qualities in a female, accounted them tightfisted, miserly, penny-pinching. To that onlooker, Hellman's lifelong financial vigilance seemed decidedly unwomanly. It generated pejorative adjectives like *grasping* and *greedy*. Hellman's daily involvement with the details of her financial affairs seems at first glance to justify the negative adjectives and even to border on hypocrisy. Her accumulated creature comforts, including expensive jewelry, fur coats, and beachfront houses, seemed to contradict her commitments to social justice in a fairer, more equitable society. But another glance suggests something of a paradox. Hellman's moral outlook (and the focus of some of her plays) centered on the corruption of money. But to live as an independent woman required her to pay close attention to the very thing she found corrupting.

Peter Feibleman attributes Hellman's relationship to money to the New Orleans experience: "She was scared of poverty," he thought, because she didn't have either looks or money as a child. She had "a contempt of the rich and an admiration of them, a contempt for money and a desire to have it."[1] But there was something else. The contradiction tells us something about how Hellman arranged her life. To live as an independent writer required financial resources. Yet, as her plays repeatedly suggested, Hellman believed that money inspired human corruption. The challenge of earning large quantities of money and remaining true to herself became

Hellman's test. We are able to reconstruct how she met the challenge by reassembling some of the legal and other documents she left behind. These might help up to understand just what a remarkable achievement it was for an unmarried woman, and a writer at that, to accumulate a small fortune without relying on family money or male support. Reading between the lines of these documents, we see not only the measure of the achievement but something of the price she paid as her personality altered to accommodate her complicated aspirations.

Hellman came to maturity in a generation when more and more women went out to work, to be sure, but when the idea of an ambitious and economically independent woman still stirred as much animosity as curiosity. To earn her living as a writer and to achieve recognition on the Broadway stage as the author of serious plays—and in Hollywood as a significant scriptwriter—required a range of qualities generally considered in the early and mid-twentieth century to be the province of men. These included a robust vocational commitment, the capacity to identify as a worker who made a living by the pen, and the self-confidence that she had something to say to the larger world. But those alone would not be enough. To sustain and ensure success, Hellman would need not only a strong voice but a forceful and demanding persona. She would need, as Feibleman put it, to make her own opportunity as a playwright to compete in a world with men.[2] As she learned to exercise these attributes, she adopted a style of public behavior that seemed a travesty of womanhood. Her reputation as an angry woman—aggressive, controlling, and rude—preceded her. Admired as a writer, she became the subject of humor and parody.

At the same time, this difficult woman accumulated the financial resources that permitted her to exercise a quintessentially female role. Those who encountered Hellman in the thirties often expressed surprise at how feminine she appeared. Her designer clothes, her gracious manners, her slim and carefully crossed ankles, the tea rose perfume all suggested a softer, more generous, and kinder persona than her public image allowed. The money Hellman earned provided the temptingly cozy environments where she entertained friends and relations in graceful style, spaces that one friend described as "elegantly furnished, but . . . comfortable."[3] Money also enabled her to affirm her principles through the generous help she could give to causes she cared about. And when the time came, her money provided for her ill father, for her dying friend

Dashiell Hammett, and for her own physical needs as she herself grew
older and sicker.

Like the hero of any Horatio Alger story, Hellman accumulated her
wealth through luck, pluck, and hard work. In the late twenties and early
thirties, when her own income was sporadic and she was still a young
adult, she relied on her husband, Arthur Kober, and then on Dashiell
Hammett. The first significant sums she earned came from the successful run of The Children's Hour in 1934 and from the lucrative employment
in Hollywood that followed it. Lillian was familiar with the Hollywood
scene, having worked as a reader before the success of The Children's Hour.
She returned afterward to work on the movie script that became These
Three, then accepted an offer from Samuel Goldwyn to write the script
for The Dark Angel. Goldwyn, pleased at her success and convinced of
her ability, offered to put her under a long-term contract. Hellman portrays this negotiation in Pentimento as an act of courtship: she enticed
Goldwyn to chase after her by disappearing to Paris. When he finally
tracked her down, he offered her "a contract with a fine clause about doing nothing but stories I liked and doing them where and when I liked. I
had become valuable to Mr. Goldwyn because I had left him for reasons he
didn't understand. For many years that made me an unattainable woman,
as desirable as such women are, in another context, for men who like them
that way."[4] The contract she finally negotiated with Goldwyn allowed her
to write two films of her own choosing per year, over a three-year period.
She would be expected to live in Hollywood during the ten-week writing
period set aside for each film, and she would be paid the then astonish-
ingly high sum of $2,500 for each working week. Writing and living in
Hollywood had its drawbacks, of course, but it not only paid very well
and regularly, it was good training.

Hellman tells us that she squandered the money she earned on drink
and parties. She called these the "wild fat" years. Perhaps. But it was in
this period that she moved from the second-class hotels and furnished
rooms in which she had been living to take up more comfortable quarters in various sublet apartments and residence hotels. She lived off and
on with Hammett, generally in apartment hotels, sometimes escaping to
more isolated places to write and occasionally creating a home at more
elegant residences such as the St. Moritz and the Plaza. By the late thirties she had begun to live well. When she traveled west by train, she oc-

cupied drawing rooms rather than sleeping compartments, or she chose to fly on the newly scheduled airlines. On the West Coast, she stayed with Hammett in rooms he took at the Beverly Wilshire Hotel. There, he notoriously partied and drank until he was out of money, then hid away until someone bailed him out or his next check came.

For all her success in Hollywood, Hellman remained contemptuous of it as a place to live and could not stay there for any length of time. Hammett often engaged in his most flagrant alcoholic binges there and gave vent to his most outrageous sexual and social behavior. By habit, he invited young women to his rooms, where they remained for days until his money gave way and his alcoholic haze lifted. Undoubtedly Hammett's free-spending ways contributed to Hellman's perception that Hollywood "stands as the most preposterous civilization of all time." But she objected as well to its flaunting of money. She could not bear "the elaborate and pretentious dinner parties" given by the film people. "You find yourself twelve at table with twelve footmen and two majordomos," she explained to one interviewer, "and then food that you'd throw right back at the counterman in a dairy lunch is set before you with fancy gestures and on gold plate."[5] Yet the commute had its benefits: she earned enough money in Hollywood to support a bicoastal life style, and she enjoyed the glamour that rubbed off on her through association with the famous and the powerful. Despite her protests about spending too freely, she lived extravagantly, and mostly in hotels. "Anybody's a fool who doesn't live in a hotel," she wrote to Arthur Kober around this time, "and me—I'm going right back to the Plaza where everything comes up in a silver service elaborate enough for royalty."[6] She was living there when she signed the contract for *The Little Foxes* in December 1938.

The Little Foxes turned into a big hit that enabled her to put a down payment on the 130-acre farm in Pleasantville, New York, that she called Hardscrabble. With a little financial help from Max Hellman and some from Hammett, she closed on the farm on June 1, 1939, and after a period of renovation, moved in the following May.[7] The farm, bought in her name alone, turned out to be everything she had hoped. In the light, airy rooms of the old house, she wrote five of her plays, following a rigorous work schedule that involved several hours at her desk in the morning, staying away from visitors until after lunch, and often returning to work in the late afternoons and evenings.

From Pleasantville, where Hellman and Hammett lived for thirteen years, it took just an hour and a half to drive to New York City. Hellman

The farm turned out to be everything she had hoped. With Hammett about 1949. (Eileen Darby)

kept a car (a Cadillac after the war) to get back and forth and never gave up on urban life. She sublet apartments—often very elegant ones like the one she occupied on the third floor of the Henry Clews house at 27 West 51st Street. Small though it was (two rooms and a kitchen and bath), the Clews house was a distinguished, mansion that added luster to Hellman's name. She moved from the Clews house in November 1941 to a somewhat larger space at 5 East 82nd Street, just off 5th Avenue. Three years later, she purchased a graceful Georgian townhouse at 63 East 82nd Street for $15,000 down and a $33,000 mortgage. She was not yet forty years old and the owner of two spacious homes, each of them bought with income she earned as a writer. The new house was just two blocks from the Metropolitan Museum of Art and in the heart of the fashionable Upper East Side that she loved. The house featured a duplex that she rented out, a triplex for her own use, a basement apartment for a resident superintendent, and two sixth-floor maid's rooms.

She purchased a graceful Georgian townhouse. (Photo by Alice Kessler-Harris)

Sixty-three East 82nd Street was not just a house purchase but a carefully explored and managed investment: Hellman first considered a partnership with the house's current owners, then asked her accountant to carefully calculate the costs and benefits of various other ownership strategies, including the lost income from other investments, the price of her own rent, and the operating expenses of the house. She subsequently invested $16,000 to renovate the plumbing and two kitchens and to install a passenger elevator. Much of the renovation was completed and supervised in Hellman's absence: she was in Moscow during the winter of 1944–45. By the time she returned in March, her apartment was ready for occupancy, and the upper two and a half floors (containing ten rooms, three baths, and a private terrace) had been rented "at a very satisfactory figure," as her lawyer, Stanley Isaacs, informed her.[8] Her lawyers successfully appealed the assessment of the house in order to lower the property taxes while raising the ceiling on the rent she could charge her tenants. Bernard Reis, her accountant, wrapped up the deal by preparing a statement showing how she had come out on the investment. The process beautifully illustrates one of the perquisites of wealth: the ability to purchase the labor of others.

As *The Little Foxes* and *Watch on the Rhine* affirmed her box-office value, Hellman became increasingly prudent in her management of her literary properties and inflexible about the financial remuneration she expected from her work. She agreed to revivals and performances only without changes or cuts of any kind, and almost never to amateur companies. If a proposed performance threatened to detract attention from a new play or draw an audience from a touring company, she often refused. She signed contracts that gave her the right to approve the director and the cast of any revival; if adaptations were necessary for a broadcast version, she wanted the right of approval. She rarely granted permission for anything but a full production of her plays, routinely refusing to permit excerpts from any of her writings to be performed onstage.

Hellman's decisions about whether to grant the rights to perform particular plays rested partially on the amount of her royalty or the payment she could expect, and here she adopted a hardheaded and unsentimental stance. On one memorable occasion, Julian Feibelman, rabbi at Temple Sinai in New Orleans and a good friend of her father's, made a mistake. He scheduled a reading of *Watch on the Rhine* without asking for permission. When the problem was called to his attention, he canceled the reading and wrote to her to apologize. Then he pleaded. Could she see her way clear, he asked, to giving them permission to do just one reading? An audience of fifty, which included her two aunts, had already been assembled. The fifty-cent admission fee would go directly to buy textbooks for poor children in the religious school. Hellman remained adamant. "It is too obvious to need much going into to say that the only way a playwright has of earning a living is to have a paying public come into a theatre, and any time people do come in without paying, he is, of course, being dishonestly cheated." Anyone who decided to read a play without paying royalties was in violation, but that somebody should decide to read a play that was still running in New York was, in her eyes, "the most impertinent I have ever heard of."[9]

If she could be sticky about permissions for idiosyncratic performances, making no exception for friends and relatives, she became positively strident when larger sums were involved. Jack Warner of Warner Bros. learned this to his sorrow when he decided to push back the release of the film version of *Watch on the Rhine*. His company had, despite wartime exigencies, completed the film in a timely fashion. But he didn't want its release to interfere with another Warner Bros. product, a wartime propaganda film called *Mission to Moscow* that was designed to assuage fears of a newly allied Soviet Union. Hellman threw a metaphorical tantrum. She insisted that *Watch on the Rhine* was equally important "and what it has to say should be said now." She had agreed to shut down the successful road tour of *Watch on the Rhine,* she wrote to Warner, "and cost ourselves a good deal of money by doing so . . . because we felt the need of the play's message."[10] Warner's efforts to reassure Lillian that a later opening would be just as lucrative did not allay her feelings of having been slighted. She was, she wrote back, concerned about the money to be sure, but she had willingly sacrificed it "because we believed we had something to say and our financial sacrifices were small in the light of it."[11] There the matter rested until, two months later, Hellman learned that Warner Bros. had scheduled the film to open in the Strand Theatre, an undistinguished and relatively small movie house. Now she was outraged and her temper unconstrained. "By the postponement of the picture, by the way it has been treated, and by the theatre at which it will open, there are few people now who are not convinced that the Warner Brothers believe it to be a minor effort. You will understand that I can only consider this treatment of my play as a violation of the principle on which the contract was originally signed." Bluntly commenting that "this letter, like the last letters, will make no difference to anybody," she announced that she "had looked forward to a future of good years with you people." Now that was over. She never signed another contract with Warner Bros.

Hellman generally defended her efforts to protect her properties as matters of principle coming out of her concern for the rights of all authors. But the record reveals so many arguments over large and small sums of money that we are led to wonder whether her defense obscured simple penny-pinching. Certainly the trivial nature of some of her dealings with *Watch on the Rhine* suggest an unfortunate penchant for haggling. She declined, in 1942, to purchase a ten-dollar audio recording of her acceptance speech when she won the Drama Critics Circle Award for the play because it was "too expensive."[12] She wanted Random House to pay her $250 rather than the $150 they offered to reprint *Watch on the Rhine,* and then settled when Bennett Cerf reluctantly agreed.[13] In 1946, she refused to forgo her royalties on the production of a Japanese version of *Watch on the Rhine* that had lost money because, as she told her agent, "I do not believe in giving away the work by which one lives . . . and I have no

interest in the rehabilitation of displaced Japanese." In her typically blunt
style, she admonished the unlucky man: "I hope you will not think it impertinent of me if I tell you that you are mistaken in recommending to
any writer the waiving of royalties for a commercial production in any
country, but particularly an enemy country."[14]

And yet Hellman could and did surrender her claims when alternative principles appealed to her or garnering payment became too difficult.
During the Second World War, and in support of the troops, she readily
gave permission for Random House to publish a special "Armed Service
Edition" of four of her plays despite the promise of only a tiny share of
the royalties.[15] When she discovered that *Watch on the Rhine* had been
performed, without permission, by the American military in Germany
and Austria, she did not ask for royalties. Rather she insisted that they be
"turned over to the proper officials of the United Jewish Appeal in those
countries."[16] And, in one of her great gestures to principle, she left her
name on *North Star* even when the final film so displeased her that it
caused a permanent breach in her relationship with Sam Goldwyn.

To be fair, she could afford these gestures because the war years—
years when the politics of the nation allied with Hellman's inclinations—
proved politically comfortable and financially lucrative for her. She sold
The Little Foxes to Goldwyn for $75,000 in 1940; she received $150,000
from Warner Bros. for *Watch on the Rhine* in 1941. She and Herman Shumlin set up their own production company to produce the film version of
The Searching Wind in 1944; Lillian owned 60 percent of the stock in this
company, Shumlin 40 percent, and Lillian got 10 percent of the gross weekly
receipts for the run of the play as well.[17] Proudly, she announced to Dash,
on army duty in Alaska, that they had called the company Dashiell Pictures, Inc. It was to be a short-lived affair. Dashiell, Inc, produced an unsuccessful film version of *The Searching Wind* and then folded in a spate
of recriminations between Lillian and Shumlin. But Lillian was now box
office magic. She partnered with Kermit Bloomgarden to produce her
next play, *Another Part of the Forest*, and sold it to Universal Pictures for
$250,000 (of which Bloomgarden got 20 percent) plus a hefty share of box
office receipts.

These sums enabled Hellman to buy two more Manhattan rental
properties, to begin her lifetime habit of investing small sums regularly
in the production of the plays of others, and to accumulate a substantial portfolio of stocks on her own account. She chose her investments

carefully, putting her money in relatively small amounts in individual blue-chip stocks and seeking financial advice from friends as well as professionals. Her largest investment in the forties was in American Telephone and Telegraph (now AT&T), in which she owned four hundred shares.[18]

Hammett, too, was doing well. Though he was not writing fiction, his army service in Alaska restricted his penchant for lavish spending. The royalties from his earlier stories and plays accumulated in accounts over which Hellman held power of attorney. Nancy Bragdon, Hellman's secretary, released small sums for one purpose or another. Hellman chose and sent presents to the people he designated when he asked. For larger amounts, he participated in a game of asking for Hellman's approval. Before he increased the support he provided to his divorced wife and their two children, he wrote to Hellman, suggesting that he wanted to do so. A couple of weeks later, he wrote, "emboldened by your silence I clear my throat again and ask you will you do whatever's necessary to . . . send them—meaning those Hammetts—their millions at the rate of $200 a week instead of at the lower rate hitherto obtaining. Thank you, Ma'am."[19] Hellman punctiliously responded. She did not hesitate to chastise Hammett when she judged that he was spending money frivolously, and she scrupulously deducted from his account the costs of the gifts he asked her to buy for herself. Hammett, for his part, participated in the game by declaring his freedom to defy her wishes—as, for example, when he proposed to invest in war bonds.

That was during the war. At its end, when America's brief friendship with the Soviet Union faded into bitter enmity, Hellman's fortunes faltered. In the war years, her plays, appearances, and appeals drew ready and sympathetic audiences. But in light of a rising fear of Soviet territorial and ideological expansion, these activities no longer seemed admirable. Her services, especially as a scriptwriter, fell out of favor. Presented by Hollywood producers with the opportunity to sign a loyalty oath in 1949, she refused, joining the list of those who would no longer be allowed to work in Hollywood. Her subsequent failure, and Hammett's, to cooperate with government investigating committees affirmed her position as at least a fellow traveler and probably a communist. Shut out of the film industry that had provided much of her income, Hellman began to worry about money.

Income tax investigations added to her troubles. The Federal Bureau of Taxation (to become known as the Internal Revenue Service in 1953) had investigated Hammett in 1950 and found that he owed taxes on his royalties back to 1943. When he got out of jail in 1951, the bureau sent him a bill for back taxes in the range of $100,000. He refused to pay, so the bureau attached all his future income. He was earning something under $5,000 a year at the time, most of it from radio adaptations of his novels and stories.

Hammett now relied fully on Hellman for support. But she too was in trouble. In March 1951, the tax bureau conducted a full-scale investigation of her income. Edith Kean, then her secretary, reported to Hellman after the visit of the inspector. He had asked not only why she needed two studies (one in Pleasantville and one in the city) but wanted a detailed breakdown of the cost of all the furniture in both; he queried her visits to the Soviet Union, France, Czechoslovakia, and England in 1947 and to Yugoslavia in 1948; he challenged her contention that her car, a Cadillac, was used only for business purposes; and he discounted the effort to claim the receipts from *Watch on the Rhine* as capital gains, declaring them taxable as income. But the most devastating questions were around Hellman's claim to losses incurred by the farm. Kean reported his comment verbatim. "Since it has steadily lost for 11 years—and no business could continue such heavy losses for so long—it should be considered as 'gentleman farming' and not a business for profit making."[20] A hefty bill for back taxes now came due.

A classified advertisement, placed in the *New York Times* in August 1951, tells the rest of the story. It also suggests how Hellman (and perhaps other victims of McCarthyism) could conflate the events of those years in ways that could be interpreted as untrue. Hellman always claimed that she put the farm up for sale after her HUAC appearance in May 1952, and in consequence of it. The advertisement tells us that the farm appeared on the market nine months before the HUAC hearing, though almost certainly in consequence of tax inquiries that were more than likely inspired by the political witch hunts for suspected communists and sympathizers. The advertisement read: "130 ACRE ESTATE, Comfortable. Homey. Restored colonial in a fairyland setting of winding lawns and wooded glens . . . As a home this estate is ideal. As an investment for subdivision, it's terrific. $75,000 firm."[21] In the event, Hardscrabble took almost a year to sell and went for $67,500. Hellman forever associated the loss of the farm with her appearance before the House Committee on Un-American Activities. In fact, its sale probably resulted from the more general political climate of the decade. But Hellman might be forgiven this conflation. She moved out of the farm shortly after her May 1952 HUAC appearance.

These postwar years into the early 1950s were surely the most difficult of financial times for Hellman. She made less money and worried about it incessantly. She pawned her jewelry to pay for bail that Hammett would not accept. She tried to make a film in London and refused to understand when her agent told her the deal was off. The unsigned contract in hand, she took off for London in the fall of 1951 and put up at Claridge's in the expectation that her expenses would be covered. Her agent, Kay Brown of MCA Management, futilely protested that Lillian had misunderstood: "As you will recall, I telephoned you and said that Charney said the deal was off."[22] Lillian, still at Claridge's, threatened to sue, backing off only when she received a settlement sufficient to cover her expenses. The sense of untouchability spread to the theater, which had no blacklist. To Joseph Losey, who withdrew a tentative offer to revive *The Children's Hour* in London, she vented her spleen. "I have just found out this morning that our negotiations with you have fallen through, and I feel that I must say that it's a little shocking to me that we went to so much trouble and so much talk for nothing. It's a new experience for me in the theatre, and I don't like it."[23]

Hellman's memories of these years tell us as much about her fears as about her financial circumstances. By her own standards she was broke, but, as her friends Morris and Lore Dickstein would put it later, Lillian's idea of being broke differed from that of ordinary people's.[24] She seems never to have fallen quite as low as her memoirs suggest. Yet she worried incessantly about whether she could continue to support her comfortable lifestyle. To keep body and soul together, she tells us, she turned to Macy's department store for employment. That story is undoubtedly false—though surely she feared that she might have had to resort to selling lingerie to make a living. Though she sold her beloved farm, she continued to live in her East 82nd Street townhouse, to maintain a staff of helpers there, and to invest in theatrical productions in which she believed. She never stopped contributing small sums to an author's investment pool, a practice that she began in 1950 and continued for the next decade and a half. Even when she was in the midst of her 1952 HUAC encounter, she invested $2,500 in Arthur Kober's *Wish You Were Here*. At the time, she had no ready cash at hand, so she asked Arthur Kober to forward the sum for her. She repaid the entire amount at the end of the year.[25] In the fall of 1952, she gave Bloomgarden $1,500 to help finance the Second Play Company production of Arthur Miller's *The Crucible*. Small but steady returns from these investments flowed into her coffers for many years. In 1955, she had enough funds to purchase an old house on Martha's Vineyard. If she was not broke, there is no question that financial worry consumed her, contributing to her irritability.

In the spring of 1953, bedeviled by the government's continuing harassment of both Hammett and Melby and fearful that she would be called once again to testify before HUAC, Hellman sought a European passport. She told Ruth Shipley, the passport officer with whom she frequently dealt, that she was badly in need of the employment that was waiting for her there. Shipley, perhaps sympathetic to Hellman's womanly pleas, acceded. Hellman left in May for what was intended to be a two-month stay during which she meant to complete a film adaptation for Alexander Korda and hoped to sign a contract that would enable her to consult with him about the work. She finished her adaptation in two weeks of relatively relaxed time in Rome, where she "felt the lifting of burdens," and then headed for London to negotiate with Korda about the film. While she was away, she wrote almost daily letters to her then secretary, Lois Fritsch, and she expected daily responses, though she did not always get them. The letters offer an unusually detailed set of insights into Hellman's fever-pitch level of anxiety about her personal affairs as well as about money.[26] And the two often intermingled to reveal the finicky and particular persona for which she was noted.

Send the wool dresses to the cleaners, she instructed Fritsch, but not to the most expensive cleaners "because they are not new. Try asking around for another medium price cleaner."[27] "Those wool dresses may look clean," she reminded Fritsch, "but they are not and shouldn't be put away until they have been cleaned." Her "favorite purple wool coat" could go to the expensive cleaner, and "the tan fur coat hat and muff to Bergdorf." Through Fritsch, Hellman conveyed orders to her housekeeper, Helen, instructing her about every detail of home care while she was gone. She should not wash "the frill around my dressing table . . . It should be cleaned." But she could do the washable blouses herself, rather than send them out, and, by the way, she should not forget to clean all the shoes and pocketbooks as well. Inquiries about money permeated the letters, along with house-hold concerns. "Have we had any money deposited?" she asked in the same breath as she wondered whether Helen had cleaned the servants' rooms and done the necessary repairs of buttons on the clothing left in the closets. "And please send promptly the box office receipts in gross dollars and our royalties."[28]

Concern about money sometimes took the form of inquiries about royalties paid or to be paid and sometimes of queries about deals under discussion or about to be consummated. These sometimes involved pro-ductions like *The Children's Hour*, then on Broadway, and sometimes advice about whether she could afford to take another mortgage. Some-times she asked if there was any income tax news, and sometimes she complained that the income tax people were holding up payments to her accounts for reasons she did not understand. She expressed relief when the money finally did come through, and then concern about whether the political situation would interfere with her capacity to earn money. "I hope nothing happens now. My movie contract could be spoiled and money is needed now for a few new reasons."

And she worried about expenses. While she waited in Rome for Korda to invite her to London and provide a place for her to stay, she com-mented on how expensive Rome was and speculated about moving to a cheaper hotel, determined to live on her expense money and to learn "to take buses, which is an experience." She checked over lists of bills to be paid as Lois sent them to her, indicating which were correct and which she wanted to protest. She berated Lois for allowing her car to remain in an expensive garage instead of driving it up to the home of friends where Dash was then living. "I have seldom felt money so foolishly thrown out as the garage bill," she wrote to her. And, finally, she asked Lois to explain to Helen that she was forced to cut back her hours because "I cannot afford to keep her all summer." Maybe, Hellman suggested to Lois, Helen "would like to come in once a week to clean, overlook apartment." Hellman would certainly want her back in September.[29]

Back home, Hellman turned to earning more of her living from the theater. Adaptations of successful existing plays seemed a promising route, and to them she now turned. Her friend (and the producer of *Montserrat* and *The Autumn Garden*) Kermit Bloomgarden owned the rights to pro-duce an English-language version of *The Lark*, a play by Jean Anouilh based on the life of Joan of Arc. Would she, Bloomgarden asked, write an

English-language adaptation for the American stage? Hellman balked. She badly needed the money, yet there were obstacles. An English adaptation already existed—made by Christopher Fry and performed without great success in London. Bloomgarden disliked the Fry version, as did Lillian when she saw it in London. Three earlier plays of Anouilh's had been presented in New York since 1950, all to mixed reviews and none of them a financial success. If she were to make a success of this one, she would need control over its content. In need of money at the time, Hellman tells us in *Pentimento* that she encouraged Bloomgarden to see if he could work out an arrangement for a new translation that she would then adapt to the American stage.[30]

Bloomgarden got to work. Anouilh's agent, Jan Van Loewen, balked at the idea of having such a famous person do the translation, fearing that his client would lose control of the piece. He proposed that the two writers work together.[31] Hellman backed off a bit. She wrote to Bloomgarden that she feared the idea of working together: "I would rather like to spare myself the problems of arguing with a man about his own play, and I have a suspicion that we would spend more time in being tactful than we would in managing any work."[32] When Bloomgarden persisted, she continued to raise problems, including the rights of the first English translator and who would have final authority over the content. She also demanded a fifty-fifty split of the proceeds and a share of the movie rights should the play be sold to the film industry. Van Loewen balked at these terms—citing, among other things, the question of whether Hellman was "politically acceptable in Hollywood." Lillian reared up in anger, insisting that "this kind of ugliness has not previously happened to me in the theatre."[33] She wrote directly to Anouilh and solicited from him an explanation and something of an apology.

Bloomgarden did not give up. Communicating now directly with Anouilh, he begged for a resolution to the problem, to which Anouilh finally conceded. "I am not opposed to the choice of Miss Hellman for the adaptation," he wrote to Bloomgarden, attributing the discord to his agent's political fears, the origins of which lay "in the working of American film producers." Still, he insisted, in the absence of any knowledge of Lillian Hellman's "style," and without having seen the adaptation, he would not guarantee her share of the movie rights. Finally he offered to return to Bloomgarden the $3,000 paid to option the play for America.[34] Bloomgarden declined the offer to withdraw, and the two compromised by agreeing to give Hellman a share of the movie rights if the play ran for twenty-five days or more on Broadway. Now there were more objections. Anouilh did not want to allow Hellman to publish her adaptation with Random House, claiming that she had agreed to too small an advance ($500 to be split with Anouilh) without informing Anouilh. Belatedly, he disclosed that he had already contracted to publish the Fry version in the United States.[35] Hellman now erupted in anger at Anouilh's bad faith, though she continued to work on the adaptation.

The production that emerged should have satisfied everyone. It earned accolades from reviewers for turning what some thought the weakest of Anouilh's works into a "beautiful production of a thoroughly vigorous play."[36] But the tension around Hellman's English-language version of *The Lark* outlived the aesthetic value of the play that appeared on Broadway. In 1966, a decade after the successful opening of Hellman's translation, Van Loewen gave permission to perform the Fry version; Hellman insisted that only her version could be performed in the United States and declined an offer of compensation. Nothing would persuade her to concede her rights to control the American production. The coup de grâce came nearly twenty years later. Hellman published her account of the episode in *Pentimento*, excoriating Van Loewen and Anouilh for their failure to acknowledge the artistic and financial success she had achieved in adapting *The Lark* to the American stage. Her play, she insisted, had been a critical success in the United States following five failed attempts by Anouilh to crack the American audience. It had made Anouilh a significant sum of money, for which she had received neither thanks nor appreciation. In response, Van Loewen penned a letter that illuminates the gender tensions that had permeated his earlier relations with Hellman. Angry that she was unwilling to acknowledge the defects of her version of *The Lark*, he wrote, "now you force me to a real spanking," and then went on to disavow any need to appreciate an adaptor whose translation was, in his view, inadequate, and who had "mutilated and amputated" a play that "but for its indestructible quality, the brilliance of the production, and of Julie Harris's performance . . . might well have been a failure." Acknowledging that vanity was endemic in writers, he concluded, with a flourish, he had "never encountered such hurt vanity as in your case."[37]

While negotiations proceeded around *The Lark*, Hellman was working on *Candide*, where, once again, she ran into problems of control and remuneration. After *Candide* closed its three-month run, Hellman insisted for artistic reasons that it not be mounted again. She didn't want to work on it anymore and she didn't want anyone else to do so either. But some of the music was magical, and in the world of musicians, Leonard Bernstein's achievement remained alive. Occasionally a two-piano concert version went out—four people sitting on stools, telling the story and singing the score. A decade later, Gordon Davidson, inspired by Maurice Peress, a friend and former assistant conductor of Bernstein's, asked if they might approach Bernstein about doing a version of *Candide* to launch a new theater in Los Angeles.[38] They wanted, Davidson says, to find simple ways to tell stories with good music. *Candide* fit the bill perfectly. Peress brought Davidson to meet Bernstein, and the three agreed to mount a twelve-performance run of the show. With extended narration that was simpler than Hellman's original, this would be not quite a full-scale production yet not exactly a concert version. Bernstein agreed to let them search through his "Pandora's box" of music omitted from the original production. "Don't tell Uncle Lillian," he warned his collaborators, fearing that Hellman would quash the effort.

The modified production that opened for a short run in 1966 was wildly successful. A new song was added strengthening Candide's character; the production caught some of the irony of Voltaire's novel and allowed the music to breathe, turning it, as Davidson says, "into a joyous beggar's opera." Hellman caught wind of it a few months after the event. She wrote asking Gordon Davidson for the script, which, with some trepidation, he sent. He received her answer weeks later. It was not as bad as he had feared. Acknowledging Davidson's talent as director and the success of the production, it went on to declare unequivocally her horror at what had been done to her work. "No-one," she wrote to Davidson, "I repeat, no-one ever changes a word that Lillian Hellman writes."[39]

The incident reveals the stubborn belief that Hellman maintained in herself and in her work. It also suggests her conception of writing as remunerative work on which she depended. Afterward, she tried to work out a way to prevent such changes from ever happening again, or at least from occurring without her knowledge. If *Candide* were to be revived, she told her agent, then not only should "Lennie, Wilbur and myself" have approval of all changes, but "if I disagree with the adaptation of the book, and Lennie should happen to agree . . . that my disagreement will have to stand—or vice versa of course."[40] Bernstein, equally stubborn, refused to give up on his music. He produced another modified version of *Candide* that was performed in Los Angeles in 1971 and then in San Francisco and at the Kennedy Center. This time, Lillian's fury knew no bounds. She had lost control and finally had little choice but to concede that Bernstein's music had a life of its own. He commissioned a new book, by Hugh Wheeler, and she agreed to take her name off any production based on that book. The struggle for control cost her the services of Robby Lantz, her devoted agent for more than a decade, who disagreed with her position in the matter. Surprisingly, it did not cost her the friendship of Leonard Bernstein and his wife, Felicia.[41]

By the late 1950s, Hellman had recouped her financial position. At various times she bought or held mortgages on rental properties in Manhattan (at 77 East 80th Street and 920 Park Avenue as well as 208 West 96th Street) and in Sunnyside, Queens. In addition to her homes in Manhattan and on Martha's Vineyard, she owned stocks and bonds worth around $200,000. She also possessed a considerable amount of expensive jewelry that she kept carefully insured: diamond pins and bracelets, antique necklaces and gold watches, several fur coats and jackets. She valued these at around $20,000.[42] Her home furnishings included expensive antiques and some valuable art objects, paintings, and prints. Together these added up to a reasonable fortune in 1960.

And yet Hellman remained worried about money and alert to opportunities to maximize both wealth and income. This mixture did not produce the best of behavior. She solicited advice from friends like Arthur Cowan, responding gratefully when he extended good advice and irritably when something went wrong. She expressed a sense of entitlement and a willingness to fight for her due, whether it was over a lost will that she was sure should have included her or the right to control Hammett's property because she believed only she could make it profitable. When she feared losing something valuable, she expressed her vulnerability peremptorily, demanding explanations, answers, and detailed accountings about everything.

Some of the most illuminating insights into Hellman's feelings of vulnerability with respect to her possessions come from her dealings with insurance companies. In the late 1950s, as her prosperity mounted, Hellman filed claims for small and large amounts: in 1958, a bathroom leak that damaged a new fur jacket in the closet below; a stolen purse, taken from an L.A. hotel room while she slept. The purse contained a diamond-studded gold powder case, a gold cigarette case, credit cards, and $640 in cash. Detectives found the purse but not the cash. She bought an expensive mink coat in January 1960 that she wanted insured; she lost a diamond pin that spring. Selma Wolfman reported that the pin turned up safely that August. She claimed a loss of several hundred dollars for household items missing, and apparently stolen, from her Vineyard house in the fall of 1961. The lost items included four Wedgwood plates, a rare old platter, six bottles of perfume, two umbrellas, a nutria fur hat, and a blanket. The total amounted to a little more than $500. In April 1962, a branch fell on the house, damaging the heating system; in August an expensive watch, left in full view on the beach when she went swimming, disappeared. Surely the police could be more careful about who they allowed on the beach, she wrote to the town authorities. In September she filed a claim for damages to goods left in storage when she moved from the Mill house to a smaller house on the Vineyard.[43]

The claims added up until they became something of a problem. Her insurance agent struggled year after year to find personal property insurance for her, only to be refused by company after company. Exasperated, she fired the agent only to discover that her new agent ran into the same difficulties.[44] In 1963, her homeowner's insurance on the 82nd Street house was not renewed: "You have presented four separate claims of losses in a three year period," wrote the unfortunate insurance agent who tried to find her a new policy. "Not that any of these claims has been large—but the fact that there have been four in the three years supposedly gives them pause, and makes them apprehensive that in a renewal period of another three years, there may be a big claim."[45] A new policy was finally found. Three years later that, too, was canceled.

Did Hellman set out to cheat insurance companies? In all likelihood, no. Her claims support that child's sense of justice that characterized all her relationships. She had paid for insurance; the losses, however caused and however minor, were real. She wanted the recompense she had paid for. After her 1962–63 debacle with insurance companies, one might think she should have been more careful. But in February 1964 she once again filed a claim. This time it was for an envelope of money ($682) that she had carried with her to a theater performance where she had been jostled, her purse opened, and the envelope taken.[46] The following September she signed a sworn statement claiming that her dressmaker had lost a package containing two expensive suits sent for alternation. She settled the claim for $800. April 1966: she reported items missing from her Vineyard home to her insurance agent—a phonograph, ten to twelve records, a transistor radio, and a Hudson Bay blanket. In July 1968, she left an expensive watch ($800) in her shoe while she went "swimming on my own beach" at the Vineyard. She claimed to have been in the water only three or four minutes. The watch was gone; she had fruitlessly raked the beach in an effort to find it.[47] This was the second such watch she had lost.

From these endlessly repeated, if minor, incidents, we learn something about Hellman's relationship to money that is more than confirmed by larger incidents. One of these had to do with how she handled the Hammett estate. When Dashiell Hammett died in January 1961, he was without resources. Lillian had supported him and paid his medical bills in the last years of his life. She estimated the cost of her support at around $40,000. In his will, Hammett named Hellman his literary executor. He divided his estate: half to daughter Josephine, one quarter to daughter Mary, and one quarter to Lillian. Then the Internal Revenue Service confiscated the entire estate in payment of back taxes. Hammett, the government claimed, owed them $163,000; New York State demanded another $10,445. Hellman offered the government $5,000 to clear the debt, which was politely refused in favor of a public sale of the assets. At auction Lillian's close friend Arthur Cowan bought the entire estate for $5,000, then gifted it to her. Lillian thus came into full ownership of Hammett's literary properties.[48]

At the time, the estate wasn't worth very much, producing by Lillian's estimate less than $500 a year in revenue. Copyrights had not been renewed, the work had not been managed well, Hammett's fiction had gone out of style. Lillian took on the task of revivifying the properties with a vengeance, paying attention to the work as if it were her own, fiercely guarding access to the property. Under her guiding hand, helped no doubt by the revival of the hard-boiled-detective-and-tough-dame style that Hammett had originated, the estate flourished. Hellman controlled Hammett's legacy tightly, asking not only for generous fees but also for the right of approval—and doing so with an air of entitlement for which some of her critics never forgave her. She turned down a 1969 movie offer of $500 for Hammett's story "Corkscrew," which she found "almost insulting," writing to her agent, "I've thought up a quite good answer, I think. Why don't you call him and say that I'll give him an option on the story for $500 if he'll give me an option on his restaurant for $500." Lillian had in mind a figure of $5,000 to option the story and $25,000 if they decided to produce it.[49] She maintained control till the end of her days, agreeing to cooperate with those who wanted to film, dramatize, or adapt Hammett's work only if she were given rights of approval. Additionally, as her agent wrote to one ultimately disappointed British television producer, "I am reasonably sure she would want financial recompense for such help."[50]

The Hammett daughters, Mary and Josephine, were at first taken aback by Hellman's possession of their father's assets but quickly came to understand that without Hellman the estate would have been worth little. Once the estate began to make money in the seventies, Hellman occasionally doled out a share of the proceeds to each of the daughters, with the lion's share going to Josephine, as Hammett had willed. Because, Lillian told them, she paid high taxes on the income earned by the estate, she kept a good portion for herself. When she died, she willed half of the income from the now-profitable estate to Josephine, Hammett's surviving daughter. The other half, including some of the profits she had derived from Hammett's work over the years, went to a trust fund in Hammett's name. The property itself remained under the control of literary executors she appointed. Money and control both entered into these arrangements. Unsurprisingly, Josephine Hammett did not resist them, although she expressed both gratitude for Hellman's successful management of her father's affairs and anger at the rigid control involved.

Hellman's adventures with Hammett's literary properties fueled suspicions of her as a greedy woman. And although much in her behavior confirms the description, she must, after Hammett's death in 1961, have felt herself truly alone. Her penchant to go after money reached a low level during her unsuccessful effort to acquire a share of Arthur Cowan's estate. She was sure that Cowan, a rich Philadelphia lawyer and sometime lover who had been her financial adviser for several years, had left her the bulk of his estate. He had, she claimed, talked all through the years about his will and "made constant jokes about what a rich woman I would be if he died."[51] When he died unexpectedly in 1964, she found letters from Cowan that corroborated her claims: one offering to start a portfolio of stock in both their names and to leave his half to her; another promising to do nothing to "diminish your share (the lioness' that is) of my estate—which by the way is something one should enjoy while alive."[52] And she insisted that her secretary could confirm her expectations. To no avail. The will could not be found. Hellman suspected the family had destroyed it.[53]

Still destined to make her own living, discouraged by the theater and disillusioned by the movies that no longer blacklisted her, Hellman found herself by the early sixties in need of substantial income to retain her comfortable lifestyle. She turned to making money in other ways. Surprisingly, she discovered that she liked to teach. Just before Hammett died, she accepted an appointment at Harvard for the spring of 1961. She went to Cambridge alone. She found the appointment satisfying—good for her ego as well as for her pocketbook. Living in a university residence normally occupied by her friend Archibald MacLeish, accompanied by her cook and housekeeper Helen Richardson, she socialized with students as well as with her distinguished colleagues. This was the first of a series of residencies at some of the nation's most prestigious universities: Yale in 1966, MIT and Harvard again in 1968, Berkeley and MIT in 1971, Hunter College in 1972. At Berkeley she earned $9,000 a quarter to teach one class and deliver one public lecture. That sum equaled the annual salary of a beginning assistant professor at the time. At Hunter, she earned $35,000 for a semester as a distinguished professor—a salary that raised some eyebrows.

This was heady stuff and Hellman thrived on it, using every opportunity to enhance her income. She was not above accepting small commissions—$700, for example, from an advertising agency to prepare five comments of one hundred words each on women's dress styles.[54] She would not go

1961: She discovered that she liked to teach. With Harvard students Robert Thurman, Peter Benchley, Charles Hart, Matthew Zion, and Frederick Gardner. (Photofest)

to speak at Iowa State University for a fee she considered too low. "Miss Hellman thinks it should be $1,200 or $1,500 whatever you think. She gets many of these offers to speak and usually turns them down," her secretary wrote to Robby Lantz. "But she may do this one if they pay more."[55] Nor would she participate at a symposium organized by *Esquire* magazine for the paltry sum of $500. "How would you like to tell them that $1,500 is the price?" she wrote to Robby Lantz, who promptly did.[56] Sometimes her requests to Lantz were crude: "What do you think about this?" she wrote to Lantz of one request. "Should I do it, or should you ask the guy how much money I get for doing it."[57]

Journalism provided something of an outlet, and in 1963 Hellman worked out an arrangement with *Ladies' Home Journal* to publish three pieces "on anything I wanted to do anywhere, with expenses paid, etc." Hellman anticipated a $5,000 fee for each piece, "a good arrangement for me because I, Saturday night, turned down a great deal of money" for a movie script. Editor Caskie Stinnett sent her to Israel to cover the pope's visit there, and to Washington to cover Martin Luther King's 1963 March on Poverty.[58] Robby Lantz, Hellman's agent, carefully negotiated the terms under which the pieces would be written. As Lantz wrote to Stinnett on signing the contract, Hellman was "particularly happy at your confirmation of the fact that no cuts or changes in Miss Hellman's material will be made without her prior express approval."[59]

By the mid-sixties, with the McCarthy period well behind her and the political activism of the civil rights movement and the New Left under way, Hellman's star once again rose. Requests for rights to perform her plays in both the United States and foreign countries poured in: *The Children's Hour* in Austria in 1966, Dresden in 1967; an Italian edition of her plays and a festival of five of her plays in Italy in 1967; *The Little Foxes* in Prague in '67; a radio production of *The Little Foxes* and *Another Part of the Forest* in Norway on December 31, 1968. The BBC inquired whether it could do *Another Part of the Forest* as well on March 28, 1960. In the United States, Hellman's popularity mounted and with it her celebrity status. A Caedmon recording of *The Little Foxes* succeeded a 1966 revival of *Watch on the Rhine* at the Cherry Lane Theater in New York. Her agents received inquiries about reviving productions of *Another Part of the Forest* and *The Little Foxes*. Television and radio stations wondered if they might do parts of *The Autumn Garden*. Finally, Mike Nichols brought in a full-scale New York production of *The Little Foxes*, which opened in New York's Lincoln Center in 1967.

But the return of good times did not diminish Hellman's sense that her popularity and her income could shift with the political winds. No matter the increase in her prosperity, she continued to exercise an ever tighter control over her financial affairs. She monitored every transaction large and small, relying on the principles that had long guided the distribution and performance of her work and scrupulously respecting the rights of others. She routinely deferred to the Dramatists Guild and the Authors' League of America over such questions as who owned performance rights to which plays in what venues, or who controlled continuing rights over plays originally signed over to producers and film companies. But she kept daily decisions over fees and production rights in her own hands. She acknowledged and made decisions about a veritable mountain of requests to reproduce her work and Hammett's from public and private groups all over the world: Norway, Czechoslovakia, Russia, Japan, France, Yugoslavia, Australia, and elsewhere. Though formally fielded by her agents, each demanded a response from her. She was called on to consider whether an amateur production one year might undermine a first-class production planned for a year later, or whether a book publication should preempt a request for a lecture or a play reading. She considered, and mostly rejected, adaptations of Hammett's work, and then of Dorothy Parker's and finally of her own. On a daily basis she decided whether to lend her name, her presence, her voice, and her pen to events small and large.

Each request demanded an individual answer from her agent, who faithfully consulted her about the price she was willing to accept for how many words, or minutes, or paragraphs, and whom she generally advised to say no unless the payment was generous.[60] Despite its prestige, she wrote to Don Congdon (who succeeded Robby Lantz as her agent), she would not allow the BBC to broadcast a forty-five-minute version of *The Children's Hour* for a "disgusting sum of money."[61] She would have to be paid $1,000 for an initial TV production of *Toys in the Attic*, she told a Yugoslav agency, and $500 for every rerun.[62] A German film producer who offered to pay her $1,500, the normal rate, for a filmed interview, was told that she would do the interview for $2,500. To make sure she got that sum, her agent set a negotiating price of $3,000.[63] Money was the bottom line, for, as she protested, she had often been cheated of her due. She'd willingly agreed to an interview with Bill Moyers in 1968, and she had also agreed to reproduce the tapes on cassettes. But when the reproducer sold the cassettes for a profit, she balked. "It is a racket, and someone is making money on it," her secretary wrote to her lawyer, Ephraim London. "Miss Hellman's point is that since the studio gets a royalty on it, shouldn't Miss Hellman get a royalty?"[64] This vigilant oversight continued all of her life.

Sometimes good causes, nonprofit organizations, and "educational" programs got a break, but not always. She would not allow her plays to be performed in South Africa, no matter who sponsored them. She could not permit a sentence or two in a women's calendar, or a paragraph in a staged celebration of women without payment. She would allow a high school student to read an excerpt of her work in a high-school auditorium only if the passage did not exceed twenty-five words. One such incident in the winter of 1976–77 is paradigmatic. When the producers could pay no fee, Hellman refused permission to allow her work to be used in a public television program intended to "highlight the important literary contribution made by women."[65] The producers reduced their request to a bare paragraph from *Pentimento* and, on the advice of counsel, informed Hellman's agent that "though they were uncomfortable doing something that will displease her," they had decided to go ahead. An incensed Hellman pushed Donald Congdon to respond. "Miss Hellman's work is in great demand and has a value in the market place," he replied, "the equity of which would surely be reduced if such free use as you propose were permitted."[66] The producer's agents and lawyers consulted, concluding that they were on solid ground in resisting payments. But Congdon, spurred on by Hellman, pursued the case: "The creative artist should not be told, as Miss Hellman was, that her work was going to be used whether she gave permission or not. Both of us found that offensive," he wrote.[67] Two months later, Hellman settled for an apology and a token fifty-dollar fee.

Hellman's hardheaded calculations did not succumb to the temptations of participating even in performances designed to celebrate her. Producer Viveca Lindfors offered her $2.50 per performance to use four lines from *An Unfinished Woman* in a show planned to highlight the role of women in letters. Lillian countered by claiming that her words were worth at least $25 per performance. After some negotiating, Lindfors offered her $5, and Lillian came down to $10. When they could not bridge that gap, Lillian abruptly pulled out. Nor did she succumb to requests for magazine interviews unless they were in connection with the publication of one of her books: she believed commercial magazines that would make a profit by publishing her spoken words should pay artists an appropriate fee. And she believed very strongly that to garner the respect it was due, she should not sell her work short.

Those who produced her plays or used her words without permission infuriated her. Not atypically, Congdon, who became her agent in the summer of 1971, wrote to object when an unsuspecting playwright inserted a few lines from *An Unfinished Woman* into a play: "This is to request an explanation from your client without delay, and to put him on notice that he has no right to use any material of Miss Hellman's without a license to do so."[68] The same lines appear repeatedly in Congdon's letters to Hellman suggesting that she remained vigilant on the principle of ownership. About a Yugoslav agency that ignored or overlooked a request for payment and performed *The Little Foxes* without permission, Congdon advised Hellman to take the tiny sum they put up after the fact and offered to "put their agency on notice that in no circumstances can they permit future performances of your work unless the theatre can pay an acceptable advance and guarantee to supply royalty statements." Hellman replied, "Yes, do this very firmly."[69]

Hellman's objections covered Hammett's work as well as her own: when a producer pleaded that he had already gone some distance toward the making of a musical based on Sam Spade, Congdon described Hellman as "affronted by the thought that professionals would go so far in developing a property they did not control."[70]

Looked at from the perspective of her ample financial resources in the late sixties and seventies, Hellman's behavior appears to be greedy. But in light of her status as an economically independent woman, the fear evoked by her blacklisting in the fifties, and the new possibilities that her celebrity status suddenly made available to her, Hellman's behavior deserves a more charitable assessment. Certainly, in the seventies, America shed whatever temptations had drawn it to the idea of cultural revolution, communal living, and a diminished concern for material goods. The New Left's vision of hippies wandering the world with all their possessions in a knapsack vanished. It was replaced by a new spirit of materialism and a new respect for corporate power. By the late seventies, a new market ideology reigned. Neoliberal ideals that glorified individual achievement and competition floated in the air and would soon replace the spirit of social responsibility that Hellman appreciated about the sixties. Hellman, approaching her seventies and still involved in every detail of her financial affairs, learned to use the market to her benefit. She understood herself as a valuable property whose protection lay primarily in her own hands and who could and should make as much as possible from a market in which she held a valuable position. Her work was, after all, her largest resource. To manage her complicated financial affairs and her literary properties, she relied on the meticulous attention of secretaries, agents, accountants, and lawyers, all of whom worked with each other, as well as with her, to ensure that her rights and interests were appropriately acknowledged and paid for. Unquestionably, she acted the prima donna. She believed in her own value and the value of her work; she expected deference. She wanted immediate attention to her affairs and thoughtful consideration of her desires. She expected accountants and agents alike not only to understand and respect her principles but to honor all her unspoken as well as spoken wishes. For this we might take her to task, but by the seventies these behaviors had become part of a tough persona and a self-protective veneer necessary to living well by her own efforts.

To guide her, Hellman hired talented literary agents who painstakingly helped her to maximize her income and advised her as to what she might and might not accept by way of remuneration. These relationships inevitably became touchy, with agents consulting with her over even the smallest decisions and eating crow when they overstepped their boundaries. Robby Lantz, who represented her in the sixties and again in the eighties, repeatedly wrote her notes about large and small requests, noting that "I think I know your answer, but don't want to answer for you."[71] The files of letters to and from Don Congdon, her literary agent in the seventies, contain similar language. After he had represented her for little more than a year, he wrote to explain why he had settled for a relatively small payment for one of Hammett's stories, apologizing at length for the arrangement. "Ordinarily, I would check any unusual request for permission to quote from Hammett's work with you," he wrote. "Because this material was to be used in a 'scholarly monograph,' and because it seemed clear that the quotes would be used in a proper fashion, I assumed that it would meet with your approval. If this assumption was incorrect, let me know and I will check all permissions with you in the future."[72] The apology seems to have worked, because Congdon eventually represented Lillian for nearly twelve years. But his deference did not diminish. Years later he continued to ask her approval for trivial decisions. "This," he would write to her in reference to one request or another, is "something you probably won't approve, and if that is so, just say the word."[73]

Their relationship could not have been easy. She quibbled about everything, asserting the most irascible side of her personality, as when she refused the author of a book on the early days of the Screen Writers Guild permission to include a photograph of herself.[74] She asked Congdon to challenge Little, Brown, publisher of her bestselling memoirs, because a statement covering December royalties did not pay off until March. Though she had signed a contract specifying the schedule, she nevertheless remonstrated: "Why in the name of God should they keep money belonging to writers two months past its proper date?" Only Congdon's assurance that this was standard in the industry prevented her from protesting "this nasty practice."[75] She made as much fuss over a $30 charge for typing a contract as over a $400 fee for altering galleys. The typing charge drew a particularly vituperative outburst: "I cannot tell you how silly I think it is to send me such a bill," she wrote to Congdon. "I find that I am totally shocked at this kind of minginess, which I can't believe is your idea. Is everybody out to annoy everybody else at any cost to themselves?"[76]

Not infrequently, Hellman overrode the authority of her agents, producing irritation and conflicting messages. After she fell out with Robby Lantz, he volunteered to give up half of his commission on the three-book contract with Little, Brown (of which *An Unfinished Woman* had been published and *Pentimento* was then under contract).[77] She insisted that she had negotiated this contract directly with Little, Brown's president, Arthur Thornhill, but agreed that he should have half of it. "I do not wish to renew the mess between you and me that need never have happened, and for which I will always feel bewildered and pained. Therefore, I agree to your proposal of one half of your commission, and to hell with all the sad mangling that goes on in this world."[78] She asked her lawyers to negotiate the rights to a piece of Hammett's for which she had previously asked Don Congdon to be responsible. Congdon, confused, complained to the lawyer, but Lillian simply dismissed the agent's concern. "Don't worry about Congdon . . ." she told her lawyer. "You and I were quite justified and no explanation need go beyond that."[79] Sometimes she simply circumvented the agent's authority by going directly to the individual with whom she was negotiating. Challenged, she resorted to stubborn language. "It does seem to me my right to insist upon certain measures that have to do with me," she wrote to Don Congdon on one occasion.[80] Congdon eventually severed their relationship, telling her, "We have come to a parting of the ways—I no longer want to represent your account."[81] Robby Lantz, who then returned to her service, reacted more generously. When, shortly before her death, she tried to find her way around him, Lantz gently took her to task. "I think it would be best if only one of us negotiates at a time . . . You pay your agent to do the agenting . . . I love you but you shouldn't burden yourself with these matters." Lillian didn't let up, and a month later he wrote again: "I beg you on bended knee to prevent people from duplicating and counter-moving on anything one has to do. It only creates major suspicion . . . and frankly serves no useful purpose."[82]

For all of her acerbic style and quarrelsome nature, this impossible woman managed to retain the services of talented literary agents, lawyers, and financial accountants, establishing with them long and loyal working relationships. Her gender served her well in this respect, for she could not only be charming and lovable, she could and did present herself as a help-less, confused woman when she wanted to garner the protection of the generally male guardians of her affairs. "I honestly believe that I do not ask very much," she wrote to Robby Lantz when he once failed her, "and when I am in trouble and need help I should get it as fast as possible."[83] When she wrote seeking explanations for some large or small confusion, she de-scribed herself, tongue in cheek, as "bewildered," "misunderstood," and pained. Occasionally she pursued answers by claiming to be an ignorant woman who needed itemized explanations of complicated statements and clarification of questionable decisions.[84] Generally, she ended these letters with declarations of love and loyalty. With astonishing frequency, she claimed to lose statements she did not understand, checks she did not wish to cash, and reports that she wanted to dismiss. When things went well, she offered expressions of warm affection, invitations to dinner, and the loan of her Vineyard house. "Helen will take good care of you," she wrote to Lantz, who borrowed the house for five days, "and please tell Shirley to let her know what you prefer in the way of food."[85]

The measure of her concern with money—and its relationship to her ability to live the good life she had carved out for herself—emerges in her relationships with accountants and lawyers as well as with literary agents. Hellman created an interlocking structure in which one checked the other and each responded to advice from as many people as she could consult. In an effort to keep track of her money, she asked Robby Lantz to forward contracts to her accountant, Ted Present, because she was "asking Present to make up a list of when and how much monies are due me, feast or famine lady that I am."[86] As her financial resources sta-bilized and she became more comfortable, her affairs became more complex and she, in turn, more dependent on the accountants and lawyers who served her. She checked with them and they checked with each other about the tax implication of royalties, property sales, and trust re-demptions. By the seventies, her accountant, Jack Klein, was paying her bills. When she had a problem with a department store or a telephone company, she, her secretary, and the accountant all consulted over how it should be handled.

If she couldn't understand what her financial advisers and lawyers were doing, or felt impatient with an explanation or a strategy, she exploded in frustration. On one such occasion, she disagreed with her former pro-ducer Herman Shumlin over how to disburse the funds that came in from the film *Spanish Earth*. For years, Shumlin had channeled Lillian's share of the money (about $200 a year) to Spanish Refugee Aid—a tax-exempt organization. In the summer of 1969, Hellman learned that the film's pro-ducer, Joris Ivens, was ill and destitute. She wanted her share of the income sent directly to him. Shumlin resisted—sending the money to Ivens would create tax problems. He asked Hellman to send the money herself. Hell-man stubbornly refused, claiming that she would then have to pay tax on the money she received.[87] The dispute went on for weeks until Shumlin caved.

Sharp-tongued she was, but apparently effective. One lawyer, who had served her well, inquired of her accountant how much he could charge her. He had, he said, accrued some $10,000 in billable hours but could not imagine billing her for much more than the $4,000 he had charged her the previous year.[88] His caution was clearly warranted. A year later, Hellman wrote to him to complain, "I really see nothing that warrants what seems to me as large a bill as this," and asked him to return her pa-pers to her.[89] The firm backed off—sending Lillian a conciliatory letter in which they agreed "to treat the check you sent . . . as a credit against fur-ther services."[90]

Twice—once with Lantz, and once with Congdon—she broke off a decade-long relationship, each time because she became convinced that the agent did not have her best interests at heart. With Lantz, the break came around the 1971 revival of *Candide*, which her partner and co-author, composer Leonard Bernstein, badly wanted to do and which she desperately did not. Lantz, who then represented both Hellman and Bernstein, was caught in the middle. Hellman, convinced that he had encouraged her to agree to the revival out of loyalty to Bernstein, be-came incensed when she discovered that he was taking a commission on a work she hadn't approved. Not wanting to quarrel with Bernstein (whose wife, Felicia, was a close friend), she severed her relationship with Lantz and, after declaring that she hated the 1971 production, agreed to pull out of the *Candide* partnership permanently, pending a new treatment that utilized none of her ideas. This proved, in the end, to be impossible, so she continued to receive royalties from subsequent productions from which her name disappeared. But she had been fond of Lantz, and, in a final bow to friendship, she agreed to let him keep half of the commission on the royalties of her old projects, channeling the rest to her new agent, Don Congdon.

Prosperity, not desperation, encouraged her to put her townhouse on the market in February 1969. She wasn't getting along with her tenants, she was tired of running the property, and the New York real estate market offered an opportunity to trade for a smaller yet fully serviced apartment.[91] She turned down an initial offer of $285,000 and sold 63 East 82nd Street in September 1969 to Theodore Zimmerman for $310,000.[92] This turned out to be a shrewd move. A couple of years later, the New York housing market declined as the city went into an economic tailspin. With the profits she reaped, Hellman was able to add to her nest egg. She agreed to hold a short-term second mortgage on the property ($220,100) at 7 percent interest, and she retained an option to live in the upstairs apartment for up to two years at a reasonable rent of $1,000 a month.

The negotiations and the move reveal Lillian's endless capacity to attend to the details of financial transactions and once again suggest her attention to the deliberations. She consulted accountants and lawyers about the best route to go with regard to taxes, the timing of new purchases, the place to put the funds released from the house, the advisability of financing a second mortgage for the buyer. She dictated notes to her secretary and wrote in her own hand on scraps of paper to remind herself about what had been agreed and what still remained to be negotiated. Her reminders overflowed the boundaries of file folders and touched the smallest details. "We have agreed that I keep storage space in the cellar, and that I keep space for the wood. If I wish to keep my washing machine downstairs in the cellar, I may do so," she wrote in a note to herself. She wanted to be sure that there would be room for her maid as long as she stayed there; she wanted the contract to indicate that her rent included gas and electricity; and she asked (and got) the new owner to paint the sixth-floor maid's bathroom as well as the live-in superintendent's apartment.[93] She carefully listed the items she would take (the sconces in her study but not the ones in the living room; the mantel in the living room, rather than the one in the hallway) and those she was willing to leave. She could part with the eighteenth-century wall panels, the ceiling fixtures in some rooms, the upstairs washer and dryer, which, however, she might use until she left. Inevitably, after the house sale was concluded, she came to dispute such issues as exactly which room the maid would occupy, where the caretaker would live, what changes should be made at Hellman's expense and which at that of the new owners. Following the negotiations and while workmen occupied the house and moved furniture, Hellman stayed in the Vineyard or traveled to California, the physical arrangements and the move itself taken care of by her secretary and helpers hired for the purpose.

Lillian's tenancy in the upstairs apartment at 63 East 82nd Street did not last very long. She found, as she wrote to a former occupant of the house, "something vaguely disturbing about living in a house you once owned and with people who have no experience in running such a house."[94] She compromised by spending as much time as she could out of town. When she moved out in October 1970, she was still perseverating over small details. She missed an English Sheraton chair that had been in a hallway, she said. It was newly upholstered. She wanted it back.[95]

The saga of the house on East 82nd Street did not end there. Hellman, having taken a second mortgage on the house, became entangled in the new owner's financial problems. For several years he paid her irregularly and occasionally skipped a payment or requested a postponement on a payment due. Hellman took all this badly, complaining that it was "embarrassing and a nuisance, and asking him not to do it again."[96] To her lawyers, she expressed concern that the house might be abandoned; she feared, she wrote them in May 1973, that "I will not have a good year next year, and I certainly cannot afford to be burdened with a house whose present condition I know nothing about and whose leases I know nothing about."[97] In fact, 1973, the year that *Pentimento* was published, turned out to be a good financial year for Lillian. But her worries persisted until January 1976, when the house was resold and the remaining loan ($83,305) repaid to her.

She quickly settled on a new apartment in one of the city's elegant buildings, at 630 Park Avenue.[98] She had sold her house for $310,000 and bought the new place for $112,650, so she could afford to renovate it to her liking. And she did, turning a traditional three-bedroom Park Avenue apartment into an elegant living space for one, with a large master bedroom and a comfortable library. The apartment also came with a second-floor room for a live-in helper. To prepare the new quarters, she left careful instructions for the carpenter who undertook to renovate the new apartment—along with the price for each job. He was to remove the sliding doors in the maid's room closets, install an electrical outlet, hang pegboard on the north wall of the kitchen, and so on. Each job had a price attached, the most expensive being the installation of a marble fireplace in the living room at a cost of between $250 and $300. After it was all done, she quibbled about small costs: why the additional $10 for a window repair, she asked. Because he had added a screen, replied contractor John Michael. Months later she was still quibbling. She could not, she said, distinguish between the front and back doorbells, and she did not understand why it had taken so long (and cost so much) to put up a shower curtain rod. If he would correct these things, she would pay his bill.[99]

To prepare for moving, Hellman hired Mildred Loftus, who also took charge of the unpacking. Together the two decided what was to be brought from the old house, what needed cleaning, what should be sold, which bookcases would need to be cut and how, which chairs to recover at what cost. But it was Loftus who got the jobs done. Hellman continued to provide detailed instructions on issues such as which books would go where, which dishes in what cabinet. Hellman thought Mildred a lifesaver, calling her "the best friend I have" and complimenting her on her arrangement of the dishes, on finding lost attachments for the shelves of the china closet, and on replacing the dining room curtains.[100] She also praised Rita Wade, who took charge of the bills and the billing, typing confirmations of all the instructions and keeping meticulous track of what was done and the cost of everything. An endless array of contractors, "rug men," and workmen handled the work itself. But Hellman was tired. From the Vineyard, she wrote her gratitude to Mildred Loftus, adding that "the weight of what I've done has been a stone around my neck and all I can do is hope that the stone will soon disappear."[101] By September, when Lillian returned from the Vineyard, the apartment was ready for her.

For all of her irascible character and her quick and angry temper, Hellman seemed not only to get along with her domestic helpers but to develop warm and affectionate relationships with many of those who worked for and with her. Chief among these were her secretaries, who generally came in for two or three days a week and who took over much of the management of her domestic as well as business affairs. Among the names that stand out: Nancy Bragdon, Edith Kean, Lois Fritsch, Selma Wolfman, and Rita Wade each stayed with her for many years, together spanning a period of almost four decades. They extended their services to supervising moves from and to houses and apartments, caring for the household and for her personal needs while she was away, and keeping track of complicated insurance, financial, and tax records. Bragdon watched over Hammett's accounts while he was in the army; Lois Fritsch fielded the IRS when Lillian ran into tax problems during the McCarthy period; Wade took care of hiring and firing a platoon of nurses as Lillian became increasingly ill at the end of her life.

She had more complicated relationships with her cooks—and, after her favorite Helen Richardson's departure, with the succession of housemaids who lived in one or another of her houses. On the one hand, Hellman seems to have treated them formally, laying out her expectations and drawing up oral and sometimes written contracts with them, expecting them to live up to their commitments and paying salaries, that were, by the standards of her day, more than fair. She scrupulously paid benefits for her household employees, including workmen's compensation and health insurance. More than once she went to bat with insurance companies on behalf of employees injured in household accidents. When her longtime cook Richardson injured her knee, Hellman asked her secretary, Selma Wolfman, to help collect the appropriate compensation; later Hellman made sure that Helen got medical attention for a shoulder injury. She did the same for other, more transient employees.[102]

But there was another side, one that went against the grain of the feminist environment of the seventies. Her instructions to newly hired employees indicated the kind of service she expected and the tasks to be performed. They were detailed, direct, and somewhat anachronistic. A 1973 "Things to Do" list instructed her new help to dust all rooms and to wipe all windowsills each day; to clean her bathroom daily and to mop the floor several times a week; to vacuum once a week "and please put the soft brush on the vacuum cleaner and vacuum all the furniture and under the cushions at the same time." Lillian wanted her bath towels washed "each time they are used," her bed linens changed twice a week, and her mattress turned every two weeks. She wanted the furniture oiled and the floors lightly waxed once a month, the ice bucket filled at noon and again at four every day, and she gave explicit instructions for laying the table and serving when guests were expected for lunch or dinner.[103] She told a twenty-five-hour-a-week helper hired in the spring of 1979 just how to get started: "You will move in Friday, April 13, around 9.30 am," she wrote to her. "You will not be expected to work each day until 12:30 or 12:45. Every Thursday when you come in at 12:45 pm you will make my bed and dust and straighten the house. Every Thursday evening if I am at home, you will either fix dinner or help me fix dinner."[104] And so on.

These detailed instructions suggest, as do the letters from women who worked for her, more of the two-sidedness of Lillian's nature. She could be extraordinarily generous and by her own lights fair. In return, she demanded not just meticulous and attentive service but caring and affection as well. Her sense of entitlement expanded as she grew older and more irascible, bringing with it displays of bad temper that often offended those who worked for her. She treated her helpers like servants rather than companions, demanding that they perform menial as well as more sophisticated tasks and insisting on promptness, cleanliness, and attention to duty. Rosemary Mahoney, one of the young women she hired, found the relationship an enormous disappointment.[105] The lists of duties allowed no room for initiative or the exercise of personal choice. They were precisely tailored to particular employees—to the full-time maid who would live in the second-floor maid's room at 630 Park Avenue as well as to the part-time summer help who came to her on Martha's Vineyard or escorted her to doctors in the years of increasing blindness. An offense could precipitate a stream of violent invective and a burst of temper that could be heard by neighbors and embarrassed her friends and visitors.[106]

To those who departed, Hellman provided instructions as detailed as those who arrived. "Give your own room a thorough dusting and vacuuming," she instructed one young woman, and "a good cleaning of the bathroom that you have been using. Please take your curtain down and give it a washing and ironing, remembering to iron it damp in order to get the sides the correct length and then rehang it." The vacuum was to remain on the bed, she reminded her helper, and the bed and pillows to be covered.[107]

If the departure was on good terms, Hellman could reach out generously. She offered a young Chinese woman employment as well as lessons in English and driving instruction. Ming Hu's English, however, proved inadequate to Hellman's needs, so she found her another job and earned the young woman's undying gratitude. Ming Hu wrote regularly to Hellman, dropped by the apartment with soup, offered her appreciation and

Her sense of entitlement expanded as she grew older. (Photo courtesy Lynn Gilbert)

massages, and presented her, in subsequent years, with a handmade night-gown and a sweater.[108] Other ex-employees wrote her affectionate and loving notes.

Given Hellman's difficult persona and her demanding nature, it isn't surprising that some of her employees could not abide her and left abruptly. Those who did so experienced her legendary wrath. She wrote a decid-edly unpleasant note to a young women who left her service for unknown reasons just after Christmas in 1980. The letter suggests something of Hell-man's increasing narcissism, as well as a paranoia perhaps aggravated by her dependence on others. But it also speaks eloquently to a conception of service that embodied loyalty and love as well as a large sense of enti-tlement.

> I am, of course, shocked that you would leave my house with-out any notification, particularly when you know that I am not well.
>
> It is my hope that nothing illegal has happened here, but cer-tainly you know that you have cost me a very large fee at the Agency, whereas if you had left one week earlier I would not have been responsible for the fee.

It is also my hope that you do not owe us any money for the telephone bill. If you do, I will have to go through proper chan-nels to collect it.

I don't think anybody in my life has ever done anything quite as unpleasant to me as you have managed; nor do I see the rea-son for it. But let us hope that nothing will come out of it that is too difficult for you.[109]

As she became older, sicker, and more needy, Hellman's irascibility and her specificity increased. So too did the speed with which a succes-sion of college and graduate students came and went. She needed these students to read to her, to take her to doctors' appointments, and to help out around the house. So she solicited from her friends and acquaintances the names of students who "would not only like to give up the summer," but who were "taking a year off from college." She offered them "a half day job from about 12 noon on" and suggested that she could help them find other employment on the Vineyard if they needed it. Much as she needed the help of these students, she could not bring herself to be kind to them: her abrupt and sometimes angry manners offended more than a few. For several years in the late seventies and early eighties she did not scruple to ask student helpers to make their homes in a tent on her Mar-tha's Vineyard lawn, suggesting that if there were no guests around they might use the house and promising them a maid's room when and if they moved to New York. Some students accepted the arrangement for the privilege of working with the great celebrity.

Nellie Mohn, a Wells College student, chose to do so in the summer of 1980. After some negotiation, Hellman hired her as a "general housekeeper and assistant secretary" in the spring of 1980, sending her a check for $125 to bind her services, which would begin on the Vineyard at the end of May. At the same time, she asked Mohn to sign a letter indicating that she understood and accepted the terms of her contract, which included providing her own tent to accommodate her for the summer. "Feel free to live in the house until your tent is well established," she wrote to her. Then she suggested that Mohn start work in the kitchen, "giving the ice box a thorough cleaning, the floors and counters a thorough scrubbing, and do the same in the room that contains the freezer and the washing machine." After that, Lillian would give her further instructions.[110] Mohn turned out to be a great success. When she left that fall, Hellman gave her a letter to take with her. In it, she described Mohn as a "young woman of extraordinary intelligence of serious education . . . of conscience, of dignity," concluding that this was "not only a letter of recommendation for Miss Mohn, it is a letter of admiration."[111]

But the case of another employee (let us call her Linda) reveals another side of Lillian's character and hints at her growing paranoia as she grew more feeble. Hellman hired Linda while she was visiting Arizona one winter. She did "not much like" her, as she wrote to a friend from whom she solicited suggestions for a replacement. But Linda stuck it out for several months before quitting. When she did so, Hellman asked her to sign a dictated statement that reads as follows:

> Dear Miss Hellman,
> This is to assure you that I have had a pleasant six months in your employment, and that we have lived by the rules of our agreement, which included my weekly salary, my airplane ticket from Tucson to New York, and half of the cost of my airfare to Charlotte, North Carolina.
> My warmest regards, and thanks.

Two days later Hellman dictated—but did not ask Linda to sign—a confused statement that began with Linda wishing Lillian success on the completion and publication of her new book and ended with Lillian offering Linda some wild game.[112]

The exchange suggests that Lillian was not in full control of her faculties at the time, but it offers a glimpse into her concern that she not be perceived as having wronged her helper. Linda bore no grudge. "I do worry for her, Rita. Please let me know how all goes," she wrote to Rita Wade a few weeks later. Then, thanking her for helping to sort the situation out, she concluded by taking responsibility for her departure: "I promise to keep working on getting a little tougher and not being so sensitive."[113] Linda was not free yet, however. Five months after she quit, she received a letter from Lillian demanding that the young woman tell her why she had not noticed that some of her jewelry had been damaged and three diamonds lost. She did not directly accuse her of theft. Rather, she wrote, "I would like to have your immediate reply of why you did not notice either one of these damages when we packed on our return . . . Please write me of any possible memory you have or any possible knowledge you might have spared me. I wait eagerly to hear from you."[114] Linda replied promptly, claiming no knowledge of the missing stones and declaring her continuing affection for Miss Hellman.

The story of Lillian's mother's will sheds more light on the question of Hellman's feelings about money. Lillian's grandmother Sophie Newhouse died in 1930, leaving her mother, Julia, a small trust fund. Grandmother Sophie Newhouse had left all the rest of her money directly to her other children. But, probably because Sophie mistrusted Julia's husband, Max, Sophie left Julia's share in trust, making her own brother, Lillian's great-uncle Gilbert, its executor. Julia in turn willed the trust to her only daughter, making small provisions to Arthur Kober and to Max's two sisters should they survive Lillian. The trust fund rankled all of Lillian's life, becoming a symbol of her mother's family's excessive engagement with money and perhaps the main source of her alienation from her mother's family. She later wrote, "I don't see my aunt Florence very often, mostly because my father quite rightly thought my grandmother's will was directed against him."[115]

When Julia died in 1935, the fund went to Lillian. From it, she initially received $900 quarterly. But Gilbert entrusted the fund to an accounting firm headed by Arthur Ernst that managed it ineffectively, eventually reducing the principal by a third. Still the trust continued to provide Lillian with an income of about $3,000 a year—a significant sum in 1940. To prevent a further erosion of its value, in 1942 Lillian asked her father to look into the situation and then hired attorney Stanley Isaacs to represent her. She encouraged him to question even small charges, because, as her secretary wrote, "Miss Hellman says to tell you not to worry about what you tell Ernst because she doesn't like him much."[116] With Isaac's guidance, Lillian tried to influence the investments made by the trust, channeling them from stocks to tax-free bonds of various kinds. When Gilbert died in 1946, he was replaced by his niece, Florence (Julia's sister and Lillian's aunt). Florence was well intentioned but utterly incompetent in financial matters and left Ernst and his successors to handle the trust at will. Over the years it continued to do badly, shrinking in value and by the 1950s providing Lillian with less than $1,500 in annual income. The relatively small sums and the declining assets added fuel to Lillian's ire: Why had her monies, alone of all the original Sophie Newhouse estate, been left in trust?

Several times Lillian demanded accountings and expressed concern at the loss of income. But in the end, she feared that the expense of scrutiny would destroy the trust entirely. Instead she sought advice on how to invest the trust's funds from her lawyer friend Arthur Cowan. Encouraged by Cowan, in 1957 she began to try to obtain access to the trust itself.[117] To no avail. Florence had been advised that turning the trust over to Lillian would encourage a suit against Florence's estate after her death. "Lillian, I am sorry," she wrote to her in the spring of 1960, "but I can't do anything about it; I can't break the law. I feel very badly and if I could I would hand it over to you but I don't want to get into any trouble."[118] Lillian responded churlishly: "It is very difficult for me to understand what Mr. Ernst means when he says you could be in any trouble, but most important to me, I feel sad and bewildered."[119]

The issue created tension for many years. Lillian simply did not understand how her aunt could continue to exert influence over money that she conceded belonged to Lillian. But in Lillian's view, her aunt shared the perspective of her mother's family, which, as she wrote to her lawyer, "talked very little about anything but money and several times Florence and I have had sharp minutes about that." This created endless ill feeling: "I see her only because my mother would have wanted it, and that amounts to about four visits a year."[120] Her friends gathered as much. One remembered "her talking all the time to some elderly aunts who were living well into their nineties because she was determined that they would leave her money."[121] Hellman's visits to Florence diminished as Florence grew older and more senile. Toward the end, she wrote a pathetic note to her niece: "Dear Lillian, What is wrong? I haven't heard from you, even on my birthday. Was it anything to do with the money for your trust?"[122]

Florence's growing senility encouraged Lillian to continue her efforts to dissolve the trust. In 1972 she hired a politically savvy lawyer, Paul O'Dwyer, who, with Florence's knowledge, petitioned the surrogate court to remove her from her position and to name him as trustee. The maneuver succeeded: Florence resigned her position on August 4, 1972, and O'Dwyer became her successor the following June. Lillian now insisted that the fund be reinvested to disregard growth and produce as much income to herself as possible. This, she told O'Dwyer, was necessary because "since I have no ability to will the trust to anybody else, my chief interest is in the highest possible yearly earnings to myself."[123] O'Dwyer continued to serve as executor until a run for political office forced him to give up the job and Lillian to seek a new strategy to control it.

All along, Lillian believed that Florence disliked and distrusted her.

Florence had, Lillian wrote to Paul O'Dwyer, "of course known about my father's anger and about my agreement with it." But this was a matter of justice. "I have no idea," she continued to O'Dwyer, "whether our petitioning for a change of executor would cause her to remove me from her will—if indeed I have ever been put there—but I think we should do it."[124] Lillian was wrong about Florence's feelings. When Florence died in 1975 she left Lillian the bulk of her estate, a sum amounting to $270,000 as well as some expensive jewelry and household objects. It took a while to clear the estate, and Lillian waxed impatient, pushing her lawyers to extract advances on the money due her and complaining that some of the jewelry left to her had gone missing. At this point in her life she did not need the money. Lillian came into her aunt's bequest at a moment in time when she was reaping many thousands of dollars in royalties from the first two volumes of her bestselling memoirs. By 1973, her accountant, Jack Klein, valued her net worth at a little more than $812,000, including $320,000 worth of securities, and her aunt's legacy made not a whit of difference in her lifestyle.

But there remained her grandmother's trust. At age seventy Lillian still had not escaped the penumbra of her mother's acquisitive family. In 1976, Florence now dead, Hellman approached a fourth lawyer, Donald Oresman of the distinguished law firm of Simpson Thacher and Bartlett to try once again. This time she succeeded. On August 15, 1977, Lillian received the news that the trust fund had been legally broken. She gave Arthur Kober's daughter, Cathy, $10,000 to fulfill her mother's bequest to Kober, paid all the fees, and inherited $132,500. She was seventy-two years old; she had lived her entire adult life under the shadow of the Newhouse family financial umbrella and had finally worked her way clear of it.

She turned now from worrying about what others would leave her to how she would distribute her own substantial assets. True to form, she worried over every detail, changing the will almost yearly in large and small ways, trying as hard as she could to control what would happen to the money she had so carefully accumulated in her lifetime. The list of beneficiaries changed as her old friends died off, but with a few exceptions she sought to leave those who remained with meaningful personal items rather than gifts of cash. To her secretaries, the choice of a piece of jewelry as well as a small amount of cash; to Annabel Nichols, a diamond bracelet; to Barbara and John Hersey, a Queen Anne table, and to Barbara a piece of jewelry too. And so it went. She named her friends and the particular item or items she wanted them to have: an antique chest or dressing table to one, a pair of candlesticks or wall sconces to another, Russian icons to a third, and then choices of anything left over to others. As each year passed, she crossed out those who had died or offended her, or added a new friend. The specificity of the final versions suggests that Lillian wanted her heirs to know that she had thought about each of them individually, that she held for each of them a particular affection that she could express only with something that was irremediably hers.

As the wills changed over the years, she left more and more of her property to Peter Feibleman, who had loved and cared for her since the mid-sixties. And yet there were strings attached that also changed over the years. She wanted to leave the cooperative apartment to him, but only if he lived in it. If he chose to sell it, then he could keep the largest part of the money it brought in—but, she wrote to her lawyers, "I would like to make the provision that he has no right to bequeath the apartment to his heirs and that if he owns it on his death the total sale reverts to my estate."[125] The Martha's Vineyard house would go to Feibleman, but additional property on the Gay Head beach would be left to the town for the use of local children. Cantankerous to the end, she sought to assign separate fiduciaries for her literary properties, as executors for her estate, and for the two trusts she established—as well as for the trust she set up for the royalties that would go to Hammett's daughters and for the Vineyard property. Her lawyers protested, finally, the "fragmented authority" that would result. Under that version of the will, they calculated, nine individuals would be involved in each decision as to any literary property. She wanted to tie her executors and literary fiduciaries to their jobs by paying them a flat fee, plus an executor's or trustee's commission on the services they rendered.

In the early eighties, when her estate was probably worth more than $2 million and would soon, by one estimate, amount to $3.5 million, she was still dithering.[126] She signed the last version of her will on May 24, 1984, just a month before she died. The will that she rewrote many times teaches us something about what history had done to her, for she wanted both to recognize those who had been kind to her and to ensure that her wealth would continue to support the work to which she had devoted her life. The final distribution of her estate suggests her need both to believe that she was loved and to use her resources to express what love she still could. For in the end money was not simply a way of sustaining herself, but a way of convincing the world that she mattered. And who could blame her, a woman alone, a woman without money or beauty, for extracting from her talent and her fame the emotional sustenance that no partner provided?

CHAPTER 8

A Known Communist

He who has seen a war and plans another must either be a villain or a madman.
—*Lillian Hellman, "Judas Goats," 1947*

It's still not un-American to fight the enemies of one's country.
—*"From America," 1949*

We are or are being made into a fearful people, and fearful people will stand for very little deviation.
—*speech at Swarthmore College, 1950*

The Communist Party was not illegal in the years when Hellman and Hammett moved into its orbit in the late 1930s. Despised and feared by some, the CPUSA commanded the loyalty of many who believed that communism augured economic democracy and social egalitarianism. Like Hellman and Hammett, many in and around the Communist Party hoped that communism would bring a fuller and more complete political democracy than any yet achieved in the Western world. They would learn that they were wrong, but at the time many clung to the idea that, whatever the defects of the existing Soviet Union, the idea of communism remained the last, best hope for a socialist nirvana. For this reason, many idealists dismissed revelations and rumors about forced collectivization of farms, the removal and forced labor of millions of peasants, fake trials and executions of senior officials, and arbitrary imprisonment of critics of all sorts in a brutal system of gulags. Later they would wonder how they could have been so blind to Stalin's malfeasances, but at the time the belief in the saving power of communism ran deep.

The reputation of communism rebounded during World War II as the United States allied with the Soviet Union to defeat Hitler's Germany. Stalin's stature and the American public's admiration for the courage of Russian soldiers increased as Americans watched its ally single-handedly—and with enormous loss of life—resist a massive assault of German troops at Stalingrad. At one with her country and its policies, Hellman could and did support the Soviet-American alliance with all the energy at her disposal. But the war's aftermath quickly ruptured the brief friendship, spawning a polarizing struggle for influence between two very different economic and political systems and a bitter stalemate as both sides sought to draw allies around the world into their orbits. As it became clear that the Soviets sought to create for themselves a series of barrier states and spheres of influence, the West became increasingly suspicious. By March 1946, only eleven months after the end of the European war, Churchill delivered the Fulton, Missouri, speech that would mark the beginning of the Cold War.

> From Stettin in the Baltic to Trieste in the Adriatic, an iron curtain has descended across the continent. Behind that line lie all the capitals of the ancient states of Central and Eastern Europe. Warsaw, Berlin, Prague, Vienna, Budapest, Belgrade, Bucharest, and Sofia; all these famous cities and the populations around them lie in what I must call the Soviet sphere, and all are subject, in one form or another, not only to Soviet influence but to a very high and in some cases increasing measure of control from Moscow.[1]

The ally had turned into an enemy, and those who had too enthusiastically supported that ally, Hellman among them, became objects of mistrust. Espousing communist ideas, once considered merely eccentric, now became subversive. Attributions of communism or excessive sympathy for communism (fellow traveling) signaled disloyalty rather than dissent. Just two months after Churchill's ominous speech, a giant railroad strike broke out in the United States, fomented by workers whose wages had been constrained during the war and who now wished to garner some of their deferred benefits. President Truman, suspecting communist leadership, declared that this was a strike of "a handful of men against their own government and against every one of their fellow citizens." On May 26, 1946, he asked Congress for authority for a government takeover of the railroads, their operation to be handled by the army.[2] Hellman described the events to John Melby in China as "absolutely unbelievable." She was in shock, she wrote, calling the day of the speech a "black, black day." Truman's speech, she thought, was "the most remarkable document ever issued by a president."[3]

The following November, Republicans, arguing that the Democrats were soft on communism, swept the U.S. midterm elections. Just two weeks after that, President Truman lashed back with a proposal to investigate the loyalty of every federal government employee. And four months later, on March 21, 1947, the president signed an executive order that gave the FBI the authority to examine the records of each of the two million employees of the U.S. government. With communist ideas now officially labeled subversive, government agencies felt free to pursue individuals. "Derogatory information" about any person could trigger a full-scale investigation even if that information came from anonymous sources. The accused lost the right to confront the accuser in open court; the FBI supplied the names of thousands of suspected subversives to 150 loyalty and security boards set up all over the nation. Accusation was tantamount to conviction, as the boards had powers of summary dismissal. The Smith Act, passed in 1940, buttressed these boards by making membership in the Communist Party illegal. Over the course of a decade, the FBI eventually investigated some four and a half million people, fostered upward of 27,000 full-scale investigations, and caused the firing of perhaps three hundred people.

Hellman was appalled. The "Truman loyalty order," she told a June 1948 audience at Carnegie Hall, "is legalizing spying on the American people." For a decade, the loyalty-security program and its offshoots would chill the heart of every American who had ever uttered a word in dissent. Reinforced by the Taft-Hartley Act (passed over Truman's veto on June 23, 1947), which required that union officers swear that they were not communists, the legislation assumed that holding communist ideas provided prima facie evidence of disloyalty. With that in mind, state and federal authorities launched a campaign of intimidation that trampled cherished rights. Gone was the notion of presumptive innocence and the promise of fair and speedy trials. Association with any group in which communists continued to work became evidence of one's guilt. The climate of fear and intimidation—Hellman called it bullying—spelled the death of the Popular Front, as social democrats and socialists quickly distanced themselves from suspected communists. It encouraged some to resign their jobs before investigations began and discouraged others from applying for jobs that required loyalty oaths. Radio and television personality Studs Terkel remembered the period as one in which "one's political beliefs served as a rationale for government monitoring."[4]

Because neither the FBI nor the loyalty boards ever had to disclose the sources of their information or the nature of their evidence, an unknown number of false accusations occurred. To facilitate their task, the FBI (prompted by the attorney general) produced a list of organizations "thought to be subversive" and those that had protected the rights of subversives. The initial list of forty-one groups indiscriminately included left- and right-wing suspects. The Ku Klux Klan, Nazi groups, and the American Civil Liberties Union found themselves among the organizations listed. Soon the list expanded to 159. Membership in any one of them implied guilt by association regardless of individual beliefs and could deny an individual a job, an education, a contract, and more. States, municipalities, hospitals, hotels all used these doubtful lists to vet teachers, nurses, janitors, and carpenters who might once have contributed money or exercised their right to dissent. Arguably, these activities gave license to Senator Joseph McCarthy, who honed the art of accusation without evidence to a science when he began his own personal campaign of intimidation in early 1950.

By the late 1940s, those who had once sought alternatives to market capitalism or been sympathetic to communism faced difficult choices. Some decided to simply walk away. Disillusioned with the Soviet Union and unable to believe in a more just United States, they dropped out of politics and hoped to slide by unnoticed. Others denounced their youthful utopian dreams, recanted their critiques of capitalism, and developed liberal positions that sought to sustain the social agenda of the New Deal within a framework of market capitalism. These were the liberals. Many who had once been communists and partisans of the Soviet Union concluded that they had simply been duped by the Communist Party, resolutely abandoned their old positions, and concluded that the Soviets threatened American freedoms. As Soviet power in the world increased, this group formed the heart of an anticommunist movement—their anger turning into bitterness about having once been misled, their audience expanding with every unpopular Soviet gambit. Men like Sidney Hook and James Burnham quickly identified themselves as Hellman's opponents.

Some partisans of communism could not let go of their illusions. They remained loyal both to communism and to the Soviet Union, rationalizing its malfeasances as the actions of a nation under threat. This was the hard-line group, the Stalinists, many of them members of the CPUSA. Hellman was not one of these. She neither admired nor feared the Soviet Union: her trips there had resulted in equal measures of romanticism about the Soviet people and cynicism about its leadership. Rather she insisted, as she remarked in a 1949 speech, that "nowadays on the Right it is fashionable to pretend that only Russia is at fault. I am sorry to say that there are too many on the Left who pretend that only the United States is at fault."[5]

Between these extremes lay a range of sometimes overlapping and limited options. Many principled progressives, including former members of the party and die-hard opponents to it, declared their horror at the methods adopted by Stalin, rejected the Soviet Union as a model, and clung, nevertheless, to the hope that some more democratic form of socialism, some more socially just social order, might emerge from the carnage of war. The reviving social democracies of Western Europe provided some hope in this respect. In the United States, liberals, socialists, Trotskyists, and others vehemently disagreed over how a new society might emerge—whether through slow changes at the ballot box or through revolutionary activity—and what it would look like. After 1949, China, Albania, even social democratic Sweden had fans; differing groups concurred only in their opposition to a specifically Soviet communism. Their conflicts with each other ultimately drowned out all possibility of alliance in the interests of creating the better world for which they all longed. But their differences did not prevent them from individually and collectively condemning both the anticommunist right and the Stalinist left.

Stalinism thus became the common enemy of left-wing factions, like the Trotskyists and former New Deal liberals, and conservatives, all of them united in their assessment of the potentially destructive power and negative ideological influence of the Soviet Union. They coalesced in support of Truman's Loyalty and Security program to weed out subversives, and in agreement with the enemies of those who still claimed allegiance to even the most abstract forms of communism. Communism, they agreed, simply bred subservience to the Soviet Union. Stalinism was no better than fascism: both produced totalitarian dictatorships inimical to freedom and democracy. In a climate of fear, hysteria ruled. Liberals and conservatives alike joined in agreement that a belief in communism betrayed the broader, more humane values of the Enlightenment in blind obeisance to a monstrous regime. To whisper the word was to query loyalty to core American values of freedom and democracy. One would have had to have been willfully ignorant not to have known about the sins of Stalin in the past, the argument went. Failure to acknowledge them now implicated the mute in the sin. To Americans of all kinds, silence connoted sympathy with communism, which, as historian Richard Pells notes, "implied organizational commitments and ties which were inimical to the interest of a democracy."[6] To those on the left, silence meant a refusal to disassociate oneself from the failed Soviet model, a continuing commitment to state-controlled, bureaucratic, and coercive forms of governing.

Efforts to identify the disloyal posed a particular conundrum to liberals. They shared the beliefs of other anticommunists in what Pells calls "the continuing danger of traitors and spies in high places, the necessity of security checks and legislative restraints to safeguard democracy, the tendency of Communists on trial to dissemble and deceive."[7] But in identifying as a foreign conspiracy those who aimed to undermine American freedoms, they found themselves supporting regulations and restrictions that threatened freedom itself. In 1947, a group of liberals including Arthur Schlesinger Jr., union leaders David Dubinsky and Walter Reuther, New Dealers Ben Cohen and Gardner Jackson, and a young lawyer named Joseph Rauh (who would later become Lillian's attorney) created Americans for Democratic Action (ADA) to defend civil rights and civil liberties and to sever any public association of liberalism with a communist agenda. "We reject any association with Communists or sympathizers with communism in the United States as completely as we reject any association with fascists or their sympathizers," they announced.[8] If communists were controlled by Moscow, part of a foreign conspiracy, and agents of a foreign power, ADA founders believed, then they would inevitably use democratic traditions to undermine them. In their view, protecting democracy required suspending democratic freedoms, including the freedom of expression, at least for a while. So they joined the anticommunist crusade and tried to distance themselves from some of its worst abuses. They challenged Joseph McCarthy's techniques, rejecting the finger-pointing strategy of guilt by association and vague accusations leveled without evidence by nameless people. At the same time, they shared such fear of subversion that they supported loyalty oaths and neither defended nor spoke up for those imprisoned under the Smith Act or charged by government committees.

Hellman interpreted their stance as sheer cowardice, adamantly insisting that in their refusal to support the civil liberties of all, liberals acted out of rank fear.[9] The committees, she said later, "made liars out of rather simple-minded people . . . who were very, very frightened."[10] Their behavior, she thought, undermined their own tenets. If she was more outspoken than most, she was not alone. While many liberals and people on the left (including Leslie Fiedler, Daniel Bell, and Philip Rahv) took anticommunist positions, others found themselves in limbo. John Kenneth Galbraith, one of the ADA's founding members and a good friend of Schlesinger's, tried to persuade his friend to change his position on civil liberties. When he failed, Galbraith limited his relationship to the ADA to economic matters.[11] A few on the left—Dwight MacDonald, Henry Steele Commager, Mary McCarthy, and Irving Howe, among them—shared Hellman's strong sense that there was more to be lost by adopting the tactics of the enemy (loyalty oaths, secret hearings, security checks) than there was in allowing communists to speak their pieces.[12] MacDonald, McCarthy, and Howe all personally rejected communism and later turned against Hellman for refusing to join their condemnation.

Hellman found herself at sea in this world of contest and conflict, comfortable in none of the competing groups. The essence of anticommunism lay in the conviction that the Soviet Union posed a large enough threat to American freedom to justify curtailing the civil liberties of Americans. She neither believed in the Soviet Union nor accepted that communists constituted an internal threat. She did believe in social justice and in the New Deal programs that fostered labor organization, enhanced economic security, and regulated corporate power. She had dealt with issues of war and peace, of greed and corruption, of fascism and antifascism in her plays and her movie scripts. Her daily life embodied all the moral certainty and outraged anger of a rebel generation. If she had briefly joined the Communist Party, she had never followed a party line. But she had friends both inside and outside the party and could not bring herself to repudiate people who, like herself, had been well intentioned. Among her friends she numbered respected New Dealers who had now become tainted. These included Archibald MacLeish, Harry Hopkins, and Henry Wallace. The accusations and name-calling made her head whirl. So she

kept her silence about the Soviets and leveled her barbs at the investigatory committees. Trying to hew a path among enemies, she earned a
reputation as a hard-liner. Liberals and conservatives alike dubbed her a
Soviet sympathizer, a fellow traveler, a known communist. Had she not
been a celebrity, perhaps none of this would have mattered. But celebrity
made her vulnerable.

Hellman returned from the Soviet Union in March 1945 convinced that
the destruction there had been so intense that the Soviets would never
want war again. As she had been moved by the suffering of the Spanish in
the Spanish Civil War, so she was touched by that of the Russian people,
who had lost as many as twenty million lives and whose destroyed cities
she had seen with her own eyes. She had stopped in London on the way
back to help with a film and, she wrote to Muriel Rukeyser, found herself
in V-2 bomb barrage. "I heard the bomb land; and then nothing happened
until the screams . . . by the time I got to the bomb hole . . . A man was sitting in the hole, one of his arms lying across from him. Two children were
lying across the street, a rubber ball between them. An old man was being
carried into a house and a woman was holding her skirt against his face."[13]
Had she seen these things? Did she imagine them? It did not matter. Lillian had had enough of war.

In the early postwar days, she lent her name to several groups that focused on how to construct an enduring peace. "There is a great deal of
war talk now," she wrote to John Melby, "and while I still don't believe it
historically possible, I would not be surprised at anything."[14] Such was
the desire for peace at the time that for a while the idea drew the support
of all kinds of individuals. In March 1946, for example, she chaired a tea
for the Women's Committee of the National Council of American-Soviet
Friendship. Held at the Soviet consulate in New York, the tea meant to
encourage notable American women to extend a hand of friendship
to Soviet women. Participants crafted a message that included the sentiment that "We dedicate ourselves anew to the furtherance of friendship
and peace among the women of all countries." It expressed the hope that the
"new world" would "bring peace, security and happiness for our children
and for us." At the time, such activities appeared relatively benign. A year
later, the group appeared on the attorney general's list of subversive organizations, and the report of this tea and the warm response to it, which
came from the Soviet Women's Anti-Fascist Committee, found its way

into Hellman's FBI file. Yet the other signatories on the message included such notables as Mrs. Dwight Eisenhower, Mrs. Franklin Delano Roosevelt, and Mrs. Mary McLeod Bethune among hundreds of others.[15]

Even as the Soviets spread their territorial umbrella over much of Central and Eastern Europe, Hellman remained a staunch believer in peaceful coexistence. "Quarrels start and quarrels end," she told one audience. "It is not right to weigh large things on small scales. It no longer matters whose fault it is. It matters that this game be stopped, and that our arms and legs and heads and faces not be used to find out who was right and who was wrong, who said what on what day."[16] To "stop the game" required talking to the enemy. Though she knew that communists "played a substantial, and often dominant, role" in many of the organizations she joined, "I did not really care; I felt as they did that the Russians really did not want war and that this was what counted most." "I was guided by a feeling that Russia would never again seek war as a means of settling international controversies," she wrote later.[17]

In light of the Cold War and evidence at the time that the Soviets had launched what Sidney Hook called a "communist peace offensive," Hellman's position seems naïve. Some of her contemporaries thought her either duplicitous or a dupe, someone used by the Communist Party to serve its nefarious ends.[18] Some have suggested that she remained a member, albeit a concealed member, of the Communist Party. Yet in the immediate postwar years, Hellman's perspective was shared by many influential people, foreign and domestic. In Western Europe, British and French intellectuals openly disputed the question of whether communism constituted a threat to the rest of the world. Almost universally, they held the opinion that if Russians wanted communism within their own borders that was their business. Nor did it surprise them that Russia, so recently the victim of a devastating attack by Germany, should want to surround itself with a barrier of sympathetic states. At the time, high-level policy makers in the American State Department, men like Dean Acheson, were still arguing that, had he lived, FDR would have accepted some of Russia's territorial aspirations.

President Harry Truman was of another mind altogether. He shared the conviction that no continuing peace could be achieved without a trustworthy partner, which the Soviet Union most definitely was not. Like Churchill, Truman was convinced that the Soviets had to be isolated, contained, confronted, and threatened by arms if their ambitions were to be stilled. Most Americans agreed. Propelled by fear, they identified the totalitarian behavior of the Soviet Union as the greatest threat to world peace. The idea of "peaceful coexistence" became a code for collaboration with the enemy, adherence to groups that supported it, an invitation to the FBI to investigate. That placed proponents of peace in an awkward position. If "peace" were construed as a communist goal, then advocates of peace became, by virtue of their beliefs, unpatriotic dupes guilty of demonstrating a foolish trust in a brutal enemy. They were disloyal Americans willing to place their country's interests second to a totalitarian Soviet Union.

Hellman worked her way through this minefield with characteristic grit and legendary stubbornness. She joined Henry Wallace's 1948 campaign for the presidency without a second thought. Wallace had been Roosevelt's third-term vice president, and, when he was eased out of the vice presidency in 1944, accepted a position as secretary of commerce. But as he came to favor political and economic cooperation with the Soviets, Truman removed him from the cabinet. Wallace's position endeared him to many advocates of peace, communists and liberals alike. In the spring of 1947, he decided to claim the issue as his own, and with the support of a new third party called the Progressive Citizens of America (PCA) began a campaign for the presidency. Hellman was a founding member of the Independent Citizens Committee of the Arts, Sciences, and Professions—one of the groups that had lent its support to the formation of the PCA. Both groups, according to the FBI, would later be cited as communist front organizations by the California Committee on Un-American Activities.[19] Lillian, Wallace's neighbor and friend, was one of seven hundred individuals who, in March 1948, helped to launch the campaign. When Wallace asked her to head up a "Women for Wallace" committee, she agreed, following up by giving several talks to women's groups—all of them emphasizing the vital role of women in any campaign to ensure world peace. Hammett stayed out of the campaign altogether.

It surprised nobody that there were communists in the campaign. Both the major-party candidates had adopted a hard line against cooperation with the Soviets, so the communists welcomed a viable candidate with a more open position regarding Soviet power.[20] But as the campaign picked up steam in early 1948, a spate of Soviet aggression raised increasing doubts about Wallace's nonconfrontational stance. In early 1948, just before Wallace announced his candidacy, the Soviets invaded Czechoslovakia, installing their own regime, loyal to Moscow. Wallace defended the new government.

In June, the communists blocked rail and road connections to Berlin, forcing the allied governments to supply the city by air. Wallace continued to argue that the United States alone was responsible for isolating the Soviet Union. In August, Whittaker Chambers named Alger Hiss, a former employee of the State Department and the United Nations, as a communist. Wallace increased the tension by adding Lee Pressman, an old-line communist and former CIO official, to his campaign staff as general counsel. And he alienated some liberals when he announced that he favored the nationalization of basic industries.

Challenged to explain the apparent leftward turn of his campaign, Wallace stumbled. Instead of asserting the rights of communists—the party was not illegal—to participate in an electoral campaign, he denied that he knew about their presence among his supporters. But Hellman, along with Paul Robeson and many others, had already been identified by the FBI as in, or close to, the party. In their eyes she was a "known communist." Fearful of the taint of communism, the campaign tried to marginalize party members, fellow travelers, dupes, anyone it felt could color it pink. Too late. Wallace supporters passed this pink or red tinge on to whatever they did afterward.

The presence of "known communists" like Lillian Hellman served only to confirm suspicions that communists had taken over. Lillian, forthright as usual, despaired at the accusations and caught the blame for the guilt they evoked. Years later Michael Straight, then a columnist for the *New Republic*, which had supported Wallace early—and one of those who pulled out of the campaign because he didn't like Wallace's left position— remembered his retreat. "I know that some hate-filled individuals like Lillian Hellman, and some foolish fellow travelers like Virginia Durr maintained, and still maintain that I acted as I did out of cowardice," he recalled.[21] But Lillian herself was having difficulty defending Wallace by the end of the campaign. In October, as the election approached, she arranged an extended trip to Yugoslavia and left the country.

Hellman came back to the United States in time to help organize the 1949 Waldorf conference. Officially called the Cultural and Scientific Conference for World Peace, the Waldorf-Astoria conference was organized by the National Council of Artists, Scientists, and Professionals (NCASP). This group was originally a division of the Progressive Citizens of America—the third party that supported Wallace's presidential party. It separated from the PCA in 1948—though it continued to boast an overlapping and sympathetic membership with the parent group. Opinions differ as to how the conference originated. Some observers insist that the NCASP was from the beginning a communist front organization and that the conference, conceived in Moscow, followed on the design of several other such meetings held in the United States and abroad in Poland and Paris. Certainly the call published in the *Daily Worker* lends itself to this interpretation. "The Cold War," it declared as it announced the conference, "is incompatible with the program of economic and social advance. The military control of science is restricting the development of science for peaceful purposes. Free exchange of information is endangered."[22] But at least some of those who supported the conference thought of it in a different way. Thomas Emerson, a distinguished First Amendment scholar and a part of the original group, hoped the conference would deal with "current issues of the day and particularly with the problem of freedom of expression and civil liberties."[23]

The best evidence we have suggests that Harlow Shapley, a distinguished astronomy professor at Harvard and a long-standing advocate of peace whom Lillian had first met about a year earlier, put together the group that initiated the call for papers. That group proposed a conference to deal "with the obstacles that block the path to peace as well as the effects of the world situation on the cultural life of the country."[24] Shapley, who was probably not a communist, may well have been a fellow traveler in the sense that he believed, in the words of historian John Rossi, that "the cause of world peace would be furthered by promoting contacts between Russia and the West."[25]

The original signatories (among them Hellman, Paul Robeson, poet Louis Untermeyer, scientist Linus Pauling, cultural critic Howard Mumford Jones, and a dozen others) included communists and fellow travelers as well as many who simply believed that, as Lillian put it, "there is no record in human civilization where wars destroyed ideologies."[26] Hellman was in good company, joined by a range of people who insisted on talking about peace and challenging the Cold War.

Eventually some six hundred individuals would agree to sponsor the meeting that took place at the Waldorf-Astoria Hotel on March 27–29, 1949. At the time, newspapers ascribed the large number to an "intellectual reign of terror." Influential communists and fellow travelers, the *New York Herald Tribune* claimed, had persuaded others to support the conference or face retaliation in the form of negative publicity.[27] Hellman had

1949: *Harlow Shapley put together the group that called for papers. (© Time &*
Life Pictures/Getty Images)

a different interpretation. "Only four years ago millions upon millions of
people died," she told the assembled participants at the opening session.
"Yet today men talk of death and war as they talk of going to dinner."[28]

Undoubtedly this was not a good time for a conference on world peace.
Tensions with the Soviet Union had continued to escalate—particularly
as questions of espionage floated to the surface. Judith Coplon, a twenty-
seven-year-old Barnard College graduate and Justice Department political analyst, was on trial for spying for the KGB. Eleven leaders of the
American Communist Party were charged under the Smith Act with
advocating the destruction of the United States. Rumors spread that the
Soviets would soon explode an atomic bomb. When it became clear that
the meeting would include participants from behind the iron curtain,
including a delegation from the Soviet Union selected by Soviet officials,
opposition rose to astronomical dimensions. These official delegates, argued critics, would be merely mouthpieces for the Soviet Union. Why
should the United States offer them a platform? The State Department

warned that the conference was likely to be dominated by communists and agreed to let in only those communist delegates who represented their countries. Eventually twenty-three delegates from behind the iron curtain were among the three thousand who attended the conference. Additionally, the State Department discovered two unauthorized Canadian communists who had evaded its scrutiny. They were immediately deported.

The American Legion and the Catholic War Veterans rounded up hundreds of members to protest outside the Waldorf-Astoria. Among them were a line of nuns through which delegates had to pass. But the most effective critique, and the one with long-lasting effects, would come from a range of intellectuals on the left who fundamentally disagreed with fellow travelers over the causes of the Cold War. To their mind, Russia bore responsibility for the escalation in tensions. The most effective guarantee of peace, they argued, was a strong military defense. Peace merely allowed the Soviets room for aggression. A conference, with delegates selected by a state that allowed no freedom of expression, could expect only to serve the cause of propaganda. Devastatingly, opponents accused conference organizers, wittingly or not, of playing into the hands of the Soviets. A handful of the six hundred sponsors encouraged Shapley to make space for critics of the Soviet Union. But Shapley and others were committed to a conference that would not castigate either side. Its intent, as Thomas Emerson put it, was "to bring together people who would discuss the possibilities of peaceful co-existence that had a clear international flavor to it."[29]

The State Department thought that under those circumstances, the conference would simply provide a platform for communist propaganda. In this it was joined by a coalition of liberal anticommunists led by Sidney Hook and George Counts and glued together by virulent mistrust of the Soviet Union. When, two weeks before the conference, some of them asked Harlow Shapley for places on the various panels, Shapley refused. They were welcome to attend the conference and to speak from the floor, he wrote to them, but the panels were already filled. Sidney Hook, incensed at the refusal, invaded Shapley's room to demand an invitation. After Shapley deftly maneuvered him out of the room, Hook and George Counts set up a counterconference at which Arthur Schlesinger Jr., Max Eastman, and others spoke. The counterconference drew as many as eight hundred people to an open-air meeting at Bryant Park, next to the New York Public Library. There, Eastman focused on the destruction of artistic freedom under Stalin and singled Hellman out for special condemnation. Dwight

MacDonald and Mary McCarthy, both opponents, registered at the Waldorf along with three thousand others. Each managed to speak from the floor for five minutes.[30]

Hellman's participation in the Waldorf conference was clearly a product of long-standing and deeply felt commitments. She was, after all, a fellow traveler, a phrase that was not yet a term of opprobrium. Yet she was a bit player in every sense, a celebrity attraction rather than an architect of the discussions in which it engaged. Her most quoted remark from the affair came after Norman Cousins unexpectedly delivered a postbanquet talk critical of the organizers. She commented then, Virginia Durr remembered, that she thought he should wait until he got home before criticizing his dinner hosts.[31] Daily newspaper accounts of controversy over the conference in the weeks before its opening hardly mention her except in the occasional lists of sponsors. At the conference itself, she sat on the dais of the opening session, chaired the banquet, and played a largely symbolic role. Afterward her name appears everywhere: among the lists formulated by the State Department and others to demonstrate the conference's subversive nature, as one of only five women among the fifty people named by *Life* magazine as communist dupes, all of whose photographs occupied a dramatic double-paged spread.[32] *Newsweek*'s highly critical account of the conference appeared alongside a photograph of her captioned "Lillian Hellman: Mastermind."

The publicity, as much as the role she played, accounts for the long-lasting association of the conference with Hellman's name. A half century later, neither the meaning of the conference nor Hellman's putative role in it had diminished. Arthur Miller, who chaired a session on the arts, credited the conference with "setting a new and higher level of hostility in the Cold War."[33] Conservative historian John Patrick Diggins conferred on the conference the honor of starting the intellectual Cold War and attributed to Lillian Hellman the feat of bringing "communist cultural celebrities together to defend the U.S.S.R."[34]

For the rest of her life and long after, Hellman's name conjured up an image of rigid, ideological commitment to Stalinism.[35] Blamed for legitimizing a delegation of "approved" Soviet writers and artists and a motley assortment of American and foreign communists to talk peace together, she was accused of being blind to Soviet repression and lacking in respect for American freedoms. She came to symbolize those who perniciously enhanced the credibility of an evil Soviet Union. The label stuck long after Stalin's death, when many liberals had begun to envision possibilities for reducing tensions with the Soviet Union. But in the late forties and early fifties, the idea that one could make peace by exchanging ideas with the enemy smacked of disloyalty. The Waldorf conference turned into an important part of the indictment of Lillian Hellman.

There is little evidence that Hellman was still a member of the Communist Party in these early postwar years, though she remained a fellow traveler. The FBI kept sporadic track of her from the mid-1940s on; its reports, which carefully noted her participation in communist front organizations and those on the attorney general's lists, agree on this question. After opening a file on her in 1941, the bureau closed it on March 15, 1951.[36] A comment from the FBI's New York office indicated simply that its confidential informants "had no knowledge of the subject."[37] Robert Newman, John Melby's biographer, concluded after a careful study of all the evidence that "Lillian Hellman was not a Communist in any significant sense, certainly not in the 1950s." Newman continues, "It is simple nonsense to call her this; sheer polemics to call her a Stalinist; and plain insanity to believe, as J. Edgar Hoover did at one time, that she was in any way disloyal to the United States of America."[38] But party membership was no longer the issue. The Waldorf conference brought into suspicion any who did not conflate democratic values with anticommunist convictions. It revealed how extensively what the historian Christopher Lasch would later call "a conspiratorial view of communism" had taken hold, how widespread the agreement among liberals as well as reactionaries "that the communist conspiracy had spread through practically every level of American society."[39] Sadly, it also suggests how easy it was in those years to target someone like Lillian—angry, outspoken, "hateful" as some thought her—and to turn her into a negative symbol.

Unsurprisingly, the conference helped to produce a series of powerful reactions. Along with the several international peace conferences that preceded and followed it, the conference stimulated Sidney Hook, George Counts, James Burnham, Arthur Schlesinger Jr., and others to create the American Committee for Cultural Freedom, a leading anticommunist cultural organization. It encouraged the CIA to get involved in a counterinitiative that involved funding the International Congress for Cultural Freedom along with *Encounter* magazine. Each of these organizations dedicated itself to spreading American ideas and ideals in an effort to combat the spread of communism. Each assumed that advocating "peace" contributed to Soviet strength, and that participation in such peace organizations demonstrated communist sympathies.

In the early fifties, Hellman believed that focusing on issues of communism and anticommunism was simply a red herring. "In all the organizations in which I have participated over the past 15 years," she wrote in an unreleased statement, she had never "heard one word concerning espionage, sabotage, force, or violence, or the overthrow of our government."[40] She would not, could not, accept a world view that situated a good United States against an evil Soviet Union. That, she thought, along with such critics of McCarthyism as *Nation* editor Freda Kirchwey, was "too easy an out . . . for it excuses policies and behavior which bear no true relationship to the danger."[41] She did not accept a definition of communism as conspiratorial. She would not play ball with those who did. The real issue, she thought, had become the repression fostered by the anticommunist campaign, and particularly the campaign's successful efforts to silence dissent in any form. From Hellman's perspective, when liberals joined the attack on communism they not only reinforced a false conception of a forceful and pervasive conspiracy to overthrow America, they inhibited the capacity of ordinary people to dissent. By empowering those who sought to suppress legitimate disagreement, they undermined democracy. In this sense, she believed, nothing less than the future of democracy was at stake. Her position earned her the enduring label of the fellow traveler. But if the term were pinned on her and many others as a derogatory label, she did not receive it as such. Rather, her consistent defense of the right to dissent conveyed her refusal to falsify a worthy American radical past.

Hellman's convictions would be put to the test, slowly and painfully, in the days after the Cold War descended. Attorney Leonard Boudin, who defended many of those attacked, would call the years between 1947 and 1954 "worse than any time" in his professional life.[42] The dragnet of loyalty and security captured Hellman's Hollywood friends first. During the war, Congress had suspended investigations into the political activities of the entertainment industry, though not before it passed the 1940 Smith Act, which proscribed written and spoken ideas intended to overthrow the government of the United States, as well as the people and organizations thought to advocate them. The provisions of the Smith Act, and the continuing investigations of California's state senator Jack Tenney, kept the issue of "un-American" activities in the public's consciousness. As the war came to an end, the House of Representatives reenergized and renamed the former Dies Committee, calling it the Committee on Un-American

Activities and providing it with subpoena power. HUAC, as it now became known, once again set its sights on the entertainment industry, focusing particularly on screenwriters who were thought to be able to exercise enormous influence on the opinions of audiences by putting subversive ideas in the mouths of unsuspecting actors. In the fall of 1947, the committee called nineteen actors and writers to testify. Some of these, most notably Adolph Menjou, Gary Cooper, and Robert Taylor, affirmed the committee's sense that communist ideas had pervaded Hollywood. Others, like Ronald Reagan, who was then president of the Screen Actors Guild, provided the names of writers thought to be subversive. Ten of the nineteen, all of them screenwriters, challenged the right of the committee to ask questions about their beliefs. To wide public support, they appealed to First Amendment protections of their rights to think and speak freely. All of the ten—including John Howard Lawson and Ring Lardner Jr., Lillian's friends and colleagues in the Screen Writers Guild since the thirties—eventually served brief jail terms for contempt of Congress.

Several days after the hearings ended at the end of November 1947, the major Hollywood producers met in New York and, in an act designed to call off the committee's investigations, fired the ten writers and agreed not to rehire them. Two days after that, the Screen Writers Guild, the organization that Hellman had worked so hard to bring to life, decided to police its own ranks. It announced that "No communists or other subversives will be employed by Hollywood."[43] The Hollywood blacklist, never formally acknowledged, had begun.

Hellman responded to these events with outspoken rage. Writing in the *Screen Writer*, the vehicle of the Screen Writers Guild, she called the hearings "sickening, immoral and degraded" and characterized the capitulation of the producers as the culmination of "a week of shame." "There has never been a single line or word of Communism in any American Picture at any time," she wrote with evident hyperbole. How could there be, she continued: "There have never or seldom been ideas of any kind." Hollywood, she thought, harbored more than its share of fearful men, "men scared to make pictures about the American Negro, men who have only in the last year allowed the word Jew to be spoken in a picture, men who took more than ten years to make an anti-Fascist picture, those are frightened men and you pick frightened men to frighten first. Judas goats." She dismissed them contemptuously as "craven men . . . trying to wreck the lives of . . . men with whom they have worked and eaten and played, and made millions."[44]

"Judas Goats" put Hellman on the record in a moment, and with a position that required a good deal of courage. It also signaled the stance she would thereafter adopt with respect to attacks on the left. She believed in freedom of thought, belief, and speech for herself and for others; she not only defended the rights of others to speak without fear or dread of consequences, but she valued those who spoke up in defense of freedom of thought and speech. She did not believe that communism endangered the United States internally, nor that the Soviet Union threatened it from outside. She despised those who knuckled under the fists of bullies, and she decried investigators who "pandered to ignorance by telling people that ignorance is good and lies even better." She had nothing but contempt for the Hollywood producers who had helped to enforce blacklists. "These great millionaires," she called them, "men powerful enough to have made and ruined the world's darlings, arrogant enough, many of them, to have led their own lives on terms outside the rest of us, would now, in solemn fear, declare that fear without shame."[45]

Still, she herself was frightened and bewildered by some of the repercussions around her own prospects. In the spring of 1948, Hellman's friend William Wyler, who had directed film versions of *These Three*, *Dead End*, and *The Little Foxes*, proposed that she adapt Theodore Dreiser's *Sister Carrie* for the screen. Hellman and Wyler talked about the plan during a European trip, and Hellman returned home to await a contract from Paramount Pictures. The contract never came. Almost three decades later, Hellman tried to reconstruct the incident in a letter to Wyler. He had confronted Barney Balaban, president of Paramount, only to be told that Hellman was unacceptable. Wyler flew to New York to talk to Hellman. As Hellman remembered the incident, he appeared at her door

> furious and angry at what had happened in Balaban's office. Balaban had told you that they could not employ me. That I was on a kind of forbidden list. You protested strongly that there was no such list and you said that Balaban took from his drawer a file which he told you was the F.B.I file on me. You were horrified that there was such a thing and you were very angry with Balaban, threatening to quit. You, Dash, and I talked about it on 82nd Street for two nights. I think . . . [46]

That was only the beginning. Lillian recalled a second story in which Harry Cohn, head of Columbia Pictures, sent her a contract "for any job I

Hellman and Wyler talked about the plan during a European trip. Here with William Wyler in 1960 on the way to Europe. (Photofest)

wanted, writer, producer, director, and that the contract sent to my house carried a clause of such mysterious words that I hastened around to ask what it meant." She discovered, she says, that it meant "I could not visit, or have visit, a prescribed list of people who were thought to be too liberal, too radical, or too talkative." Hellman remembers "laughing at the sheer gall of it, sure that they couldn't be serious."[47] But they were to have the last laugh. In 1950, the right-wing newsletter *Counterattack*, whose sponsors included former FBI agents, published a list of 150 entertainment-industry individuals believed to be communists. *Counterattack* editors made a point of going after people who were well known and had reputations to hurt. The detailed information they collected about Hellman's activities could only have come from the FBI.[48] Hellman, her name on the latest list, now knew she was excluded from the American movie industry.

   She watched now, her world in chaos, as her friends and acquaintances allied themselves with those who championed curtailing civil liberties. Some of the most liberal organizations refused to protect the rights of communists. Americans for Democratic Action, founded in 1947 to preserve the New Deal, took a strong anticommunist position in order to preserve its own legitimacy. Traditional defenders of the First Amendment like the American Civil Liberties Union refused to defend the rights of those suspected of communism to speak.[49] Both organizations willingly purged their memberships in order to defend their anticommunist credibility. Trade unions fell into line, policing themselves, though often only after fierce fighting and internal political tensions. Hellman's own Screen Writers Guild agreed to eliminate communists from leadership positions. Universities followed suit. Though at first the American Association of University Professors issued a statement insisting that faculty members could be dismissed only for acts of disloyalty, not for Communist Party membership, it never so much as publicized the names of dozens of institutions that fired suspected party members.[50] The Board of Regents of the University of California dismissed thirty-two faculty members who refused to sign loyalty oaths in 1950. Three years later, thirty-seven institutions (including Yale, Stanford, and Brown) agreed that since "loyalty, integrity and independence are incompatible with membership in the Communist party . . . party membership extinguishes the right to a university position."[51] Their stance effectively curtailed the "full academic freedom . . . guaranteed to professors and scholars," for it was assumed that not cooperating with government investigatory bodies was tantamount to admission of Communist Party affiliation.

Hellman responded, naïvely perhaps, but nevertheless with stubborn refusal to concede to fear. On numbers of occasions she had demonstrated her own willingness to stand by her convictions. By the late 1940s she was a celebrity who had lent her name to causes that she believed would further her visions of equality—against racism, for world peace, and on behalf of social justice. Many of the organizations she had joined— she counted thirty-nine of them in a list she prepared in 1952—appeared on the attorney general's list of subversive organizations. Some of the petitions she had signed explicitly attacked HUAC, calling on Congress to abolish it and the Supreme Court to declare that it imposed censorship.[52] The FBI duly reported these attacks as indications of Hellman's continuing attachment to communism.[53] She also lent her name to an endless number of dinners and appeals on behalf of a variety of an eclectic series of groups that included the United Jewish Appeal, the American Jewish Congress, Ethical Culture, FDR's Four Freedoms Award, and, after the president's death, the National Committee for Roosevelt Day. Some of these were front organizations in the sense that the Communist Party led them into paths consistent with Soviet policies at the time. Others were formed by non–party members, though they welcomed communists and everyone else who shared their goals. Hellman did not distinguish among these groups, participating in one after another, seemingly paying little attention to their leadership: "I joined a great number of organizations which I believed were dedicated to peace and to other humanitarian aims," she would write later.[54]

She must have felt something akin to panic as she tried to sort out what was happening to her world. "I had never, during my grown life, lived in a period of reaction and I did not identify it quickly," she wrote a decade later.[55] Repeatedly she faced moments when decisions about how to act tormented her. As a member of the board of the Authors' League of America, she was asked in 1950 to sign an affidavit testifying that she was not a member of the Communist Party. She agonized over the decision, deciding at last to sign it: "If it must be done now then it must be done and that is all there is to it." But she asked to speak to the issue at the next meeting, and she accompanied her affidavit with a statement of protest condemning "the requirements of affidavits of this sort as violating my constitutional freedom of opinion and association."[56] "We are—or we are being unnaturally made into—a fearful people," she warned an audience of Swarthmore College students around the same time.[57]

She and Hammett, who was then living part of the time in his 10th Street apartment in New York, and part of the time with her, remained under sporadic surveillance. In July 1951, as Hammett was preparing to go to jail for refusing to reveal the names of contributors to a bail fund for Communist Party leaders, the FBI came to call. They were both at home when a team of agents knocked on the door of her Pleasantville farm to search for eight Communist Party leaders whom they believed were in hiding there. Hellman denied knowing anything about the fugitives, and a search of the farm produced no trace of them.[58]

Hoping to find work in Europe, Hellman decided to travel there. This was a familiar scenario. Ring Lardner Jr. recalled that during this period he was reduced to working incognito for Hellman's friend Hannah Weinstein, who had taken her family off to England, where she set up the television production company that produced the first Robin Hood series using blacklisted Hollywood writers.[59] But Hellman was not desperate enough to write under an assumed name. She had traveled to Europe in 1948 with some success, and in early 1951 she applied for a new passport. But now she ran into trouble. In 1950, Congress passed the Subversive Activities Control Act, also known as the McCarran Act, which contained a provision denying passports to communists. The decision to grant a passport rested in Ruth B. Shipley's State Department Passport Division. Mrs. Shipley needed to be convinced that Lillian was not a communist. Hellman, with a potential job waiting for her in Paris—an adaptation of Ibsen's *The Doll House*—pleaded her case and then waited. Desperate, in July she told Shipley that she would lose the job if she delayed her departure. "I am not a Communist. I am not a member of the Communist Party," she wrote. "In the past I have been a member of many left wing organizations but, while I have made many foolish decisions in my life, I have never done anything which could be called by any honest person, ugly or disloyal or unpatriotic."[60]

The passport came through a week later. It was too late. Her European counterparts backed off and refused to sign the contract she had so carefully negotiated. She set off for London anyway, eager to leave a United States where Hammett was heading to jail for refusing to reveal names to an investigatory committee. The two had agreed that she should get out of the way if possible. And she was still hoping for work. She departed despite warnings from her lawyers that the trip might be futile and that she had no grounds to press for a completed deal, preceded and followed by an angry flurry of telegrams, including one from her agent, Kay Brown, that insisted that "the responsibility for going to Europe was entirely yours." It tells us something about her state of mind that Hellman not only went, but that she felt unfairly treated by those who had warned her off. She wrote to Henry Beeson, Gregory Zilboorg's secretary, to report testily that she was at loose ends. "My original plan was to make a movie in France but I'm afraid that offer has been withdrawn."[61] When he suggested that she meet with Zilboorg in Switzerland, she wrote to say that she could not, and though she would not admit it, her restricted passport would not have allowed it. She consulted her lawyers about legal action only to be told that she had "no grounds for action. Because of the delay in connection with the passport, these people in the meantime changed their minds."[62] Kay Brown wrote to express sympathy that the expected contract had not materialized and to hope that "an assignment which you might like comes up for you in London."[63] But if Lillian had no legal ground to stand on, she continued to press her case until the Ventura production company agreed to pay her travel costs and expenses.

Hellman returned to the United States in the fall of 1951, Hammett in jail, to find the dragnet was moving ever closer. In the 1947 Hollywood hearings, her closest colleagues, including John Howard Lawson and Ring Lardner Jr., were among those who went to jail. But in 1951, when investigations of the entertainment industry resumed, she saw her friends turn tail and confess. In turn Larry Parks, Clifford Odets, Budd Schulberg, and Elia Kazan cooperated with investigating committees and implicated others. Kazan argued that he needed to protect his livelihood. "I'd hated the Communists for many years and didn't feel right about giving up my career to defend them," he wrote in his autobiography.[64] Others simply saw no reason to protect a Communist Party they had come to despise. They not only publicly renounced communism but agreed to reveal everything they knew, including the names of those with whom they had worked. After all, to refuse to identify oneself as a former communist implied that one had something to cover up. And once one revealed one's past, cooperating with investigatory committees provided the best evidence of sincere contrition. Offering the names of other once and future party members not only provided the government with a huge list of potential subversive suspects that HUAC and the FBI could question, but it meant that those named, in turn, could name still others. The list could expand indefinitely.

The trouble, as Hellman and others quickly understood, was that the process rewarded the informer and encouraged people to exaggerate their knowledge. "The good American," noted Ted Thackrey in the left-wing *New York Compass*, "is the informer and the conformist who is willing to confess that associations once regarded as innocent must have been evil . . . and that those associates must be denounced by name no matter how tenuous the association, how vague the memory."[65] The behavior, Hellman perceived, produced "confessions of sin that never happened." She thought this "one of the comic marks of the years between 1948 and 1958," when many men "marched themselves before committees to confess what they never knew, beg pardon for what they had never done."[66]

Hellman did not and could not believe that Americans would remain silent in the face of such injustice. Her sense of bewilderment is palpable. All around her, friends and acquaintances positioned themselves with respect to the assault on the left. As they did so, the lines between and among them with respect to the sanctity of civil liberties sharpened. She was, she wrote just a decade later, "a very frightened woman," and she felt "the sadness of watching people be punished for so little—because the truth is that the radical or liberal movement in America was always very small and almost always very foolish. But then fools also have a right to justice and to freedom." At first she laughed "at anybody's right to deny that."[67] But her laughter was short-lived. Hellman was not among those who frighten easily, she had written "Judas Goats," and yet she was afraid. Her hero in this period was Anton Chekhov, in whom she had become interested in early 1950 and whose collected letters she would soon edit and publish. From Chekhov she copied into her notebook an early statement that reflected her disillusionment with her colleagues. "I do not believe in our educated class, which is hypocritical, false, poorly educated and indolent; I don't believe in it even when it suffers and complains for its persecutors emerge from its own bosom," Chekhov had written.[68] Hellman shared the belief and wished she could emulate his courage.

Hellman's Armageddon came when she was called before the House Committee on Un-American Activities in the spring of 1952. For several years she had preached defiance of the investigatory committees, suffered from the movie industry's blacklist, and watched her friends weigh the impossible choice of cooperating with the committees, going to jail, or losing their livelihoods. Now it was her turn. She was part of an entertainment industry that had been targeted for several years; she had made no secret of her sympathy for world peace or racial equality, both key programs of the CPUSA. And she knew that her name had come up before HUAC and other committees on several occasions. In a list of names he turned over to HUAC in July 1950, FBI informant Louis Budenz had identified Hellman as a party member from 1937 to 1945.[69] Her name surfaced again during an April 1951 investigation of her friend Dorothy Parker, and a third time when former party member Martin Berkeley identified her, the following September, as having attended a meeting at his California home in the late thirties. Still, the call came at a particularly difficult time. Hammett had just been released from a four-month jail term; Julius and Ethel Rosenberg sat in jail, each under sentence of death. Joe McCarthy was at the peak of his career.

When the subpoena arrived, Hellman lost her cool. By her own account, she tasked the African-American man who delivered it with serving an inglorious master. Finally she succumbed to the numb calm that comes, as she put it later, from knowing that "there is nothing to do but to face trouble with a roped control."[70] She consulted one lawyer and then another before she came to the man who would finally counsel her through the episode. He was Joseph Rauh, a founding member of Americans for Democratic Action and a liberal anticommunist who had not previously represented admitted communists. This was not, he later told

Hellman, entirely his choice. Rather he sensed that potential clients who remained within the Communist Party chose to follow the advice of party lawyers, even when they sought him out. He could not, he thought, represent them, because they could not be fully open with him.[71] But Hellman was different. She had, he wrote to her as they tried to frame her defense, "made it quite clear in our talks that you genuinely disagree with the activities of the Communist Party . . . and recognize that you were wrong in joining the Party." Rauh believed that Hellman refused to distance herself from the party or to acknowledge her error in joining up because of "your feeling that somebody might think you were saying so because you were afraid of public opinion rather than because that was your true view."[72] He counseled her to set aside her fear of public opinion and to admit that she had been wrong in joining the party. She refused. Only later did he begin to understand why. She believed, he wrote shortly after *Scoundrel Time* began to attract attention, that "it only added to the witch hunt to criticize Communists and Communism—even rationally and thoughtfully."[73] Rauh disagreed with that position. He did not believe, as Hellman did, that attacking communists would simply play into the hands of the committee. "It seems to me that the struggle for freedom is a two-front war against both communists and their right wing opposition," he would confess later. But he admired her stand, and "the courage with which she held it."[74]

With Rauh, Hellman confronted the Hobson's choice she now faced. She was, Rauh's assistant Daniel Pollitt recalled, terrified. When she came into the office, "she was very polite and she didn't interrupt. I thought she was extremely frightened."[75] Still, she was adamant that she would not name names. Rauh thought she "would even have accepted jail before naming names. What she really wanted to do was tell the committee off without violating the law and that is what she ended up doing."[76] But how would she behave? She could choose to answer no questions about her relationship to the Communist Party and simply take the Fifth Amendment against self-incrimination, as others had done. But that course suggested that she had something to hide. Though those who had taken it had avoided jail, they had not shed the taint of communism. School boards routinely fired teachers who pleaded the Fifth Amendment; employers would not hire them; Hollywood refused them jobs. She could admit her earlier association with communism, repent the mistake, and apologize. That option curdled her blood. She had done nothing of which she was ashamed. As she later told Rauh, if she had briefly joined the Communist

Party, she had never taken it seriously. To confess to a wrong she did not feel would be tantamount to groveling before the bullies of the committee. Besides, if she confessed she would be asked for the names of those she had encountered in the party. Rauh tried to persuade committee counsel Frank S. Tavenner Jr. and member Richard Nixon to allow her to testify in executive session. But the approach came to nothing.

In the end Rauh and Daniel Pollitt devised a halfway strategy, to which she agreed. She could, as she wished, tell the committee "under oath everything about yourself but nothing about anyone else."[77] Rauh cautioned her about the risk involved: if the strategy failed, it would invite a citation for contempt and the jail sentence she hoped to avoid. But Rauh and Pollitt thought they might pave the way by appealing to public opinion. They would hedge her refusal to testify about others with a letter to the committee in which she would offer to answer anything they wanted to know about her if they agreed to ask her about no one else. That letter would explain the dilemma in which the committee put her and others like her, and appeal to their sense of decency. Rauh was almost sure that committee chair John Wood would refuse this overture, and he advised Hellman to prepare a public statement that she could release to the press after the committee hearing, explaining her position.

This second, public statement was never released, but in some ways the various drafts that Hellman composed provide what is possibly the most accurate assessment of her association with the Communist Party. She joined in 1938, "attended very few Communist party meetings in Hollywood in 1938–39 and an equally small number in New York in 1939–40. I stopped attending meetings or taking part in Communist Party activities in the latter part of 1940 and severed all connection with the Party." Under Rauh's prodding, she added a sentence admitting that she was "wrong about the Communist Party"; she had joined out of a misplaced idealism, and she had no bitterness with those with whom she associated in the party. She would not, she wrote, "become the instrument for damaging these lives and those of their families."[78] Together she and Rauh completed this statement as she drafted the initial version of the letter she would send to committee chair John Wood. She did not wish to claim the Fifth Amendment privilege against self-incrimination, she wrote to Wood: "I am ready and willing to testify before the representatives of our Government as to my own opinions and my own actions, regardless of any risks or consequences to myself." She could not and would not answer questions about other people. The letter, duly rejected, left her and Rauh fearful of what would happen next.

On the morning of the hearing, May 21, 1952, Dan Pollitt and Joseph Rauh picked Hellman up, a bundle of nervous energy. She had tried to calm her nerves the day before by shopping and was wearing the fruits of her expedition. Newspapers described the "blonde, forty-six and trim figured" Hellman wearing "a close-fitting black hat and a tailored brown-and-black checked silk dress."[79] As she took the stand, she "clenched a handkerchief in clasped hands." The hearing started slowly, and then twenty minutes in, counsel Frank Tavenner asked her whether it was in fact true that she had been present at a June 1937 meeting in the home of Martin Berkeley. Hellman ducked the question. "Most seriously I would like to ask you once again to reconsider what I have said in the letter," she replied. "In other words," said Tavenner, "you are asking the committee not to ask you any questions regarding the participation of other persons in the Communist Party activities." Hellman's back rose: "I don't think I said that, Mr. Tavenner."[80]

Then Chairman Wood, in a mistake he must have long regretted, suggested the letter be entered into the record. Rauh had brought with him copies he intended to distribute to the press after the hearing. Now he seized the opportunity. Dan Pollitt jumped up and passed copies of the letter to waiting hands.[81] Briefly, it looked as if Rauh would be disciplined for causing the letter to be distributed, but it had been entered into the record, which forced the committee to read it out loud. Ten more minutes of fruitless questioning later, the committee closed the hearing. It had been exactly thirty-seven minutes long, and it would situate Hellman as a heroine.

As Pollitt whisked her out of the hearing room, a dazed Lillian Hellman did not fully realize what had happened. She had won, a triumphant Rauh told her when he joined them later in a local coffee shop. She had defeated the committee; she had given no names and would serve no jail time. Rauh attributed the victory to her letter. In it, Hellman eloquently asked the committee to respect "simple rules of human decency and Christian honor" by not forcing her to betray people who had never done any harm. "I was raised in an old-fashioned American tradition, and there were certain homely things that were taught to me: to try to tell the truth, not to bear false witness, not to harm my neighbor, to be loyal to my country," she had written. "To hurt innocent people whom I knew many years ago in order to save myself is, to me, inhuman, and indecent and dishonorable. I cannot and will not cut my conscience to fit this year's fashions even though I long ago came to the conclusion that I was not a political person and could have no comfortable place in any political group."[82] The letter was now public, its plea for decency part of the public record. She had stood up to the committee by articulating a defiant moral position that quickly caught the American imagination.

Public and private praise poured in. LILLIAN HELLMAN BALKS HOUSE UNIT, headlined the *New York Times*.[83] Journalist Murray Kempton contrasted her behavior with that of others who debased themselves by confessing to sins they had not committed. This was a "courageous act of conscience," he concluded, "worthy of a lady."[84] One precious tribute came from Brooks Atkinson, the *New York Times* drama critic who had previously taken her to task for writing melodrama. He wrote to compliment her: "If we are to have a society that is not totalitarian and in which people do not denounce each other, as they do in Communist Russia and did in Nazi Germany, your attitude has a basic moral force that every lover of the American system must adhere to. It is the code of honor among civilized people of all national origins."[85]

Hellman reveled in this position. "It was like a wedding here yesterday, with strange people getting happy," she wrote to her friend Bill Alfred two days later, enclosing some of the newspaper clippings. "I must say the New York papers treated me fine . . . *The Mirror*, maybe, best of all."[86] She had been surprised to learn that when her name was mentioned at a luncheon at the American Jewish Congress, "the ladies applauded loud and long." The euphoria continued for a while. "I am a local heroine," she wrote to Melby a week after the event.[87] To Rauh she gushed, "The reaction here has been just too good to believe. There has been the largest amount of mail I have ever received about anything, and an equally large number of telephone calls." She sent her "deepest thanks and absolute conviction that we did everything as well as we could do it, and that the legal decisions you make were sound and thoughtful, and no matter what comes from them I will be fully satisfied and happy."[88]

Privately, she was not as confident. To Melby she complained about part of the strategy he had developed, regretting that she had agreed to deny Communist Party membership for the two years before the hearing and to take the Fifth Amendment for questions before that point: "I am sorry that I didn't take the legal risk and go back 13 years. I think it was the only unwise decision that Rauh made and stupid of me to have followed it."[89] For all her courage at the HUAC hearing, she could not hide a sense of vulnerability. To Melby she confessed to being "foolishly restless and frightened to be alone. That is new for me, and I don't like it."[90] She had difficulty working—difficulty that persisted through the summer, forcing her to set aside work on her new play and to focus instead on the Chekhov introduction. "One of the penalties of this year," she told Melby, "has been a restless refusal to sit down and work, or even to read or think." In the same letter, she elaborated: "I have got myself into kind of a bad, aimless state of depression and discomfort . . . I am doing foolish things, and feeling foolish things."[91]

The things she was doing were not only foolish, they were sometimes narcissistic and unprincipled as well. The Pleasantville farm sold, Dash rented the cottage in Katonah from their old friends Helen and Sam Rosen; Lillian often joined them there for a Saturday-night dinner. The Rosens were close friends and loyal supporters of Paul Robeson, with whom Hellman had fought for an end to racial segregation in the army during the war. Robeson, then still either in or close to the Communist Party and himself hounded by various government investigating agencies, was at dinner one night shortly after Hellman's HUAC hearing. Helen Rosen recalled watching Hellman, who "evidently did very well in public but was shivering inside of herself." That night "when she came into the kitchen to get her drink, leaving Paul and Dash and Sam in the other room, she gave me hell for having Paul there when she was there. I couldn't understand what she was talking about. She was in a fury, and she said, 'I've had a terrible time. I've been followed, my phone is probably tapped, and of all people to walk into—I don't need to be in the same room with Robeson!'" Helen tried to calm her down. "I said, 'Lillian, take it easy. He's your friend, he's my friend, he's our friend. You've been through the worst, what is this all about?'" The response from a still enraged Lillian was simply, "'Well it's too much, everything's too much.'"[92]

And indeed, Hellman was still suffering. Her victory over HUAC enraged political enemies on the right who remained convinced that she was a communist and that her clever strategy had enabled her to escape punishment. How could a woman who refused to cooperate with a government committee claim to be acting in the American tradition? Was it possible for political dissenters, for rebels and radicals, to love their country? Was it fair to allow those who refused to divulge their past commitments to hide behind claims of truth telling? Advocates of security turned on her old lover and continuing friend, John Melby. Melby was by then a well-regarded senior State Department officer stationed in the Philippines who visited Hellman on his not infrequent visits to the United States. The most recent visit, in Philadelphia, occurred just a month before her HUAC hearing. And he had briefly seen her just after the hearing itself. His association with Hellman drew the attention of the Department's Loyalty-Security board, which targeted him for investigation even before her HUAC hearing and picked it up with intensity afterward. To accuse Melby of disloyalty, his biographer Robert Newman tells us, was absurd. Since 1947, Melby had become a valued China hand with an unblemished record and a lengthy list of supervisors all attesting to his loyalty. "With his rock-ribbed reputation for anti-communism," Newman tells us, Melby and his lawyer "were sure that no puny guilt by association with a playwright who was also a friend of eminent officials, could do him in."[93]

But drifting away from Hellman did not protect Melby from the investigations of government committees. In late June 1952, the Loyalty-Security Board repeatedly grilled him about his relationship with Lillian Hellman. Convinced that she was a dangerous communist and that his admitted association with her convicted him of duplicity, the board continued to ask him about her communist associations. Two days later, Melby and Hellman met in Joseph Rauh's office. Lillian wanted to clear his name by appearing as a witness for Melby. Rauh, worried about her future as well as Melby's, counseled against it. Melby, increasingly worried about Lillian's political past, wavered but, according to Newman, finally gave in to the board and admitted that Hellman might well have had a past about which he did not know. For months the Loyalty-Security Board dueled with Melby, with Lillian on the sidelines, begging to appear as a witness on his behalf. If she could convince the board that she was not a communist and had herself never been disloyal, then the board would have no evidence of his disloyalty, no grounds to dismiss him. But when she finally testified in February 1953, the committee asked her nothing about her politics—they were already convinced on that score—and fastened instead on the repeated evidence of a devoted and committed relationship. John was fired the same spring of 1953 that Hammett was called before McCarthy's Permanent Subcommittee on Government Investigations to explain why so many of his detective stories could be found in government libraries overseas.

Hellman, a fresh new passport in hand, once again granted to her by Mrs. Shipley (who could not have issued it had she believed Lillian to be a

communist), left for an extended visit to Europe, where she again hoped
to find work. Though she could leave the country, Hellman never outran
her public image as a communist. She had defeated the House Committee
on Un-American Activities, to be sure, satisfying those who railed against
its violations of elemental civil liberties. But she had not squelched the
increasingly certain, though surely mistaken, public perception that
she was a communist. Repeatedly the label came back to haunt her—a
powerful weapon in the accusatory arsenal leveled against her. She might
evade the "known communist" label to emerge as a "fellow traveler" in the
late fifties and sixties, only to descend to the level of "unrepentant Stalinist"
in her later years. The labels suggest less about Hellman's beliefs and practices than about the public mind-set from which they emerged. They tell
us something about the long-lasting fear generated by Soviet communism
and the McCarthy period, and the search for suspects during an intermi-
nable Cold War. And they lead us to wonder how Hellman—whose major
sins were a continuing if misguided hope, an outspoken and voluble rebellion, and an angry and stubborn refusal to bow to bullies—managed
to become the public face of Stalinism for as long as she did.

CHAPTER 9

The Most Dangerous Hours

I see a road in this lovely land, crowded with people I liked and re-spected being pushed aside as the gay and very mischievous face of Joe McCarthy moves steadily faster than they do and so may catch up with us once again.

—Lillian Hellman, 1970

You have grown up in a country that has possibly come closest to its most dangerous hours if you believe that the corruption of liberty, the invasion of personal freedom is the sin of sins, the final sin.

—commencement address, Mount Holyoke College, 1976

How does one make a free womanhood, or a liberated womanhood, unless there are jobs and opportunities for women to have?

—American Scholar Forum, 1972

The lessons of the McCarthy period remained with Hellman for the rest of her life even as the hysteria of the Red Scare subsided. The 1950s wit-nessed the emergence of a solid middle-income class in the midst of unprecedented prosperity; at the same time, under Dwight Eisenhower's leadership a positive national consensus grew around some of the most contentious innovations of the New Deal years, including old-age pensions, unemployment insurance, and welfare support for the poor. But fear of war and subversion faded more slowly. After the Communist Control Act of 1954 declared the Communist Party "an agency of a hostile foreign power" and "a clear and present and continuing danger to the security of the United States," the party itself shrank into a tiny hard core of perhaps five thousand members, of whom one third might have been undercover FBI agents. The following December, the U.S. Senate censured Joseph McCarthy for impairing the dignity of the chamber. Yet HUAC continued to investigate the influence of communist thought in academia, education, and the entertainment industry. J. Edgar Hoover's FBI did not cease its search for communists, and it labeled "pink" or "red" those who supported liberal causes such as trade unionism and the burgeoning civil rights movement. Nor did the Subversive Activities Control Board stop investigating federal employees accused of affiliation with communist front organizations. Loyalty oaths became commonplace in states and educational institutions.

Hellman remained blacklisted by the movie industry throughout the decade, as did actors, directors, and screenwriters of all kinds. She survived the ordeal by working in the theater, where, bolstered by her fame, she continued to attract an audience. Slowly, she reemerged as the celebrity she had once been. Her adaptation of *The Lark* drew wide acclaim and played for more than six months. The 1956 musical version of *Candide* added to her luster even as it failed at the box office. Though she vowed after the disappointment to leave the theater scene behind her, she wrote one more great play, *Toys in the Attic*, which opened in February 1960. Some say it was her greatest play.[1]

Feeling more economically secure, she bought a house on Martha's Vineyard in 1955. There she befriended a distinguished group of literary neighbors who included novelist John Hersey and his wife Barbara, Sue and John P. Marquand, cartoonist Jules Feiffer, and, later, William and Rose Styron. Putting politics behind her, she socialized with an eclectic group of celebrities and intellectuals and met and grew to like some of the leading liberals of the moment. She made friends with Senator John Kennedy's speechwriter Richard Goodwin, who shared her love of fishing; she came to know McGeorge Bundy, then dean of Arts and Sciences at Harvard, and Arthur Schlesinger Jr., an advocate of Adlai Stevenson's presidential aspirations. Both Bundy and Schlesinger were noted for their liberal anticommunism. In the same period from the late fifties to the early sixties, she established intimate friendships with conservative columnist Joseph Alsop, Philadelphia lawyer Arthur Cowan, and CBS news executive Blair Clark. She might have disagreed politically with each of these individuals, but all of them remained lifetime friends.

With the election of John Fitzgerald Kennedy and the shift from a political climate of fear to one of hope, the honors and the work poured in. Bundy paved the way to a teaching job at Harvard, where she took her first crack at teaching a seminar of undergraduate students. She did not want, she said, to teach them how to write plays but to teach them how to write. "Are there students," she asked Bundy, "who are interested as I am, in the relation of drama writing to all other writing?"[2] In 1963, she won election to the American Academy of Arts and Letters, an honorary degree from Douglass College, and another from Wheaton College. The film version of *Toys in the Attic* appeared that summer. As the blacklist lifted, Hellman accepted an offer from Twentieth Century Fox to write the movie script for *The Chase*, a play written by Horton Foote that would be directed by Arthur Penn and feature Marlon Brando, Jane Fonda, and Robert Redford. She didn't like the way the film turned out, but still, she was back in the swing again. This was only part of it. More honorary degrees came from Brandeis in 1965 and Mount Holyoke in 1966. Visits abroad to attend openings of her plays spiced her days: Moscow in the fall of 1966, London and Paris in the spring of 1967, Paris and Moscow the following fall. At home, Mike Nichols mounted a first-class revival of *The Little Foxes* in 1967. Lillian Hellman was in full celebrity mode once more.

But in the sixties, the political debate took on a new shape, and Hellman once again found herself a target of criticism. President Kennedy's electoral victory and his desire to return to the domestic visions of FDR, the emerging civil rights and antiwar movements, and, later, the claims of feminism all seemed to Hellman to signal a newly energized population. At Harvard in the spring of 1961, she met with a small group of students whose critical minds she admired. She welcomed their incipient turmoil as an indication that students, among others, were emerging from the apathy of the fifties. At Harvard, and later at the Massachusetts Institute of Technology, the University of Chicago, and Yale and in the commencement addresses and lectures she gave at prestigious colleges and universities around the country, she invariably told her audiences to remember the lessons of the fifties: to be courageous, not to give in to bullies. Not to stand up for what you believe, she repeated to a generation of students, was the greatest dereliction of civic duty.[3] Hellman vigorously applauded the emergence of what came to be called a New Left, especially when, as at the 1968 Democratic convention in Chicago, young people turned their attention to political protest. She loved it when young people demonstrated "spunk" or courage.

Others on the left as well as on the right mistrusted students and despised the New Left. The young, they argued, lacked a sense of history, knew nothing of the perils of Marxism, and romanticized nonconformist and aesthetic lifestyles.[4] Around her, especially among the New York intellectuals and in the anticommunist left, Hellman heard only criticism of students. Cultural leaders such as Irving Howe thought them guilty of undermining a necessary vigilance against the Soviets. The controversy severed old political alliances and realigned partnerships. Sidney Hook and Irving Kristol opted to seek shelter by moving increasingly toward a right-wing stance. Socialism, they thought, would inevitably lead to totalitarianism of either the communist or fascist variety. To avoid that fate, they opted for programs that would suppress socialist impulses or socialist ideas. In the name of preserving democracy, oblivious to the cost to freedom of expression and civil liberties, an increasingly conservative minority targeted anything that did not look like free-market individualism. In their view, government intervention on behalf of the disadvantaged (African-Americans, migrant workers, women, the poor) constituted a slippery slope that would end, they thought, in totalitarianism. Focused around magazines like *Encounter* and *The New Leader*, most of this group, as historian Alan Wald puts it, "not only denuded themselves of past radicalism but developed sophisticated rationalizations for tolerating the essence if not the precise McCarthyite form of the witch-hunt."[5]

All through the sixties and into the early seventies, majority opinion deviated from this view. Men such as Philip Rahv, editor of *Partisan Review*, cultural critic Dwight MacDonald, and *Dissent* editor Irving Howe sought a distinctively American path toward the social-justice goals of the old left. Convinced that the future of American transformation lay in distancing themselves from communism in any form, they sought to recreate an audience for liberal or socialist programmatic change. *Partisan Review* and *Dissent* became the voices of transformative, noncommunist change.

Hellman did not participate in, and perhaps was even oblivious to, the sectarian arguments. Her politics remained a moral politics vested in the belief that too much attention was being paid to the Soviets, too little to civil liberties in America. For her the legacy of the McCarthy period rested in defending decency and loyalty and, most of all, in the courage to defend one's beliefs. So she hovered on the fringes of all these groups, continuing to value social change while for the most part ignoring unfounded sporadic accusations that she remained faithful to communist ideas. Her celebrity as a survivor of HUAC shielded her from explicit attack; her refusal, even in the sixties, to denounce Stalinism or to turn away from friends who clung to their own principles, rendered her politically untrustworthy to the continuing idealists. She was not, by their standards, an intellectual: she lacked what Irving Kristol called critical intelligence. When in the early 1960s some of the younger generation of the New York intellectuals (Jason Epstein, Robert Silvers, Barbara Epstein) founded the *New York Review of Books*—a magazine explicitly designed to foster conversation on the left outside the realm of the old Communist Party debates—Hellman was simply irrelevant. Friends and acquaintances including Robert Lowell, John Hersey, and John Marquand wrote for the *NYRB*; Hellman remained marginal.

In the politics of the sixties, the largely nonideological choices of activist students (and the New Left into which they merged) appealed to Hellman. She liked the fact that young people were standing up for something: they had what she called "spine." At a 1968 political rally, she declared with pleasure, "Our children black and white have caught up with our hypocrisies, and whatever our doubts about their actions or their methods, they have a right to sneer at us."[6] She would later describe their protests "as a mixed bag of the good and the foolish." The good part, she thought, was "the insistence upon examination of what they had been told, taught, and read." The bad consisted of "the taking over of college offices, damaging of files, bullying of teachers, and so on." But she did not condone the sending in of police to quell the protests of "good-natured young men and women with much to complain about that needed complaint."[7] Nor, on the other side, did she have much patience for the youth movement that questioned parental, political, and corporate authority, promoted sexual liberation, and suspected that anyone over thirty was already part of an unredeemable establishment. She considered this emerging counterculture (dropping out, turning on, communal living, flower power) mere foolishness. She later applied the same label to the cultural expressions of the women's movement.

The rise of grassroots efforts by southern blacks to stand up for themselves stirred Hellman deeply. The civil rights movement, she noted in her journal, was "the first deeply felt movement since the Spanish Civil War," an indication that people could not "live long on non-something" without belief. Recalling her own political epiphany, she scrawled notes in her own hand: "suddenly something like 1930s has appeared again and man is once more angry that other men don't eat very well, get snubbed and insulted, haven't proper rights."[8] Hellman never participated in the ongoing strategy sessions and debate as she had with efforts to eliminate Jim Crow from the army in the forties. This time around, she found a way to support the cause of civil rights by doing what she did best: raising money and writing.

In the summer of 1963 Hellman persuaded *Ladies' Home Journal* to send her as a journalist to report on the August 28, 1963, March on Washington organized by Martin Luther King Jr.'s Southern Christian Leadership Conference and a coalition of labor union and civil rights groups. To prepare the article, she did her usual job of research, clipping pieces from several newspapers and familiarizing herself with the Civil Rights Act then before Congress. She interviewed protest organizer Bayard Rustin along with a range of young southerners, many of them marchers in previous demonstrations. Among her contacts were two virulent southern opponents of civil rights, Louisana's senator Allen Ellender and Alabama's John Sparkman. She scrawled notes from her informants in a three-by-five notebook—to which she also included references to hair appointments, lists of expenses, and instructions she wanted to convey to her secretary at home. The notes reflect something of her feelings. Of a jail in Alabama, she noted "toilet facilities—toilet in room they slept" and "food was 2 times 5AM & 6PM. Grits & gravy & bread & no sugar for coffee." On another occasion, she recorded: "Treated girls as bad as boys. Electric prodders used on private parts . . . Police came in during night and used electric prodders. 24 girls to a cell—3 beds or 4 beds . . . Struck some of girls on breast."[9]

The piece that finally emerged, called "Sophronia's Grandson goes to Washington," used the device of her beloved nurse Sophronia (whose viewpoint was that of the old paternal order) to imagine what it would have been like for a young black man to be speaking up for himself. In it she mocked the positions of traditional racist southerners and told stories about the way protesting blacks faced beatings, dogs, and electric cow prodders. Graphic descriptions of Sheriff Dewey Colvard of Etowah County, Alabama, "putting a cow prodder to the breast of a girl" and later to the testicles of a boy provoked a denial and demand for retraction, to which the *Ladies' Home Journal* acceded.[10] Though Hellman did not deny having falsely named the sheriff, she insisted that she had accurately depicted the spirit of the events. "My article in all important matters tells the truth," she wrote brashly. "What is true should not be obscured by the fear of lawsuits."[11] Years later she would reject this logic when she was the victim of a similar rationale. But at the time, she hid behind her heritage "as a white woman born in the South" to insist on the veracity of her interpretation.[11] Some of her southern readers respectfully disagreed. They dismissed her efforts to excuse what one called her "slanderous defamation of Mr. Colvard's character" and insisted that "Lillian Hellman's birth was a geographical accident; she is not a Southerner."[12] And yet many saw this small confrontation as a courageous intercession in a much larger struggle. "I know that your experience will not keep you from speaking out against injustice wherever you see it," wrote her lawyer when, somewhat apologetically, he sent her his bill at the conclusion of the case, "and that your stand will ultimately be vindicated and approved."[13]

For all of her sympathy with the purposes of the march and her anger at the methods of those who resisted black protest, for all of her insistence that "the argument for States' rights was now reduced to the argument for the right of each police department to act as they saw fit," she could not restrain her impatience with the slow pace of change.[14] White people shared the blame for this, she thought. "What is interesting now," she reminded herself, recalling her frequent injunctions against silence, is "where the white man had been all those years—very few of us will protest unless the victim makes us."[15] She gave no quarter even to her friends. Folk singer Pete Seeger remembered her dismissing the words of "We Shall Overcome," the song that became the anthem of the movement. "She didn't like the song," he recalled. "She said, 'someday, someday . . . That's been said for too long.'"[16]

The same mixture of sympathy, relief, and impatience pervaded Hellman's attitude toward antiwar movements of the sixties. Between 1961 and his death in 1963, President Kennedy slowly escalated American military commitments to Vietnam. Hellman remained uninvolved during this period. She was, after all, a friend of McGeorge Bundy, now a Kennedy adviser, and she still enjoyed fishing with Richard Goodwin. But in 1964 and 1965, as President Lyndon Baines Johnson stepped up American troop presence, Hellman's anger mounted; her old desire for peace rose. She could not bear an acquiescent silence in the face of policies that she abhorred. But what could she do? In 1965, her former Harvard student and now good friend Fred Gardner came up with an idea to establish coffeehouses outside army bases where GIs uncomfortable with the war could talk with like-minded souls. Hellman loved the idea. She offered Gardner $5,000 and the use of her Peugeot for a year to get the project off the ground. The idea worked, and Gardner, along with his partner, Donna Mickelson, established a GI coffeehouse network that provided neutral territory for conversation. After they were taken over by more ideological antiwar activists, the role of the coffeehouses diminished.[17]

Later, Hellman translated her opposition to the war into support for Eugene McCarthy's 1968 presidential candidacy. The campaign, headed up by her good friend Blair Clark, included old friends and new ones, all of them opponents of the war. She joined them and McCarthy on countless platforms and at rallies to articulate the moral stance that was her trademark. There she chose to remind audiences of the importance of articulate leadership in the service of just causes. At a huge Madison Square Garden event organized by Hannah Weinstein, she noted how easily Joseph McCarthy prevailed "often unopposed by those who had not been so frightened of liars and bullies when Roosevelt was there to give them the courage evidently lost on the day he died." Not to protest in the face of a war cloaked in democratic words, she told that audience, was to share the sin of hypocrisy. "We have allowed our government to kill an innocent people, as they explained that their death was for their own good."[18] When she received the 1969 National Book Award for *An Unfinished Woman*, she asked her audience why they were not disturbed "by the death of young men they have in majority, silently agreed to send across the world against a people who never harmed them, into a war they do not understand."[19]

In light of the war in Vietnam, politics took on a new dimension. Hellman's resonant moral pleas suggest that she closely identified her own Cold War experiences with those of the young people who challenged a war they opposed. They too risked castigation and exclusion for their opinions. Her messages begged audiences to overcome the fears she still shared with them and to get out and do something. "So many of us climbed into that bed of pain in those years," she reminded her own generation, "and have stayed there ever since."[20] Her stance brought her closer to elements of the left and New Deal coalitions—who now defined their politics as liberal and social democratic—and especially to the New York intellectuals. Their shared opposition to the war in Vietnam, their common desire to expose America's malfeasances around the globe in the name of democracy and freedom, temporarily obscured deeply rooted disagreements over the Soviet Union. To this group, Hellman brought her luster as a "moral beacon," her reputation as a brave opponent of McCarthyism.[21]

Hellman's moral credibility increased when she began to speak out with respect to the intellectual dissent that boiled up in the Soviet Union in the late fifties. Censorship remained rigid behind the iron curtain, but underground (samizdat) publication of stories and novels enabled writers to circulate their work privately and to smuggle it out of the Soviet Union for publication abroad, often under false names. Writers and printers caught circulating work in this way, rather than subjecting it to official censored channels, risked long jail sentences and confiscation of their possessions. In the winter of 1965–66, the Soviet authorities tried two writers, Yuli Daniel and Andrei Sinyavsky, for criticizing the regime in articles smuggled out of the Soviet Union and published in the foreign press. After a well-publicized show trial, the court found them guilty and leveled sentences of hard labor—seven years for Daniel and five for Sinyavksy. But in contrast to earlier years, when Russian intellectuals remained silent and communists abroad supported the regime, in 1966 the dissidents attracted vocal support inside and outside the Soviet Union. Hellman joined the public outcry against the regime's intolerance. In 1938 she had done exactly the opposite, signing a statement in support of the Moscow trials that condemned several writers to death. She had not spoken up when actor and director Solomon Mikhoels was executed in 1948. Nor did she utter a word when the poet Itzik Feffer, whom she met during a 1943 visit to the United States, died in a Soviet prison in 1952. Her voice now signaled misgivings about her previous rationalizations of Soviet repression. Catherine Kober Zeller, her goddaughter, remembers her around this time "as standing up, or pacing, furious at herself, with all the intensity of her fury, for not having seen through what was going on in Russia." Kober Zeller adds, "I felt, at that moment, that she hated herself for it."[22]

Hellman visited the Soviet Union the following spring to attend a theater festival. She was warmly received by a regime that still recalled her wartime expedition. Her old friend and interpreter Raisa Orlova, now married to Lev Kopelev, one of the country's leading dissenters, took her under her wing. This put her in an awkward position when she received an invitation to address the fourth national congress of the Union of Russian Writers in the spring of 1967. She accepted reluctantly, not wanting to offend the regime. Still, she had to decide whether to support the regime's refusal to tolerate dissent or cast her lot with the dissenters. She chose to do the latter, offering the group a sharply worded message urging them to remain true to their values regardless of state pressure to follow a particular line. "Intellectuals—and by intellectuals I mean men who believe in the power of reason—can continue in the hopes they once had only if they come together to speak honestly of past mistakes and present problems." Intellectuals, she insisted, "almost never wish to imprison men for speaking words they do not like . . . all intellectuals believe in freedom and many of them have an honorable record of fighting for it. No medals need be given for that fight: freedom is the essence of thought, the blood on the paper. Without freedom the intellectual will choke to death and his country will gasp for air. Thus the demand for it is the measure of true patriotism."[23] She might have been speaking of the United States just fifteen years earlier. Back in the United States, she found herself publicly proclaimed as a champion of Soviet dissent. Not yet comfortable as an opponent of the regime, Hellman hedged. She had not meant to imply that writers opposed the Soviet system; she said only that they wanted to be able to express themselves freely within it.[24]

She clung more persuasively to that argument when she lashed out at novelist Anatoly Kuznetsov, who fled the Soviet Union for England in the spring of 1969. Unlike Alexander Solzhenitsyn, who preferred to suppress his work rather than see it censored, Kuznetsov published censored editions that conformed to bureaucratic demands. His compliant behavior (which included denouncing novelists Andrei Sakharov and Yevgeny Yevtushenko for failing to cooperate with the Soviet authorities) earned him a trip to Britain, where he immediately sought asylum. Once safely out of Soviet reach, the forty-year-old Kuznetsov published an incendiary attack on what he remembered of the Soviet Union in his youth. The Western press and literati welcomed Kuznetsov as a friend and ally. Lillian refused the consensus. She knew, she wrote in a *New York Times* piece, that intellectuals in the Soviet Union were in turmoil; and she knew as well the disgusting pressure exerted by "the semi-literate bureaucrats, who suppress and alter manuscripts, who dictate who can and cannot be published." But Kuznetsov, she argued, protested only when it was safe to do so. Palpably bitter, she concluded her piece: "I'd like to bet that he'll soon pay us a visit and the dinner party lists are already being drawn up. After dinner in a chair by the fireside—the favorite position of Whittaker Chambers once upon a time—he will speak to the guests of freedom but somebody should tell Kuznetsov that freedom earned by betraying innocent friends is a contradiction of terms."[25]

Hellman surely relived the experiences of the early fifties when she watched her friends choose how to behave under pressure of investigation. But the Kuznetsov episode reminded others more of 1938, when she had rationalized her support for what she should have seen as an evil regime. In attacking Kuznetsov for cowardice, she seemed to expose her own hypocrisy. Commentaries in the *New Yorker* and *Time* magazine noted that Hellman was "scarcely in a position to demand that a Soviet writer risk his liberty and perhaps his life, by making open protests on Soviet soil."[26] Hellman angrily accused William Shawn, editor of the *New Yorker*, of "misinterpretation presented under the covering banner of 'fact.' "[27] Her agent, Robby Lantz, objected that *Time* had returned to "the old pastime of witch-hunting and red-baiting."[28] And yet Hellman resisted the notion that her piece in any way defended the Soviet Union. "I didn't mean to 'champion the USSR' or anything else," she wrote to a sympathetic correspondent. "I meant only that I didn't like what Mr. Kuznetsov had to say about his friends."[29]

For all of the renewed attention, Hellman remained in the late sixties unsure of how to situate herself. Her friend Anne Peretz and Catherine Kober Zeller both remember her as mildly depressed, though she continued to teach regularly and to lecture widely.[30] Her plays and the film versions of *The Little Foxes* and *The Children's Hour* received renewed attention. But she was a playwright whose time had passed. She knew, she would say later, that she didn't want to write any more plays, but she also knew that she "wanted to go on being a writer . . . I had to find some other form to write in."[31] That form turned out to be the memoir.

In 1966, she persuaded Bennett Cerf (Hammett's old editor at Random House) to publish a collection of Hammett's fiction for which she would write an introduction. The effort proved transformative. Hellman refused the temptation to write biographically about her "closest . . . most beloved friend," trying instead to capture some of the feeling of the man she had both loved and fought with for "thirty-one on and off years."[32] Moving from memory to memory, she produced a remarkable essay infused with love and affection, with pride in Hammett's idiosyncrasies, and with pleasure at her own capacity to cope with them. But it was an essay that, critics argued, placed her too centrally in Hammett's life and claimed too much for the importance of their relationship. It revealed more about her than about him. The piece proved to be a model for the memoirs to which she would soon turn.

Hellman came reluctantly, and with great insecurity, to the idea of writing a memoir. She didn't like the idea of writing about herself; she feared writing about others. Besides, she didn't know who might publish it. Relationships had soured with Random House, which had put most of her plays into print, and she wasn't getting along with Alfred Knopf over the Hammett stories. Stanley Hart, an editor at Little, Brown, was at the time actively pursuing her. But she was uncomfortable. That company had, in 1951, parted with Angus Cameron, then a young editor of left-wing proclivities. It had also, unforgivably, apologized for publishing politically "dangerous" authors and named Lillian Hellman among them. Cameron recalled that Hellman came to him before she signed with Little, Brown and the two agreed that "it was many years ago and people are all different there."[33] After she overcame her doubts and signed the book up, Hellman worried that she "wouldn't like it when I finished it," and insisted on a clause that allowed her to return the advance without penalty if she didn't like the final product.[34] Even after she sent the manuscript in, she lingered over the details. William Abrahams, who served as her editor and became her friend, was in near despair at the end. "Lillian telephoned to say that she was uncertain about one passage," he wrote to his boss. She wanted lawyers to check whether the words in a particular film had been spoken by actors or written as subtitles. Abrahams thought she had "a case of jitters brought on by giving up the manuscript to the printer."[35]

The final product, An Unfinished Woman, proved to be an intriguing mix of incisive commentary on herself and others punctuated by reflective and emotive anecdotes. About one third of it is a roughly chronological account of her growing-up years. Another chunk replicates heavily edited diary entries of her trips to Spain in 1937 and to Moscow in 1944–45. The rest consists of three character sketches. "Hammett" reproduces much of her introduction to The Big Knockover. "Dorothy Parker" depicts the "tangled fishnet of contradictions" that represented her own sense of herself. The final story, of her longtime housekeeper Helen, is, in the words of one critic, "a subtle study in race relations and the liberal conscience, shaped like a story."[36] Hellman's parents, relatives, and friends emerge from behind curtains of memory, each starring in a story of love or disappointment or hope. As a memoir must, An Unfinished Woman reveals less of the lives it puts forward than of an inner Hellman.

But the book worked. Admiring reviewers described it as "a record of personal discovery" that captures "the deepest of feelings, coming plain, and meant to be that, enlarged nonetheless by its clarity and infectious in its precision."[37] A British reviewer suggested that Hellman had taken "the very personal fragments" of her life and merged them to reveal a "personality of real beauty."[38] Another complimented the writing as "lucid, flinty, vulnerable," and averred that "the compressed prose is diamond hard and sometimes brilliant and the dialogue is like one pithy speech after another out of a Hellman play."[39] If reviewers complained about the silences—"the omission of any discussion about her political passions, her life in the theater, her sexual appetites"—they interpreted them generously, seeing in them confessions of vulnerability, measures of her continuing effort to find herself. They appreciated her modesty, her search for integrity, her need for solitary moments. "She has given us a detailed portrait of a person who doesn't want to be portrayed," wrote Christopher Lehmann-Haupt in the New York Times.[40] Critics almost universally complimented An Unfinished Woman for its "rare imagination and literary skill," at least one noting that it revealed "with an almost sad reluctance" the unexpected personal story of a great American playwright. Hellman, one concluded, had drawn a portrait of a complex woman, at once shrewd and difficult. The self of An Unfinished Woman was simultaneously shy and frightened and "an adventurous rebel." This was a book in which everyone could find "a mirror, and an image," concluded Life magazine.[41]

Released at the end of June 1969, An Unfinished Woman climbed to eighth on the New York Times bestseller list within a month. It stayed on top for three full months, winning the National Book Award for 1969 and launching Hellman on her new career as memoirist. She was excited and delighted. She signed a new contract with Little, Brown, with the proviso that she continue to work with her editor, William Abrahams, who had now relocated to California. Again the honors poured in: visiting professorships at MIT and Berkeley in the spring of 1971, and then a distinguished professorship at Hunter College for the spring of 1973. Hellman, by all accounts, loved to teach and took students seriously. She thought carefully about what she wanted to convey to them and commented copiously on her students' work. They, in turn, often wrote to tell her how meaningful her classes were. Elected to the Theater Hall of Fame in 1973, she won a woman-of-the-year award from New York University's alumnae club the same year.

The book could not have been better timed, appearing just as a new young generation of women's movement activists cohered into a political force. The women's liberation movement had built rapidly in the sixties, emerging from women's growing discontent with limited roles in the home and rampant discrimination in the workplace. It was fueled as well by a powerful civil rights movement that involved black and white women in the struggle for freedom, and nurtured by a search to end the war in Vietnam that encouraged women as well as men to challenge the twin gods of manliness and wartime bravado. *An Unfinished Woman* caught the crest of the moment. It followed on a year of rapid and almost invisible organizing that included the emergence of radical women's groups like Red Stockings and the increasing success of a three-year-old National Organization of Women. It paralleled the spread of small consciousness-raising groups designed to allow women to "speak bitterness" and to confront a growing sense that private life was lived in the context of public decisions as well as shaped by them. The year 1969 followed on a widely publicized August 1968 protest action against the Miss America pageant in Atlantic City, which demanded an end to the fetishizing of women's bodies. It was the year that young women began to understand and to repeat the mantra "The personal is political." And it preceded an August 1970 mass march by women who celebrated the fiftieth anniversary of women's suffrage with banners that read WOMEN STRIKE FOR PEACE AND EQUALITY.

Nineteen sixty-nine was also the year that tensions emerged between the political and cultural strands of the women's movement. Radical feminists urged women to focus on changing the organization of personal life and familial relationships. If women eliminated the demeaning attributes of language and lifestyle, thought radical feminists, if they controlled their own reproductive choices, if they resisted limited gender roles, they could win equality between the sexes. These changes would require overturning a patriarchal power structure whose insidious effects materialized in the everyday actions of men and women. To radical feminists, questions of chivalry—who opened car doors or held coats or walked nearest the sidewalk—mattered as symbols of the larger patriarchy. Liberal feminists, to whose ideas Hellman's came close, believed, in contrast, that economic opportunity held the key to gender equality. The first step, they thought, should be to drop the barriers to women's education, occupational choices, and career aims by fighting for legislative and policy changes that would provide access to job training and professional education, make available credit and financial resources, and ensure fair treatment in the workplace for women regardless of their family status.

Hellman was already in her mid-sixties when women's liberation became a movement, and she was approaching her seventies by the time the conflict between liberal and radical feminists became apparent. Ironically, perhaps, her own remarkable successes as a playwright drew attention at the time because she had achieved them as a woman. Hellman, who had never wanted to be identified as a "woman playwright," now found herself a heroine to women who admired her achievements because of her identity, not her politics. Her readers focused as well on the unorthodox lifestyle she celebrated in *An Unfinished Woman*. The long-term relationship with Dashiell Hammett, the several abortions of which she made no secret, the sexual liaisons in which she continued to indulge even as she grew older: all these turned her into a model for the new women's movement.

Yet the Lillian Hellman dramatized in her memoir bore little resemblance to the Hellman her friends and lovers knew. The strident and outspoken persona that Hellman memorialized presented another side in private. She could, says Feibleman, "walk into a room very quietly and sit down, and the room would turn to her, and people wanted to get to know her or wanted to be in her good graces. She was very electric, electrifying, magnetic." Nor was she, in real life, sexually adventurous or aggressive. Peter Feibleman describes her as shy sexually, a description that affirms the femininity that others noticed in private moments. She was, says Feibleman, "very passive, very unaggressive, very feminine—one of the most feminine women I've ever known. The bark and the bite were political or emotional. Never sexual, never sexual."[42]

This second Lillian, this woman who, to paraphrase Feibleman once again, both lived her life and performed it, made no secret of her contempt for issues of cultural change. She believed she had become successful as a result of her own talents and efforts, not as the result of her sexually liberated lifestyle. She had earned her way to the top, and her success had given her access to political culture that promised to shape the world. She had deployed her fame to espouse political causes that could address issues of racial and gender equality. She had used her visibility to help organize screenwriters in the 1930s; she had relied on her talent to raise her voice in the fight against fascism and on her celebrity to raise funds for causes she cared about in the forties. Hellman had done all this without particularly focusing on women's issues, though always with an eye to the collective strengths of politically mobilized women.

To Hellman, women's equality was never a goal in itself. Rather, she believed in equality as a vehicle for achieving national and worldwide political progress and the good society she imagined. From early on, women's failures to help each other had systematically disappointed her. While political emancipation had led to advances for individual women, in her early forties she wrote, "it has nowhere gone in quite the most desirable direction." She expected that since women had always been underdogs, they "would become the most advanced, the most liberal." She hoped that because women "suffered from the deprivation of certain basic human rights" she would be "in the forefront of the fight for others' human rights," and she anticipated that "because she is the giver of human life, she would be also the most zealous guardian of it—instead she is often the most bloodthirsty."[43] These lessons stuck with her. At a Women for Wallace luncheon during Henry Wallace's 1948 presidential campaign, she accused her female audience of being "remarkably indifferent to the problems of our time . . . Another generation gave us the vote and either we have not used it at all or we have too often used it for the wrong issues and the wrong men . . . another generation worked hard to establish us as equal people, capable of doing more than giggling at dinner tables, or scrubbing floors for those who did. We responded with little enough gratitude, little true interest, in the affairs of our country or the state of the world."[44]

To Hellman, "career" women, as the postwar world defined them and as the new women's movement of the late sixties and early seventies proposed to empower them, did not automatically harbor the kinds of values necessary to political progress. Career women who adopted the aggressive strategies and power-grabbing mentality of successful men would only emulate their politics. And while she understood that wealth ruled the world, she believed that most real wealth was inherited from husbands and fathers rather than earned, so it was folly to assume that women with careers would exercise significant amounts of power. In her view only a broad education, one not oriented toward a particular career, could lead women and men to decide how to live their lives and to define their own values. "Pick yourself a few decent standards and stick by them," she advised one audience."[45]

Despite her skepticism, *An Unfinished Woman* spoke directly to the lives of the young women then marching. Its depiction of a sexually free, politically engaged, and economically successful life, a life filled with love and friendship, with courage and determination, resonated with a generation of young women in search of models. In direct and clipped prose, less reminiscence than an evocation of self, Hellman recalled a life lived not by the standards of her mother's generation or those of the postwar young, but by those whom she so frequently called "my generation." These standards, as she remembered them, were rooted in integrity and honesty, in a lack of pretense and an absence of sentimentality. "My generation," she would say repeatedly, "didn't emulate the standards of their mothers; they chose to go their own ways." Rejecting conventional modes of being, Hellman painted herself, as one reviewer noted, as "impatient with 'lady stuff' . . . attracted towards dangerous places and brave intelligent men."[46]

Lillian shrugged off the adulation. She did not believe that women's liberation could or should be a matter only or primarily of sexual freedom. In the series of tours and interviews and invitations that followed the publication of *An Unfinished Woman* and then, four years later, *Pentimento*, Lillian expressed her impatience with what she thought of as the diversionary tactics of the current women's liberation movement. They had taken their eyes off "the problems implicit in our capitalist society."[47] Middle-class white mothers had failed to teach their daughters values like courage, loyalty and integrity, warning them that these were "unfeminine, unfashionable qualities," inconsistent with "the qualities that will get you a husband."[48] The result, she argued, was a generation of women without real values. From these generalizations she exempted black women and poor women, who, since they had always needed to work, had developed more substantial characters. The educated white woman, in her eyes, bore responsibility for women's bad name.

These views undermined Hellman's position in the women's movement. In 1972, in the heady moments of women's liberation, Hellman moderated a panel on the "condition of women today." Panel members—seven distinguished women writers, novelists, and critics—had been invited by Hiram Haydn, editor of the *American Scholar*, to record a conversation that he later published in the pages of the journal. The exchange began with a question originally suggested by Hannah Arendt: "What will we lose if we win?"[49] The debate, which took place in mid-May, was sometimes heated and often acerbic. In it, Hellman revealed her sense of what being a woman meant to her. Unsurprisingly to anyone familiar with her life, she argued that the most significant issue for women was economic independence. Nothing mattered, she repeatedly asserted to panelists who generally disagreed with her, as much as good jobs for women. "Equal wages, equal opportunities" seemed to her the crucial issues. When another panelist sought to override these concerns, telling her, "That goes without saying," Hellman replied sharply, "I'm afraid it doesn't go without saying. I think one of the troubles with women's liberation is that it has not touched women of the so-called lower classes, deprived classes. It's really been a movement of intellectuals and well-heeled middle-class ladies. It's too bad." Challenged by African-American novelist Alice Walker to explain why black women, who had historically earned their own livings, nevertheless remained sweet and compliant to their men, Hellman replied that such behavior "pays better." Nor did she credit cultural issues with paving the way to change. Dismissing impatiently the significance of "who takes out the garbage and who takes care of the children," deriding the debate over whether women should or should not burn their brassieres, she returned insistently to the idea that "the liberation of people comes about through economic equality. Men could not put women down if women were truly equal."[50]

Hellman repeated this theme endlessly, offering herself as the archetype of the successful woman who had achieved renown and a substantial fortune on her own merits. "It seems to me a question of what dignity is about," she told that 1972 audience, and dignity in her mind involved "economic equality, spiritual equality," the capacity to meld a satisfying personal life with fulfilling wage work. Dignity manifested itself in a refusal to idealize marriage and motherhood. That made her insufficiently womanly to some, and decidedly masculine to others. Perhaps she was something of a throwback, for even as she drew on the models of the twenties to flout the gender assumptions of the seventies, she insisted that she was merely following the conventions of the most interesting people of her generation. "Enlarging the norms is good for everybody," said Elizabeth Janeway, who hoped for a broader conception of what a woman could be.[51] Lillian Hellman agreed. She had, she thought, done her bit to do just that.

In some respects, Lillian was repeating what she had always said: she hoped women might acquire what she variously called self-respect or dignity. She believed women could achieve these only if they had the possibility of earning their own livings. Lack of economic independence produced ugly emotions and despicable acts, as she had written in two of her best plays. Regina of *The Little Foxes* challenged her brothers, took the life of her husband, and risked the love of her daughter to acquire control of family resources. The two aging sisters in *Toys in the Attic* remained so

invested in the love of their younger brother that when his newfound success threatened to reduce his dependence on them, they sabotaged him
rather than allow him to reverse roles. Nobody was better at drawing the
portraits of women who, like those in her mother's family led frustrated
lives that revolved around the desire to have, to keep, and to construct
something of their own; nobody was better at articulating the sense that
women's traditional economic dependence undermined their capacity to
be unselfishly loving; nobody better captured the ambivalence of women
whose emotional dependence was forged in their inability to control their
own money.

To the goal of a women's movement that could produce self-respecting
women and free them from the internal pressures and tensions of pretense
and self-abnegation, Hellman remained faithful even as her own fame and
wealth grew. Despite her consistent vanity—she carefully cut and dyed her
hair, dressed modishly, and wore perfume daily—she ridiculed the attention paid to issues of language, insisting on being addressed as Miss Hellman rather than the clumsy *Ms.* She preferred to be published by general
literary publishing houses and magazines rather than those dedicated to
"militant feminist publications," but she would settle for publication by
such houses over no publication at all.[52] She turned a deaf ear to pleas to lend
her name or her funds to feminist causes. Nor did she particularly identify,
as a writer, with women's issues. Rather, as she told a series of graduating
college students, she hoped that young women would "speak out for the
benefit of others" and wished for them that they "have something to do
with making the country what it must and ought to be."[53]

For Hellman, the important symbiosis, the tension that called young
women to act, was between work and politics rather than between money
and love. In the spring of 1975, she gave a commencement address at Barnard, which she later published in the editorial pages of the *New York Times*
and then republished in the college issue of *Mademoiselle* magazine. In the
various drafts of this address she connected the threads of her concern
with what women would become. The world ahead of them, she told the
graduates, was a troubled one, and America was filled with people who
misused power to make it worse. But these graduating women had a responsibility to connect their book learning with what was happening in the
world. America would grow better only if they undertook the responsibility of examining their lives and their goals. To do that, they first needed to
make a living. "How can there ever be liberation of women," she asked,

"unless they can earn a living?" Ibsen's Nora, she noted, "having slammed the door and opened it for women's liberation," was embraced by students but not really recognized for what she did or couldn't do. What happened to Nora after she slammed the door? she asked. And then answered her own question: "The talk of brassieres or no brassieres, who washes the dinner pots, whether you are a sex object . . . has very little meaning unless the woman who slams the door can buy herself dinner and get out of a winter wind."[54]

To Hellman, who had managed to do far more than get out of a winter wind, the lessons of women's freedom were clear. Hellman hoped that a women's movement would be a means to an end—the end being a more engaged and politically informed community of citizens. She wanted to eliminate boundaries imposed by class and wealth in order to assure the personal and cultural freedom that could lead women to make a better world. And she made no secret of her contempt for women who used wealth conspicuously or wastefully. *My Mother, My Father and Me*, her last attempt at writing for the theater, mocked the aridity of a 1950s family whose life focused on the meaningless consumption of a vapid mother and the empty goals of her purposeless teenage son. The lesson of these shortcomings was hard to miss: if she was going to argue for real values, she would have to put her own on the line. And her own commitments were laid out in the books that brought her a second chance at celebrity. All her life she fought for decency, self-respect, and dignity that could be achieved only by self-support and political engagement in the struggle for a better world.

Small wonder, then, that for all that she was idolized by the young feminists of the 1970s, Hellman could not fully identify with the modern version of women's liberation. In that 1972 panel, Elizabeth Janeway and Carolyn Heilbrun among others tried to tell her that questions of life's meaning and purpose, of socialization and self-confidence, could not be disentangled from those of economic opportunity and freedom to choose jobs. Hellman thought otherwise. By herself, through hard work and talent, she had achieved money, status, and fame in her lifetime and by her own hand. She was a self-made woman. Her capacity to live freely—her sexual liberation, her personal freedom—rested on the economic foundation she built for herself. Young women, she thought, could choose to emulate her unorthodox lifestyle—to emulate her capacity "to walk out if somebody insults me"—only if they were economically independent. But the younger generation of women reserved their adulation for her style. They admired her brash and outspoken stance, her ability to smoke and to swear and above all her courage in living by her own rules of personal conduct. "I was so bored. I got so nasty," she told an interviewer about that famous panel. "Nobody seemed to be talking about economics."[55]

Even as she became popular among young women of the 1970s, she did not call herself a feminist. When, in 1976, interviewer Barbara Walters asked her how, in the face of her skepticism about women's liberation, she accounted for her status as something of a "cult figure," Lillian replied, only half tongue in cheek, "It is probably due to the fact that I lived with a man so very long without marrying him." "Do you think they say she really did it when nobody else dared to?" Walters asked. Lillian replied, "Well, you know the younger generation always thinks that nobody did anything before they did it . . . I wish it were something more solid." Walters pursued the issue, asking Hellman how she felt about "women's lib." Lillian replied, "I think it is an excellent theory," and continued, "It certainly should be fought for, probably on any ground one can fight it." But she punctuated each assent with a qualifier: "I wish they'd get more on economic equality than who wears what brassiere," she added. And again, "I don't think it can be fought for in the foolish ground."[56] Still, Walters would not let go. How was it, she asked, that she didn't identify with women's liberation, "even though you would be perhaps one of the heroines of it"? Hellman responded: "I stayed out of it because I realized I would get into arguments over it; I once conducted a forum on it with very intelligent and educated ladies and I was so in disagreement with most of them I thought I'd better not do this again."[57]

She did not, after that 1972 debate, get into any more fights with adherents of women's liberation, but she did stick to her guns and in so doing earned the veneration of a generation with whom she had declared herself at odds. For years after that 1972 forum, she told whoever would listen that she had been misunderstood then and that she continued to be misunderstood. "I don't have to tell you how deeply I believe in women's liberation," she told interviewer Bill Moyers.[58] But in the same breath, she repeated her assertion that "it all comes down to whether or not you can support yourself as well as a man can support himself—whether there's enough money to make certain decisions for yourself, rather than a dependence."[59] Hellman clearly met this test. She placed the demands of women's liberation in the context of the life she had shaped for herself and found them wanting. She never stopped admiring the spirit and gumption of the young women who acted in the name of women's liberation, and she never stopped hoping to convince them that economic independence was their best hope for expanded personal rights and freedom—and that this in turn would lead to the better world that she had so long envisioned. "I'm with the movement in theory," she said. "Most of its goals are excellent, although I'm uncomfortable with some of the slogans. Wearing or not wearing a bra is terribly unimportant. It's being able to buy that bra yourself—that's important."[60] If Hellman could not admit to being a feminist by the standards of the seventies, she was certainly one by her own.

In 1970, disturbed by what she saw as the increasing repression of the Nixon administration, Hellman saw an opportunity to do exactly what she had hoped her friends and colleagues would do in the McCarthy period, exactly what she had been urging students to do in the 1960s: to stand up for what they believed. As early as 1968, Hellman was already worrying out loud about the re-emergence of surveillance techniques and the possibility of a new McCarthyism.

She had good reason to worry. In April 1968, the assassination of Martin Luther King Jr. produced a wave of despair in the black community. Two months later, Robert Kennedy—who, as attorney general, had led his brother's campaign to secure voting rights for Southern African-Americans—died at the hands of another assassin. Parts of a disjointed civil rights movement formed a black liberation faction to demand black power; some members of the Black Panthers, who organized breakfast programs for poor children, resorted to weapons amid a rhetoric of self-protection. Radical fringe groups like the Weather Underground splintered away from mainstream protest movements to organize a campaign of bombings and demonstrations that would lead to revolutionary change. Violence mounted on other fronts too. The war in Vietnam was going badly: national security adviser Henry Kissinger and President Nixon had formed a tight cabal to make decisions about how to run it. Even the State Department found itself excluded from policy decisions. Matters got worse when, in the fall of 1969, the air force secretly began bombing Cambodia. As opposition mounted and peace marchers challenged the power of the military industrial complex, government surveillance stepped up. National Guard efforts to defuse peace protests turned ugly.

The administration responded to the turmoil with heightened repression. In the name of order, and to counter what it called subversion, the

Justice Department and the FBI infiltrated a wide variety of political organizations thought to be threatening. Lists of those under surveillance grew. The FBI, joined by the Central Intelligence Agency (CIA), escalated an already massive campaign to subvert left-wing organizations by encouraging "deep cover" agents to act as provocateurs. Operation Chaos, originated by the CIA in 1967, collected 7,200 files on Americans within national borders; army intelligence spread one thousand agents among the protest groups; the FBI's Cointelpro (Counter Intelligence Operation) sent anonymous letters to left-wing groups designed to set off quarrels and foment internecine warfare. The undercover agents did their jobs well, provoking violence where none might have occurred. Twenty-eight members of the Black Panther political party were killed in 1969. The same year, Greensboro, North Carolina, undercover agents incited militants to bomb stores and ambush police, providing the weapons that enabled them to do so. Police, hearing rumors, called in the National Guard; one student died. In the meantime, opposition to the war reached a fever pitch: as many as a third of draftees were not showing up for their induction dates. As they had done before, law-enforcement agencies blamed communist infiltration and influence. But the hammer and sickle no longer frightened the young. Campus protests escalated; in May 1970, four students died when National Guard troops opened fire on a peaceful demonstration at Kent State University in Ohio.[61]

Hellman had not forgotten that Nixon was a key player on Joseph McCarthy's Government Operations subcommittee. Nor had the wounds she sustained in that period healed. In February 1970, she began to talk about how to resist what she saw as a new period of repression. Robert Silvers, editor of the *New York Review of Books*, recalled the moment: "She felt strongly that the old rot was setting in and that there was a need for a new group of citizens—writers, artists, scientists, lawyers—who would, so to speak, be on guard—a group that would be willing to speak out in defense of constitutional rights against the dangers of bullying, devious secret government."[62] Starting with a group of trusted friends, including Blair Clark, her old pal Hannah Weinstein, and her fishing partner John Hersey, Hellman cajoled others into organizing resistance. In April, she invited Telford Taylor, a former Nuremberg prosecutor and now a professor at Columbia Law School, into a small group called the Committee for Public Justice. Convincing Taylor of the need for such a committee, wheedling a little, adding self-deprecatory comments—"It's been a big job for me and I am not very good at it"—she persuaded him to become active.[63]

From this narrow circle the group spread to include Norman Dorsen, then general counsel of the ACLU and later to become its president; Jerome Wiesner, a well-known scientist, Lillian's neighbor on Martha's Vineyard, and soon to become president of MIT; cartoonist Jules Feiffer; and Burke Marshall, a former assistant attorney general in charge of civil rights and then a deputy dean at Yale Law School. Recruiting members was not, apparently, a difficult job: Roger Wilkins, a former assistant U.S. attorney general, then consultant to the Ford Foundation and the committee's first chair, recalled his own decision to join up. It emerged, he wrote, from a frightening experience in the summer of 1967, when he was surrounded by

> fellow-citizens . . . six of them were kneeling and pointing guns at me and some of them were calling me nigger. I thought then that to be a free man in America was perilous indeed . . . For myself I vowed in that moment of terror to fight, if I survived, as hard against the spirit of repression and intimidation . . . as I would for equal justice for all Americans. That is why, in the atmosphere of the spring of 1970, I eagerly joined with other citizens to form the Committee for Public Justice.[64]

When the group reached more than a dozen names, its members circulated their friends and relations in a letter drafted by Norman Dorsen, revised by Hellman, and sent over the signature of Burke Marshall. "What we propose to do is based on the belief that this country has entered one of its recurring periods of dangerous political repression," the letter, written on May 25, said. "What we are setting up is a kind of early-warning system against the erosion or invasion of the basic freedoms."[65] An accompanying letter spelled out the purpose of the newly named Committee for Public Justice. Hellman's sensibilities shine through every line. "Once again it becomes necessary for citizens to perform the high public duty of resisting the repressive efforts of the state," it began. Then, deftly combining the interests of minority groups with those of antiwar protestors, it continued, "The nation has often endured times when the refusal of the government to recognize the right and aspirations of the weak and the poor and of political dissenters has led to periods of hate and intolerance." The statement cited ten "grave invasions of individual liberty" that had occurred, among them official threats to the independence of mass media; repression of dissent at the 1968 Democratic convention; invasion of privacy by wiretapping and eavesdropping; bills to authorize preventive detention; malign neglect of the rights of the black minority and of poor people generally; and an official blacklist of respected and qualified scientists. Quoting Justice Louis Brandeis to the effect that "the greatest menace to freedom is an inert people; that public discussion is a political duty; and that it should be a fundamental principle of the American Government," the statement concluded:

> We cannot now stand silent in a period of repression. We must remind the country and our elected representatives that only enduring principles of justice are fundamental to the common good and that all or any violations must be strongly resisted now and in the future with full strength and force. How can this be done? We know that the lawless activity of the government is often obscured because the public does not know the facts, or is given a distorted version of the facts by the authorities. We know that the rights of unpopular political dissenters are sometimes overridden not only in police action and in the courts but in the legislatures themselves. When such threats to constitutional rights arise, we intend to investigate them, to criticize them and to draw the attention of the public to them."[66]

Within three weeks, the group had attracted twenty more names, and these quickly expanded to provide a roster of distinguished women and men in every field of business and the arts, of law and the sciences, letters and literature. On it were people of every political persuasion from former communists and fellow travelers to anticommunist liberals. Some of these were Lillian's friends from other political causes; many were social admirers and acquaintances. Some joined because they agreed with the call to speak out against a "lawless government" or responded to the ringing cry that "We were born free and intend to remain so." Lillian's strong ties to Hollywood served her well. Movie stars and directors Paul Newman, Shirley MacLaine, Donald Sutherland, Warren Beatty, Candice Bergen, Marlon Brando, and Mike Nichols joined at her invitation. So did others in the arts, including Leonard and Felicia Bernstein and George Kirstein. Writers, critics, editors: William Shirer, William Styron, Richard Poirier, Robert Silvers, Martin Peretz, and Robert Coles signed up. Lawyers, union leaders, academics, scientists, and philanthropists added their names. They were joined by political and policy people including the Children's Defense Fund's Marian Edelman, Congressman Charles Goodell, EEOC member Aileen Hernandez. And the list kept growing.[67]

The group could not have been assembled without Hellman. To put it together, she traded on the personal qualities for which she was often disliked: she deployed her celebrity status, she alternately demanded and cajoled, and she attracted both vigorous opponents of the Soviet Union and casual supporters of peaceful coexistence. Leon Friedman, the group's third executive director, described as her goal "to energize the political community, to focus on public problems and to do something about them."[68] People put their names on the letterhead because they were her friends, to be sure: "I joined largely because she asked me to," Telford Taylor admitted when he was still unsure of the CPJ's prospects.[69] But they donated money, legal expertise, and time because they believed in the cause that the CPJ espoused. If they were not all friends of Hellman's, they were friends of friends, acquaintances who believed in defending civil liberties, a group so diverse that only a Lillian Hellman, who had credibility in the worlds of both celebrity and the intellect, could have brought it off. It was not only that "she knew everybody," as an early executive director, Stephen Gillers, recalled. It was that "she willingly picked up the phone to call them."[70]

In the summer the CPJ hired its first director, Luis Sanjurjo, and housed him in space donated by Lillian's friend Sue Marquand (wife of the writer John Marquand) on West 57th Street. Lillian had so far spearheaded the fund-raising efforts of the organization. She had, in the words of an executive committee report, "exhausted herself and also her sources for these kinds of funds."[71] That summer the executive council, chaired by Roger Wilkins, took formal responsibility. But Lillian remained unrelenting in her pursuit of support and supporters. She hosted executive council meetings in the Park Avenue apartment to which she moved in the fall.[72] Singlehandedly she raised the money to keep the CPJ going during its first year, soliciting her friends to provide contributions.

By the late fall of 1970, the CPJ was ready to go public. With flair worthy of Hellman, the organization called a news conference at the Overseas Press Club on November 17, 1970, where Ramsey Clark, among others, explained the group's origin as a consequence of the FBI's increasingly ideological bias, accusing the bureau of "having an end before it" and of seeking "facts to fit that end."[73] The *New York Times* covered the event sympathetically—describing the CPJ as "an organization of prominent private citizens . . . concerned that the nation has entered a period of political repression." It did not mention that uneasiness at invasions of public privacy had spread into the corners of Congress, where North Carolina's conservative Democratic senator Sam Ervin and others had begun to raise issues of military surveillance of civilians, unauthorized wiretapping, federal blacklists of scientists, and intimidation of the national media. Hellman's name appeared in the last paragraph of the *New York Times* article as one of several founding members. But the *Washington Post* singled her out for attention: "Playwright Lillian Hellman, the principal organizer of the group, also spoke at today's news conference. She said she felt impelled to do something last spring because some of us thought we heard the voice of Joe McCarthy coming from the grave."[74]

The CPJ followed its opening salvo with a full-page announcement that appeared in the *New York Times* on December 15, 1970, and placed the Bill of Rights at the heart of its mission. "This is your Bill of Rights. It is 179 years old. It is being killed," the advertisement announced. In small type, it reprinted the Bill of Rights along with an annotated list of the ways the current government eroded it. "These violations of the Constitution," it concluded, "are not isolated instances. They represent a dangerous trend toward repression and neglect of rights, for which the present administration bears a major responsibility."

The FBI, still in its Cold War mode, reacted vigorously. In their view, Hellman's presence in the CPJ immediately identified the organization with communism. Apparently at J. Edgar Hoover's personal request, the bureau produced a document that identified the CPJ's leaders and pinpointed their previous political activities. These thumbnail sketches, which tell us little about the individuals the FBI followed, reveal the bureau's particular interest in their political lives and especially in the issue of communism. Telford Taylor earned a negative review for many reasons, including his membership in the left-wing Lawyers Guild in 1942, his membership in the "Carnegie Endowment for International Peace which cooperated with the Soviet Government," and the fact that he had represented many CPJ members in court and before congressional committees. The report complained about Robert Silvers, editor of the *New York Review of Books*, because in 1964 he "reportedly used individuals

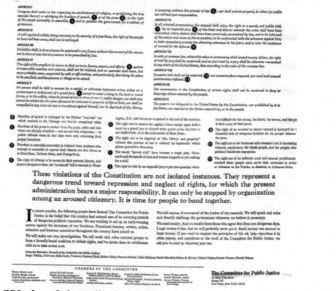

1970: *The CPJ placed the Bill of Rights at the heart of its mission. (From advertisement in the* New York Times*)*

with 'leftist tendencies' to review books dealing with security matters and the U.S. Government." It identified Norman Dorsen as a supporter of "the aims of the National Emergency Civil Liberties Committee, a cited organization." Additionally, it trashed Dorsen as one of a number of law professors who attacked the department's claim that the "Government may wiretap and bug domestic organizations considered subversive without court supervision." Dorsen stood accused, as well, of participating in a TV debate that included notorious left-wingers like Abbie Hoffman and Rennie Davis. And so it went.[75] Former assistant attorney general Burke Marshall got off lightly, accused only because he was "not considered a friend of the FBI" while he was in the Civil Rights Division. Of Hellman, who was cited as active in at least eighteen subversive organizations in the 1940s and identified then as a known communist, the worst that the FBI could say was that new information revealed her support of New Left and antiwar groups. "She was one of the speakers at the Second Annual *Nation* Conference of the Committee of Concerned Asian Scholars, described as a New Left-type group made up of students and instructors which is against the war in Vietnam and supports the government of Communist China."[76]

While the FBI investigated, the Committee for Public Justice got to work. Its first projects reflected the eclectic base of its membership: a project on child labor, another on women's prisons that featured an investigation of the Women's House of Detention on Greenwich Avenue. These drew little attention. But the CPJ's greatest coup was soon to come. In the spring of 1971, egged on by Hellman, the executive council decided to tackle an overreaching FBI directly. Lillian called on her friends Milton and Elinor Gordon to provide funds for a conference scheduled for the following fall. Burke Marshall, then a member of the executive council, asked his old friend Duane Lockard, dean of the Woodrow Wilson School at Princeton University, to host the conference on the site of the school. The two joined Norman Dorsen as co-chairs of the conference. The group issued a press release announcing that it planned to assemble a group of some fifty knowledgeable citizens to "make a scholarly and objective inquiry" into the role of the Federal Bureau of Investigation in American society.[77] In the interest of fairness, Duane Lockard sent a letter to J. Edgar Hoover, inviting him or a representative to attend.[78]

Hoover declined the request, insisting that "no worthwhile purpose could be served by an FBI representative attending an inquiry casting him in the role of defendant before even the first fact is brought out, and condemned by the 'judges' before trial begins."[79] His refusal was accompanied by eight single-spaced pages explaining why the FBI, an efficient and fair organization, had no need to defend itself and suggesting that the CPJ instead invite a representative from the organization of retired FBI agents. The CPJ promptly issued the invitation.

Hellman could not have been more pleased. The CPJ, then barely a year old, acknowledged Hoover's letter for what it was: a welcome sign of the committee's public influence. The letter, as political journalist Tom Wicker proclaimed in the introduction to the book that followed the conference, "splendidly exemplified why its sponsors thought the conference necessary."[80] In claiming that the FBI needed no defense, Hoover provided the best justification for a "scholarly effort to improve our understanding of the functioning of an important American institution."[81] The CPJ circulated the letter to illustrate its growing presence in conversations around civil liberties.

For its part, the FBI also reprinted and distributed Hoover's letter, seemingly unaware that with every copy it sent out, it enhanced the visibility of the CPJ. To its correspondents, it revealed the biased backgrounds of its speakers, hoping to discredit them and the conference by convicting them of guilt by association. But this strategy often got tangled in the knot of past politics. When Allan Brownfield, a small-time political activist, tried to curry favor among FBI officials by producing a forceful piece for *Roll Call* challenging the credibility of the conference as nothing less than an attack on the FBI, bureau officials identified him as having had unsavory communist associations in the past and reluctantly recommended ignoring the piece.[82]

The FBI could hardly be faulted for its opposition to the CPJ, nor for believing that the conference would not deal evenhandedly with the bureau. Still, the bureau's extraordinarily defensive response produced precisely the effect it sought to avoid. Hoover's letter dramatically escalated newspaper coverage of the conference and public awareness of it. Even as announcements of the call to the conference emerged, the FBI encouraged the formation of "Friends of FBI" to raise money for its defense. The group pleaded for donations on the grounds that "the FBI and J. Edgar Hoover are now being subjected to the degradation of a vicious partisan attack by self-serving politicians, their supporting media and certain radical elements that ultimately seek the destruction of all law and order in the United States."[83] It circulated a cartoon depicting itself as the victim of a hanging judge; it asked one of the invitees, William Bittman, to inform on what was happening there. The bureau also did what it could to discredit the conference by asking sympathetic newspaper columnists (including students from the Princeton University newspaper) to denounce the CPJ as a liberal, or left-leaning organization. The bureau's trepidation led it to closely track the amount of press the conference drew, as well as the content of favorable and unfavorable articles. In the aftermath, its agents dismissed most of the conference presentations as lies, freely distributing phrases such as "wholly false," "a collection of baseless and twisted allegations," and "a tissue of lies" to dismiss those it did not like. It deployed words like *fatuous* and *slanted* to describe some papers and accused one presenter of "twisting facts to suit his own ends." Other presentations appeared to agents to be "filled with errors and distortions" or "half truths, unsupported assertions and outright lies."[84]

From the perspective of Hellman and the CPJ, the conference was an enormous success. They had brought together critics from a variety of political perspectives (New York City's police commissioner, the editor of the *Nation*, two retired FBI agents, a distinguished Yale Law School professor) to challenge the FBI's repressive strategies against dissenting political groups. The conference sparked national press coverage that drew attention to the FBI's single-minded focus on national security and its lack of regard for civil liberties. It positioned the CPJ as a player in a dialogue that would continue for several years. Crucially, the conference legitimized reasonable criticism and dissent—one of Hellman's main goals—and dramatically reduced the fear of name-calling. A day after the conference closed, the *Washington Post* published an extensive account of the conference that included a quote from an unnamed government official who complained that "those left-wingers are not only after a pound of flesh now, they are trying to make money for another pound later." The piece closed with a reference to a House floor speech by Representative Richard Ichord, whom the FBI had approached early on. Ichord took the floor to disparage the provenance of the Committee for Public Justice by asserting that in 1951 Hellman had been "identified as a member of the Hollywood chapter of the Communist Party U.S.A."[85] To no avail. This time neither the public nor the "left-wingers" associated with the CPJ would bite. A second piece, set beside the first, described conferencegoers as "painting a grim picture of a police state disregarding constitutional liberties and repressing political dissent by use of informers, wiretaps, electronic surveillance and agents provocateurs."[86] But none of these pieces made as much of a splash as the spirit of the conference itself.

The CPJ used its leverage to advantage, broadening its membership to some eighty "prominent citizens." It also turned the CPJ into a visible player against repression and encouraged an even broader representation of membership that soon came to include such political antagonists as Victor Navasky and Arthur Schlesinger Jr. Hoover died in 1972, a few months after the conference closed. His successor, acting director L. Patrick Gray, quickly arranged a meeting with three representatives of the CPJ. The *New York Times* trumpeted the organization's victory in a headline that declared THE FBI AGREES TO HEAR ITS CHIEF CRITIC.[87] And when Congress settled down to confirm Gray as permanent director, the CPJ's Norman Dorsen drew national attention for pointing out that there had never been a real congressional investigation of the FBI.[88] Five years later, the CPJ once again received an invitation to testify in hearings to approve Gray's successor to the post of director. Bureau records reveal its subsequent concern to fend off the kinds of inquiries that the CPJ conference had provoked and to work out some method by which the FBI could ap-

pear to be more amenable to oversight while maintaining a necessary secrecy and without actually ceding authority to Congress.

Finally, and most important, the conference signaled a turn in the politics of liberalism. No longer barricading themselves behind an anticommunist shield lest they be associated with communism, liberals promoted
the civil liberties of all. The turnabout rejuvenated a languishing American Civil Liberties Union, which soon took the CPJ under its umbrella.
Hellman reveled in this shift of opinion, and the rapid succession of CPJ
activities that followed confirmed her sense that if people would simply
stand up and speak, they could maintain the freedom that was their heritage. When, on June 13, 1971, the *New York Times* published the Pentagon
Papers—a top-secret history of the unfolding war in Vietman compiled by
the Defense Department and made available by Daniel Ellsberg—the federal government immediately convened a grand jury in Boston to investigate their release and to consider bringing criminal charges. In the furor
that followed, the CPJ turned its attention to the grand jury system, asking if it was fulfilling its historic function to "check the power of the state
by filtering prosecutions . . . through a group of disinterested citizens," or
whether the system was simply serving as a "rubber stamp for indictments
the government wants to secure."[89] At the daylong conference that followed the following May, the CPJ confirmed its reputation for pointed
investigation.[90]

The organization's concern with the increasingly secret operations of
the federal government produced several other significant achievements.
A conference on secrecy in May 1973 resulted in a book edited by Norman Dorsen and Stephen Gellers called *None of Your Business*. In December of that year, while the Watergate scandal was still unfolding, the
CPJ sponsored a conference on the subject of "Watergate as a Symbol"
and to encourage the investigations by Senator Sam Ervin into the Nixon
administration's abuse of power. Asked by a popular magazine if she
identified with the witnesses who faced the Ervin committee, Hellman
replied, "I envy the courtesy with which they are treated. Villains do better
than any of us innocents who were called before House or Senate committees in the 1940s and 1950s."[91] The following year, the CPJ took a lead
role in filing suit to release the tapes made in the Nixon Oval Office. While
this was going on, during the winter and spring of 1974, the CPJ inquired
into the operation of the Justice Department. In February 1974, director
Stephen Gillers and his soon-to-be successor Leon Friedman issued a
report on "courtroom disruption" that exposed the false premise behind

a crackdown on courtroom discipline and protested "summary contempt proceedings" that permitted judges to discipline lawyers to whom they took a dislike—sometimes for defending unpopular clients. Hellman played no role in organizing this conference. But she delighted in seeing one of McCarthy's chief ploys overturned.

Soon the Committee for Public Justice was everywhere: its name and its spokespersons routinely punctuated articles and news briefs that questioned the authority of government surveillance efforts, challenged presidential secrecy, and called for scrutiny of FBI and CIA activities. More than once the CPJ was mentioned on the floor of Congress, often in negative statements inserted by representatives who were routinely thanked by the bureau for their cooperation. More than once the CPJ testified before Congress, thriving on the publicity and taking every opportunity to insert its voice into debates about civil liberties matters. When she addressed conferences or made public statements on behalf of the CPJ, Hellman never failed to connect the event with past moments of silent acquiescence. She told a June 1975 meeting, called to explore reports that the CIA had kept track of student radicals and antiwar activists, that twenty-five years after the McCarthy period, she still felt the need to understand how individual freedom could be so easily invaded.[92] In 1977, when newspapers began to note the emergence of a neoconservative movement, she turned her attention to raising money for a conference that would investigate the "swing to the right." Recalling the public inattention that had led to an undeclared war and the fostering of "crooks and liars in high places," Hellman urged CPJ supporters to speak up against "efforts . . . to reconstitute the power and legitimacy of government security and investigative agencies whose irresponsibility and violation of civil rights had been exposed as scandals."[93] The conference took place that fall. Finally, in 1977, the CPJ joined with the ACLU and the Center for National Security Studies to propose a bill that would prohibit the FBI from engaging in political surveillance and curb its efforts at eavesdropping and wiretapping except in criminal cases.[94] The bill was never passed though CPJ pressure did produce briefly effective guidelines.

All this activity was funded through Lillian Hellman's efforts and her personal connections. Her verve and her spirit, her shamelessly demanding insistence, and her absolute confidence in the justice of the CPJ's mission held sway. Bravely, the CPJ asserted its voice in the interest of transparency, and increasingly Lillian called on her celebrity friends to raise money and speak out for the organization. She tapped Ruth Field and the Field Foundation; she softened up her rich friend Max Palevsky—computer entrepreneur and venture capitalist. She lent her name to one benefit after another, shamelessly glorifying in adulation and contributions.

A March 6, 1975, "Citizen's Town Meeting" in Los Angeles, called to disclose domestic surveillance activities of the CIA, featured film star Warren Beatty. The benefit attracted Jacqueline Onassis, Jane Fonda, Ryan O'Neal, and other stars, and proved so popular that Hellman quipped she'd run out of tickets.[95] Six months later, Hellman's old friend Hannah Weinstein, a distinguished Hollywood producer and herself a victim of McCarthyism, orchestrated a benefit for the Committee for Public Justice around Lillian Hellman's seventieth birthday. For $150 apiece, contributors heard a dozen actors read from Hellman's plays and memoirs and then adjourned for dinner at Gallagher's steak house. Hellman

1975: Increasingly Hellman called on her celebrity friends to raise money. Here with Warren Beatty at a tribute to Hellman. (Photofest)

basked in the glory of extensive coverage of both herself and the event.[96] The movie *Julia*, released in 1977, became the occasion of a third benefit. A trip to Los Angeles persuaded Robert Redford to host yet another glamorous benefit for the CPJ.

Though there is little doubt that without Lillian Hellman the Committee for Public Justice could not have survived, Hellman exerted little influence over the daily workings of the committee, the projects it chose, or the books and papers it produced. The substantive issues and the strategies for addressing them were the brainchildren of the lawyers and others who sat at monthly meetings and determined the direction of the organization.[97] Hellman attended most of the meetings of the executive board, hosted many of them at her Park Avenue apartment and occasionally at her Vineyard home, and lent her name to every activity that the CPJ undertook. With Hannah Weinstein and Bobbie Handman, she dominated logistical decisions about food and drink, driving the small staff crazy as she repeatedly changed her mind about benefits and entertainments. Yet, except for reasserting the purposes of the organization, she took no part in debating the issues. She could be disruptive at meetings, drawing attention away from substantive matters. She fussed over small details, making Saturday-morning phone calls to Stephen Gillers to check that nothing had been overlooked and harassing some of the later executive directors. The record suggests that, far from being passively "outmaneuvered," "checkmated," and "cajoled"—to use one biographer's derogatory description—the brilliant legal and intellectual minds in the CPJ enthusiastically developed the projects that successfully drew attention to instruments of government repression.[98]

The CPJ lasted as long as Lillian had the energy to mobilize resources for it, petering out as she became sicker in the late seventies and as controversy mounted over her veracity. By then, its agenda had largely been subsumed into a revitalized ACLU. Still, for as long as she lasted, she supported the organization's efforts to move questions of civil liberties to the forefront of the public agenda and to maintain public awareness of the dangers of silent acquiescence. She stuck by that agenda, leading the Committee for Public Justice to a position as an honored and effective organization that educated the public in a decade permeated with lies. The CPJ benefited, to be sure, from the changing climate of the seventies—a decade when President Nixon led a delegation to Communist China, J. Edgar Hoover's death provided an opportunity for the FBI to alter its agenda, and Congressional Committees began to take up the issue of secrecy.

Within that context, Hellman briefly helped to reframe the agenda and move the United States from attacks on communism to self-examination. In so doing, she and the CPJ exposed the harm done by those who insisted on exaggerating the power of Soviet Communism. Her efforts helped to heal a breach on the left by uniting people of different political and social perspectives in the interest of civil liberties. At the same time, she exposed herself to a new set of attacks that emanated from those who still believed her guilty of subversion.

CHAPTER 10

Liar, Liar

I don't know what the hell the truth is, maybe just not lying.
—*Harvard lecture, 1961*

What a word is truth. Slippery, tricky, unreliable.
—*from* Three, *1978*

Lillian Hellman, I think, is tremendously overrated, a bad writer, a dishonest writer. Every word she says is a lie, including "and" and "the."
—*Mary McCarthy, 1979*

Lillian Hellman died in 1984, in the midst of a scandalous lawsuit, fighting for her honor and her integrity against accusations of lying. There is more than irony in this, for Hellman struggled all her life to sort out the meaning of truth and to adhere to a high standard of honesty. She had, she tells us in the story of Bethe Bowman, learned as a child the damage that could be done by lying and vowed then and there never to tell a lie, under penalty of torture and the guillotine.[1] She sometimes thought of herself, as she once said, as "too honest." Indeed, asked by Dashiell Hammett to identify her worst fault, that's the one she recorded.[2]

But what was truth? Efforts to find the answer to that question permeate Hellman's work: *The Children's Hour* rotates around a lie told by a disturbed thirteen-year-old girl that destroys three lives and a cherished school for girls. *Dark Angel*, her first movie script, focuses on a white lie, meant to hide a marriage, that subjects the hero to a dangerous wartime mission he might otherwise have avoided—and to a lifetime of blindness. *The Little Foxes* turns on a lie about a theft of bonds whose discovery places Regina in a position of power and allows her to win a financial victory over her brothers. *Toys in the Attic* features a young wife from whom truth is withheld who then becomes the unwitting instrument of her husband's ruin. How is it that the writer who spent so much of her energy defending truth became known as the archetype of liars? The answer to that question lies less in Hellman's life than in the historical debates that consumed her final decade.

Hellman continued to puzzle over questions of truth, and particularly its relationship to memory, as she developed her lectures and talks in the 1960s. At a 1960 University of Michigan reading of *Toys in the Attic*, she told an audience that wanted to hear something of the history of the play that she could "not remember all or much" of what they wanted to know. But, she promised, "I will certainly be more accurate tonight than I will be next year or next week."[3] She told a group of Harvard students in 1961 that her memory had always been poor. When she offered to recall for them her memories of the theater, she paused to warn them that she hoped they would be "accurate and as truthful as anybody can make memory, which is not very truthful at all."[4] Though she admitted that she could not remember where she was at particular times, she did not apologize for her "extremely cranky memory."[5] She understood, as she would say later, that memory "is not the same thing as what happened in the real minute of pleasure or pain."[6] Over and over again, whether the stories were about herself or about others, she deflected the notion that memory could point to truth. "I have no memory for dates," she told Hammett biographer Diane Johnson, along with a story about how a dozen people she knew each remembered Hammett in a different way.[7]

The struggle to tell the truth and to recognize that truth itself was elusive persisted all her life. She did not know if it was a writer's task to tell the truth, or what truth meant, she told her Harvard students. Though she kept notebooks, carefully researched and recorded details, and certainly "tried to get things right," she never escaped her dictum that "truth is larger than the truth of fact."[8] When she turned to writing memoirs in the mid-1960s, questions of truth and memory came to the fore in a literal as well as a metaphorical sense. She had, she confessed in the last paragraph of *An Unfinished Woman*, never known "what I meant by truth, never made the sense I hoped for."

Later, after the trouble started, people would return to *An Unfinished Woman* to challenge the literal truth of what she had written. She shrugged off the factual discrepancies. It was no secret that she had a poor memory. She had been speaking about it for years. "I have little sense of time and often when I have tried to walk back through memory's lane I have stumbled in the dark and lost my way," she wrote in 1967.[9] In this respect, Hellman differs little from most memoirists who practice an art that relies exclusively on their unchallengeable memories and distances itself from anything called objective truth. As one commentator remarked, "She heightened things, she shuffled them around, she remembered some things and repressed others."[10] Hellman admitted that she could not have written her memoirs without "a feeling for fiction, some belief that what I was writing about was interesting or dramatic."[11] Doris Lessing would have approved. "There is no doubt fiction makes a better job of the truth," she wrote trenchantly.[12]

When she wrote *Pentimento*, which Little, Brown published in 1973, Hellman gambled that she could construct her vivid, beautifully written, sharply characterized stories about her past with the license of the fiction writer. The title itself, as she announced in the epigram, refers to the painter's practice of reconceiving an old image as "a way of seeing and seeing again." To editor William Abrahams, she confided that "the accuracy or lack of accuracy of my memory was not important."[13] And in the book she wrote, "I wanted to see what was there for me once, and what is there for me now."[14] She did not want to describe the book as a memoir. "For reasons best known to cranky authors, I am anxious that this book not be thought of as sequel to *An Unfinished Woman*, but as a book of portraits," she wrote to an editor at *Esquire* who wanted to publish an excerpt from it.[15]

In the seven stories of *Pentimento*, Hellman chose to revisit scenes of her childhood and young womanhood to see if she could recapture the feelings evoked by some key moments. Repeatedly she warned her readers that she was simply writing what she remembered, that she doubted her capacity to remember: What she wrote was her version of what happened, but others, she readily conceded, might remember things differently. "I know all I have written here," she wrote in *Pentimento*, "or I know it the way I remember it, which of course may not be the whole truth."[16] The book, written in the style she had introduced in *An Unfin-ished Woman*, was filled with words unspoken, questions unasked and unanswered, places never again visited, and people, once encountered, never again known. "I was never to be angry with him again," Hellman might write. A few pages later she would maintain, "I was never to see her again," and shortly afterward, "we were never to talk about it again." The phrases infused the stories with an air of mystery and suspense that enhanced their intrigue and her own centrality, for they suggested that the unwritten words held secrets never to be unlocked.

Many read into her prose a reflection of her personality, seeing in it either a "Hammett-like parsimony" or an elliptical and evasive quality. Others described "a rich, murky, Henry Jamesian" quality that could be "wildly elusive and vague."[17] Those who thought her tough, direct, and honest, as did a *New York Times* book critic, declared that she wrote "a prose as brilliantly finished as any that we have in these years."[18] They admired her "elegantly simple style" and, somewhat hyperbolically, de-scribed it as shining "with a moral intelligence, a toughness of character that inspires even as it entertains." Critic John Leonard, who penned that phrase, added, "the prose is as precise as an electron microscope."[19] But those who caviled at the image of a courageous and honest Hellman thought her writing style "irritating" rather than "slight and charming." It was, said one critic, imitative of "a time when Hemingway and Ham-mett made it seem fresh, new and appropriate."[20] Another described her style as "obdurate, flat and mannered" and flailed her as a "virtuoso of the ellipsis."[21] The contrasts may be less aesthetic assessments than ex-pressions of feeling about the author.

Each chapter in *Pentimento* purports to tell a story about other people yet begs us to understand what she tells us about herself. In the first story, Lillian's distant cousin Bethe arrives from Germany, rejects the family's advice to marry a dependable relative, and ends up living disreputably with a minor-league crook. We never know whether Bethe existed, or in what form. But it does not matter. The story Lillian tells of how, as a teen-ager, she defied parental injunctions and tracked down her cousin illus-trates the rebellious spirit of which Lillian was so proud. The second story, "Willy," portrays an uncle by marriage who becomes a mysterious, much-admired gunrunner and wealthy fruit importer. Looking behind the words, we find a provocative tale of adolescent Lillian's emerging sense of sexuality. A story about Hellman's life in the theater reveals her discomfort with the one arena that generously embraced her. "I always knew that I was seldom comfortable with theatre people," she writes.[22] Describing her tormented relationships to the actors, directors, and producers who collaborated with her in her life's work, Hellman articulates her continuing sense of isolation even as she became a celebrated playwright. Once again we are pulled by a powerful magnetism rooted in the doubt, confusion, and anguish she expresses with every anecdote. "Turtle," ostensibly a story about an animal she and Hammett trapped and then killed, turns into a meditation about survival and her fear of death. The final story, titled "Pentimento," is an extended reflection on race relations, constructed around the tale of a talented young black man who could not bring himself to participate in a corrupt scientific world.

The centerpiece of the book—the essay that attracted the most attention and was widely reprinted—is "Julia," a mostly fictional story of Hellman's effort to smuggle a hat full of money to her friend Julia in Berlin. The money is destined to save the lives of Jews, communists, and socialists stuck in a hostile Austria in the late 1930s. The story describes a fearful young Lillian who, contemptuous of her own cowardice, agrees to undertake the dangerous mission. Julia appears in it first as Hellman's closest childhood friend, whom she admires beyond reason and to whom she cannot say no. She reappears as a crippled resistance fighter whose loss of a leg symbolizes the danger Hellman imagines. Here then is a story about a loyal and loving friend willing to risk untold danger to serve an important cause. This was the woman Hellman wanted to be. More tellingly, the story casts aspersions on those who refused to risk their lives and fortunes when, during the McCarthy period, they would not "rescue" people under attack.

Lest there be any doubt about the message Hellman wanted to convey, another story in the collection—one that most reviewers dismissed as inconsequential—makes it explicit. "Arthur W. A. Cowan" is on its face a story about a rich Philadelphia lawyer with whom Hellman had a long relationship and who became something of a financial adviser. Cowan is a good guy. He is rich, very rich, as Hellman tells us, and his politics very conservative, but he nevertheless spends his money to support the cause of freedom, including the freedom to advocate unpopular causes like communism. Hellman uses the story to open up the questions she would pursue in her next memoir, *Scoundrel Time*, and which she claims there to have feared writing about for so long. She tells us that she knew all along that the reason for what she calls the "bitter storm" inside her "was not due to McCarthy, McCarran, Nixon and all the rest, but was a kind of tribal turn against friends, half-friends, or people I didn't know but had previously respected . . . Others, almost all American intellectuals, had stood watching that game, giving no aid to the weak or the troubled, resting on their own fancy reasons."[23] Cowan, in contrast, spent a portion of his fortune to defend communists and others.

All these stories reveal the self-dramatizing Hellman. They paint portraits of the woman Hellman wished she had been: the self who, given an opportunity, would have overcome her fears to act with a rare courage. But the voice is also that of the moral Hellman, the Hellman who could not and would not stop talking about the way she and others should have acted in times of stress. The book revealed Hellman, as Mark Schorer put it in the *New York Times*, in the "character of an extraordinary woman with rare powers of self-analysis, a woman both proud and self-assured but without a taint of self-importance, a woman of rare wisdom."[24] Critic Christopher Lehmann-Haupt put it even more strongly: "These portraits of others add up to nothing less than a self-portrait of Miss Hellman, an autobiography of her soul."[25] Hellman was "an emancipated woman for her period," wrote a *Ms.* magazine reviewer, "showing us, with sensitive, wise perceptions, where we have been and where it remains for us to go."[26] The praise and the months of bestseller status demonstrated Hellman's success in the battle for celebrity. She had won, hands down.

Whether the stories in *Pentimento* and *An Unfinished Woman* were factually "true" or not mattered less to readers and critics at the time they were published than the "cultural" and "interpersonal" truths they conveyed. Biographer Louise Knight notes that these forms of truth are necessarily produced by a narrator constructed "to serve the author's rhetorical purposes."[27] Hellman was such a narrator. Her childhood recollections re-created images of place and time, fears and interactions that defined the sensibilities of a moment for her readers. Her ability to describe her own weaknesses, her sexuality, her failed ambitions humorously and without self-pity appealed to readers not because they faithfully recorded what really happened but because they evoked moments of awareness with which readers could identify. Putting herself at risk, she appealed to audiences of all kinds. She located herself in the middle of her stories, unafraid to chastise and to celebrate herself in the same sentence, willing to let go of the story after it had reached its dramatic moment. If Hellman's stories tended to cast her in a good light, if they offered an image of a woman in the middle of an adventure, if they celebrated her achievements at the expense of others and mocked the personalities of the great and famous women and men she knew, all of this contributed to the legend of a resilient woman with a strong moral spine. The writer Alice Munro might have been speaking for Hellman when she wrote, of her own memoir: "I put myself in the center and wrote about that self as searchingly as I could. But the figures around this self took on their own life and color and did things they had not done in reality . . . You could say that such stories pay more attention to the truth of a life than fiction usually does. But not enough to swear on."[28] Memoirist Joel Agee put it differently. "Everything in this book is true," he wrote of his own memoir, "but not everything is precisely factual."[29]

If Hellman won the battle for celebrity, the battle for history had yet to be fought. Some critics, most notably John Simon, felt cheated by Hellman's focus on herself. Simon protested that Hellman's stories were not *pentimenti*—they lacked a subtle interplay "between what was and is, or what was and is no more." He complained that the portraits constituted Hellman's effort to complete the autobiography she had started in *An Unfinished Woman*. They camouflaged, in his view, her own persona in the same melodramatic style that infused her plays. She had drawn no portrait of Julia, complained Simon, "however great and tragic she may have been . . . the acts of bravery and devotion that we actually read about are Miss Hellman's."[30] Critic James Lardner disagreed. "She exaggerated many things," he wrote shortly after her death, but "you knew more about her times after reading her than before, and there are many more matter-of-factly reliable chroniclers about whom that could never be said."[31]

When it came to the third volume of her memoirs, *Scoundrel Time*, questions of historical truth came to the fore. Hellman had long been unable to write about the McCarthy period for reasons she claimed not to understand. "I wish I knew why I couldn't write about it. If I knew it I could do it," she told interviewer Bill Moyers in the spring of 1974.[32] But she did know, and the feelings ran deep. In *Pentimento*, she reflected on the "bitter storm that the McCarthy period caused, causes, in me . . . it was as if I had been deprived of a child's belief in tribal safety. I was never again to believe in it and resent to this day that it has been taken from me." She held intellectuals responsible: "It is eccentric, I suppose, not to care much about the persecutors and to care so much about those who allowed the persecution," she wrote, pointing her finger at "American intellectuals."[33] To Nora Ephron, shortly afterward, she was more specific: "I don't remember one large figure coming to anybody's aid . . . I suppose I've come out frightened, thoroughly frightened of liberals.

Most radicals of the time were comic, but the liberals were frighten-ing."[34] Fear, Hellman thought, fear of isolation, fear that nobody would stand up for her, fear that she lacked the courage to stand by her friends, led her to take refuge in silence. "I had only one way out, and that I took: to shut up about the whole period."[35]

In the early seventies, as the war against communism in Vietnam wound down and a disgraced Richard Nixon left office, Hellman prepared to speak. Her friend Peter Feibleman warned her against doing so: too many of the old actors were still alive, he said. But it was time for Hellman to put the past behind her. She wanted, most of all, to record the emotional truths of her experience. She had already made the decision to write about the McCarthy years when she had an accident that would shape the style of the book. The summer before she started to write, traveling in Europe with Billy Abrahams and Peter Stansky, she had a small stroke. It did no visible damage beyond landing her briefly in a Paris hospital. This was probably the first of several small strokes that successively brought emotion to the surface and left her with a reduced ability to control outbursts of anger. Likely, the strokes released some of the pain and anger that had festered for more than twenty years.[36] "I don't want to write about my historical conclusions," she says in the beginning of *Scoundrel Time*. "If I stick to what I know, what happened to me, and a few others, I have a chance to write my own history of the time."[37] *Scoundrel Time* is "mostly about me," she told interviewer Rex Reed shortly before the book appeared. "I've forgotten about historical background and stuck to personal feelings, and I think that's worked out better."[38] But when Hellman turned her private pain into public statements, she discovered that her truth differed dramatically from the truths of some others. The result was to set off a storm of anger that she might have anticipated.

Scoundrel Time retold the story of the McCarthy period through the lens of Hellman's 1952 appearance before the House Committee on Un-American Activities. HUAC was the scourge of the entertainment in-dustry, and Hellman's appearance before it was part of the committee's long campaign to uncover the radicalism thought to permeate the film industry at the time. When she sat down to write the book, Hellman could remember odd details about her appearance: the Balmain dress and the expensive new hat she had bought to comfort herself and boost her confidence; the probably apocryphal voice from the gallery that con-gratulated her afterward. But she had only sketchy memories of prepar-ing for her ordeal, and almost none of the thirty-seven minutes she endured before the committee. To jog her memory and help her reconstruct the circumstances around her appearance, she wrote to Joseph Rauh, her lawyer at the time, and others. Had they not prepared a letter and a statement? she asked. Why had Rauh distributed the letter rather than the statement? How did it happen that Rauh had copies ready to distribute to the press? What had happened after the hearing ended? Rauh replied with detailed answers, sending along copies of her testimony, her letters and memoranda documenting the emergence of their strategy and the sequence of events. Many of these made their way into *Scoundrel Time*. In that sense, the book is literally accurate.

But Hellman was after something more. "If you survive something," she said shortly after the book came out, "it's hard to remember the terrible pressure on you when you believe that survival is not possible."[39] She wanted to capture the prevailing sense of confusion and fear generated by continuing investigatory commissions, the fury at their power to destroy lives without evidence, the helplessness of individuals faced with a Hobson's choice of maintaining their capacity to earn a living by telling committees what they wanted to hear or staying silent and risking jail. Above all she wanted to express her blinding contempt for people (she labeled them liberals and cowards), under no threat themselves, who betrayed their own commitment to liberty and freedom of speech for fear of being tarred with the brush of communist sympathy. These were the American intellectuals, who "had stood watching that game, giving no aid to the weak or the troubled, resting on their own fancy reasons."[40] In a refrain that permeated *Scoundrel Time*, she told interviewer Nora Ephron, "I wasn't shocked in the way so many people were. I was more shocked by the people on my side, the intellectuals and liberals and pretend radicals . . . I mean, I wasn't as shocked by McCarthy as by the people who took no stand at all."[41]

For all the pithy and direct language of *Scoundrel Time*, Hellman's position took the moral high ground: she had stood up for the ordinary American values of decency, honesty, and integrity while many had, like cowards, given way. For those who cooperated with the investigatory committees, she had only scorn: "Some of them . . . had sprinted to demean themselves, apologizing for sins they never committed, making vivid and lively for the committees and the press what had never existed." Dismissing the committees as made up of "men who invented when necessary, maligned even when it wasn't necessary," she declared that from them she expected nothing. The shock and anger, the sense of betrayal came rather "against what I thought had been the people of my world." She had believed, she wrote, that "the educated, the intellectual, lived by what they claimed to believe: freedom of thought and speech, the right of each man to his own convictions, a more than implied promise, therefore of aid to those who might be persecuted. But only a very few raised a finger when McCarthy and the boys appeared." These, then, were the scoundrels: the American intellectuals who would not "fight for anything if doing so would injure them."

One after another, she skewered with forceful language those who had not lived up to her standards of honor. Elia Kazan, Clifford Odets, the columnist James Wechsler, and her old friends Lionel and Diana Trilling all fell victim to her angry words and wittily venomous barbs. Their silence, she continued, allowed McCarthy to quash freedom of thought, opening the door to a continuing witch hunt. It encouraged intellectuals to sell their souls to the CIA (as had recently been revealed), which used their names to foster thinly disguised propaganda through sponsored magazines and the Congress for Cultural Freedom. Appeals to the fear of communism accounted, in her view, for the disastrous war in Vietnam and the ascendance of Richard Nixon.[42] Hellman gave no quarter, dismissing the rationalizations of the silent as cowardice and "pious shit." "Lives were being ruined and few hands were raised in help," she wrote accusingly. "In every civilized country, people have always come forward to defend those in political trouble." Why not in the United States? She thought the answer obvious. "These men and women, too eager to secure themselves and their material possessions, were too often the children of immigrants, determined to keep what they had earned."

The first reactions to *Scoundrel Time* took Hellman's story at face value, affirming her sense of decency and applauding the moral courage she had shown before HUAC. Repeatedly and admiringly, they echoed the line that had resonated in 1952 and turned Hellman into a heroine: "I cannot and will not cut my conscience to fit this year's fashions." Friendly critics described Hellman's story as "compelling," brave, and written with "plainspoken vigor." *Time* magazine alluded to her personal code of morality: "She was brave because her private code would not allow her to be anything else."[43] Her friends Richard Poirier and Robert Coles pitched in admiringly. What one does at a moment when one is faced with earning a living or losing one's honor, declared Coles, was a measure of character. Hellman had not flinched. She had made that difficult choice with "explicit, unhedged moral decisiveness."[44] *Scoundrel Time* soared to the top of the bestseller lists, where it remained for twenty-one weeks. "I found the kind of unwritten code of honor and decency, which she feels she has lived by, extremely moving and touching," said the distinguished British critic Marina Vaizey. "It felt truthful to me."[45] Hellman had earned a right to tell her story as she remembered it, said journalist Murray Kempton, "thanks to her superb hour of resistance to banal chic."[46]

And yet there were dissenters. A few reviewers noted that the book contained false notes. *Scoundrel Time* accused James Wechsler, for example, of being a friendly witness before HUAC. In fact he had been called before McCarthy's Government Operations subcommittee rather than HUAC, and he hotly contested Hellman's attribution of friendliness. Wechsler, who had an unimpeachable record of opposition to McCarthyism both in print and before the committee, had decided for perhaps misplaced strategic reasons to give the committee some names they already had. Doing so, he believed, would enhance his credibility in the fight against McCarthyism. Hellman found this rationalization absurd but under threat of a lawsuit agreed to modify her characterization of Wechsler in subsequent editions of the book.[47] Critics also noted that Hellman had incorrectly described the use of the pumpkin in which Whittaker Chambers had hidden rolls of microfilm later used to convict Alger Hiss of perjury. While Hellman had insisted that none of the microfilm was ever useful, they pointed out that two rolls of it were in fact used as evidence at the trial.

The "scoundrels" (some of whom Hellman identified as the editors of magazines like *Commentary* and *Partisan Review*, and many of whom had once been her friends) did not remain silent for very long. In accusing them of not coming to her aid, Hellman called their morality and decency into question. But their view of history was quite different from Hellman's, and on that basis they refused to cede the high ground. In 1976, those who had once counted themselves among the New York intellectuals and their allies still perceived communism as a very real threat. They remembered the postwar period as a difficult moment when even those who had opposed McCarthyism felt that their first obligation was to challenge Stalin, who, in their view, constituted a powerful enemy of freedom and world peace. From the anti-Stalinist perspective, those who cooperated with the committees were heroes rather than collaborators. Those who denounced the committees were the real cowards. They deserved the contempt of all right-thinking Americans, not their gratitude. As William Buckley, an old-fashioned conservative, noted, anyone who was a communist in that period was complicit in the deaths of ten million people.[48]

Beyond crude politics, the economic crisis of the 1970s played a crucial role in the reception of *Scoundrel Time*. Stagflation—the unholy combination of high unemployment and inflation—along with the decline of the industrial Midwest left economists in a quandary over how to reduce joblessness without increasing inflation. The old liberals of the 1950s who had once battled over whether centralized planning and the socialization of the economy was a viable alternative to capitalism now wondered whether some sort of industrial planning along with a greater attention to social justice and equality might improve the economic outlook.[49] They were resolutely opposed by social commentators who insisted that such a return to socialist ideas posed a danger to the American way of life. Blaming the breakdown in self-discipline and individual entrepreneurship on the 1960s cultural revolution that advocated resistance to authority and promoted a new sexual and personal freedom, conservatives gathered under the umbrella of what would become known as neoconservatism. The most vociferous among them (including *Encounter* editor Irving Kristol, philosopher Sidney Hook, sociologist Nathan Glazer, and Hellman's former friend Norman Podhoretz) linked America's economic woes to its failure to confront the Soviet Union. America's prosperity and safety, they argued, lay in a vigorously aggressive posture toward the Soviet Union that would revive free-market economies at home and abroad. Supporting traditional family and gender values at home and establishing democracy and free markets everywhere would save an America that had lost its way. Allying themselves with traditional conservatives and with liberal anticommunists, neoconservatives sought to foster a more stable world order in which the United States would play a leading role. By 1976, when *Scoundrel Time* appeared, neoconservatives were on the cusp of acquiring a powerful ideological presence. To them the book, in Nathan Glazer's words, was more than naïve: it trivialized the real dangers of "an awesome power that was, after the defeat of Hitler, unquestionably the enemy of freedom throughout the world."[50]

Hellman had a very different view of history. She had never believed, and did not in 1976 believe, that communism constituted a threat to American freedom. To be sure, she had once thought that social justice would be best served by following the Soviet example, and into the sixties she still hoped that the Soviet Union could reform itself. But she had long ago abandoned any commitment to Stalinist Communism. She was an American patriot, convinced that the route to a nonracist and more egalitarian America lay in defending freedom of thought, the capacity to dissent, and curbs on the power of money. For all that she had briefly been a member of the CPUSA who now recognized the sins of Stalinism, she no longer advocated utopian beliefs that had once made sense to her and to millions of others. And she could not, even symbolically, kick a man when he was down. Though Hellman acknowledged three times in *Scoundrel Time* that she had wrongly believed ideas that she now rejected, her sense of decency, her code of loyalty, forbade her from turning on others whose intentions had been good. "Think of what it would be like," remarked her goddaughter Catherine Kober Zeller. "She sees through the politics, hates herself for having supported it, but can't say anything for fear that if she says it, it will look as if she's betraying her friends."[51] After all, as she wrote in *Scoundrel Time*, "Whatever our mistakes, I do not believe we did our country any harm."[52]

To skeptics, Hellman's stance seemed like rank hypocrisy. Had she simply been blind? She had, after all, early on attacked fascism (which in the eyes of many of the liberal anticommunists was simply another version of totalitarianism). How could someone "who pictures herself as a heroine defending intellectual and cultural freedom" defend a system now known to have destroyed millions of lives at the whim of Stalin, asked Sidney Hook.[53] *Scoundrel Time*, they argued, was simply an obfuscation of Hellman's longtime support of the Soviet Union and of the totalitarian policies of Stalin. Her work for "world peace" in the late forties and early fifties, they charged, was ample evidence of her political naïveté and of her continuing acquiescence to the communist line. How, Sidney Hook asked, could she have portrayed the Soviet Union to be peaceful and freedom-loving at a time when "dissenting or non-conforming intellectuals were being martyred in Communist countries?"[54] Her silence in 1952, and her continuing silence in the sixties, provided tacit support for what President Ronald Reagan would label an evil empire. Either she was a hypocrite and a liar or she was, in their language, an unregenerate Stalinist.

Hellman could not apologize for something she could not see. In her view, communism posed no real threat to the United States, but attacks on freedom of thought and speech did. Her position was reinforced by a turn in historical interpretation that occurred in the 1960s. A new group of revisionist historians led by William Appleman Williams, then at the University of Wisconsin, began to seek new explanations for U.S. military and economic involvement in the world. Particularly in Latin America and South Asia, they traced American foreign policy back to a relentless search for power and influence.[55] These New Left historians suggested that the United States was as single-mindedly self-interested as any nation. Driven by economic impulses, the United States had followed its own ideological bent into the world, imposing on allies a vision of freedom and democracy that ran roughshod over the wills of indigenous peoples. The new view recognized the brutality of Stalinism and the failures of the Soviet system even as it acknowledged the Soviet Union's territorial and ideological goals. It suggested not so much an apology for the Soviet Union as an effort to understand the dynamics of national self-interest. And there was the rub. Far from being an innocent defender of freedom, the United States, revisionist historians suggested, enacted a foreign policy as much in pursuit of power and economic influence as any in the world. This view both emanated from the ongoing war in Vietnam and fuelled opposition to it.

Furious opponents of the Soviet regime held New Left historians at least partly responsible for undermining American security by ignoring the excesses of communism while they critiqued America's search for power. The new truth, wrote former liberal Nathan Glazer, was inspired in great part "by the unending flow of volumes of apparently serious research revising the history of World War II and its aftermath." Referring back to the McCarthy period, he emphasized the consequences of the research. "Young scholars now believe that the congressional committees investigating Communism represented a totally unjustified attack on the freedom of thought, speech, and action of progressive-minded Americans . . . and that those investigations posed a greater danger to this country's liberties than Communism itself ever did."[56] These views, for which *Scoundrel Time* provided juicy evidence, could not be allowed to go unrefuted. As Richard Falk perceptively noted, "the success of *Scoundrel Time* would, if not challenged, endow its views of the McCarthy period in the early 1950s with an authoritative status."[57]

Hellman probably never fully appreciated the dimensions of the conflict into which she landed. Yet she enthusiastically endorsed historian Garry Wills, who her publisher suggested might write the introduction to her book. And Wills fully endorsed the new view of history. His lengthy introduction quickly became part of the problem—singled out by reviewers as proposing a biased and problematic view of the Cold War. In his view, that Cold War was incited not by Russian territorial aggression, not by efforts to impose communist regimes in Greece and Turkey, but by Truman's efforts to appease anticommunists by imposing loyalty and security oaths on government employees. Wills believed that the loyalty-security program had encouraged the climate of fear that led directly to the flaunting of civil liberties by congressional committees and other investigatory bodies. In turn, the failure of liberal intellectuals to stand firm against McCarthyite tactics led the authorities to believe that they could trample the civil liberties of opponents to the war in Vietnam, New Left dissenters, and protesters against the Democratic convention in 1968. That, in turn, had given credence to Richard Nixon's successful run for the White House and to the culture of surveillance that his administration sustained. To this extent, Hellman and the New Left historians held common ground.

The parallels between Hellman's ideas and those identified with revisionist history fueled the ire of Hellman's critics—former liberals, traditional conservatives, and neoconservatives alike. In an influential piece, *New York Times* cultural critic Hilton Kramer identified *Scoundrel Time* as just one among "a new wave of movies, books and television shows" that were "assiduously turning the terrors and controversies of the 1940s and 1950s into the entertainments and best-sellers of the 1970s." He traced this wave back to "academic historians" who had redrawn "the history of an earlier era along . . . often fictional lines." "For a decade," he argued, they "have been laboring to persuade us that the Cold War was somehow a malevolent conspiracy of the Western democracies to undermine the benign intentions of the Soviet Union." The point of *Scoundrel Time*, in his view, was "to acquit 60's radicalism of all malevolent consequences and to do so by portraying 30's radicalism as similarly innocent, a phenomenon wholly benign, altruistic and admirable."[58] Arthur Schlesinger Jr., historian, political adviser to presidents, and a friend and longtime dining companion of Hellman's, dropped Kramer a note declaring his wish that the article "could be made required reading for everyone born after 1940."[59] Hellman, who had dined with Schlesinger just the day before the article appeared, promptly wrote him a scathing note: "In my cricket book, you don't sit next to people at dinner in apparent friendship and not tell them that you have publicly embraced their attacker."[60] Schlesinger forwarded it to their mutual friend, Joe Rauh, with a one-sentence comment: "Now I am on the enemies list too."[61]

As in so many instances, Hellman had turned herself into the center of a controversy waiting to happen. She had challenged the morality of the anticommunists who had betrayed their nation by refusing to defend freedom of speech. She had called them scoundrels, accused them of undermining the values they held dear. In reply, the neoconservatives unleashed all the fury of morally wronged victims, the personal venom of opponents bent on destruction. These attackers were not after her to tell the "truth": what they wanted was a confession of "sin." What right did she have to claim moral authority, this woman who could not get her facts straight, who placed herself at the center of a struggle in which she was at best a peripheral player? Why believe someone who still publicly denied her participation (and that of her longtime friend and companion Dashiell Hammett) in the Communist Party, who hypocritically overlooked the millions of murdered and destroyed lives in Stalin's Russia even as she wept over her own lost financial security? What right did she have to claim that she had done no harm? By refusing to cooperate with the investigations, some asserted, she had reinforced the credibility of a totalitarian system and prolonged the life of McCarthyism. If this fight was to be fought on the basis of virtue and morality, then Hellman's virtue was fair game.[62]

In the storm that followed, there was no halfway house, no resting place. In the view of critics, hypocrisy—rather than decency and honor—characterized Hellman's behavior. Where, asked conservative columnist and editor Melvyn Lasky, was her "responsibility as a writer and intellectual, supposedly committed to the truth, in a 'scoundrel time' of Soviet slave labour camps and mass purges"?[63] Sidney Hook eagerly offered his services as a book reviewer to Commentary magazine because she kept silent about the behavior of communists while excoriating the congressional committees whose excesses "do not begin to compare to genocidal Stalinist practices that Lillian Hellman staunchly defended up to a few years ago."[64] Conservative pundit William F. Buckley took her apart for claiming to be a champion of the "negro" people when her behavior, as she described it, was rude and dismissive: she had insulted the black employee who delivered the subpoena to her door, and she had tried to divert Dorothy Parker's estate away from the NAACP toward more radical groups. And she expected people to lie while she herself claimed allegiance to truth.[65] Why, asked William Phillips, an editor of Partisan Review, should one risk one's honor to defend those who hid behind the Fifth Amendment because they didn't want to reveal the truth about themselves? "Some were communists, and what we were asked to defend was their right to lie about it."[66] Hypocrisy, wrote Lasky, "was a bottomless well."

Additional questions revolved around Hellman's veracity in a broader sense. *Scoundrel Time* proclaimed Hellman's devotion to decency and honor. But her critics accused her of painting a "guileful" self-portrait, one that called into question her honesty, especially around political issues. The issue of how close she had been to the Communist Party once again reemerged. In *Scoundrel Time*, and in several interviews afterward, she denied ever having been a party member. Her own statements to Joseph Rauh suggest that this was in fact technically untrue—though it is almost certainly the case that her association was brief and not very active. *National Review* editor William Buckley, tongue in cheek, described her relations with the communist movement as "a marriage, but for the paperwork."[67] Nor did Hellman's several confessions of past errors of belief redeem her in the eyes of critics. Her acknowledgments were too muted, too vague, insufficiently anti-Stalinist. Walter Goodman, author of a book about HUAC, asserted that her admissions were simply the work of "a skilled writer who knows that the best way to persuade readers of one's honesty and right-thinkingness is to concede that one has made passing mistakes."[68]

These unfriendly critics and others concluded that she had crossed a line. She was not entitled to what Murray Kempton, who had admired her courageous 1952 performance before HUAC, described as the position of a "hanging judge." "I have never quite understood," wrote Kempton, "upon what altar Miss Hellman's moral authority was consecrated."[69] William Buckley concurred, avowing that at best she was a conspirator who had lent the enemies of the United States a helping hand. "Those who wittingly helped [the communists], even if they paid no party dues, were morally as guilty in the deceptions they practiced. They were engaged in helping to destroy the open society whose benefits and freedoms they enjoyed."[70]

Just a few months after the release of *Scoundrel Time*, with its ringing attack against liberals for refusing to defend free thought, an episode involving Diana Trilling raised the moral issue to a different level. Just before he died in 1975, Lionel Trilling published a piece in the *New York Review of Books* in which he reaffirmed his long-standing belief in the honor and veracity of Whittaker Chambers. Trilling and Chambers were classmates at Columbia, where Trilling had since spent most of a distinguished career. His piece clearly implied the guilt of Alger Hiss, for if Chambers told the truth, then Hiss lied. Hellman took a few sentences in *Scoundrel Time* to lament that the Trillings could not see things her way.

She did not understand, she wrote, how old and respected friends like the Trillings "could have come out of the same age and time with such different political and social views from my own."[71] Diana Trilling, just then preparing a new collection of essays for publication, included one that defended liberal anticommunism and introduced it by dismissing political attacks on her position as having "diminishing intellectual force."[72] Little, Brown— her publisher and Hellman's—asked her to remove this oblique attack on one of its bestselling authors. Trilling refused and took the book elsewhere.

The episode put Hellman in an impossible position. As far as we know, she never did bring pressure on her publishers to remove the offending lines, though most people who knew her describe Hellman as capable of doing so. Trilling herself wrote to Hellman shortly after the story broke to make clear that she had "never in conversation with the press assigned any responsibility whatsoever to you for the censorship of me. On the contrary, I have told reporters that you were far too intelligent to have done this."[73] The New York Times, which broke the story, suggests that Hellman first heard about the incident from its reporter and, when she read the offending words, simply laughed.[74] When the Times interviewed Diana Trilling, its readers learned that Trilling had been excluded from the summer social scene on Martha's Vineyard at Hellman's behest.[75] Nobody now remembers that, but several of Hellman's friends found the notion plausible.[76] At the time, the truth hardly mattered. Those who heard the story—and the press covered it in juicy detail—delighted in the possibility that Hellman had directly or indirectly brought pressure on her publishers to demand the retraction and at least implicitly suggested that her friends might not wish to associate with Trilling. The incident inspired further suspicions of hypocrisy, even glee at the thought that Hellman, self-proclaimed champion of free thought, wanted to censor a rival.

It also added zest to a series of unrelenting criticisms of her person, and most especially her capacity for self-aggrandizement. "I can't stand her," wrote one critic, who nevertheless went on to praise the book. "I can't stand the person . . . No writer I have ever come across is so convinced of her own absolute superiority, *and* innocence, *and* nobility."[77] William Buckley thought the book mistitled. It should have been called "The Heroism of Lillian Hellman during the Darkest Days of the Republic," he wrote in the pages of the *National Review*.[78] Despite the criticism, Alfred Kazin thought Hellman's posturing effective. "It has convinced the generation that has grown up since the fifties that the author was virtually alone in refusing to name past or present communist party members to the House Un-American Activities Committee."[79]

Nor did critics hold back on the most personal forms of ridicule. William Buckley refused her even the benefit of her hard-earned reputation as a playwright, scornfully dismissing Garry Wills's attribution of her as the "Greatest Woman Playwright." That, he wrote, was the same as talking about "the downhill champion on the one-legged ski team."[80] Who else but a woman, asked Murray Kempton, would write about the Balmain dress and the hat she purchased so that she would feel good at her HUAC hearing? Was she afraid of going to jail? Did she decry the victimization of herself and others? Melvyn Lasky dismissed these fears as "an embarrassing insensitivity to history" in the age of the gulag and the gestapo.[81] Kempton thought that she had turned to Joseph Rauh because of his reputation for saving clients from jail.[82] "The best way to sell one's courage," wrote Walter Goodman, "is to make much of one's weaknesses."[83] Kazin, perhaps tongue in cheek, averred that she had escaped jail because "not only was she a woman amid all these shambling and shamefaced witnesses and congressional inquisitors, she was vivid, as always, brave yet somehow wistful, and a famous playwright."[84] Everyone agreed that she was a snob, repeatedly recalling her allusions to cooperative witnesses as the "children of timid immigrants" from whom nothing better could have been expected.[85]

Hellman found the biting mockery and the personal criticisms hard to take. More than once she responded to them with letters to editors and demands for retractions. A review of *Scoundrel Time* in the *Baltimore Sun* began by interpreting Hellman's photograph on the front and back covers of the book: "The masculine pose, Harris tweed coat, and casual cigarette convey that air of sassy androgyny cultivated by forties movie heroines."[86] The covers, continued the review, "seem products of the same carefully cultivated self concept, sophisticated, butch, and gutsy." Hellman took umbrage. She was not wearing a tweed coat at all, she wrote to the publisher, but a suit. "It does not matter that the clear intimation that I am a Lesbian happens to be a lie. It is low down stuff. I guess maybe the lowest I ever read in a respectable newspaper."[87] What, she wanted to know, could be done about this extraordinary review? When George Will wrote a column that described *Scoundrel Time* as including misrepresentations of herself, she demanded that he show her where she had done that: "You have, of course, every right to disagree or criticize my opinions . . . but that does not give you the right to say that I lied without saying where I lied."[88]

Hellman remained adamant about her position, becoming angrier with each passing attack. She produced a brief introduction to a collected edition of her three memoirs in which she unapologetically defended her work, including *Scoundrel Time*. "I tried in these books to tell the truth," she wrote. "I did not fool with facts. But of course that is a shallow definition of the truth."[89] Then she started working on her fourth book of prose. This one would be called *Maybe*, a word she frequently used to describe her sense that she could no longer tell what she believed and what she didn't. Unlike her earlier books, which gloried in rich anecdotal detail and obfuscated uncertainty behind her witty tongue and tough style, *Maybe* reeks of self-doubt. She had hinted at the doubt in the introduction to the collected volumes published just a year before. Hellman asks of those books, "What didn't I see during the time of work that I now see more clearly?" And yet, she goes on to say, she is no wiser now than when she wrote them. Of truth, she is convinced that "I can be sure I still do not see it and never will."[90]

To be sure, all three books of memoir declare Hellman's uncertainty about memory and truth. *An Unfinished Woman* ends with a single word: "However." *Pentimento* starts with an explanatory paragraph that describes an ongoing effort at "seeing and seeing again." *Scoundrel Time* concludes with an intriguing idea: "I tell myself that was then, and there is now, and the years between then and now, and the then and now are one." But in *Maybe* Hellman turned her story into an ode to self-doubt, a defense of the revelations of memory whose value lies not in its capacity to speak truth but in its ability to expand the unconscious. The book contains barely a hint of the tough-minded and willful woman of the three previous volumes. This Lillian is weak, vulnerable. She focuses on what she cannot know rather than on what she can. In that sense, *Maybe* reflects some of the torment of the years that followed the release of *Scoundrel Time*. At one level it explores the elusiveness of memory; at another it asks what kinds of truths memory can reveal. In the end, Hellman commits herself to writing about what she sometimes calls the "truth of her memory" or "the truth as I saw it." If there is another truth somewhere, she cannot write about it.[91]

Neither memoir nor fiction, *Maybe* seems to oscillate between the two. It interweaves a series of encounters with a distant friend named Sarah Cameron with ruminations about herself, her sexuality, her relationships with men. While Sarah is a dreamlike fantasy figure who flits in and out of Hellman's life, Hellman uses her as a guide to her own memories. Early in the book, for example, Hellman recalls a period in her life when a destructive sexual episode with a man named Alex left her feeling as if she "smelled down there." For years, she tells us, she took as many as three baths a day and could take no pleasure in sex. Then Sarah, at a chance lunch, tells Hellman that she laughed off a similar experience with Alex, and Hellman is magically cured of her negative feelings about herself. How much of Sarah is Hellman's alter ego we do not know. Sarah is the occasion for Hellman to tell us that memories fail, that memory is inaccurate, that names and dates disappear, that she might have seen what she could not have witnessed, that she cannot remember what she must have experienced. All this provides justification for *Maybe* and, not incidentally, a response to the attacks generated by the publication of *Scoundrel Time*. Repeatedly Hellman insists that though she may not know—perhaps cannot know—the literal truth of what happened and when and where events took place, there is nevertheless truth in the tale she tells.

Maybe was already in press when, early in 1980, novelist and literary critic Mary McCarthy lit a match to the firestorm that would serve as a metaphor for the twentieth century. The moment provided a ready supply of fuel: everywhere one looked, small conflagrations were already erupting. There was confusion and concern about the changing roles of women; debate over the legitimacy of sexual preference and the value of the traditional nuclear family; declining opposition to left-wing ideologies, including communism, and a resulting escalation in the politics and language of anticommunism; the rise of identity politics as a factor in domestic and world politics; the vanishing influence of the intellectual; and the simultaneous rise of a popular, seemingly mindless, celebrity culture. All these created a tinderbox of politics and emotion, and the aging Lillian Hellman seemed to have provided a spark to each of them. In the conflagration lay questions petty and mean, twinges of common jealousy and sparks of rage. When the fire died down, Lillian Hellman's reputation was reduced to ashes.

On October 18, 1979, McCarthy arrived at the studios of the Educational Broadcasting Corporation to tape an interview with talk show host Dick Cavett. She had a new novel to publicize, *Cannibals and Missionaries*—her first in eight years. She hoped for the kind of success that would bring her back into the limelight. Cavett looked forward to the interview: "She was lively, witty, opinionated, and striking on camera," he recalled later.[92] The interview was going smoothly when, in response to a question about "overrated writers," she mentioned, among others, Lillian Hellman, "who I think is tremendously overrated, a bad writer, and a dishonest writer, but she really belongs to the past." Cavett followed up. What was dishonest about Lillian? he asked. Cavett knew Hellman reasonably well. He had occasionally had dinner with her, previously interviewed her on his show, and claimed to like her a lot. "Everything," McCarthy replied. "I said once in some interview that every word she writes is a lie, including *and* and *the*."[93] The audience laughed; the moment passed, and Cavett went on to other arenas. The network lawyer complimented him afterward on a "nice show," and the tape was stashed away in preparation for its scheduled air time on January 24, 1980.

Two months later, alone in her bedroom, Lillian watched the show on a cold Saturday night. Ill with emphysema and almost blind, she listened to Mary McCarthy accuse her of being a liar. Worn down by the accusations of Stalinism and unwarranted sympathy for the Soviet Union that followed the publication of *Scoundrel Time*, tired of the never-ending negativity about her personal life, and defensive about her rumored greed, she was unprepared for this new assault. The following morning, she picked up the phone and called her old friend and lawyer, Ephraim London, one of the two people to whom she dedicated *Maybe*. She wanted to know if there were grounds for a lawsuit. Ephraim London agreed that there might be. Still in a fury, she called Dick Cavett, demanding to know why he hadn't defended her. She would be suing "the whole damn bunch of you," Cavett recalled her telling him.[94]

Mary McCarthy, at home in her Paris apartment, heard rumors of a pending lawsuit and at first laughed them off. On February 18, a process server knocked on her door and handed her the formal notice. She claimed disbelief. Cavett's question caught her unaware, she protested, and Lillian's name came to the forefront accidentally. Surely her opinion was not actionable. Notes from Cavett's assistant that day suggest that Mary McCarthy was dissembling. Several days before the interview, the assistant noted, she had offered McCarthy a range of questions, including the one about overrated writers. "When I asked if she'd like to discuss which writers are overrated and which underrated and suggested that it could be like a game, she was delighted," the assistant alerted Cavett.[98] Afterward, McCarthy continued to deny that Lillian had been on her mind. But that seems unlikely. For more than forty years the two had shared a climate of hostility, their trajectories running along parallel paths, their opinions conflicting and confronting as they avoided personal encounters.

Seven years younger than Lillian, an acknowledged beauty with a winning smile, Mary McCarthy was, like Lillian, a woman with a quick wit, a bad temper, strong political opinions, and "famous for her malice."[96] Both women had married young and divorced fairly quickly. Both had lived sexually adventurous lives, abused alcohol, and achieved success in worlds generally reserved for men. Each had a passion for good food and drink and generous hospitality.[97] But there the similarities ended. McCarthy, graduating from Vassar in 1933 as a self-declared socialist, had soon chosen Trotskyism, rather than the Communist Party, as her ideological home. From the beginning she despised what she called the brutality of Stalinism and vigorously opposed the Soviet Union. She became the only female to participate in reviving the *Partisan Review*—champion of the non-Stalinist left—in the late 1930s, and served as its drama critic for many years.

The two women were on opposite sides of a 1930s cultural divide that preceded, and continued long after, their contretemps. McCarthy, who had once been called "the first lady of American letters," thought of herself as "a mind" to whom reasoning was natural.[98] Along with her good friend, philosopher Hannah Arendt, and unlike the marginal Hellman, she understood herself as a significant voice among intellectuals. In the 1950s and '60s she wrote literary criticism for some of the country's most influential publications, including the *New Republic*, *Harper's*, the *Nation*, and the *New York Review of Books* as well as *Partisan Review*, all of them magazines that paid minimal attention to Hellman and for which Hellman only rarely wrote. Hellman's desire to appeal to a broad audience as a playwright and essayist countered her appeal to intellectuals who thought of her as decidedly middlebrow.[99] And Hellman's eagerness to immerse culture in political debate offended the partisans of highbrow, and theoretically apolitical, culture. As a drama critic for more than a decade, McCarthy pretty much ignored the plays of Lillian Hellman. They were, she would later claim, destined for a mass audience and not interesting to her or her readers. She reviewed Hellman's film *North Star* negatively, finding its romanticization of the Soviet Union unpalatable. McCarthy likely did not know at the time that Hellman, too, had found the final film lacking in the same respect. A decade later, McCarthy trashed *Candide*.[100] When asked, she could remember referring to Lillian only once, comparing Hellman's "oily virtuosity" to the greater talents of Eugene O'Neill and other modern playwrights.[101]

McCarthy's relationships with men also took a different trajectory from Hellman's. After her first marriage to aspiring actor Harold Johnsrud ended, she lived for a couple of years with Philip Rahv, one of the editors of *Partisan Review.* She left him to marry Edmund Wilson, with whom she had a son and whom she credits for inspiring her to write the novels that would make her literary reputation. But Wilson was not her Hammett. McCarthy left him after seven years for another man, Bowden Broadwater, whom she married in 1946. Broadwater in turn gave way to a fourth husband, James West, whom she met and with whom she fell in love in 1960 while on a State Department–sponsored tour of Eastern and Central Europe. West was a State Department officer in Warsaw at the time. By 1980, McCarthy had been happily married to Jim West for nearly twenty years.

All the while, McCarthy maintained a feisty political persona distinctly at odds with Hellman's. They occupied opposite sides of the Stalinist divide in the thirties: Hellman strongly supported the Soviet Union in that decade, while McCarthy deeply mistrusted it. Hellman traced their differences back to the Spanish Civil War, when help to those fighting Franco came largely from the Soviet Union. Hellman welcomed that help, failing to see that it came at the price of communist control over the forces fighting Franco and oblivious to the atrocities that communists committed in an effort to sustain their influence. McCarthy, along with George Orwell, John Dos Passos, and many others, condemned the Soviet policy of trying to eliminate opponents of Franco who did not agree with the Soviets. She blamed people like Hellman for the murder of opposition leaders and for the ultimate defeat of the Loyalists. McCarthy claims to have had "angry words with Hellman about the Spanish Civil War" at a small dinner at the home of Robert Misch, then head of the elite Wine and Food Society. Hellman denied that she ever attended such a dinner, and remembers meeting McCarthy in the apartment of Philip Rahv shortly after she came back from Spain.[102]

There is no disagreement about where the two stood with relationship to Leon Trotsky, archenemy of Joseph Stalin. Hellman believed that the Soviets, if they could only get rid of internal enemies, might achieve the revolution to which they aspired. Leon Trotsky was, in her eyes, one of those enemies, justly exiled. McCarthy thought the opposite. Trotsky had been exiled, she believed, for opposing Stalin's dictatorial visions. He had no wish to overthrow the Soviet state, only to reform it. The question, investigated in 1938 by a commission led by distinguished philosopher John Dewey, roiled the left. When Dewey's commission exonerated Trotsky of evil intent, McCarthy wholeheartedly supported its conclusions. Hellman excoriated the commission and signed a petition defending the Soviet Union's notorious Moscow show trials as legitimate efforts to police itself internally. Hellman's position, McCarthy argued later, echoed the Stalinist line. By turning a blind eye to Stalin's sins, Hellman had indirectly participated in the murders of thousands of innocent people. Hellman later refused to condemn the 1939 Nazi-Soviet pact—clear evidence, in McCarthy's view, of her subservience to the Soviets. But Hellman never admitted guilt.

Resonances of these political differences lasted during occasional encounters through the years. The two attended a dinner in 1948; McCarthy remembers the event taking place in the home of Harold Taylor, president of Sarah Lawrence College. She describes Hellman "sounding off to some students about how John Dos Passos betrayed the Spanish Loyalists because he didn't like the food in Madrid!" McCarthy maintains she embarrassed Hellman by offering to tell the students why Dos Passos broke with the loyalists. Hellman, she recalled, "started to tremble."[103] Hellman remembers the same dinner as having taken place at the home of Stephen Spender. She left early, she remembers, because "two male students came over to tell me that they felt it was their duty to report that I had been asked to Spender's in order to be 'baited.' "[104] Spender affirmed Hellman's recollection that the dinner was at his home but noted that there were only girls present and that Hellman and McCarthy had been invited together for no other reason "than to please these girls . . . We have never in our lives," Spender continued, "deliberately invited people who disliked each other."[105] McCarthy alleged that Hellman held a grudge against her for her dissenting role at the 1949 Waldorf conference, where McCarthy spoke from the floor in objection to the presence of authorized Soviet participants. Hellman, a sponsor of the conference, claimed not to have known that McCarthy was present, and in any event to have been among those who encouraged the voices of dissenters.

The personal and the political slipped into petty jealousies and touched trivial issues as well as large ones. Hellman skipped out of a theater festival in Edinburgh where Mary McCarthy turned up. After a futile request to her agent to get her out of the gig, she told a friend that she planned to give herself "a vacation from the warlock smile of Miss Mary MacCarthy [sic]."[106] McCarthy, in turn, claimed to remember, thirty years after her encounter with Hellman at Sarah Lawrence, that Hellman "had rather aging wrinkled arms, bare and on them were a lot of gold and silver bracelets—and all the bracelets started to jangle."[107] Hellman, hearing this story, replied that she found it "particularly comic since I was in my very early forties, and arms don't age quite that fast, and I never wore dangling bracelets in my life."[108]

Discomfort and jealousy manifested themselves as well within the overlapping intellectual circles to which the two women belonged. Hellman began to mingle with the New York intellectuals and the *Partisan Review* crowd in the late fifties and sixties. She drew close to Philip Rahv and Edmund Wilson, one a former lover of McCarthy's and the other a former husband. She socialized with Robert (Cal) Lowell, his wife, Elizabeth Hardwick, and with Lowell's school chum Blair Clark, all of them close friends of McCarthy's.[109] Try as she might, Hellman never became fully a part of the New York intellectual community in which Hannah Arendt and Mary McCarthy figured. This might not have been entirely her fault, for, despite the presence of Arendt, Hardwick, and McCarthy, the New Yorkers did not generally take women seriously as intellectuals.[110] Hellman did try to get to know Arendt. "Hannah and I met a number of times for dinner and lunch through the many years before her death . . . and never mentioned Mary McCarthy."[111]

The history of feuds and jealousies came to a head in the years just before the Dick Cavett show aired. Ever since the 1940s, Hellman had been engaged in the effort to raise money for refugees who had fled Spain after Franco's victory in 1939. In 1969, Dwight MacDonald, friend to both McCarthy and Hellman and an independent anticommunist, persuaded her to become a sponsor of Spanish Refugee Aid, then the most important vehicle for aiding the now aging and ailing refugees of the conflict. Spanish Refugee Aid identified itself as both antifascist and anticommunist. It was run by MacDonald's former wife, Nancy. Its sponsors included, among many others, Arthur Schlesinger Jr., Roger Baldwin of the ACLU, Mary McCarthy, and Gabriel Javsicas. All of their names, along with Hellman's, appeared on SRA letterhead for 1970 and after. Javsicas, a Russian-born and German-educated anarchist, had been briefly imprisoned by Franco's regime in 1964 when he tried to make contact with anarchist opponents of the dictator.

After the publication of *Scoundrel Time*, Javsicas noticed that Hellman was a member of the board and began a campaign to oust her.[112] In close communication with McCarthy, to whom he copied much of his correspondence, he insisted that he would resign if Hellman were not removed from the board. "She is a nasty, hard headed homo sapiens knowing full well what she was doing when she viciously attacked us for presuming to question Stalin's right to exterminate our fellowmen," he wrote.

> Nor can it be said that she has repented. She is as good a Stalinist propagandist as ever, voluntarily spreading the Tchekist line that the mass murder of intellectuals and peasants under Stalin was a sin, a slight aberration of Stalin in an otherwise admirable human experiment. This woman is also an unconscionable liar, a hypocrite who sends me monthly appeals to join her so-called Committee for Public Justice (no less) while condoning the censorship exercised by her publishers against a friend who presumed the mildest disapproval of her politics . . . Supposing we had unmasked a Nazi among our sponsors who condoned the extermination of the Jews, would you vote to retain such a person?[113]

In April 1978, the board voted to drop Hellman as an SRA sponsor. MacDonald, who had invited Hellman onto the board, intervened. When the board met (in Javsicas's absence) the following September, he persuaded its members to reinstate her. Furious, Javsicas submitted a letter of resignation and wrote to Mary McCarthy to encourage her to resign too. Nancy MacDonald begged him to rethink: "I think it is all very foolish and wish you wouldn't do it. After all you do believe in the work we are doing and Lillian is hardly an impediment to it."[114] McCarthy, too, offered to resign in an ambivalent letter to Nancy at the end of November. "Gaby has sent me copies of his letters to you on the subject of Lillian Hellman," she wrote. "I'm sorry to say that I thoroughly agree with him and feel, though with pain, that I should ask for my name to be removed too from the list of sponsors . . . How in the world did it happen that she was invited to join? I had no knowledge of it at all." The letter was signed "with my love."[115]

For months after that—into the spring and summer of 1979—Javsicas, Mary McCarthy, Dwight MacDonald, and Nancy MacDonald exchanged letters and phone calls airing the issue of whether or not Hellman was still a Stalinist, deserving of ostracism. Finally, by the end of June the issue had boiled down to a question of choice: "Are you going to maintain Hellman rather than Mary?" Javsicas asked Nancy MacDonald.[116] In July

James Farrell, persuaded by Javsicas, resigned from the board. But then the tide turned. Dwight MacDonald convinced McCarthy to change her mind, not because she thought any better of Hellman but because she and others had "kept silent for so long." McCarthy wrote apologetically to Javsicas about her change of heart: "My present feeling is that if Hellman does something new that we can and ought to object to, the whole question could be reopened."[117] McCarthy sent this letter a week before she taped the Dick Cavett show.

Nor did the antagonism end there. Javsicas expressed concern at McCarthy's comment. By now he had become so obsessed with having Hellman removed that he went to small claims court to ask for the return of his $160 contribution. McCarthy tried to persuade him to drop the action. "It will probably have the reverse effect of creating sympathy for the very undeserving Hellman," she wrote to him.[118] Still, Javsicas persisted, eventually alienating everyone including Mary McCarthy, who rescinded her resignation and volunteered to contribute to some of the SRA's legal fees if necessary. All this occurred just as her own legal problems with Hellman descended, suggesting that Hellman had been much on McCarthy's mind in the months before and after she went on the Dick Cavett show. Her claim afterward not to have thought much about Hellman during the months before seems patently false.

To defend herself in a lawsuit that she hoped at first would simply die, McCarthy began searching for proof of Hellman's falsehoods. From Castine, Maine, she wrote that summer to friends and friends of friends, reminding them of the lawsuit and asking them for help. In snowball fashion, evidence accumulated. McCarthy asked her friend Jon Randal what he remembered; he put her in touch with Martha Gellhorn, who suggested that she contact Charles Collingwood. Her old friend Stephen Spender put her in touch with Muriel Gardiner, who turned her on to John Hite, an expert on European railway timetables between the wars. Several people suggested she contact Sidney Hook and Diana Trilling, but she balked at the idea of allying with such politically incompatible bedfellows. And so it went. By November she could write that "I spent my workless summer rather fruitfully on this."[119] The stress was enormous. She worried about money and she developed a bad case of shingles in July, which did not dissipate until November.

Unsurprisingly, the search turned up enormous amounts of evidence demonstrating that Hellman had embroidered stories, dramatized and inflated her own role in them, conveniently consolidated different versions of the same tale, and misremembered dates and their relationships to events. These were all acknowledged techniques deployed by Lillian over the years, and all "deeds that countless good writers have committed," as one commentator put it.[120] McCarthy understood that her own memory could be faulty too. Indeed, when Stephen Spender confirmed Hellman's account of the 1948 meeting at Sarah Lawrence College, she began to doubt herself: "They're so sure, and so had I been," she wrote to her lawyer.[121] Self-doubt did not stop McCarthy from taking great comfort in discovering small and large aberrations in Hellman's stories. She wrote about them to friends and acquaintances to jog their own memories and to confirm her sense that Hellman routinely lied. In the process, McCarthy constructed a mountain of information that, added together, seemed to confirm the reputation of Lillian Hellman as a liar.

In November she asked Carol Gelderman, who was just then negotiating a contract to write McCarthy's biography and who conveniently resided in New Orleans, to check to see whether the "Willy" story in *Pentimento* was true or not. She had spoken to a friend who "recognized much of this material, but as belonging to the public domain rather than to Hellman or her family."[122] Gelderman and a student searched the record, interviewed neighbors, and read old newspapers. They concluded that the figure of Willy was a fiction—a composite made up of the husband of her great-aunt and the husband's nephew by marriage. This and other trivial differences led Gelderman and McCarthy to conclude rather gleefully that it would be easy to label her a liar. And Hellman had, in a literal sense, lied. She had conflated Willy's house with that of his nephew; she had invented a visit of her great-aunt to the farm in Pleasantville; she claimed that Willy had been "thrown out" of the big company he created, when in fact he had quit; she described Willy as dying in bankruptcy when, it seemed, his wife and daughter had "rejected the estate because it contained nothing but debts."[123]

In these ways, McCarthy produced a fat file of "lies." Hellman could not have gone on an errand in the time she claimed it had taken her. The big dining room in which she remembered a conversation happening probably didn't exist in the house in which she put it; a giant doll's house that Lillian remembered as having contained elaborate furniture contained only simple objects. Her cousin Bethe would have been eaten up by mosquitoes had she been naked when Hellman saw her hanging clothes on the line. Southern azaleas did not have an odor, much less the sweet scent that Hellman attributed to them. Hellman sometimes claimed to speak fluent French in a patois that resembled the Marseilles dialect, and at others declared herself unable to make herself understood. There were plenty of lies to be found in Lillian's books, and McCarthy had no difficulty identifying many of them. "I have a feeling that she will be sorry she sued," Gelderman concluded after her search ended.[124]

But what did these lies reveal about Hellman or about the 1970s? McCarthy needed enough evidence to exonerate herself from the charge of libel. To her it did not matter how trivial the lie or what its meaning. We cannot blame McCarthy for the consequences of the kind of search she conducted, nor for her efforts to bias her sources. Nor can we accuse her of living in a glass house: McCarthy found herself trapped in several small lies of her own and confessed her propensity to mendacity in a newly published autobiography.[125] She was, after all, defending herself from what she thought of as a vindictive lawsuit; she needed all the ammunition she could get. And Hellman made an easy target. Her brilliant storytelling, published under the rubric of the memoir; her propensity to fudge in the interest of a good story; her skill for manufacturing realistic detail—all these made literal truth easy to demolish. Hellman would be exposed as someone who had tried to turn herself into the heroine of her own life. She had, as Irving Howe would later put it, turned her life with Hammett into a myth.

McCarthy attacked the myth directly when she tried to illuminate Hellman's politics. Often her letters asked for information that would demonstrate that Hellman was still the unregenerate Stalinist her friends assumed. Could Mrs. Sheila Hale, McCarthy wrote to a woman to whom Hellman had apparently been unpardonably rude, provide information about an incident in which Hellman had called Solzhenitsyn insane and claimed that the gulag was a total invention? If true, wrote McCarthy, "It gives the lie to her pretense of . . . having had her eyes opened to the sins of Stalin."[126] Sheila Hale replied promptly, if somewhat cautiously. There was some truth in what McCarthy had heard, she wrote—Hellman had called Solzhenitsyn insane. But this was after a good dinner with a few close friends, and she had never said his numbers were "a total invention," only that "he had exaggerated the numbers of prisoners in the Gulag."

Accurate or not, the conversations around the lawsuit helped to revive and spread Hellman's reputation as a Stalinist. William Buckley aimed an opening salvo: "What Lillian Hellman specialized in, during almost two bloody decades," he wrote shortly after the lawsuit became public, "was precisely in cutting her conscience to fit the whims of Joseph Stalin."[127]

McCarthy avidly sustained that notion, even as she claimed that "examples of [Hellman's] political dishonesty, unless especially flagrant, aren't what's needed in a case of this kind."[128] Hellman, who remained critical of dissidents who earned their freedom by betraying others, had at this point roundly condemned the Soviet repression of intellectuals and allied herself with Solzhenitsyn.[129] McCarthy nevertheless took advantage of the fear and suspicion of Stalinism sparked by the newly resurgent neoconservative movement to fan the dying flames of an old battle. She described Hellman in her letters as a "virtually unreconstructed" Stalinist. "Maybe the organization has something on her which has kept her a captive all these years," she wrote. "A friend close to the CIA tells me he is convinced that she was an *agent,* literally on the payroll, in the Forties and possibly Fifties."[130] She triumphantly called the attention of her friends to an article in *Harper's* that referred to Hellman's "decades long affair with the dashing Communist, Joseph Stalin."[131]

McCarthy's effort to tarnish Hellman as an unregenerate Stalinist encouraged sparks to fly in unanticipated directions. McCarthy quickly tried to stamp them out. She learned early on that Diana Trilling wanted to participate in a defense committee on McCarthy's behalf. But McCarthy mistrusted Trilling and believed that she had her own motives for wanting to help. "The intrusion of Diana affects me disagreeably," she wrote to her lawyer.[132] Later she elaborated: she would resist the idea of a defense committee "even if it came from other sponsors rather than from that Cold-War Bellona."[133] Above all she resented the fact that Trilling seemed less interested in raising money for McCarthy's defense than, in Trilling's words, "to mobilize sentiment on Mary's behalf and extrude Lillian from the community of the fair-minded."[134] When Sidney Hook, who earned his political stripes as an anticommunist and had since moved to the far right, offered to provide McCarthy with evidence of Hellman's political misdeeds, McCarthy found the offer repugnant.[135] This was another offer she wanted to refuse.

As the details of McCarthy's search began to coalesce, they turned all of Hellman's life into a trough of suspicion in which truth was the first casualty. When McCarthy contacted Martha Gellhorn, Hemingway's third wife and a distinguished journalist, Gellhorn responded eagerly. She would cooperate "with pleasure and would do the same for anyone against all liars and self vaunters as I am sick of the lot."[136] From Castine, Maine, McCarthy mailed to Gellhorn in London a copy of *An Unfinished Woman.* Gellhorn replied before she had finished it: "As I read this book, I think it's ALL lies," she wrote to McCarthy, adding that she thought the book "egomaniacal malarkey."[137] Later, she added, "everything she writes is self praise and all rot."[138] Gellhorn had already made up her mind about Hellman based on an earlier experience with her. She had met Hellman first on the boat that took both of them to Europe in the summer of 1937. Gellhorn resented Hellman, who, accompanied by her friends Dorothy Parker and Alan Campbell, traveled first class. In Paris, Gellhorn, not yet married to Hemingway, kept a low profile and then joined Hemingway to travel with him to Spain. Hellman claimed to have seen a good deal of Hemingway in the weeks before they left for Spain. Gellhorn, deeply involved with him, denied it. The three would meet again in Valencia.

Gellhorn, digging enthusiastically into the material that McCarthy sent her, filled McCarthy with advice about how to go about her research: "You should take specific statements and demolish them—make her out to be what she is, a self-serving braggart."[139] Gellhorn advised going for the jugular: "Specific details, wherever she actually names a place, a street, a fact: simply prove it cannot be true." Find out, she told McCarthy, whether Lillian was actually on the Russian front, as she claimed to have been in *An Unfinished Woman*. Gellhorn doubted it. How could she have perched in a dugout with a glass wall? How could a grenade be thrown at her if she was five hundred feet from the enemy lines?

McCarthy pursued these leads with zest. At Gellhorn's suggestion, she wrote to John Hersey, who had shared some of Hellman's Moscow experiences and accompanied her partway to the front. Hersey, who had since become one of Hellman's closest friends, disappointed McCarthy. He had not personally witnessed the event, he replied. Hellman's interpreter and companion, Raisa Orlova, who had been with her at the front and recently defected, was just then publishing a memoir of her own. Recalling the trip to the front, Orlova described Lillian's courage under machine-gun fire and "during the moments that brought us close to death." She was, according to Orlova, "clever, sharp witted, and often full of anger."[140] McCarthy dropped her inquiry into Hellman's experience under fire to follow more promising leads.

Particularly sure of herself about events in Spain during 1937, Gellhorn denied that Hellman could have been there for as long as she claimed. She mocked Hellman's self-proclaimed courage under bombing that could not have happened and accused her of making up encounters with Hemingway that she could not have had.[141] McCarthy could neither confirm nor deny most of Gellhorn's stories and in the end did not use them, but Gellhorn persisted. Inspired by McCarthy's search, she set to work on an article based on her research. Resentment infected her quest. "I cannot bear liars, apocryphiars," she explained to McCarthy to justify her continuing interest. "As a reporter, I regard them as wicked, deforming the news and the facts. As a writer, I consider that fact and fiction are totally different and I object fiercely to lying. And besides I do despise self aggrandizement in a general way."[142] Gellhorn did not use the word *liar* in the piece that the *Paris Review* published in June 1981.[143] Cautioned by the editors, she invented instead the euphemism *apocryphiar* and acquiesced grumpily when the same editors altered the essay's title from "Close Encounters of the Apocryphal Kind" to "Plume de Guerre."[144]

But she did her best to demolish Hellman's account of her experiences during the Spanish Civil War and her encounters with Hemingway. Hellman, Gellhorn claimed, could not have been as close to Hemingway as she protested, for he was simply not in the locations at the times Hellman described. He could not, for example, have been with Gustav Regler at the Stork Club at the time that Lillian recalled Hemingway challenging Hammett to bend a spoon with one elbow. Gellhorn insisted Hemingway was abroad at the time of the purported meeting. Nor could Hellman have read the manuscript of *To Have and Have Not* during one Paris night. The manuscript, Gellhorn claimed, was in press at the time. Besides, Gellhorn wrote to friends, Hemingway could not stand her.

The piece drew wide attention despite the fact that Gellhorn's veracity was itself called into question. When she leveled accusations of lying against Stephen Spender (former editor of the neoconservative publication *Encounter* and, incidentally, former lover of Muriel Gardiner and friend to Mary McCarthy), Spender responded dismissively, telling her that her memory was faulty.[145] Yet he and the world at large continued to hold the opinion that her account of Hellman's lies was substantially correct. A year later, in 1981, he cited Gellhorn's piece as evidence for asserting that Hellman was no more than a "fiction writer and a plagiarist."[146]

Eventually the idea that Lillian was no more than a liar spread to every detail of her life. "Being a liar is deeper than politics—ingrained, surely," wrote McCarthy to a friend.[147] Was Hellman really born in New Orleans? What about the two aunts: had Hellman made them up too? How old was she? McCarthy suspected that Hellman had deducted a year or two from her age and enthusiastically broadcast her suspicions to Gellhorn, who promptly exaggerated the difference. Hellman, Gellhorn guessed, had probably been born between 1899 and 1901. Indeed Hellman did routinely (and in the fashion of many women of her generation as they grew older) deduct a year and sometimes two from her age. She was born in 1905. But the casual accusations against her veracity descended to an ugly level of callousness. When witnesses could not be found to support Hellman's stories, McCarthy suspected that she had deliberately chosen anecdotes that could not be verified. To CBS news anchor Charles Collingwood, who could not find information about a CBS radio broadcast that Hellman claimed to have made from Madrid in October 1937, McCarthy wrote, "There's an unusually high mortality rate among witnesses to her doings wherever she was."[148] Gellhorn agreed with this assessment: "That's the clever side of mythomanes," she wrote to McCarthy, "they wait until everyone is dead (except me) before they really go to town."[149]

The coup de grâce came from the story of Julia, the fifth chapter of *Pentimento*, which purported to describe Hellman's courage in aiding antifascist resistance in 1937 Austria. The story became a film starring Vanessa Redgrave as Julia and Jane Fonda as Lillian. Released in the fall of 1977 at a fund-raising party for the Committee for Public Justice, it produced immediate accolades for Hellman. European editions of *Pentimento* followed, along with invitations to read the story and describe her experiences to college audiences. Suddenly Hellman turned into the beautiful blonde she had always wanted to be; she became the courageous woman of her fantasies and an icon of twentieth-century womanhood. But was this Lillian's story or someone else's?

Julia had long been rumored to be based on the life of Muriel Gardiner, then a psychiatrist living just outside Princeton, in Pennington, New Jersey, and the only American woman known to have worked in the Austrian resistance. Lillian shrugged off the rumors, insisting that although she had heard them, nobody had ever publicly come forward. She said she had never received a letter that Gardiner claimed to have sent her, pointing out the similarities between her life and Julia's. She and Gardiner shared one friend in common—a lawyer named Wolf Schwabacher who had talked about Hellman to Gardiner and who could easily have shared Gardiner's story with her. But Lillian insisted that the story was that of her pseudonymous friend. Though her memory was poor—as she wrote in *Pentimento* and repeated in interviews—she remembered this story absolutely. Instead of retreating as the rumors began to spread, Hellman elaborated on them. Before McCarthy's interview, before the lawsuit, she told one interviewer that "nothing on God's earth could have shaken my memory about" Julia.[150] To another, she described in great detail how she had discovered the fate of Julia's baby from the doctor who treated Julia in London at her death.[151]

McCarthy learned about Muriel Gardiner in the summer of 1980, probably from Stephen Spender, once Gardiner's lover and still a close friend. She wrote immediately to Gardiner, who responded positively. But Gardiner did not want the story repeated. McCarthy wrote to a friend that "the distinguished professional woman who has come to recognize herself as the original of Julia" was "hesitating as to whether to offer a deposition." And then, perhaps projecting her own feelings onto Gardiner, McCarthy added, "She has been warned that Hellman is a dangerous antagonist, quick to revenge herself."[152] When Gardiner subsequently published an account of her experiences in the resistance, she did not claim the identity of Julia. Instead she merely acknowledged that she "had often been struck by the similarities between my life" and that of Hellman's heroine.[153] But others noted that Gardiner, like the fictional Julia, was born to a wealthy family, studied at Oxford, went to Vienna to be analyzed, and there enrolled in medical school. Crucially, as Gardiner pointed out, Julia had worked in the Austrian resistance—the Austrians could identify only one American who had been so active. And she was Muriel Gardiner.

Was this, then, a lie? Most likely, Hellman concocted the outlines of Julia's story from the comments she had heard about Muriel Gardiner from Schwabacher. After Gardiner's book appeared, Hellman went to some lengths to contact Gardiner, only to be rebuffed. To her friend and psychiatrist George Gero, who tried to arrange a meeting, Hellman wrote that she feared McCarthy would "use the publicity on Gardiner's book to discredit my word on everything."[154] Later she reported to him that her lawyer, Ephraim London, "was very frightened of her and so indeed am I."[155] London, increasingly disturbed by the idea that Hellman had invented Julia, pressured Hellman to reveal the name of Julia's family. She tried to convince him that she should not mention Julia's last name with a story so convoluted and fanciful that those named in it could only laugh at the whole cloth out of which it was made.[156] But the puzzle is why Hellman tried to keep this story going for so long; why she could not admit that, though she might have been inspired to invent the tale from the little she knew of Gardiner's life, most of the story came out of her fantasy life, out of her desire to be the courageous woman she imagined she might be.

This was not the first time Hellman had created and kept spinning a long-running tale that could not have been true. There was her insistent saga to Blair Clark about an aristocratic foreigner and the child she claimed to have borne him. She invented a story about why she kept changing her age, which she told with a straight face to Hunter College colleague Alex Szogyi. Her father, she said, was a gallant gentleman who never wanted her to know her age, and by the time she was interested enough to ask, "the hospital in which she was born had burned down and the records were lost."[157] Nor was it the first time that she had built on the experiences of others (including family members) to construct portraits or stories out of her imagination. She was, after all, a dramatist, and self-dramatization was her strength. Unaccountably, she continued to stand by the veracity of the Julia story.

By continuing the tale, by appropriating the outlines of somebody else's life, Hellman overstepped the bounds of memoir, crossed an invisible line, and—in the context of the lawsuit against Mary McCarthy—revealed her lying habits. Conversations around the lawsuit quickly deteriorated into name-calling, venom, and malice. Hellman was a "Bloody vindictive old broad," wrote CBS reporter Charles Collingwood to McCarthy. Hellman supporters responded in kind: "I have been incensed since I heard about that 'bitch' Mary McCarthy's attack on the television. You have more in your ASS than she has in her brain," wrote Sam Jaffe to Hellman. Hellman replied, "Dear Sam, Thank you very much."[158]

The swiftly unfolding events quickly turned friends into enemies. When Norman Mailer begged the two women, in print, to reconcile, Richard Poirier wrote a passionate defense of his old friend Hellman. Mailer responded with a personal note that he copied to several of the literati. "Your righteous mind and sulphurous bottom," he wrote to Poirier, "produce much brimstone."[159] Hellman promptly broke off a thirty-year friendship with Mailer. "I am sorry about you and me," she wrote to him, "genuinely sorry."[160] Hellman reached out to Barbara Epstein—an editor at the New York Review of Books with whom she had long been close. Epstein responded cautiously, indicating her distress at the lawsuit and hoping that they could "meet again soon."[161] Then in private correspondence with McCarthy, Epstein expressed her distaste for Hellman. She refused Hellman's subsequent requests to meet. Hellman expressed only a little regret at this. "My lawsuit against Mary McCarthy," she wrote to her friend Dorothy Pritchett, "has caused Barbara to increase her already very stern dislike of me. She actually told me that she thought it was disgraceful of me to take so crazy a statement seriously and to cause McCarthy pain."[162] Bob Silvers, editor of the New York Review of Books and for a decade Hellman's colleague in the Committee for Public Justice, rallied to McCarthy's side. A year or so after the lawsuit was filed, he wrote to McCarthy to tell her that he had denounced Lillian's suit to her face: "Since then silence from her and most of her friends."[163] Elizabeth Hardwick (also part of the *New York Review of Books* circle and the ex-wife of Lillian's friend Robert Lowell) had offended Lillian in 1967 with a scathing review of a revival of *The Little Foxes*. Now she tried to organize her friends to write a public letter condemning the suit. The letter, she suggested, would support Mary McCarthy's position that she was entitled to express her opinions freely.[164]

But Hellman remained staunch in the face of criticism. Bill Alfred, who had arranged her first job at Harvard, wrote to tell her that he hadn't called to talk about the suit because "I would have to tell you that I think it mistaken."[165] Hellman replied with uncharacteristic dispassion. "I don't think we will ever agree about the Mary McCarthy mess . . . You must know from the tone of my letter that I was offended by yours. But that, of course, will heal, and has nothing to do with an old affection, and one that I hope can soon be mended."[166] Bill Styron wrote her a letter of apology when a reporter quoted him saying that the lawsuit "was unfortunate all around." Hellman accepted the apology, which was filled with admiration and praise, telling him, "I am deeply glad we can continue in great friendship with each other."[167]

Some took sides on the grounds that the rich, vindictive Lillian wanted to pursue the lawsuit merely to bankrupt McCarthy. Hellman, irascible and old, they suggested, wanted only revenge. Rumor spread that the lawsuit would cripple McCarthy financially and wreck her health.[168] Hellman had little sympathy. "Quite simply I feel I was treated in a most brutal fashion and, while I have no desire to ruin her, or anybody else, I have heard no words of apology or attempt to make one."[169] Lillian, McCarthy's friends carped, was represented without charge by her old friend Ephraim London. But McCarthy was no victim. Though she worried about the money the lawsuit would cost, especially if it went to trial, she desperately wanted victory. Two years into the proceedings, she received a $25,000 contribution from an anonymous "angel" and around the same time bought herself a new fur coat.[170] Lillian insisted throughout the entire ordeal that money was not the object. Honor was at stake. McCarthy's assertions of lying, she argued, constituted the last straw in a long campaign to undermine the integrity that Hellman held so dear. Egged on by friends, one of whom wrote, "Here's hoping you get every nickel she's got," she withheld

1983: She grew increasingly frail. (Photofest)

public comment about McCarthy's refusal to say she was sorry.[171] In the meantime, and over London's objections, Hellman sent several checks to cover some of the cost of court expenses. "Please, please, please," she wrote to London, "If you do not accept any money from me, I will become an even greater cripple than I am."[172]

All this took second place to the most forceful argument against the suit, and perhaps the one that rankled most. Increasingly, the literati focused their discontent on what they viewed as Hellman's attack on freedom of expression. Hellman's suit, insisted her detractors and some of her friends, violated an unspoken code of writers. As Gellhorn put the case to McCarthy, "Miss H, by resorting to libel law, has broken an ancient and noble tradition of writers, which is to call each other any names they like, in print, insult not law being the proper behavior."[173] Herself the victim of blacklisting, Hellman was now thought to be engaged in muffling the free expression of others, leading some to say that she embraced the First Amendment only in her own defense. When Hellman dismissed Stephen Spender's support of Mary McCarthy as coming from someone who had "long been a member of the anti-Hellman group," he responded quickly.[174] He had never heard of an "anti-Hellman group," he told her, and then later explained his opposition to the suit. "I think such cases, whatever the provocation, lower the status of literature. A writer, after all, is someone who believes in the power of words, and if he wishes to defend himself he can do so in language without resort to the law."[175] Others thought the suit could have devastating effects. "Should it be successful," Charles Collingwood wrote to McCarthy, sympathetically, "it would have the most inhibiting effect on critical comment within whose bounds of propriety your observations certainly fell."[176]

Hellman, bothered by this line of attack, consulted Burke Marshall, distinguished law professor at Yale and an active member of the Committee for Public Justice. Marshall gave her little comfort, but he was in an odd position. He was an old friend of Renata Adler, once Lillian's protégé and now on McCarthy's side. Lillian turned to him in 1983, as the suit dragged on, to ask whether he could support her position in the suit. Marshall replied in the negative. "I think the courts should be left out of that kind of business and that it should be left up to dispute in other places."[177]

Through almost four years, while the lawsuit bounced around, Hellman grew increasingly frail. What was left of her eyesight diminished rapidly. Sometimes she could hardly breathe. Often she had to be carried in and out of public appearances that she stoutly refused to cancel. Still, she had one more victory to savor. McCarthy's lawyers tried to get the courts to issue a summary judgment against the case on the grounds that Lillian Hellman, as a public figure, was fair game for criticism. Ephraim London responded by claiming that Hellman was not a public figure at all. The claim drew loud chortles from some of Hellman's enemies. But it persuaded Judge Harold Baer Jr., who, after many months of delay, refused the plea. "In addition to being a person of general notoriety," Baer wrote in May of 1984, "a public figure must be someone who is involved in a public issue, question, or controversy."[178] Siding with Hellman, the judge reminded the participants of McCarthy's deposition. Hellman might not consciously have lied, McCarthy conceded there. She was not speaking of "'prevarication per se' or a conscious intent to state an untruth." "I don't mean literally nothing when I say 'nothing in her writing rings true,'" McCarthy said. "I don't mean of course . . . say perhaps 70 per cent of her factual statements are probably true . . . I mean the general tone of unconvincingness and falseness." Asked directly if she thought that all of Hellman's writings were in fact lies, she replied: "I would say, no."[179] Under the circumstances, to call Hellman a "dishonest writer," the judge concluded, "crosses the boundary between opinion and fact."[180]

Both sides now regeared for action. McCarthy promptly hired distinguished First Amendment lawyer Floyd Abrams to represent her in court. Hellman claimed to relish the court trial that would soon occur. The trial never happened. Hellman grew sicker and more irascible by the day, and a month later she was gone. McCarthy, hearing the news, expressed sorrow only that she would not get her day in court.

CHAPTER 11

Life After Death

Life owes it to you to die your own way.
—*Lillian Hellman, Harvard lecture, 1961*

You don't necessarily have to like her, but you should understand her.
It's more about empathy than sympathy.
—*William Luce*

It may be that her life, with its strong loyalties, combative courage and
abiding hatred of injustice, will eventually be considered her greatest
theatre.
—*Robert Brustein*

Lillian Hellman died in her home on Martha's Vineyard on June 30, 1984,
a few days after her seventy-ninth birthday. The night before, Bill Styron
carried her into a small dinner party at John and Barbara Hersey's. She
ate and drank almost nothing, but she was in good spirits and planned a
fishing expedition for the next morning. Anecdote has it that she propo-
sitioned a guest at dinner, inviting him back to her place for a nightcap.
He declined the playful request. She returned home after dinner to the
care of her nurse and housekeeper and died quietly in the night. The
coroner listed the death as coronary arrest, but most likely the underlying
cause was the emphysema from which she had suffered for years.

Her death was no surprise. Over a period of several years, Hellman had become increasingly frail. Bronchial problems caused by her ubiquitous cigarettes impeded her blood circulation and contributed to heart failure; a series of small strokes reduced her ability to walk and eventually to eat by herself; glaucoma and cataracts reduced her eyesight to near zero. Hellman's eyesight became so poor by the winter of 1980 that she could no longer read a printed page. At that point her helpers began to write in large spiral-bound notebooks, using bold markers to make block letters. The notebooks contain schedules and plans, as well as reminders to Lillian. The one she kept from February to March 1980, while she was in California, includes a poignant comment on her troubles that winter. A single page, written in block letters, contained the words: "MARY MACARTHY QUOTE ON THE DICK CAVETT SHOW: EVERY WORD SHE WRITES IS A LIE INCLUDING 'AND' AND 'THE.'"[1]

That was the winter that Hellman spent in San Francisco, where she celebrated the publication of *Three*, a single-volume edition of her memoirs. Billy Abrahams, her editor, arranged a tribute to the book at the Marin County Veterans' Center and agreed that he and Peter Feibleman would host the event. As it turned out, Hellman was too weak to make the trip without help, and Abrahams and Feibleman together assisted her onto the stage. Abrahams introduced her to an enthusiastic crowd, telling them that she was ill but that "she said if she had to, she'd come by ambulance. And in fact, she did."[2] Her appearance, said Abrahams, demonstrated her "indomitability." Peter Feibleman pitched in to read a section of *Pentimento* for her. Hellman read two pages from a new afterword she wrote for *Scoundrel Time*. "I am angrier now than I hope I will ever be again," the piece concluded, and then went on to say that she wanted to take the moral stand she tried to avoid taking when she wrote *Scoundrel Time*. "I never want to live again to watch people turn into liars and cowards and others into frightened, silent collaborators. And to hell with the fancy reasons they give for what they did."[3] The audience gave her a rousing ovation, and Lillian left in a limousine followed by two ambulances, one of them filled with friends, just in case.

The next day, the writer Kay Boyle wrote to her friend Jessica Mitford, also Lillian's friend. She was, she wrote, shattered by the "macabre performance" of the previous evening: "The ambulance might have been a hearse from which they lifted the poor, desperately ill, emaciated creature that Lillian has become." She blamed William Abrahams and the publishing house for "its total horror of exploitation." And she spluttered that "that terrible liquid cough that shook her was like a sound from the grave."[4] Little did she suspect that Lillian had in fact insisted on appearing.

Lillian gave everyone trouble in those years, her irascibility and impatience rising with increasing infirmity. Friends withdrew from her withering tongue: embittered by her stubborn refusal to abandon the suit against Mary McCarthy, they stopped seeing her. But many remained loyal, forgiving her temper tantrums and reveling in her continuing ability to make fun of everything and everyone.[5] Unable to withstand northern winters, she moved each year to California, where she took rooms for herself and her nurses at the Beverly Wilshire hotel or rented houses from absent friends. The nurses who cared for her wrote of their plight to Rita Wade, Hellman's secretary, who coordinated their efforts from New York. After one particularly difficult period at the Beverly Wilshire, one wrote to describe the "absolutely incredible" and "miserable" time that Hellman had given her and her coworker. The registered nurse who replaced them the following year wondered if she could survive Hellman's "mental abuse." She had, she reported, won one battle: she convinced Lillian that no nurse could sleep, night after night, on a couch in the sitting room. She persuaded Hellman to hire an aide to relieve her at night. "I am going out of my mind," she protested. "What am I doing as Lillian Hellman's personal slave? Pray for me!!"[6] All the nurses complained of Lillian's tightfistedness about money, the requirement that they send each receipt, no matter how small, to Rita on the day it was acquired, and Hellman's insistence that they notify Rita immediately if they cashed checks. The nurses, with Rita's acquiescence, passively resisted these instructions, notifying Rita when and as it seemed appropriate.

Over a period of about eighteen months, Hellman ate less and less and lost weight rapidly until she was down to about eighty pounds. Still she accepted invitations, allowed her friends to carry her from cars to restaurants, and invited guests for dinner. Often she was, as her friend Robert Brustein described, "carried into the house, placed in a chair, and fed her food," little more than "a bedridden Job imprisoned inside a broken bag of bones."[7] In California, Hannah Weinstein came to visit while she could. In New York and on the Vineyard, Annabel Nichols read to her several times a week, providing one of Hellman's few sources of pleasure. Her nurse described her at the end to Peter Feibleman as a woman who "is half paralyzed, legally blind; she's having rage attacks that are a result of strokes; She cries at night; she can't help that. She can't eat. She can't sleep. She can't walk."[8] And still she could hold a room with her offbeat humor, or interrupt a dinner conversation with a withering disagreement that always began with a rasping "forgive me" before she launched a tirade. Most of her friends thought she survived these last years not on food but on anger.

Everyone remembered the anger. To be sure, Lillian had been bad-tempered and irascible all her life. But, as Brustein noted, before her illness "her anger was more focused; after, it became a free-floating, cloud-swollen tempest that rained on friend and foe alike."[9] Peter Feibleman agreed; he believed that her personality changed after the small strokes she suffered in the mid-seventies. Most of her good friends took the anger in stride, understanding that it was not directed at them personally but rather, as John Hersey described it, constituted "a rage of the mind against human injustice."[10] Anger, Hersey thought, was "her essence." Bill Styron agreed.

1983: Still she could hold a room. (©Bettmann/CORBIS)

He, among others, bridled at her quarrelsome nature, regularly refusing to speak to her after a spat about one insignificant thing or another. He recalled one such incident over how to cook a Smithfield ham that kept them apart for an entire summer.[11] In the end Styron, like Hersey, believed the "measure of her anger was really not personal, but cosmic, directed at all the hateful things she saw as menacing to the world."[12]

To the end, Hellman retained her capacity for fun—the continuing, wicked humor—that her friends cherished. At their last dinner together, William Styron recalled, "We carved up a few mutually detested writers and one or two mediocre politicians and an elderly deceased novelist whom she specifically detested...I remember that gorgeous cackle of laughter which always erupted at moments when we were together...which followed some beautiful harpooning of a fraud or a ninth-rater."[13] Like Styron, those who spent the most time with her balanced anger against this capacity for humor. Alex Szogyi, a Hunter College professor, caught her two-sidedness. She was "naturally contentious and cantankerous," he wrote, "in a manner that was humorous or disturbing, depending on one's proximity."[14] Her old friend Jules Feiffer commented on "the girlishness, the brattishness and incredible sense of fun." Asked what she missed most about Lillian, Maureen Stapleton replied, "She made me laugh more than anybody I've ever known." She was "deeply funny. Deeply funny."[15]

Vanity and pride persisted even as Hellman's body deteriorated. Each morning she got up, dressed carefully, and applied heavy makeup and mascara.[16] Too ill to go very far or to do very much, she nevertheless surrounded herself with all the acroutrements of elegance to which she was accustomed. On one two-month trip to California, she instructed Rita Wade to send her four handbags (gray, red, the Blair Clark bag, Hannah's brown bag) and three evening bags (rose, black, and gold) along with an assortment of shoes and coats.[17] Her nurse, convinced that Hellman did not need heavy coats in California, suggested that Rita simply ignore that part of the instruction. Just days before she died, Hellman showed up at a party at Patricia Neal's house, looking divine in a "magnificent Russian amethyst necklace."[18] Regularly she lied about her age. Bill Styron recalled that she deducted six or seven years just days before she died. She had been doing this all her life, Styron thought, "not as vanity, but as a kind of demonstration that she was hanging on to life."[19]

Peter Feibleman—her friend, for awhile her lover, and the man whom she later called her son—learned of Lillian's death in his Los Angeles home. Though he knew she was close to the end, he had been waiting

1981: To the end, Hellman retained her capacity for fun. (©Bettmann/CORBIS)

impatiently in California for the galleys of their coauthored cookbook to arrive. He wanted to bring them to her. In some ways, the cookbook, *Eating Together*, effectively capped her life. Unable to see, she dictated most of it and listened as recipes and portions of it were read back to her. Many of the recipes emerged from memories of New Orleans; others came from her travels over Europe and her New England experiences. A sprinkling (added as an afterthought) came from Hannah Weinstein's Jewish kitchen. They were all peppered with commentary, not about food but about the occasions on which she had eaten the dishes and with whom. Because the two authors could not agree on which dishes to feature, they divided the book into two parts labeled "Her Way" and "His Way." It was the only kind of collaboration she could tolerate. Peter arrived on the Vineyard two days late, without the manuscript, and just in time to participate in the funeral arrangements.

The funeral was an impressive affair. Two hundred people, many of them celebrities, some of them her Vineyard neighbors, gathered under a crop of pines at Abel's Hill cemetery in the village of Chilmark to say good-bye. The theme of the day was not her anger or humor or vanity or love, though these were often mentioned, so much as her ability and desire to communicate. Jules Feiffer recalled her capacity to speak across generations, "to effortlessly engage the old, the young, the middle-aged, the left, the middle, the right, and just about anyone except on occasion the women friends of the men she admired." Patricia Neal remembered her eagerness to find out about her daughter Lucy's plans and noted that "she was very eager to help the next generation." Jerome Wiesner, the former president of MIT who had helped to found the Committee for Public Justice, remarked on "her special caring for students and her excitement in helping them to learn and grow and . . . the enormous enthusiasm and love with which they responded." And Peter Feibleman cried as he recalled her last conversation with him. When he asked how she felt, she replied that she was suffering from "the worst case of writers' block I ever had."[20]

Lillian Hellman's body may have been in her grave, but quickly it became apparent that she would find no rest there. A residue of ill will, still very much alive, continued to corrode an already damaged reputation. Within days after her death, the quarrels about her name and her reputation resumed. Letters poured into William Abrahams (who, in addition to being her editor at Little, Brown and her friend was also one of three literary executors), whose agreement to undertake an authorized biography of Hellman had just been announced. Many of the letters praised and complimented her "courageous stand against the infamous [Joseph] McCarthy."[21] Others suggested that controversy would continue. "You will be at the mercy of this frightful old harridan as an arbiter of verification for allegations, often contradictory, which she commonly made and which history repeatedly refutes," wrote one New Yorker.[22] "Writing an *authorized* biography of Lillian Hellman is like trying to square a circle. I feel sorry for you," wrote another correspondent.[23]

The notion that she was a liar not only persisted but took on a life of its own. Just days before she died, questions of Hellman's veracity resurfaced in a *Commentary* article written by Samuel McCracken, which purported to establish definitively that "Julia" was mere fiction.[24] Christopher Hitchens affirmed and sealed Hellman's fate as a liar in a few paragraphs that appeared in the *Times Literary Supplement* two days after the funeral. There he declared that McCracken demonstrated "every verifiable incident" of the Julia episode "false or unconvincing."[25] Though he heard about Hellman's death before the piece went to press, he wrote, he "saw no reason not to leave" the piece as it stood. No one, he thought, would disagree that she was a liar.

Hellman did not think of her stories as lies. She was, after all, a dramatist who used the material at hand to invent tales. She made up stories about herself, her mother's family, her father's past. All her life she used the experiences of friends, wars, and journalistic forays to make up stories. Like Ibsen, she believed that drama was meant to make a point, not just to entertain. She never claimed a good memory; she always said her books were portraits, inventions, so she wrote memoirs that were not memoirs, fulfilling the mandate that memoir is the art of lying. If her work exaggerated or misplaced incidents, or engaged in self-dramatization, she believed that she had lived a life of integrity, honesty, and trust. The difference between her opinion of herself and the opinions of others earned her the tag of hypocrite.

Then there was the moralism. That Lillian was a moralist, nobody would want to deny. That she proclaimed her moral principles loudly—in her plays and her memoirs and at every public opportunity—must have irked friends and enemies alike. She fully earned the labels of self-righteousness and self-aggrandizement that her critics leveled at her. But these labels might have disappeared after her death had she chosen not to replay her courageous stance before HUAC and to taunt others about their behavior then. She was, after all, a woman whose memoirs had been praised as "moral beacons for the generation coming of age, telling of an effort to remain truthful to one's convictions in the face of the forces of dishonesty and repression."[26] The claim to a higher morality could only have been humiliating to the targets of Hellman's attack.

The label of Stalinism, too, became indelibly affixed, plausible because it melded with that of the liar. Hitchens fended off potential criticism of his easy acceptance of McCracken's piece, which, he admitted, "goes on to cite examples of her lack of scruple in the political world." Such criticism, he wrote with skillful innuendo, would come from members of "Miss Hellman's faction" who "will say that it is motivated by the dislike of her opinions which inspires the rest of the magazine." The *New York Times* received letters that insisted that even as Hellman was being praised as a great playwright, she be remembered for her skill "in moralizing even at the expense of truth, honor, and common sense." This was a woman, the writer reminded readers, who "accepted the murderous crimes of J. Stalin, never questioned."[27] Soon, identifying Hellman as a "Stalinist" became simply a matter of course, lightly tossed off as one among many adjectives used to locate her presence.[28]

After death, every crack and crevice in Hellman's literary record seemed to reveal a Stalinist cast. If she had refused in 1953 to support a presentation of Anne Frank's story that was specifically Jewish, it must be that she was not only anti-Semitic but that she was then trying to cover up the deaths of Jewish nationalists in the Soviet Union.[29] If her plays were melodramatic, wrote one distinguished biographer, so were her politics.[30] In her will, she created three trusts: one to protect her piece of the beach on the Vineyard for the use of local children; a second, named for her, to help deserving writers anywhere in the world. Hellman intended the third fund, named for Dashiell Hammett, to be used for the "promotion and advancement of political, social and economic equality, civil rights and civil liberties." She requested that fiduciaries distribute the revenue from this fund in accordance with "the political, social and economic beliefs, which of course were radical, of the late Dashiell Hammett who was a believer in the doctrines of Karl Marx."[31] The clause demonstrated to all and sundry that Hellman herself continued to be a believer.[32]

Attributions of Stalinism quickly became part of Hellman's public reputation, their ugly implications tarnishing many who had never met her. When conservative pundit William Buckley sought to impugn the reputation of presidential candidate Bill Clinton by going after Hillary Rodham Clinton, he traced her association with leftist groups. Mrs. Clinton, had, he wrote, chaired the New World Foundation ("one of the most left-leaning foundations in America"), on whose board had sat one Adrian DeWind, who in the 1970s had been a member of the Committee for Public Justice, an organization "formed to attack the FBI" and whose founder was none other than "Lillian Hellman, a member of the Communist Party well after she reached the age of puberty."[33]

Soon Lillian Hellman's name evoked a visceral, negative response. She had pretended to moralism, argued her detractors, and spent a lifetime railing against silence in the face of evil. Yet she had remained silent before HUAC rather than speaking up. To call her a hypocrite was simply to identify what was the case. Hellman, critics argued, never repented her self-righteousness, her lies, and her self-aggrandizements. To label her a communist was to offer a simple description. Had she not, after all, "year after year, held the Soviets blameless for all their crimes?"[34] Nor did she get credit for courage. "She was awarded laurels for valor," wrote William Wright, one of her biographers, "in spite of others quietly going to jail for the same, but less well-worded bravery."[35] So well accepted did these assertions become that within a decade after her death, the mention of her name produced vituperative, visceral responses. None but a fool could believe she was other than an apologist for Stalin. Friends and admirers retreated in the face of the onslaught. Some quietly denied that Lillian had any con- tinuing association with Stalin. Others, giving a little, defended her brilliant way with words and acknowledged that she was loath to fully acknowledge the Stalinist horror and quick to criticize those who did. Evidence to the contrary, the general consensus was captured in a 1997 biography of the Hellman-Hammett relationship, which was described by one reviewer as a chronicle "of their love affair with Stalinism."[36]

Within a decade after her death, and continuing into the twenty-first century, Lillian Hellman's name came to serve a symbolic purpose. Invok- ing it negatively became shorthand for designating one's own place in the political universe, a way of capturing what had gone wrong with the twen- tieth century, of explaining one's own behavior in the face of evil. To seize on Hellman and attack her created solidarity with those who had always opposed communism and who had not succumbed to the politically naïve temptations of a New Left, who, with the dawning of neoconservatism, stood solid in the face of the nation's enemies. To assail her revealed the assailant as a patriot, polishing his image and turning accusations of cow- ardice and betrayal into the virtuous partisan. This was precisely the line taken by some of Hellman's detractors. After her death, but not before, film producer Elia Kazan, who had named names and subsequently suf- fered from Hellman's accusations in Scoundrel Time, vented his fury on "this bitch with balls" who spent the last fifteen years of her life "canoniz- ing herself." As if exonerating himself from responsibility, he continued, "I believe now she wanted me to become the villain I became."[37]

In this context, Hellman's sexuality became fair game: just another example of her perverse and unattractive nature, another source of resent- ment. It wasn't just that she slept with men. She was plain, and she slept with whomever she pleased, and then remained friends with them after- ward. She was plain and she claimed a great love who reciprocated her affection; she was plain, and even at the end of her life she attracted men to her side. "Most women as plain as Hellman would have slunk off into a comfortable marriage or sublimated their amorous side altogether," wrote William Wright.[38] But Lillian had done the opposite, turning herself into a seductive and sexually attractive woman. This clearly galled some men. Kazan accused her of using sex to gain her political ends. "She was able to ease what she seemed to have considered her misfortune of birth . . . by gathering men around her, living testimonials to her allure." Kazan continued, revealing his offended manhood with every word: "Once, it is said, she kept a house in which she provided hospitality for a cadre of vigorous intellectuals . . . the chosen"—he went on to name those involved in this household, and claimed "to admire the lady for providing herself with this mini-harem." This was the kind of setup many males have secretly yearned for, he insisted, extending tribute to Hellman for doing what other men and woman were not brave enough to do.[39]

Distasteful stories about Lillian's sexuality surfaced from every corner. Elia Kazan avowed that she had come on to him but that he had resisted—he would have preferred someone else.[40] Stanley Hart insisted that he had to sleep with her to get her signature on a contract with Little, Brown, and that he left her when the sexual interest palled.[41] Occasional newspaper columns insinuated that there was something odd about Hellman's penchant for young men, or hinted of Hellman's secret love for women: "Hellman detractors, of which there are many," one insisted, "have often hinted that she had lesbian tendencies and point out her play 'The Children's Hour' and the film 'Julia' as examples of her fondness for unusually close female relationships."[42] At the same time, other detractors described with complete certainty her inability to get along with women.

There is no doubt that she was a difficult woman, impassioned, tempestuous, transgressive with regard to gender roles. "She went after what she wanted the way a man does," Elia Kazan commented.[43] She was demanding, peremptory, and often rude. And she could be vindictive and sometimes vengeful. Such qualities, often forgiven in death, might have been judged differently had Hellman not been female, or a displaced southerner, or come from a Jewish background, or appealed to highbrow rather than middlebrow audiences. But Hellman was all of these things, and in acting against the grain she distanced herself from communities of support, turning into the rebellious individual she always imagined herself to be.

Her loud and contentious nature identified her, stereotypically, as a Jew, as did her concern for money onstage and off. But Hellman's Jewishness was by no means her most dominant identity, nor did it constitute a religion or a politics. Rather it was a source of comfort and reassurance. So she alienated those who identified with Jewish spiritual content as well as those who supported the state of Israel. If she thought of herself as a southerner, she reserved her southern charm and hospitality for those she cared about. In private she exhibited joy at creating hospitable environments and sharing her talent as a cook. In public, Hellman deployed her southern heritage like a trump card to claim the last word against racists and bullies.

The speed with which Hellman's image came to personify evil in some minds did not entirely mask her skills as a playwright and memoirist. If she was the most evil of people to some, she was still a treasure to others. Her continuing popularity and her ability to attract an audience rankled many. William Luce's play *Lillian*, mounted just months after her death, drew reactions that spoke to both of these. Conceived while she was still alive, the play linked together passages from Hellman's three memoirs. Before she died, she listened as the finished version was read to her, and she approved. Several actresses turned down the role before Luce showed the script to Zoe Caldwell, who immediately accepted the challenge. Caldwell's husband, the distinguished Robert Whitehead, agreed to direct the one-woman play. Whitehead had earlier directed some of Arthur Miller's plays with no political fallout.

There was no question that the play effectively captured Lillian, nor that Caldwell's acting brilliantly rendered what one fan described as "the soul of your Lillian." Caldwell prepared for the role carefully, consulting with her friends and visiting Hellman's old New Orleans home. She, who did not smoke, puffed continuously onstage and off; she manicured her nails in just the careful way Lillian would have done. Two hours before curtain every night, she made herself up by fitting a large molded nose to her face; each night she wondered why Lillian, always impeccably dressed and vain of her appearance, had not had her nose fixed. She concluded that Lillian wore the nose as "a badge of courage."[44] Before every performance, Caldwell splashed on a little of the tea-rose perfume Lillian generally wore. Her performance captured Lillian so well that the actress disappeared into her. "I saw a woman whom I shall never forget become a woman whom I have long admired and have never forgotten," wrote one fan. "Mesmerizing . . . brilliant . . . extraordinary," wrote another.[45] The one-woman play toured the Midwest and parts of the South before opening in New York in January 1986, then going on tour again in both Europe and America.

Despite the fact that Caldwell so effectively captured Lillian Hellman, leading audiences to share the pathos of her childhood and her life in the theater and with Hammett—or perhaps because of it—the play risked once again popularizing a woman now buried. Critics, unhappy with seeing Hellman resurrected, took the occasion, in the words of one of them, "to say more about Lillian Hellman than to discuss the biodrama they were offered."[46] Again and again they followed glowing descriptions of Caldwell's performance and Whitehead's direction with attacks on Luce and on Lillian herself. The performance might be a tour de force, one critic averred, but he did not understand why it avoided "the issue of whether she was a Communist at any time in her life."[47] Luce, said another, "misrepresented Hellman by glossing over the more controversial aspects of her life and by whitewashing her notorious career as a playwright, a mendacious memoirist, a relentless Stalinist, and a vindictive, self-serving celebrity."[48] Luce responded by telling everyone that Hellman had final approval of the script: "She wouldn't let me use any words of my own. I call it a job of carpentry."[49] But he stood by his work.

Discontent with Hellman surfaced once again as reviewers commented on her "profound contempt for virtually everyone with whom she came into contact" or noted "her bitterness and petty vindictiveness," her "steely presence," or the "meanness and transparency" of her nature. "The larger issue," one thought, "is how such a vile person could have exercised so much influence on a culture she so haughtily despised."[50] In the *New York Times*, Frank Rich savaged the play. Caldwell, he began, "surely captured the seething physical presence of Hellman." But Caldwell was "chained to a sanitized Hellman portrait," Rich continued, a portrait that omitted her "controversial attack on fellow liberals with whom she parted ways" as well as "her scathing portraits of friendly witnesses before the House Un-American Activities Committee."[51] When the play opened in London the following fall, critics followed suit. The play failed to pay attention to Hellman's politics, trumpeted the *Observer*, headlining a full-page review, THE LIFE AND LIES OF LILLIAN HELLMAN. Caldwell's performance was brilliant: "The only snag is that Hellman's autobiographical works are full of lies." Nor could the author resist throwing in a negative comment about Hellman's politics: "She certainly never said a word against Stalin until long after Khruschev's denunciation; and she very rarely criticized Russia."[52]

Like a cat with nine lives, Lillian Hellman survived this criticism. Her work continued to reach the stage, repeatedly revived into the turn of the new century. Regional theaters turned to *The Autumn Garden* and *The Children's Hour* in the 1990s. The decade after the new century began, New York theaters mounted major productions of *Another Part of the Forest*, *Toys in the Attic*, and *The Little Foxes*. In London in 2011, a new production of *The Children's Hour* drew packed audiences. Late-night television regularly showed the films into which Hellman had poured her heart:

Dead End Kids, Dark Angel, The Little Foxes, and *The Children's Hour* all became staples. And Hellman herself continued to inspire public attention. Nearly twenty years after Hellman's death, Nora Ephron's *Imaginary Friends* (a reflection on the relationship of Mary McCarthy to Hellman) hit the boards. The play, which opened in New York in December 2002, was described by one reviewer as "an uncomfortable cross between vaudeville and conventional musical comedy."[53] Another called its story that of "a feud between two politically engaged, exceptionally feisty women within a literary world of men."[54] In what may well be the supreme irony, in 2010 the Committee for Recognizing Women in Theater established its "Lilly Award" in honor of Lillian Hellman, the playwright who never wanted to be placed in the company of "women playwrights." Gloria Steinem offered the invocation at the first award ceremony.

If we can attribute to Hellman's persona some of the virulence of the charges against her and her continuing hold on the American imagination, much of the explanation for her continuing presence surely lies in the twentieth-century moment. During her lifetime, Hellman's political positions remained remarkably consistent, taking on different colors as the political climate changed. Critic Richard Bernstein has noted that "the posthumous reexamination has to do with the playing out of old battles between American liberals and conservatives, or to put this another way, between anti-Communists and those who felt that American anti-Communism was more dangerous than Communism itself."[55] Hellman belonged in the latter camp, along with a goodly number of the intellectuals of her generation. But in the late twentieth century, victory went to those who defined communism as the enemy of national security. Each new revelation of espionage, every document that revealed a close relationship between the Comintern and the CPUSA, strengthened the hand of anticommunists. Though most American radicals, like Hellman, never involved themselves in party activities, the idea that government investigatory committees had been right to demand retraction, apology, and information took hold. Even after the communist threat had passed, her critics remained furious that Hellman had never been called to task for failing to acknowledge its seriousness. Hellman was forever viewed through the lens of a persistent communist threat.

Patterns of association that seemed ordinary or benign to observers of the forties and even of the fifties turned, by the late seventies, into evidence of guilt. In Hellman's case, the unbroken pattern stemmed from her fateful 1930s decisions with respect to the Spanish Civil War, the Moscow trials of 1937, and her refusal to denounce the Nazi-Soviet pact of 1939. In the eyes of detractors, these demonstrated her commitment not only to communism but to Stalin. She committed further sin, in the eyes of detractors, when she remained silent about that commitment in her appearance before HUAC. That made her a liar and justified unsubstantiated assertions of "fealty to a foreign power." All the while, so the story went, she never wavered in her sympathy for Stalin. That made her an irredeemably evil person. Worse, instead of silently suffering the slings and arrows of persecution, she rewrote the story, turning her escape from a jail sentence into a moral claim to courage and heroism. This tendency to self-aggrandizement, most readily confirmed by what was seen as the theft of the Julia story from an innocent woman, was in this context simple confirmation of Hellman's evil nature. To those who saw the world through the schisms of the twentieth century, Hellman's effort to redeem her good name from Mary McCarthy constituted "the mark of high Stalinism."[56]

And yet it is precisely this extremely negative view of Hellman that illuminates her role in twentieth-century America. The Stalinist label undermined not only the personal integrity of the accused: it was meant to discredit her conception of virtue and decency as well. Her life and work proclaimed the benefits of certain kind of moral society, one that would care for its poor and excluded members, protect democracy against bullies in uniform or not, and provide the freedom to live by one's own lights. Casual accusations of Stalinism incorporated these goals within the penumbra of deception that included lying and self-aggrandizing behavior. Hellman's deep and continuing antagonism to anticommunist appeals suggests that she understood that they would engender cynicism of the entire progressive agenda. She feared—not wrongly, it turns out—that anticommunism could and would be used to unite disparate groups in opposition to the larger moral principles of a progressive politics. This, she insisted—when, for example, she pointed to the role of anticommunism in fostering the Vietnam War—would unleash American power on an unsettled world. It would foster a new morality rooted in a money ethic that would dominate all spheres of life. In the twenty-first century the retreat of social democracy, progressivism, and liberalism and the rise of neoliberalism and neoconservatism bring us to a new appreciation of Hellman's strident and continuing outbursts.

Judgments about Hellman's behavior still come out of the battles over who was right and who was wrong in that midcentury conflict. "We understand something about Lillian Hellman," wrote Hunter College professor

Alex Szogyi, "when we look at her life—but we understand as well what some of the salient cultural imaginings of the twentieth century were—and we see in the paradoxes of Lillian Hellman's life—some of the tensions of a difficult century." Those tensions reflected the competing moral claims of different world views as Hellman tried to sort out what was virtuous and how to behave. The woman who wanted to become a great playwright became a celebrity instead; the woman who aspired to the company of the century's great intellectuals fought fierce battles with them; insecure, fearful, and politically naïve, she espoused particular political positions that fostered discord rather than consensus. Out of a desire to protect dissent, she dedicated much of her life to the cause of civil liberties; in return, she earned the Stalinist label. To become the beautiful, audacious, and courageous Julia of her imagination, she invented a world in which she did not live. That invention brought her castle tumbling down.

When we look back now, we notice the compromises that Hellman made in order to maintain moral consistency in a challenging world. We see in them the complicated circumstances in which many well-intentioned people found themselves caught. Hellman retreated from none of these issues. She wrote, she took positions, she acted on her beliefs as her conscience moved her. She was alternately damned and respected for her pronouncements, the variation less a function of her will and her choices than of the changing times in which she lived. The same sexual behavior that others emulated in the 1920s appeared predatory by the 1960s; the brave search for economic independence in the 1930s seemed, to radical feminists of the 1970s, to be insufficiently feminist. And the commitment to a better world that so many people shared in the Depression years seemed by the 1960s and '70s to be sheer folly.

The divided world in which Lillian lived her adult life would disintegrate after 1990 when the Soviet Union collapsed and, some would say, the twentieth century ended. But the conflicts in which she became a lightning rod continue to attract attention and mold the political arena. There are still no easy answers to the questions that Hellman confronted around the meaning of traditional family life, the price of commitments to racial and ethnic egalitarianism, the corrupting power of money, and the precariousness of the search for political utopias. Nor are there solutions to women's desire for economic independence or the hoary question of the relationship of art to politics. These lacunae make her life worth examining not for her sake, but for ours.

Acknowledgments

It gives me great pleasure to record, finally, my appreciation for the many favors that have come my way during the decade that I've been working on this book. The small and large kindnesses that have helped this project along have made researching and writing a genuine pleasure. They constitute a tribute to the community of scholars who I've come to love and value. The book began to take shape during a year spent at the Radcliffe Institute for Advanced Studies. In Cambridge, Susan Ware prodded me into thinking about what historians might make of Hellman's life, and a wonderful group of colleagues and friends pushed away the resistance I felt to taking on anything that resembled biography. To Nancy Chodorow, Lizabeth Cohen, Nancy Cott, Gish Jen, and Radcliffe Institute Director Judith Vichniac, thank you. At the National Humanities Center a few years later, I enjoyed the company and the criticism of a distinguished group of colleagues led by Geoffrey Harpham and Ken Mullikin and including Sheryl Kroen, Alex Rosenberg, Bill Sewell, Jan Goldstein, Mimi Kim, Sheryl Kroen, and Sarah Shields. I also benefited from the extraordinary services of a splendid staff.

The formidable collection of Lillian Hellman's manuscripts at the Harry Ransom Center at the University of Texas in Austin yielded up its riches under the expert guidance of Richard Workman and with the efficient help of Patricia Fox. I am grateful for their kind assistance, as well as for the efforts of Andi Gustavson and Linda Briscoe Myers in finding and reproducing photographs. At the Tamiment Library Kevyne Baar helped me navigate swiftly through a range of materials. At Stanford University's Cecil H. Green Library, Polly Armstrong and Sean Quimby were especially helpful. Ruth Milkman, Linda Gordon, and Allen Hunter facilitated visits to Los Angeles and Madison, Wisconsin, respectively. Sal Cline prompted a visit to Hardscrabble Farm and to Katonah, New York. Peter Feibleman provided generous encouragement and a range of introductions.

I've relied on a comfortingly large range of student help over the years, much of it from Columbia's wonderful undergraduates who brought an astonishing array of computer skills and enthusiasm to their tasks. I've benefited as well from sterling graduate students who tracked down crucial pieces of information and helped me think through problems large and small. In alphabetical order, I want to say thank you to Leah Aden, Jessica Adler, Zeina Alhendi, Sarah Brafman, Sarah Dunitz, Nell Geiser, Stephanie Harrell, Emma Curran Hulse, Suzanne Kahn, Cristina Kim, and Sarah Kirshen.

Many people became engaged in this project in ways I could not have anticipated. Their kindnesses have surprised me and energized my work. Some sent programs from new productions of Hellman's plays, forwarded comments on contemporary efforts to write memoirs, took photographs of her various homes, and recalled fleeting meetings with her. Others offered contacts with her friends and colleagues, allowed me to read chapters of their own work prior to publication, shared anecdotes and insights, and corrected mistaken notions. Most of all, they provided a level of enthusiasm that kept me going through the rough spots. I wish I could say thank you to each of them personally. In lieu of that I send warm affection to Brooke Allen, Uri and Michal Alon, Rosalyn Baxandall, Louise Bernikow, Barbara Black, Zoe Caldwell Whitehead, Anita Chapman, Mary Marshall Clark, Blanche Wiesen Cook, Claire Coss, Michael David-Fox, Eric Foner, Lynn Garafola, Linda Gordon, Allen Hunter, Andrew Kessler, Lucy Knight, Julia Mickenberg, Ruth Milkman, Dinitia Smith, Kitty Stalberg, Peter Stansky, Richard Stern, Ray Stollerman, Carole Turbin, and Michael Wrezsin. I owe special thanks to Norman Dorsen, Stephen Gillers, and Leon Friedman, who helped me to understand the Committee for Public Justice, and to Annabel Davis-Goff for her incomparable insights. I am especially grateful to Peter Feibleman for sharing his memories and his thoughts so graciously.

To Lila Abu Lughod, Susan Crane, Victoria de Grazia, Marianne Hirsch, Jean Howard, Martha Howell, Dorothy Ko, Sharon Marcus, Carol Sanger, and Pamela Smith—feminist scholars at Columbia who have generously critiqued my ideas over the years—I owe a special debt of gratitude. I didn't always love their sharp criticism, but I continue to value their commitment to making our work better. I've tried out various parts of the book on audiences at Russell Sage College, Northwestern University, the University of North Carolina, and the Columbia University School of Law, where I delivered a Barbara Black lecture. I have learned much from seminars sponsored by the Arthur and Elizabeth Schlesinger Library at Harvard University, the workshop in Twentieth-Century Politics and History at Columbia, the Women Writing Women's Lives biography group at the City University of New York, and the National History Center series at the Woodrow Wilson Center in Washington, D.C.

To those who read the entire manuscript and provided the trenchant criticism that drove me back to the drawing boards, I bow my head in appreciation. Rachel Brownstein, Doris Friedensohn, Eugene Goodheart, Judith Smith, and Amy Swedlow deserve far more than a simple thank-you, and I hope they will know how heartfelt this one is. Peter Ginna has encouraged this project from the start. It has been a privilege to be able to work with a skilled and caring editor whose enthusiasm never flagged. Thanks, too, to the helpful staff at Bloomsbury, including Pete Beatty, Laura Phillips, and Sara Mercurio.

Bert Silverman read the pages of each chapter as they came out of the printer, and then read the entire manuscript again and again and again. I could not have completed this book—indeed I probably would never have started it—without his critical eye and his impassioned intellectual challenges. Nor could I have completed it without his warm and caring partnership at home. I dedicate this book to the grandchildren we share together in the hope that they will grow up to be just like him.

Notes

Abbreviations

BCASC	Brooklyn College Archives & Special Collection, Brooklyn College Library
CCOH	Columbia University Center for Oral History Collection
HRC	Harry Ransom Center, University of Texas at Austin
LOC	Library of Congress
RBML	Rare Book & Manuscript Library, Columbia University, NY
SML	Seeley Mudd Library, Princeton University
SUL	M1125, Department of Special Collections, Stanford University Libraries
TM	Tamiment Library/Robert F. Wagner Labor Archives, New York University Libraries
TTP-CLS: 11–0–8–108	*Telford Taylor Papers*, Arthur W. Diamond Law Library, Columbia University, NY
VCU	Vassar College Library
WHS	Wisconsin Historical Society

Introduction

1 Carl Rollyson, *Lillian Hellman, Her Legend and Her Legacy* (New York: St. Martin's Press, 1988); Deborah Martinson, *Lillian Hellman: A Life with Foxes and Scoundrels* (New York: Counterpoint, 2005).

2 This information has been assembled with the generous help of Richard Workman, archivist at the Harry Ransom Center, University of Texas at Austin.

3 Annabel Davis-Goff, interview by author, September 2, 2010.

4 LH to Diane Johnson, September 13, 1978, box 62, folder 4, Lillian Hellman Collection, Harry Ransom Center, University of Texas at Austin, Austin, TK.

5 Carol Kolmerten, "Writing Modern Women's Lives," *American Quarterly* 50:4 (1998): 849–59.

6 LH to Donald Erickson, May 23, 1973, box 124, folder 1, Lillian Hellman Collection, HRC.

7 See especially William Wright, *Lillian Hellman: The Image, the Woman* (New York: Simon and Schuster, 1986) and Joan Mellen, *Hellman and Hammett: The Legendary Passion of Lillian Hellman and Dashiell Hammett* (New York: Harper Collins, 1996).

8 Pete Seeger is a case in point. See Daniel Wakin, "This Just In: Pete Seeger Denounced Stalin over a Decade Ago," *New York Times* (September 1, 2007).

9 Robert Newman, *The Cold War Romance of Lillian Hellman and John Melby* (Chapel Hill: University of North Carolina Press, 1989), Appendix I.

10 Patricia Meyer Spacks, *The Female Imagination* (New York: Knopf, 1975), 306, 309.

11 David Denby, "Escape Artist: The Case for Joan Crawford," *New Yorker* (January 3, 2011), 65.

12 Charles McGrath, "Muriel Spark: Playing God" *New York Times Book Review* (April 25, 2010).

1. Old-Fashioned American Traditions

1 U.S. Bureau of the Census, *1900 Census of Population and Housing*, Cincinnati Ward 2, Hamilton, Ohio, roll T623 1274, p. 3A.

2 Wedding guestbook, box 119, Folder 4, Lillian Hellman Collection, Harry Ransom Center, University of Texas at Austin.

3 Zoe Caldwell, interview by author, September 24, 2010.

4 LH to Diane Johnson, September 13, 1982, box 62, folder 4, Lillian Hellman Collection, HRC.

5 Bertram Wallace Korn, *The Early Jews of New Orleans* (Waltham, MA: American Jewish Historical Society, 1969), 22.

6 Julian Beck Feibelman, "A Social and Economic Study of the New Orleans Jewish Community" (doctoral thesis, University of Pennsylvania, 1941), 134.

7 Ibid., 3. See also Leo Shpall, *The Jews in Louisiana* (New Orleans: Steeg Printing and Publishing Co., 1936), and Lillian Hellman, *An Unfinished Woman: A Memoir*, 1st Back Bay paperback ed. (Boston: Little, Brown and Co., 1999).

8 Feibelman, "A Social and Economic Study," 134, 3.

9 Korn, *The Early Jews of New Orleans*, 228.

10 James Kern Feibleman, *The Way of a Man: An Autobiography* (New York: Horizon Press, 1969), 66.

11 Christine Doudna, "A Still Unfinished Woman: A Conversation with Lillian Hellman," *Rolling Stone* (February 24, 1977): 54.

12 Leonard Reissman, "The New Orleans Jewish Community," in Leonard Dinnerstein and Mary Dale Palsson, eds., *Jews in the South* (Baton Rouge: Louisiana State University Press, 1973), 288.

13 Alfred O. Hero Jr., *The Southerner and World Affairs* (Baton Rouge: Louisiana State University Press, 1965), 481.

14 Eli Evans, *The Provincials: A Personal History of Jews in the South* (Chapel Hill, NC: University of North Carolina Press, 2005)

15 Ronald Bern, *The Legacy* (New York: Mason Charter, 1975), ch. 8.

16 W. J. Cash, *The Mind of the South* (1941; repr., New York: Vintage, 1991), 332–33.

17 Feibelman, "A Social and Economic Study," 134.

18 Lillian Hellman, "East and West: *The Provincials: A Personal History of Jews in the South by Eli Evans*," *New York Times Book Review* (November 11, 1973), 421.

19 Ibid.

20 Lillian Hellman, "Typescript: Harvard Lecture No. 2," Spring 1961, box 44, folder 6, p. 5, Lillian Hellman Collection, HRC.

21 Lillian Hellman, *An Unfinished Woman* (Boston: Little, Brown, 1969), 12.

22 Lillian Hellman, "Typescript: Harvard Lecture No. 1," Spring 1961, box 44, folder 6, p. 5, Lillian Hellman Collection, HRC.

23 Hellman, *An Unfinished Woman*, 15.

24 Zoe Caldwell, interview by author, September 24, 2010.

25 Lillian Hellman, *The Little Foxes*, in *The Collected Plays* (Boston: Little, Brown, 1971), 145.

26 Ibid., 188.

27 Hellman, *An Unfinished Woman*, 32. See also Peter Adam, "Unfinished Woman," in Jackson Bryer, ed., *Conversations with Lillian Hellman* (Jackson, University of Mississippi Press, 1986), 230.

28 Hellman, *An Unfinished Woman*, 15.

29 Ibid., 13.

30 Ibid., 3–4.

31 Ibid., 5.

32 Lillian Hellman, diary, c. 1923, box 97, folder 1, Lillian Hellman Collection, HRC.

2. A Tough Broad

1 Lillian Hellman, untitled and unpaginated typescript in response to an advertising agency's request to prepare five one-hundred-word comments on women's dress and style, spring 1963, box 40, folder 5, Lillian Hellman Collection, Harry Ransom Center, University of Texas at Austin.

2 Ann Scott, "After Suffrage: Southern Women in the Twenties," *The Journal of Southern History* 30 (August 1943): 298–318.

3 Lillian Hellman, *Pentimento* (Boston: Little, Brown, 1973), 46–47.

4 Susan Ware, "Unlocking the Porter-Dewson Partnership," in Sarah Alpern et al., *The Challenge of Feminist Biography* (Urbana, IL: University of Illinois Press, 1992), 63

5 Ibid. See also Susan Cahn, *Sexual Reckonings: Southern Girls in a Troubling Age* (Cambridge, MA: Harvard University Press, 2007).

6 Otto Weininger, *Sex and Character: An Investigation of Fundamental Principles* (Bloomington, IN: Indiana University Press, 2005).

7 Lillian Hellman, diaries, November 28, 1922, box 97, folder 1, Lillian Hellman Collection, HRC.

8 Lillian Hellman Kober, "Perberty in Los Angeles," *American Spectator* 3 (January 1934): 4.

9 Lillian Hellman Kober, "I Call Her Mama," *American Spectator* 2 (September 1933): 2.

10 Lillian Hellman, diaries, April 22, 1924, box 97, folder 1, Lillian Hellman Collection, HRC.

11 *An Unfinished Woman*, 33. "I have often asked myself whether I understood the damage that so loveless an arrangement made on my future," she wrote in *An Unfinished Woman*, 32. These questions are raised as well in *Maybe* (Boston: Little, Brown, 1980), the last of her autobiographical volumes.

12 Ibid., 36.

13 Ibid., 41

14 Muriel Gardiner, *Code Name "Mary": Memoirs of an American Woman in the Austrian Underground* (New Haven, CT: Yale University Press, 1983), 33.

15 LH to "Baby," c. early 1930, box 1, folder 20, Arthur Kober Papers, Wisconsin Historical Society, Madison, WI.

16 LH to Arthur Kober, c. June 1934, box 1, folder 20, Arthur Kober Papers, WHS.

17 LH to "Dear Babe," c. summer 1934, box 1, folder 20, Arthur Kober Papers, WHS.

18 *An Unfinished Woman*, 32; *Pentimento*, 43.

19 Lewis M. Dabney, *Edmund Wilson: A Life in Literature* (New York: Farrar, Straus and Giroux, 2007), 271.

20 Margaret Harriman, "Miss Lily of New Orleans," *New Yorker* (November 8, 1941): 22.

21 Elia Kazan, *Elia Kazan: A Life* (New York: Knopf, 1988), 324.

22 Christine Doudna, "A Still Unfinished Woman: A Conversation with Lillian Hellman," *Rolling Stone* (February 24, 1977): 55.

23 Lucius Beebe, "An Adult's Hour Is Miss Hellman's Next Effort," *New York Herald Tribune* (December 13, 1936): 2.

24 Harriman, "Miss Lily of New Orleans," 22.

25 Fern Maja, "A Clearing in the Forest," *New York Post* (March 6, 1960), M2.

26 Ernestine Carter, "Lillian Hellman," *Sunday Times* (October 19, 1969), 55.

27 LH to John Melby, December 30, 1945, box 81, folder 7, Lillian Hellman Collection, HRC.

28 LH to William Abrahams, box 21, folder 5, William Miller Abrahams Papers, M1125, Department of Special Collections, Stanford University Libraries, Stanford, CA.

29 LH to "Dear Babe," c. fall 1934, box 1, folder 20, Arthur Kober Papers, WHS.

30 LH to Arthur Kober, June 1934, box 1, folder 20, Arthur Kober Papers, WHS.

31 LH to "Dear Babe," c. fall 1934, Box 1, Folder 20, Arthur Kober Papers, WHS.

32 Austin Pendleton, interview by author, December 12, 2009. See also Diane Johnson, "Obsessed," *Vanity Fair* (May 1985): 79. For a different version of the story, see Peter Feibleman, *Lilly: Reminiscences of Lillian Hellman* (New York: William Morrow, 1988), 168.

33 Johnson, "Obsessed," 79.

34 David Denby, "Escape Artist: The Case for Joan Crawford," *New Yorker* (January 3, 2011): 65–69.

35 Zoe Caldwell, interview by author, September 24, 2010.

36 Patricia Meyer Spacks, *The Female Imagination* (New York: Knopf, 1975), 306.

37 This story is pieced together from Hellman, *Pentimento*, 13–14, and Richard Layman, *Shadow Man: The Life of Dashiell Hammett* (New York: Harcourt Brace, 1981), 166–67.

38 Doudna, "A Still Unfinished Woman," 55.

39 Lillian Hellman, Typescript: "I was speaking of Hannah Weinstein," box 41,

folder 7, Lillian Hellman Collection, HRC. Patricia Neal, interview by author, August 26, 2010.

40 Lillian Hellman, typescript, box 77, folder 1, William Miller Abrahams Papers, SUL.

41 Doudna, "A Still Unfinished Woman," 55.

42 LH to John Melby, spring 1946, box 81, folder 7, Lillian Hellman Collection, HRC.

43 LH to John Melby, c. August 1946, box 81, folder 7, Lillian Hellman Collection, HRC.

44 LH to "Maggie darling," c. 1947, box 1, folder 20, Arthur Kober Papers, WHS.

45 LH to Maggie Kober, May 10, 1950 and May 22, 1950, box 1, folder 20, Arthur Kober Papers, WHS.

46 Catherine Kober Zeller, interview by author, November 19, 2009.

47 LH to Arthur Kober, telegram, August 14, 1941, box 1, folder 20, Arthur Kober Papers, WHS.

48 LH to "Dear Mr. Kober," November 12, 1941, box 1, folder 20, Arthur Kober Papers, WHS.

49 LH to Mr. and Mrs. Arthur Kober, telegram, May 29, 1943, box 1, folder 20, Arthur Kober Papers, WHS.

50 LH to Arthur Kober, telegram, December 18, 1947, box 1, folder 20, Arthur Kober Papers, WHS.

51 LH to "Arthur Baby Darling," August 4, 1948, box 1, folder 20, Arthur Kober Papers, WHS.

52 Ibid.; LH to Arthur Kober, telegram, June 13, 1941, box 1, folder 20, Arthur Kober Papers, WHS.

53 LH to Arthur Kober, telegram, December 31, 1947, box 1, folder 20, Arthur Kober Papers, WHS.

54 Lillian Hellman, "Typescript: Arthur Kober's Funeral," no date, box 42, folder 10, Lillian Hellman Collection, HRC.

55 Dashiell Hammett to LH, January 21, 1943, box 77, folder 6, William Miller Abrahams Papers, SUL.

56 Dashiell Hammett to LH, February 12, 1944, box 77, folder 8, William Miller Abrahams Papers, SUL.

57 Dashiell Hammett to LH, November 25, 1943, box 77, folder 6, William Miller Abrahams Papers, SUL.

58 Dashiell Hammett to "Dearest Lily," September 13, 1944, box 77, folder 8, William Miller Abrahams Papers, SUL.

59 Dashiell Hammett to "Dearest Lily," November 5, 1944, box 77, folder 8, William Miller Abrahams Papers, SUL.

60 Dashiell Hammett to "Dear Lilishka," October 26, 1943, box 77, folder 6, William Miller Abrahams Papers, SUL.

61 Dashiell Hammett to LH, January 29, 1943, October 11, 1943, November 16, 1943, December 10, 1943, December 22, 1943, box 77, folder 6, William Miller Abrahams Papers, SUL.

62 Dashiell Hammett to Maggie Kober, March 10, 1945, box 77, folder 8, William Miller Abrahams Papers, SUL.

63 Dashiell Hammett to "Lily dear," March 1, 1945, box 77, folder 8, William Miller Abrahams Papers, SUL. He signed off, "Love and kisses and things," instead of the usual "much love darling." Ten days later, Hammett wrote once again to complain of her silence (March 10, 1945); again on March 13, he wrote, "I am doing my best not to attribute it to anything." Finally, on March 15, he received two letters from her (one dated March 5), and told her "it was awful nice being on your mailing list again."

64 LH to John Melby, April 17, 1946, box 81, folder 7, Lillian Hellman Collection, HRC.

65 Robert P. Newman, *The Cold War Romance of Lillian Hellman and John Melby* (Chapel Hill: University of North Carolina Press, 1989), ch. 12.

66 Letters in Max Hellman file, box 66, folder 4, Lillian Hellman Collection, HRC.

67 Elaine Tyler May, *Homeward Bound: American Families in the Cold War Era* (New York: Basic Books, 1988), ch. 1.

68 Patricia Neal, interview by author, December 15, 2005.

69 Reminiscences of Helen Van dernoot Rosen (1994), on page 44, in the Columbia University Center for Oral History Collection.

70 Appointment book, 1960, box 78, folder 8, Lillian Hellman Collection, HRC.

71 Appointment book, 1960.

72 Johnson, "Obsessed," 79–81, 116–19.

73 Most of this comes from a typescript written by Blair Clark, box 71, folder 11, William Miller Abrahams Papers, SUL.

74 Richard Locke and Wendy Nicholson, interview by author, June 4, 2007.

75 Blair Clark, "Typescript: Lillian Hellman," box 71, folder 11, William Miller Abrahams Papers, SUL.

76 Ibid., 4.

77 Richard Locke and Wendy Nicholson, interview by author, June 4, 2007.

78 Peter Feibleman, interview by author, August 4, 2002.

79 Stanley Hart, "Lillian Hellman and Others," *Sewanee Review* 107 (Summer 1999): 409.

80 Ibid., 401

81 Ibid., 418

82 Ibid., 408.

83 Edmund Wilson, *The Sixties*, ed. Lewis Dabney (New York: Farrar, Straus and Giroux, 1993), 547.

84 Norman Podhoretz, *Making It* (New York: Random House, 1967), 117, 118.

85 John Hersey, "Lillian Hellman, Rebel" *New Republic* (September 18, 1976): 26

86 Peter Feibleman, interview by author, August 4, 2002.

87 Ibid.

88 Richard Locke and Wendy Nicholson, interview by author, June 4, 2007.

89 Morris and Lore Dickstein, interview by author, March 24, 2005.

90 Shirley Hazzard to William Abrahams, February 14, 1970, folder 36, box 77, William Miller Abrahams Papers, SUL.

91 LH to Robby Lantz, no date, box 72, folder 6, Lillian Hellman Collection, HRC.

92 Morris and Lore Dickstein, interview by author, March 24, 2005.

93 Personal communication with Anne Navasky, July 2010.

94 Morris and Lore Dickstein, interview by author, July 21, 2010.

95 Maureen Howard, interview by author, January 27, 2010.

96 John Hersey to Victor Pritchett, January 23, 1986, box 133, folder 2, Lillian Hellman Collection, HRC. Hersey noted that Dorothy Pritchett, Barbara Hersey, and Annabel Nichols were exceptions.

97 Elizabeth Hardwick, "The Little Foxes Revived," *New York Review of Books* (December 21, 1967): 4.

98 Bobbie Handman, interview by author, May 31, 2005.

99 Exchange of letters and telegrams can be found in box 77, folder 5, Lillian Hellman Collection, HRC.

100 Bobbie Handman, interview by author, May 31, 2005.

101 LH and Dina Weinstein correspondence, February 23, 1981, May 11, 1981, and April 29, 1981, box 91, "Dina Weinstein (1981–82)" folder, Lillian Hellman Collection, HRC.

102 Catherine Kober Zeller, interview by author, November 19, 2009.

103 LH to Ann Tiffany, January 29, 1973, box 3, "January to October 1973" folder, Harold Matson Company, Inc. (New York, NY) Records, Rare Book & Manuscript Library, Columbia University, New York, NY.

104 LH to Lois Fritsch, no date, box 122, folder 2, Lillian Hellman Collection. Also, LH to William Alfred, May 26, 1961, box 20, Papers of William Alfred, Brooklyn College Archives & Special Collections, Brooklyn College Library, Brooklyn, NY.

105 Dabney, *Edmund Wilson*, p. 506. Note that Dabney remembers this apartment as being on 5th Avenue. In fact, it was on Park Avenue.

106 LH to William Alfred, March 29, 1971, box 51, folder 12; LH to William Alfred, January 5, 1972, box 51, folder 26; William Alfred to Richard de Combray, March 28, 1978, box 53, folder 8, William Miller Abrahams Papers, M1125, SUL.

107 LH to Arthur Thornhill, April 12, 1976, box 3, "January to December, 1976" folder, Harold Matson Company, Inc. Records, RBML; LH to Don Congdon, early February 1982, box 47, folder 10, Lillian Hellman Collection, HRC. See also reply, Alice Wexler to LH, February 9, 1982, box 47, folder 10; Margaret Mills to LH, June 16, 1982, box 45, folder 5, Lillian Hellman Collection, HRC.

108 Lillian Hellman, memo, May 24, 1978, box 41, folder 7, Lillian Hellman Collection, HRC.

109 Morris and Lore Dickstein, interview by author, March 24, 2005.

110 Howard Kissel, "Lillian Hellman: Survival and the McCarthy Era," *Women's Wear Daily* (November 5, 1976): 28; Austin Pendleton interview by author for Bernstein story.

111 Lillian Hellman, "Typescript Lists: Europe Trip, April 1950, " box 102, folder 6; Lillian Hellman, "European Trip 1951," box 102, folder 7; Lillian Hellman, "European Trip, 1968," box 102, folder 8; Lillian Hellman Collection, HRC.

112 Leonard Bernstein to LH, c. 1956, box 4, folder 8, Lillian Hellman Collection, HRC.

113 According to Peter Feibleman, after Christina Stead died, Hellman anonymously contributed $10,000 to Stead's estate to benefit Stead's surviving father. Peter Feibleman, interview by author, August 4, 2002.

114 Felicia Geffen to LH, July 8, 1963, box 45, folder 5, Lillian Hellman Collection, HRC.

115 Morris and Lore Dickstein, interview by author, March 24, 2005.

116 Quoted in Jack Kroll, "Hollywood's New Heroines," *Newsweek* (October 10, 1977): 79

117 Richard Stern to William Abrahams, July 22, 1984, box 71, folder 10, William Miller Abrahams Papers, SUL.

118 Robby Lantz to LH, September 29, 1965, box 29, folder 6, Lillian Hellman Collection, HRC.

119 LH to "Dearest Billy," September 22, 1970 box 50, folder 36, William Miller Abrahams Papers, SUL.

3. A Serious Playwright

1 William Alfred, "Typescript of Alfred's Introduction to Hellman's Harvard Lectures," spring 1961, box 44, folder 6, Lillian Hellman Collection, Harry Ransom Center, University of Texas at Austin.

2 Hellman, "Typescript: Harvard Lecture No. 1," spring 1961, box 44, folder 6, 6A, Lillian Hellman Collection, HRC.

3 Hellman, "Typescript: Harvard Lecture No. 2," Spring 1961, box 44, folder 6, 2–3, Lillian Hellman Collection, HRC.

4 Lillian Hellman, *Four Plays by Lillian Hellman* (New York: Modern Library, 1942), vii.

5 The film, produced by Irving Thalberg and released in 1932, starred Greta Garbo, John Barrymore, Joan Crawford, Wallace Beery, and Lionel Barrymore. It won an Academy Award for Best Picture.

6 Lillian Hellman, "Light Reading Good of Its Kind," *New York Herald Tribune Books* (November 28, 1926); Lillian Hellman, "A Moral Immorality," *New York Herald Tribune Books* (December 4, 1927).

7 Lillian Hellman, "Futile Souls Adrift on a Yacht," *New York Herald Tribune Books* (June 19, 1927).

8 Peter Feibleman, interview by author, August 4, 2002.

9 LH interview with Harry Gilroy, "The Bigger the Lie," *New York Times* (December 14, 1952): sec. 2, 3. Hellman was never happy with *Dear Queen* and only halfheartedly tried to get it produced. "We are absolutely cold on the damn play and I doubt whether we do much good by it," she wrote to Arthur Kober after tinkering with it for years. LH to Arthur Kober, June 1934, box 1, folder 20, Arthur Kober Papers, Wisconsin Historical Society, Madison, WI.

10 Hellman, "Typescript: Harvard Lecture No. 1," 10.

11 Gilbert W. Gabriel, "'The Children's Hour,'" *New York American* (November 21, 1934): 13.

12 Ibid.

13 Robert Benchley, "Good News," *New Yorker* (December 1, 1934): 34.

14 George Jean Nathan, "The Theatre," *Vanity Fair* (February 1935): 37.

15 Brooks Atkinson, "Children's Hour," *New York Times* (December 2, 1934): sec. 10, 1.

16 Brooks Atkinson, "'The Children's Hour,' Being a Tragedy of Life in a Girls' Boarding House," *New York Times* (November 21, 1934): 23.

17 Percy Hammond, "The Theatres," *New York Herald Tribune* (December 9, 1934): 5.

18 Robert Garland, "'Children's Hour': A Moving Tragedy," *New York World Telegram* (November 21, 1934): 16; Benchley, "Good News," 34.

19 Typescript: Yiddish-to-English translation of critique by N. Solovey, *Daily Forward* (November 24, 1934), box 50, folder 4, Lillian Hellman Collection, HRC.

20 Percy Hammond, "'The Children's Hour': A Good Play About a Verboten Subject," *New York Herald Tribune* (November 21, 1934): 16.

21 LH to Mr. H. J. Whigham, January 2, 1935, box 50, folder 4, Lillian Hellman Collection, HRC. See also the controversy over the title of *The Children's Hour*, *New York Times* (November 17, 1935): 3.

22 LH interview with Harry Gilroy, "The Bigger the Lie," *New York Times* (December 14, 1952): sec. 2, 3, 4.

23 Ibid., 4.

24 "Children's Hour Banned in Boston," *New York Times* (December 15, 1935): 42.

25 The *New York Times* followed the dispute closely. See "American Play Banned," *New York Times* (March 12, 1935): 24; "Fight Boston Play Ban," *New York Times* (December 16, 1935): 22; "Boston Sued on Play Ban," *New York Times* (December 27, 1935): 15; "Children's Hour Ban Extended," *New York Times* (December 18, 1935): 33.

26 Lillian Hellman, "Typescript: The Children's Hour," no date, box 50, folder 36, 3, William Miller Abrahams Papers, M1125, Dept. of Special Collections, Stanford University Libraries, Stanford, CA.

27 Lillian Hellman, "Typescript: Days to Come," no date, box 50, folder 36, William Miller Abrahams Papers, SUL.

28 Joseph Wood Krutch, "Plays, Pleasant and Unpleasant," *Nation* (December 26, 1936): 769; Richard Watts Jr., "Class War," *New York Herald Tribune* (December 16, 1936): 22.

29 Lucius Beebe, "An Adult's Hour Is Miss Hellman's Next Effort," *New York Herald Tribune* (December 13, 1936): sec. 7, 2.

30 Terry Curtis Fox, "Early Work," *Village Voice* (November 6, 1978): 127. Fox continued, in remarks that evoked Hellman's battle with HUAC: "All people, Hellman tells us, have their failings: they are to be understood. But when those failings spill out onto other people, they become something which is no longer private and which cannot be overlooked. Hellman does not mind cowardice, but she will never countenance betrayal." For the circumstances of the play's revival, and for Hellman's efforts to extend the production, see correspondence from November and December 1978 in the papers of Harold Matson Company, Inc. Records, Rare Book & Manuscript Library, Columbia University New York, NY.

31 Lillian Hellman, *Pentimento* (Boston: Little, Brown, 1973), 160–61; this section first appeared in the *New York Review of Books*, "Flipping for a Diamond" (March 30, 1973).

32 Lillian Hellman, "The Art of the Theater I," *Paris Review* 33 (Winter/Spring 1965): 91; LH to "Dearest Art," box 1, folder 20, Arthur Kober Papers, WHS.

33 Lillian Hellman, "Typescript: Theatre," box 31, folder 16, 2, Lillian Hellman Collection, HRC.

34 Hellman, *Pentimento*, 163.

35 The quotation is from Tish Dace's review of a 1978 revival of *Days to Come*. See "Hellman: Beyond the Topical," November 2, 1978, box 52, folder 9, Harold Matson Company, Inc. Records, RBML.

36 Beebe, "An Adult's Hour," 2.

37 Krutch, "Plays, Pleasant and Unpleasant," 769.

38 Arthur Miller, *Timebends: A Life* (New York: Grove Press, 1987), 230.

39 Ibid.

40 John Gassner, *The Theatre in Our Times: A Survey of the Men, Materials and Movements in Modern Theatre* (New York: Crown, 1954), 11

41 Jacob H. Adler, *Lillian Hellman* (Austin, TX: Steck-Vaughn and Company, 1969), 6.

42 Ibid.

43 Lucius Beebe, "Stage Asides: Miss Hellman Talks of Her Latest Play, The Little Foxes," *New York Herald Tribune* (March 12, 1939): sec. 6, 1.

44 Hellman, "Typescript: Harvard Lecture No. 1," 2–3.

45 Ibid., 3.

46 Lillian Hellman, "Typescript: Smith College," April 15, 1955, box 43, folder 1, 6, Lillian Hellman Collection, HRC.

47 Hellman, "Typescript: Harvard Lecture No. 1," 3.

48 Hellman, "Typescript: Smith College," 6; Lillian Hellman, "Typescript: Smith/MIT," April 15, 18, 1955; Lillian Hellman, "Typescript: Swarthmore," April 6, 1950, box 43, folder 1, Lillian Hellman Collection, HRC.

49 Hellman, *Four Plays*, viii

50 Robert van Gelder, "Of Lillian Hellman," *New York Times* (April 20, 1941): X1.

51 Hellman, *Pentimento*, 199.

52 LH to Arthur, late 1930s, box 20, Arthur Kober Papers, WHS.

53 Lillian Hellman, "Typescript: Wellesley Address," March 22, 1951, box 43, folder 1, Lillian Hellman Collection, HRC.

54 Hellman, *Four Plays*, xiii.

55 On her gift for drawing character, see Adler, *Lillian Hellman*, 19.

56 Hellman, *Four Plays*, xiii.

57 Hellman, *Pentimento*, 193.

58 Hellman, "The Art of the Theater I," 89.

59 LH to "Dearest Art," no date, box 1, folder 20, Arthur Kober Papers, WHS.

60 Hellman, "The Art of the Theater I," 83.

61 Beebe, "An Adult's Hour," 2.

62 Hellman, "The Art of the Theater I," 68.

63 Hellman, *Four Plays*, x.

64 Lillian Hellman, typescript, "The Children's Hour," 1.

65 Lillian Hellman, "The Time of the Foxes," *New York Times* (October 22, 1967): sec. 2, 1.

66 Hellman, "The Art of the Theater I," 83.

67 Ibid.

68 Hellman, "Typescript: Swarthmore Address," 6, 7.

69 Reminiscences of Harold Clurman (1979), on page 131 in the Columbia University Center for Oral History Collection.

70 Hellman, *Pentimento*, 202–3.

71 Hellman quoted in Gretchen Cryer, "Where Are the Women Playwrights?" *New York Times* (May 20, 1973): 129.

72 Jerome Weidman, "Lillian Hellman Reflects Upon the Changing Theater," *Dramatists Guild Quarterly* 7 (Winter 1970): 22.

73 Walter Kerr, "Whose Play Is It?" *New York Times* (October 12, 1969): SM66.

74 Remiscences of Harold Clurman (1979), on page 132, CCOH.

75 Austin Pendleton, interview by author, December 12, 2009; and Pendleton to author, personal communication, August 14, 2011.

76 Hellman, "Typescript: Harvard Lecture No. 1," 10–11.

77 Austin Pendleton, interview by author, December 12, 2009.

78 Hellman, "The Art of the Theater I," 72; Hellman, *Pentimento*, 162–63.

79 Hellman, "The Art of the Theater I," 68.

80 Hellman, "The Time of the Foxes," sec. 2, 1.

81 Miller, *Timebends*, 231.

82 Weidman, "Lillian Hellman Reflects," 20.

83 This idea first put forward by Edith J. R. Isaacs, "Lillian Hellman, A Playwright on the March," *Theatre Arts* 28 (January 1944): 20.

84 LH to Arthur Kober, 1935, box 1, folder 20, Arthur Kober Papers, WHS.

85 Beebe, "An Adult's Hour," 2.

86 Joseph Wood Krutch, "Unpleasant Play," *Nation* (February 25, 1939): 244; James Eastman, "Image of American Destiny: The Little Foxes," *Players* 48 (1973): 70–73.

87 Beebe, "Stage Asides," in Jackson Bryer, *Conversations with Lillian Hellman* (Jackson: University Press of Mississippi, 1986), 7.

88 Transcript from interviews by Gary Waldhorn and Robert Murray, "Yale Reports," June 5, 1966, box 30, folder 10, Lillian Hellman Collection, HRC.

89 Lillian Hellman, "Theatre Pictures: Excerpts from a Theatrical Journal, Remembered in Subacid Tone," *Esquire* (August 1973): 64.

90 Lillian Hellman, *The Collected Plays* (Boston: Little, Brown, 1971), 188.

91 Atkinson, "Children's Hour," sec. 10, p. 1.

92 John Mason Brown, "Tallulah Bankhead and 'The Little Foxes,'" *New York Post* (March 11, 1939): 8. Brown credited Bankhead with "creating the kind of villainess even the Grand Guignol has never been able to match."

93 Brooks Atkinson, "Tallulah Bankhead appearing in Lillian Hellman's Drama of the South, 'The Little Foxes,'" *New York Times* (February 16, 1939): 16.

94 Joseph Wood Krutch, *American Drama Since 1918: An Informal History* (New York: G. Braziller, 1967), 132

95 Richard Watts, "The Little Foxes," *New York Herald Tribune* (February 16, 1939): 14.

96 Stark Young, "Watch on the Rhine," *New Republic* (April 14, 1941): 498.

97 Hellman, *Four Plays*, x–xi.

98 Lillian Hellman, "Typescript: Harvard Lecture No. 3," spring 1961, box 44, folder 6, 5, Lillian Hellman Collection, HRC.

99 The critic Barrett Clark agrees with Hellman on this point: "Melodrama is melodramatic not because it is violent or striking but because it uses violence for violence' sake." See Barrett H. Clark, "Lillian Hellman," *The English Journal* 33 (December 1944): 524. Thanks to Emma Hulse for making this connection.

100 Hellman, "The Art of the Theater I," 70; Richard Stern, "An Interview with Lillian Hellman," May 21, 1958, box 1, folder 23, Richard Stern Collection, Special Collections Research Center, Regenstein Library, University of Chicago, Chicago, IL.

101 Hellman, *Pentimento*, 180. See also Lillian Hellman, "Back of Those Foxes," *New York Times* (February 26, 1939): sec. 9, pp. 1, 2, and Richard Lockridge, "Lillian Hellman's 'The Little Foxes' Opens at the National Theater," *New York Sun* (February 16, 1939): 12. Lockridge described the plot as touching melodrama now and again, but "touches it effectively."

102 Thanks to Anita Chapman for pointing out that *The Little Foxes* took on new life after the arrest of Bernard Madoff for constructing a financial Ponzi scheme in 2008.

103 John Gassner, *The Theatre in Our Times: A Survey of the Men, Materials, and Movements in the Modern Theatre* (New York: Crown, 1954), 78.

104 Adler, *Lillian Hellman*, 17.

105 Richard Watts Jr. "The Theater: Miss Hellman's Play," *New York Herald Tribune* (February 26, 1939): sec. 10, 1.

106 Lillian Hellman, "Author Jabs the Critic," *New York Times* (December 15, 1946): 3.

107 Walter Kerr, "Voltaire's Candide as a Light Opera," *New York Herald Tribune* (December 26, 1956): sec. 4, 1.

108 Margaret Harriman, "Miss Lilly of New Orleans," *New Yorker* (November 8, 1941): 22.

109 Beebe, "Stage Aside," in Bryer, ed., *Conversations*, 10.

110 George Jean Nathan, "Playwrights in Petticoats," *American Mercury* (June 1941): 750.

111 Harriman, "Miss Lilly of New Orleans," 22.

4. Politics Without Fear

1 Peter Feibleman, interview by author, August 4, 2002.

2 This story is drawn from Nancy Lynn Schwartz, *The Hollywood Writers' Wars* (New York: Knopf, 1982), Christopher Dudley Wheaton, "A History of the Screen Writers' Guild (1920–1942): The Writers' Quest for a Freely Negotiated Basic Agreement" (doctoral thesis, University of Southern California, January 1974), and Brian Neve, *Film and Politics in America: A Social Tradition* (London: Routledge, 1992).

3 Reminiscences of Albert Hackett (1958), on page 26 in the Columbia University Center for Oral History Collection.

4 Wheaton, "A History of the Screen Writers' Guild (1920–1942)," 82.

5 LH to Arthur Kober, June 1934, box 1, folder 20, Arthur Kober Papers, Wisconsin Historical Society.

6 Harvey Klehr, John Earl Haynes, and Kyrill M. Anderson, *The Soviet World of American Communism* (New Haven, CT: Yale University Press, 1998), 280.

7 On the history of the Popular Front, see especially Michael Denning, *The Cultural Front: The Laboring of American Culture in the Twentieth Century* (London: Verso, 1996), 10–12.

8 Hammett to Mary Hammett, September 11, 1936, in Richard Layman, ed., *Selected Letters of Dashiell Hammett, 1921–1960* (Washington, DC: Counterpoint, 2001), 107.

9 Ibid., 111.

10 Richard Layman, *Shadow Man: The Life of Dashiell Hammett* (New York: Harcourt Brace, 1981), 171.

11 Betsy Blair, *The Memory of All That: Love and Politics in New York, Hollywood, and Paris* (New York: Knopf, 2003), 195–96.

12 Patrick McGilligan and Ken Mate, "Alvah Bessie," in Patrick McGilligan and Paul Buhle, eds., *Tender Comrades: A Backstory of the Hollywood Blacklist* (New York: St. Martin's Griffin, 1999), 97.

13 Lawson interview in Dan Georgakas and Lenny Rubenstein, *The Cineaste Interviews on the Art and Politics of Cinema* (Chicago: Lakeview Press, 1983), 197.

14 A. Scott Berg, *Goldwyn: A Biography* (New York: Knopf, 1989), 267

15 This story is fully explored in Schwartz, *The Hollywood Writers' Wars*. See also Ian Hamilton, *Writers in Hollywood: 1915–1951* (New York: Carroll and Graf, 1990), chs. 7 and 12.

16 Dan Katz, *All Together Different: Yiddish Socialists, Garment Workers, and the Labor Roots of Multiculturalism* (New York: New York University Press, 2011).

17 Patrick McGilligan, "Maurice Rapf," in McGilligan and Buhle, eds., *Tender Comrades*, 508.

18 This interpretation follows Schwartz, *The Hollywood Writers' Wars*, 99–103.

19 Philip Dunne interviewed by Douglas Bell, October 29, 1989, 142, Oral History Collection, Margaret Herrick Papers, Academy of Motion Picture Arts and Sciences, Beverly Hills, CA.

20 Ibid.

21 Schwartz, *The Hollywood Writers' Wars*, 172. The successful negotiating team included Dore Schary, Boris Ingster, Mary McCall Jr., Charlie Brackett, Ralph Block, and Sheridan Gibney.

22 Reminiscences of Albert Hackett (1958), on page 26, CCOH.

23 Ibid., 27.

24 Patrick McGilligan and Ken Mate, "Allen Boretz," in McGilligan and Buhle, eds., *Tender Comrades*, 115.

25 Dalton Trumbo, *Time of the Toad: A Study of Inquisition in America* (New York: Harper and Row, 1972), 7.

26 See especially Gerald Horne, *The Final Victim of the Blacklist: John Howard Lawson, Dean of the Hollywood Ten* (Berkeley: University of California Press, 2006), ch. 6.

27 Most elements of the act were declared unconstitutional by the Supreme Court in 1957. See *Yates v. United States*, 354 U.S. 298.

28 Larry Ceplair and Steven England, *The Inquisition in Hollywood: Politics in the Film Community, 1930–1960* (Garden City, NY: Doubleday, 1980), 257.

29 Hammett to Mary Hammett, September 11, 1936, in Layman, ed., *Selected Letters*, 109–10.

30 Hellman incorrectly places this showing in March 1938 and recalls it with pleasure in *An Unfinished Woman* (Boston: Little, Brown, 1939), 67.

31 Lillian Hellman, *An Unfinished Woman*, 82. On Katz, see Ronald Radosh and Allis Radosh, *Red Star Over Hollywood: The Film Colony's Long Romance with the Left* (San Francisco: Encounter Books, 1996), 47–48. Katz, probably a lover of Hellman's, was executed by the Czech Communist regime after the Second World War.

32 Hellman, *An Unfinished Woman*, 82.

33 Lillian Hellman, "A Bleached Lady," *New Masses* (October 11, 1938): 21.

34 Lillian Hellman, "Day in Spain," *New Republic* (April 13, 1938): 298.

35 Ibid.

36 Lillian Hellman, "The Word Noble," *The Village Fair Almanac* June 28–30, 1938, box 2, folder, 1938, Millen Brand Papers, 1906–1980, Rare Book & Manuscript Library, Columbia University New York, NY.

37 Lillian Hellman, "Day in Spain," 298.

38 D. D. Guttenplan, *American Radical: The Life and Times of I. F. Stone* (New York: Farrar, Straus and Giroux, 2009), 113–14.

39 Lillian Hellman, "The Word Noble."

40 Lillian Hellman, "The Lyons Den," *New York Post* (July 22, 1938): 12. Clip courtesy of Justin Jackson.

41 Edward Barsky, "Typescript: Address of Dr. Edward Barsky: Hotel Astor," March 22, 1945, Edward Barsky Collection, box 2, folder 37, 1, Tamiment Library/Robert F. Wagner Labor Archives, Elmer Holmes Bobst Library, New York University Libraries, New York, NY.

42 Lillian Hellman to Alvah Bessie, July 14, 1952, Veterans of the Abraham Lincoln Brigade Records, ALBA 019, box 12, folder 5, TL.

43 This story is in chapter 10.

44 Deborah Martinson, *Lillian Hellman: A Life with Foxes and Scoundrels* (New York: Counterpoint, 2005), 131–32, attributes Hellman's political commitment and awakening to her fall 1937 trip to Paris, Berlin, Moscow, and Spain.

45 Milton Meltzer, "Hollywood Does Right by 'The Little Foxes,'" *Sunday Worker* (August 24, 1941): 7.

46 Memo submitted by Louis Budenz, no date, Investigative Name Files, box

24, "Lillian Hellman" folder, National Archives and Records Administration, RG233, Records of the House of Representatives House Un-American Activities Committee.

47 Statement by Miss Lillian Hellman, draft, April 28, 1952, 1-2, box 71, "Lillian Hellman, 1950-57" folder, Joseph Rauh Papers, part I, Manuscript Division, Library of Congress. The statement was drawn up before Hellman's 1952 HUAC hearing but was never publicly released.

48 "A Statement by American Progressives," New Masses (April 3, 1938): 32.

49 Catherine Kober Zeller, interview by author, November 11, 2009.

50 On the complex motives behind the positions taken by intellectuals to Soviet atrocities, see Michael David-Fox, Showcasing the Great Experiment: Cultural Diplomacy and Western Visitors to Soviet Russia, 1921-1941 (New York: Oxford University Press, 2011).

51 Quoted in Guttenplan, American Radical, 108.

52 FBI report, "Lillian Hellman," June 18, 1941, box 119, folder 1, 1-2, Lillian Hellman Collection. Harry Ransom Center, University of Texas at Austin.

53 Sam Jaffe interviewed by Barbara Hall, April 25, 1991, 264-65, Oral History Collection, Margaret Herrick Papers.

54 "Sees Finnish Aid Imperiling Peace," New York Times (January 21, 1940): 27

55 Hellman's fullest version of the story is in "An Evening with Lillian Hellman," Bulletin of the American Academy of Arts and Sciences 27, no. 7 (April 1974): 19; a slightly different version is in Lillian Hellman, Pentimento (Boston: Little, Brown, 1973), 183.

56 Hellman, Pentimento, 184.

57 Typescript, "Statement by Miss Lillian Hellman," draft, April 14, 1952, box 71, "Lillian Hellman, 1950-57," folder, 2. Joseph Rauh Papers, LOC.

58 This story comes from Roy Hoopes, Ralph Ingersoll: A Biography (New York: Atheneum, 1985), 5.

59 Ibid., 401

60 Lillian Hellman, "The Little Men in Philadelphia," PM (June 25, 1940): 6.

61 Several sets of these files are now located in the archives. The first set collected by Peter Benjaminson is now in box 119, folder 1, Lillian Hellman Collection, HRC. The second, collected by Robert Newman, was also donated to Harry Ransom Center. The William Miller Abrahams Papers, Stanford University Libraries, also includes some originals. They differ in minor ways.

62 Hellman, Pentimento, 186.

63 Alvah Bessie, "Watch on the Rhine," New Masses (April 15, 1941): 26; Ralph Warner, "Watch on the Rhine: Poignant Drama of Anti-Fascist Struggle," Daily Worker (April 4, 1941): 7.

64 Ibid., 195.

65 These names culled from records of the U.S. House of Representatives, House Un-American Activities Committee, Master Name Index, box 291, NARA, RG233.

66 Memo from special agent in charge (SAC) to director, FBI, December 19, 1951, box 4, folder 3, William Miller Abrahams Papers, SUL.

67 Martin Bauml Duberman, *Paul Robeson* (New York: Knopf, 1988), ch. 12.

68 This event was sponsored by the women's division of the Joint Anti-Fascist Refugee Committee at the Hotel Commodore on December 14, 1943. Apparently a thousand guests lauded her for her aid to the loyalists. FBI report, box 119, folder 1, Lillian Hellman Collection, HRC.

69 FBI files, March 23, 1945, box 4, folder 3, William Miller Abrahams Papers, SUL.

70 FBI report, August 18, 1944, box 119, folder 1, Lillian Hellman Collection, HRC.

71 FBI memo, October 7, 1944, box 119, folder 1, Lillian Hellman Collection, HRC.

72 FBI report, October 14, 1944, box 119, folder 1, Lillian Hellman Collection, HRC.

73 Lillian Hellman, "Russian Diaries," box 103, folder 3, 2–3, 4, 10, 11, Lillian Hellman Collection, HRC.

74 Ibid., 3.

75 Ibid., 10, 11.

76 Lillian Hellman, "I Meet the Front-Line Russians," *Collier's* (March 31, 1945): 68; Lillian Hellman, "Russian Diaries," 6.

77 Raisa Orlova, *Memoirs* (New York: Random House, 1983), 117.

78 Hellman, "I Meet the Front-Line Russians," 71. For Hellman's behavior at the front, see Raisa Orlova, *Memoirs*, 116–17.

79 Lillian Hellman, "I Meet the Front-Line Russians," 71. In *An Unfinished Woman*, 163, the gift is described as "a cigarette lighter made from a gun barrel."

80 FBI memos, January 2, 1945, February 9, 1945, March 27, 1945, May 17, 1945. Copies of these files are located in box 74, folder 1, William Miller Abrahams Papers, SUL.

81 SAC, New York, to director, FBI, March 17, 1947, box 119, folder 1, Lillian Hellman Collection, HRC.

5. An American Jew

1 On issues of identity, see Judith Smith, *Visions of Belonging* (New York: Columbia University Press, 2004); Matthew Jacobson, *Roots Too: White Ethnic*

Revival in Post-Civil Rights America (Cambridge, MA: Harvard University Press, 2008); and especially David Hollinger, *Cosmopolitanism and Solidarity: Studies in Ethnoracial, Religious, and Professional Affiliation in the United States* (Madison: University of Wisconsin Press, 2006).

2 Irving Howe, *A Margin of Hope: An Intellectual Autobiography* (New York: Harcourt Brace, 1982), 251.

3 Edmund Wilson, *The Thirties: From Notebooks and Diaries of the Period* (New York: Farrar, Straus and Giroux, 1980), 313.

4 Mary McCarthy, *How I Grew* (New York: Harcourt Brace Jovanovich, 1987), 45.

5 Ibid., 215. Such examples of the silence of Jews about their backgrounds are not unusual. See, for example, Reminiscences of Kitty Carlisle Hart (November 15, 1978), on page 407, in the Columbia University Center for Oral History Collection.

6 Dashiell Hammett to LH, no date, box 75, folder 3, William Miller Abrahams Papers, M1125, Department of Special Collections, Stanford University Libraries, Stanford, CA.

7 Dashiell Hammett to LH, April 5, 1944, box 77, folder 9, William Miller Abrahams Papers, SUL.

8 Dashiell Hammett to LH, February 25, 1944, box 77, folder 8, William Miller Abrahams Papers, SUL.

9 Dashiell Hammett to LH, January 8, 1944, box 77, folder 8, William Miller Abrahams Papers, SUL.

10 Dashiell Hammett to LH, July 24, 1944, box 77, folder 8, William Miller Abrahams Papers, SUL.

11 LH to "Darling Arthur, darling Maggie," no date, box 1, folder 20, Arthur Kober Papers, Wisconsin Historical Society, Madison, WI.

12 LH to "Arthur Baby Darling," August 4, 1948, box 1, folder 20, Arthur Kober Papers, WHS.

13 Carl Rollyson, Lillian Hellman, *Her Legend and Her Legacy* (New York: St. Martin's Press, 1988), 418

14 Sylvia Drake, "Lillian Hellman As Herself," in Jackson Bryer, ed., *Conversations with Lillian Hellman* (Jackson, MS: University Press of Mississippi, 1986), 29.

15 Mary McCarthy, *Intellectual Memoir: New York, 1936–1938* (New York: Harcourt Brace Jovanovich, 1992), 60–61.

16 "Under Forty: A Symposium on American Literature and the Younger Generation of American Jews," *Contemporary Jewish Record* 7 (February, 1944): 15. Trilling's position echoed that of his African-American contemporaries Ralph Ellison and Lorraine Hansberry, who also preferred not to

be so identified with their race as to foster expectations that they could or would write only as black people. Thanks to Judith Smith for pointing this out to me.

17 Lionel Trilling in ibid., 15–16. For more on Trilling's Jewishness, see Alexander Bloom, *Prodigal Sons: The New York Intellectuals and Their World* (New York: Oxford University Press, 1986), 22.

18 Muriel Rukeyser in ibid., 6.

19 Delmore Schwartz in ibid., 13.

20 Muriel Rukeyser in ibid., 6.

21 Lillian Hellman, *An Unfinished Woman* (Boston: Little, Brown, 1969), 5.

22 Lillian Hellman, "The Lyons Den," *New York Post* (July 22, 1938).

23 "Miss Hellman and Miss Ferber discuss Jewish Author's Plight," *New York Herald Tribune* (January 10, 1940): 19.

24 Robert Kall, "Equality Magazine is True Crusader for Jewish Rights," *Jewish Examiner* (April 28, 1939): 1.

25 Judith Smith, private communication with author; and Smith, *Visions of Belonging*, 28–33.

26 FBI confidential report NY 100-25858, undated, 16, 17.

27 Lillian Hellman, *The North Star: A Motion Picture About Some Russian People* (New York: Viking Press, 1943), 75.

28 Lillian Hellman, "Russian Diaries," 4, Lillian Hellman Collection, Harry Ransom Center, University of Texas at Austin.

29 Ibid., 6.

30 Ibid., 9, 10, 12.

31 Ibid., 12. (Also in the Russian Diaries she noted on January 26 on her way to Cairo, "BOAC manager resented Jews in Palestine," 12.)

32 These names are culled from the long lists that LH provided to her lawyer, Joseph Rauh, in 1952 just before her HUAC appearance. Untitled list, part 1, box 71, "Lillian Hellman, 1950–57" folder, Joseph Rauh Papers, Part I, Manuscript Division, Library of Congress.

33 It does not excuse Hellman to say that she was not alone. Paul Robeson, who is said to have met Feffer in Moscow just before his death, also refused to condemn the Soviet regime.

34 Alfred Kazin, *New York Jew* (New York: Knopf, 1978), 194.

35 Arthur Miller, *Timebends: A Life* (New York: Grove Press, 1987), 155–56.

36 Bloom, *Prodigal Sons*, 141, 143; Martin Peretz, interview by author, June 22, 2009.

37 Norman Podhoretz, *Ex-Friends: Falling Out with Allen Ginsburg, Lionel*

and Diana Trilling. Lillian Hellman, Hannah Arendt, and Norman Mailer (New York: Free Press, 1999), 124.

38 Elaine Tyler May, *Homeward Bound: American Families in the Cold War Era* (New York: Basic Books, 1988).

39 Victor Navasky, *Naming Names* (New York: Penguin, 1981), 109–11.

40 Ibid., 109.

41 Irving Howe, *A Margin of Hope*, 198.

42 LH to William Alfred, February 19, 1959, box 20, Papers of William Alfred, Brooklyn College Archives & Special Collections, Brooklyn College Library.

43 On the question of self-hatred among Jews, see Susan Glenn, "The Vogue of Jewish Self-Hatred in Post-World War II America," *Jewish Social Studies* 12 (Spring 2006): 95–136.

44 Anne Frank, *The Diary of a Young Girl* (Garden City, NY: Doubleday, 1952). This interpretation follows Lawrence Graver, *An Obsession with Anne Frank: Meyer Levin and the Diary* (Berkeley, CA: University of California Press, 1995), ch. 1.

45 Meyer Levin, *The Obsession* (New York: Simon and Schuster, 1973) 35.

46 Stephen J. Whitfield, *In Search of Jewish American Culture* (Waltham, MA: Brandeis University Press, 1999), 173.

47 Saul Bellow, *Letters*, ed. Benjamin Taylor (New York: Viking, 2010), 196. Thanks to Eugene Goodheart for calling these letters to my attention.

48 Levin, *The Obsession*, 73. See also 102.

49 Ibid., 65

50 Levin, *The Obsession*, 72–74. See also Ralph Melnick, *The Stolen Legacy of Anne Frank: Meyer Levin, Lillian Hellman, and the Staging of the Diary* (New Haven, CT: Yale University Press, 1997).

51 Levin, *The Obsession*, 72.

52 This is the argument of, among others, Melnick, *The Stolen Legacy of Anne Frank*.

53 Kermit Bloomgarden to investors, May 16, 1958, box 53, folder 1, Lillian Hellman Collection, HRC. Statement from Pinto, Winokur and Pagano, Accountants, June 30, 1970, box 53, folder 1, Lillian Hellman Collection, HRC. See also box 52, folder 10. The $25,000 figure is my calculation based on the one half of one percent investment that LH made.

54 LH to William Alfred, February 19, 1959, box 20, Papers of William Alfred, BCASC.

55 Ibid.

56 LH to "Dear Joe," January 22, 1974, box 72, folder 10, William Miller Abrahams Papers, SUL.

57 Quoted from American Masters, "The Lives of Lillian Hellman," production of PBS, 1998.

58 Martin Peretz, interview by author, June 22, 2009.

59 Podhoretz, *Ex-Friends*, 124.

60 Lillian Hellman, *Scoundrel Time* (Boston: Little, Brown, 1976), 38–39

61 Ibid., 83.

62 Sidney Hook, "Lillian Hellman's Scoundrel Time," *Encounter* 48 (February 1977): 86.

63 Christine Doudna, "A Still Unfinished Woman: A Conversation with Lillian Hellman," *Rolling Stone* (February 24, 1977): 54.

64 Hellman, "East and West: *The Provincials: A Personal History of Jews in the South*," *New York Times Book Review* (November 11, 1973): 421.

65 Hellman, *Pentimento*, 196.

66 Glenn, "The Vogue of Jewish Self-Hatred," 95–136.

6. The Writer as Moralist

1 "An Evening with Lillian Hellman," *Bulletin of the American Academy of Arts and Sciences* 27 (April 1974): 19.

2 Lillian Hellman, *Pentimento* (Boston: Little, Brown, 1973), 152.

3 Hellman, "The Art of the Theater I," *Paris Review* 33 (Winter/Spring, 1965): 84.

4 Lillian Hellman, "Typescript Prepared for Circle in the Square Talk," February 8, 1953, box 43, folder 2, 7, Lillian Hellman Collection, Harry Ransom Center, University of Texas at Austin.

5 Lillian Hellman, *The Collected Plays* (Boston: Little, Brown, 1971), 275.

6 Stark Young, "Watch on the Rhine," *New Republic* (April 14, 1941): 499.

7 Wolcott Gibbs, "This Is It," *New Yorker* (April 12, 1941): 32.

8 Young, "Watch on the Rhine," 499.

9 Brooks Atkinson, "Lillian Hellman's 'Watch on the Rhine' Acted with Paul Lukas in the Leading Part," *New York Times* (April 2, 1941): 26.

10 Brooks Atkinson, "Hellman's 'Watch on the Rhine,'" *New York Times* (April 13, 1941): sec. 9, 1.

11 George Jean Nathan, "Playwrights in Petticoats," *American Mercury* (June, 1941): 752.

12 Morris Frumin to LH, April 5, 1942, box 91, "Watch on the Rhine/Business Correspondence," folder, Lillian Hellman Collection, HRC.

13 Richard Watts Jr., "The Theaters," *New York Herald Tribune* (April 2, 1941): 20.

14 Ralph Warner, "'Watch on the Rhine' Poignant Drama of Anti Fascist Struggle," *Daily Worker* (April 4, 1941): 7; Walter Bernstein, *Inside Out: A Memoir of the Blacklist* (Cambridge, MA: Da Capo Press, 2000), 138–39.

15 Warner, "Watch on the Rhine," 7.

16 Albert Maltz, "What Shall We Ask of Writers?" *New Masses* (February 1946), 19. See also the discussion of this issue in Daniel Aaron, *Writers on the Left: Episodes in American Literary Communism* (New York: Harcourt Brace and World, Inc., 1961), 387.

17 Lillian Hellman, "Typescript: Swarthmore," April 6, 1950, box 43, folder 1, Lillian Hellman Collection, HRC.

18 Dan Georgakas, "The Revisionist Releases of North Star," *Cineaste* 22 (April 1996): 46.

19 Lillian Hellman, "Russian Diaries," box 103, folders 1 and 2, Lillian Hellman Collection, HRC.

20 Theodore Strauss, "Of Lillian Hellman: A Lady of Principle," *New York Times* (August 29, 1943): X5.

21 Theodore Strauss, "The Author's Case: Post Premiere Cogitation of Lillian Hellman on 'The North Star,'" *New York Times* (December 19, 1943): X5.

22 Mary McCarthy, "A Filmy Vision of the War," *Town and Country* (January 1944): 72.

23 Ted Strauss, "The Author's Case," *New York Times* (December 19, 1943): X5.

24 Hellman, "The Art of the Theater I," 84.

25 Dashiell Hammett to LH, March 21, 1944, and February 9, 1944, box 77, folder 8, William Miller Abrahams Papers, M1125, Department of Special Collections, Stanford University Libraries, Stanford, CA.

26 Dashiell Hammett to LH, March 10, 1944, box 77, folder 7, William Miller Abrahams Papers, SUL.

27 Ibid.

28 Dashiell Hammett to LH, March 15, 1944, box 77, folder 7, William Miller Abrahams Papers, SUL.

29 Dashiell Hammett to LH, April 17, 1944, box 77, folder 8, William Miller Abrahams Papers, SUL.

30 Hellman, "The Art of the Theater I," 84.

31 Hellman, *The Searching Wind*, in *Collected Plays*, 337.

32 Ibid.

33 Ibid., 334–35.

34 Hellman, *The Little Foxes*, in *Collected Plays*, 188.

35 Kappo Phelan, "The Searching Wind," *Commonweal* 40 (April 28, 1944): 40.

36 Howard Barnes, "The Searching Wind," *New York Herald Tribune* (April 13, 1944): 16.

37 Lewis Nichols, " 'The Searching Wind' " *New York Times* (April 23, 1944): sec. 2, 1.

38 "Hellman's New Play," *Washington Times Herald* (April 21, 1944): 27.

39 Wolcott Gibbs, "Miss Hellman Nods," *New Yorker* (April 22, 1944): 42.

40 Ralph Warner, "The New Lillian Hellman Play," *Daily Worker* (April 17, 1944).

41 Ralph Warner, "On Broadway," *Daily Worker* (April 27, 1944): 8.

42 Burton Rascoe, "Has Miss Hellman Disappointed the Party?" *New York World-Telegram* (April 22, 1944): 27.

43 Ibid.

44 Stark Young, "Behind the Beyond," *New Republic* (May 1, 1944): 604.

45 Hellman, "The Art of the Theater I," 85

46 Sam Sillen, "Lillian Hellman's *Another Part of the Forest,*" *Daily Worker* (November 25, 1946): 11.

47 Brooks Atkinson, "The Play in Review," *New York Times* (November 21, 1946): 42.

48 John Mason Brown, "And Cauldron Bubble," *Saturday Review* 29 (December 14, 1946): 21, 23

49 Kappo Phelan, "Another Part of the Forest," *Commonweal* 45 (December 6, 1946): 202.

50 Joseph Wood Krutch, "Drama," *Nation* 163 (December 7, 1946): 671.

51 John Chapman, "*Another Part of the Forest* Makes *The Little Foxes* a Mere Warmup," *New York Daily News* (November 21, 1946): 67.

52 LH to Arthur Kober, c. 1935, box 1, folder 2, Arthur Kober Papers, Wisconsin Historical Society, Madison, WI.

53 Fred Gardner, "An Interview with Lillian Hellman," in Jackson Bryer, ed., *Conversations with Lillian Hellman* (Jackson, MS: University Press of Mississippi, 1986), 119.

54 Richard Watts Jr., "Miss Hellman's New Play is Fascinating Drama," *New York Post* (November 21, 1946): 40.

55 Joseph Wood Krutch, "Drama," *Nation* (December 7, 1946): 671.

56 John Chapman, "*Another Part of the Forest,*" 67.

57 Jacob Adler, *Lillian Hellman* (Austin, TX: Steck-Vaughn Company, 1969), 42

58 Richard Watts, "Lillian Hellman's New Play is Fascinating Drama," 40.

59 Millie Barringer, "Lillian Hellman Standing in the Minefields," *New Orleans Review* (Spring 1988): 64.

60 Stephanie de Pue, "Lillian Hellman: She Never Turns Down an Adventure," in Bryer, ed., *Conversations*, 186.

61 Kappo Phelan, *"Another Part of the Forest,"* 201–2.

62 Hardwick, "The Little Foxes Revived," *New York Review of Books* (December 21, 1967): 4.

63 Lillian Hellman, "An Interview with Tito," *New York Star* (November 8, 1948): 1, 8. Additional pieces in this series appeared on November 4, 5, 7, 9, and 10, 1948.

64 "The Theater: New Play in Manhattan," *Time* (November 7, 1949): 37; " 'Montserrat' " Adapted from the French of Emmanuel Robles by Lillian Hellman," *New York Times* (October 31, 1949): 25; Howard Taubman, "Lillian Hellman Play Revived at the Gate," *New York Times* (January 9, 1961): 17.

65 Hellman, *Pentimento*, 198.

66 "The Autumn Garden," *Commonweal* 53 (April 6, 1951): 645.

67 Robert Coleman, "Autumn Garden Harps on Depressing Theme," *Daily Mirror* (March 8, 1951): 32.

68 "The First Team Takes Over," *New Yorker* (March 17, 1971): 52.

69 John Beaufort, "Openings on Broadway," *Christian Science Monitor* (March 17, 1951): 6.

70 Harold Clurman, "Lillian Hellman's Garden," *New Republic* (March 26, 1951): 21–22.

71 Lillian Hellman, "Typescript: Connecticut College," January 9, 1952, box 43, folder 1, 1, Lillian Hellman Collection, HRC.

72 Ibid., 2.

73 Hellman, "Typescript: Swarthmore."

74 Lillian Hellman, "Typescript: Smith/MIT," April 15, 18, 1955, box 43, folder 1, 1, Lillian Hellman Collection, HRC.

75 Lillian Hellman, handwritten note on notecard, box 43, folder 2, Lillian Hellman Collection, HRC.

76 Lillian Hellman, "Typescript: Harvard Lecture No 2," 4.

77 Eric Bentley, "Hellman's Indignation," *New Republic* (January 5, 1953): 31.

78 Hellman, *Pentimento*, 202.

79 Quoted in Stewart H. Benedict, "Anouilh in America," *Modern Language Journal* 45 (December 1961): 342.

80 Lillian Hellman, undated/untitled typescript (probably an early draft of her introduction to *The Selected Letters of Anton Chekhov*), box 43, folder 7, Lillian Hellman Collection, HRC.

81 Lillian Hellman, ed., *The Selected Letters of Anton Chekhov* (New York: Farrar, Straus and Company, 1955), ix.

82 Ibid., xi.

83 Ibid., x.

84 Lillian Hellman, undated early typescript of notes toward an introduction to the letters of Anton Chekhov, box 43, folder 6, Lillian Hellman Collection, HRC.

85 Robert Lethbridge, "Introduction," Emile Zola, *Germinal* (New York: Oxford University Press, 1943), vii.

86 Richard G. Stern, "Lillian Hellman on Her Plays," *Contact* 3 (1959): 119.

87 Lillian Hellman, typescript: draft of *Candide*: "The Inquisition, Part One," box 9, folder 5, Lillian Hellman Collection, HRC.

88 Quoted in Arthur Gelb, "Lillian Hellman Has Play Ready," *New York Times* (November 9, 1959): 35.

89 Weidman, "Lillian Hellman Reflects upon the Changing Theater," *Dramatists Guild Quarterly* 7 (Winter 1970): 22.

90 Mary McCarthy, "The Reform of Dr. Pangloss," *New Republic* (December 17, 1956): 30.

91 Hellman, *Toys in the Attic* in *Collected Plays*, 758.

92 Jacob Adler, "Miss Hellman's Two Sisters," *Educational Theatre Journal* 15 (May 1963): 117; Austin Pendleton, interview by author, December 12, 2009, confirms this judgment.

93 Walter Kerr, "It's Gone About as Far as It Can Go," *Los Angeles Times* (April 21, 1963): N29.

94 Hellman, "Typescript: Harvard Lecture No. 1," 2.

95 Hellman, "Typescript: Connecticut College," 1.

96 Irving Drutman, "Hellman: A Stranger in the Theater?" *New York Times* (February 27, 1966): 11.

97 Lillian Hellman, undated note in preparation of publication of *The Selected Letters of Anton Chekhov*.

98 Transcript from interviews by Gary Waldhorn and Robert Murray, "Yale Reports," June 5, 1966, box 30, folder 10, Lillian Hellman Collection, HRC.

99 Gelb, "Lillian Hellman Has Play Ready," 35.

100 Gretchen Cryer, "Where Are the Women Playwrights?" *New York Times* (May 20, 1973): 129.

101 Lillian Hellman, typescript with handwritten corrections of work that later

appeared in *Pentimento*, no date, box 31, folder 16, Lillian Hellman Collection, HRC.

102 Marilyn Berger, "Profile, Lillian Hellman," in Bryer, ed., *Conversations*, 267.

103 Waldhorn and Murray, "Yale Reports."

104 Thomas Meehan, "Q: Miss Hellman, What's Wrong with Broadway? A: It's a Bore," in Bryer, ed., *Conversations*, 45–46.

105 Lillian Hellman. "Typescript: Swarthmore."

106 Gardner, "An Interview with Lillian Hellman," 115.

107 Stern, "Lillian Hellman on Her Plays," 119.

108 Adler, "Miss Hellman's Two Sisters," 117

109 Walter Kerr, "The Theater of Say It! Show It! What Is It?" *New York Times* (September 1, 1968): 10.

110 Lillian Hellman, "Scotch on the Rocks," *New York Review of Books* (October 17, 1963): 6.

111 Drutman, "Hellman: A Stranger in the Theater?" 11.

112 Hardwick, "The Little Foxes Revived," 4.

113 "Preserve us all, when friendship tires like this," wrote Penelope Gilliatt in response. See Penelope Gilliatt, "Lark Pie," *New York Review of Books* (February 1, 1968): 9. For other examples of this exchange, see Edmund Wilson, "An open letter to Mike Nichols," *New York Review of Books* (January 4, 1968); Richard Poirier, "To the Editor," *New York Review of Books* (January 18, 1968); Felicia Montealegre, "Raising Hellman," *New York Review of Books* (January 18, 1968).

7. A Self-Made Woman

1 Peter Feibleman, interview by author, August 4, 2002.

2 Ibid.

3 Morris and Lore Dickstein, interview by author, March 24, 2005.

4 Lillian Hellman, *Pentimento* (Boston: Little, Brown, 1973), 164–65.

5 Lucius Beebe, "An Adult's Hour is Miss Hellman's Next Effort," *New York Herald Tribune* (December 13, 1936): 2.

6 LH to Arthur Kober, no date, box 73, folder 2, William Miller Abrahams Papers, M1125, Department of Special Collections, Stanford University Libraries, Stanford, CA.

7 She paid off the mortgage in January 1942.

8 Stanley Isaacs to LH, March 2, 1945, box 66, folder 6, Lillian Hellman Col-

lection, Harry Ransom Center, University of Texas at Austin. The initial rent on the apartment was $4,000 a month, a hefty sum in 1945 and one that the Office of Price Administration initially contested (Irving Schwartzkopf to Office of Price Administration, September 11, 1945, box 66 folder 7, Lillian Hellman Collection, HRC).

9 LH to Rabbi Feibelman, November 13, 1941, and Julian Feibelman to LH, November 5, 1941, box 91, "Watch on the Rhine" folder, Lillian Hellman Collection, HRC.

10 LH to Jack Warner, March 9, 1943, box 91, "Watch on the Rhine" folder, Lillian Hellman Collection, HRC.

11 This and the following quotes are from Jack Warner to LH, March 12, 1943, and LH to Jack Warner, March 24, 1943, box 91, "Watch on the Rhine" folder, Lillian Hellman Collection, HRC.

12 LH to Audio Subscriptions, Inc., July 19, 1942, box 91, "Watch on the Rhine/ Correspondence and Statements" folder, Lillian Hellman Collection, HRC.

13 LH to Bennett Cerf, July 5, 1944, box 91, "Watch on the Rhine/Correspondence and Statements" folder, Lillian Hellman Collection, HRC.

14 LH to Hal Keith, August 27, 1946, box 91, "Watch on the Rhine/Correspondence and Statements" folder, Lillian Hellman Collection, HRC.

15 LH to Bennett Cerf, November 8, 1943, "Watch on the Rhine/Correspondence and Statements" folder, Lillian Hellman Collection, HRC.

16 LH to Mr. Jelinek, July 12, 1947, "Watch on the Rhine/Correspondence and Statements" folder, Lillian Hellman Collection, HRC.

17 William Abrahams, notes, box 77, folder 1, William Miller Abrahams Papers, SUL.

18 Lillian Hellman, schedule of securities, December 31, 1944, box 103, folder 9, Lillian Hellman Collection, HRC.

19 Dashiell Hammett to LH, April 5, 1944, box 77, folder 8, William Miller Abrahams Papers, SUL. See also Dashiell Hammett to LH, January 8, 1944, box 77, folder 8 and Dashiell Hammett to Nancy Bragdon, June 4, 1944, box 77, folder 6, William Miller Abrahams Papers, SUL.

20 Edith Kean to LH, March 24, 1951, box 91, "Watch on the Rhine (Tax matters, 1951)" folder, Lillian Hellman Collection, HRC.

21 Copy of the ad from the *New York Times*, August 1951, box 65, folder 1, Lillian Hellman Collection, HRC.

22 Katherine Brown to LH, August 23, 1951, box 53, folder 52, Lillian Hellman Collection, HRC. Letters that follow are September 1, 1951, and October 12, 1951, box 53, folder 52, Lillian Hellman Collection, HRC.

23 LH to Losey, February 5, 1953, box 5, folder 6, Lillian Hellman Collection, HRC. Losey apparently held no grudge. Twenty years later, he asked Hellman

to write a script from Conrad's *The Secret Sharer*. Hellman was intrigued but ultimately refused. Joe Losey to LH, June 30, 1972, and LH to Joseph Losey, July 18, 1972, box 3, "June–November, 1972" folder, Harold Matson Company, Inc. (New York, NY) Records, Rare Book & Manuscript Library, Columbia University, New York, NY.

24 Morris and Lore Dickstein, interview by author, March 24, 2005.

25 Letters between LH and Arthur Kober, box 71, folders 2–9, Lillian Hellman Collection, HRC.

26 Letters from LH to Lois Fritsch, typed or handwritten on stationery from the Eden Hotel-Roma or the Hotel Dorchester in London, undated, box 122, folder 2, Lillian Hellman Collection, HRC.

27 Ibid.

28 LH to Lois Fritsch from Eden Hotel-Roma, undated, box 122, folder 2, Lillian Hellman Collection, HRC.

29 LH to Lois Fritsch from the Dorchester, London, undated, box 122, folder 2, Lillian Hellman Collection, HRC.

30 Hellman, *Pentimento*, 200.

31 Jan Van Loewen to LH, March 1953, box 72, folder 8, Lillian Hellman Collection, HRC.

32 LH to Kermit Bloomgarden, February 26, 1954, box 72, folder 8, Lillian Hellman Collection, HRC.

33 LH to Jean Anouilh, April 13, 1954, April 23, 1954, and May 10, 1954, box 72, folder 8, Lillian Hellman Collection, HRC.

34 Kay Brown to Jean Anouilh, May 12, 1954, and Jean Anouilh to Kay Brown, May 19, 1954, box 72, folder 8, Lillian Hellman Collection, HRC.

35 Jan Van Loewen to Kay Brown, December 13, 1955, and Kay Brown to Jan Van Loewen, December 15, 1955, box 72, folder 8, Lillian Hellman Collection, HRC.

36 Stewart Benedict, "Anouilh in America," *Modern Language Journal* 45 (December 1961): 342.

37 Jan Van Loewen to LH, January 18, 1974, box 72, folder 8, Lillian Hellman Collection, HRC.

38 Maurice Peress interview with Gordon Davidson, August 17, 2010, unpublished, Los Angeles, CA. I am grateful to Maurice Peress for providing this material and the insights that follow from it.

39 Maurice Peress, interview by author, August 19, 2010.

40 LH to Robby Lantz, February 8, 1966, box 72, folder 6, Lillian Hellman Collection, HRC.

41 LH to Leonard Bernstein, November 22, 1971, box 122, folder 16, Lillian Hellman Collection, HRC.

42 Selma Wolfman to Arthur Richenthal, December 13, 1962, box 70, folder 1, Lillian Hellman Collection, HRC.

43 These claims are in box 68, folder 3, Lillian Hellman Collection, HRC.

44 Hellman's secretary detailed the history of these insurance company cancellations and refusals over a five-year period to her lawyer, Oscar Bernstein, concluding, "Since December 15, 1962, Kermit Bloomgarden's agent, an agent from Arthur Richenthal and a third agent have all tried to get a policy but without success." Selma Wolfman to Oscar Bernstein, May 17, 1963, box 70, folder 1, Lillian Hellman Collection, HRC.

45 Philip Stern to LH, May 31, 1963, box 70, folder 1, Lillian Hellman Collection, HRC.

46 LH to Calvin Siegel, February 27, 1964, box 70, folder 1, Lillian Hellman Collection, HRC.

47 LH to Kurtis Sameth Hill, Inc., July 29, 1968, box 70, folder 1, Lillian Hellman Collection, HRC.

48 Draft typescript, "Deposition by Lillian Hellman, June 1962"; O'Dwyer and Bernstein to Mrs. Josephine Marshall, March 19, 1963; box 56, unfiled materials, Lillian Hellman Collection, HRC.

49 LH to Ronald Bernstien, August 29, 1969, box 72, folder 6, Lillian Hellman Collection, HRC.

50 Donald Condon to Norman Swallow, May 10, 1978, Hellman/Hammett Estate Files, Harold Matson Company, Inc. Records, RBML.

51 LH to Oscar Bernstein, January 14, 1965, box 54, "Hammett Estate" folder, Lillian Hellman Collection, HRC.

52 LH to Oscar Bernstein, May 24, 1965, box 54, "Hammett Estate" folder, Lillian Hellman Collection, HRC.

53 Hellman, *Pentimento*, 258.

54 Lillian Hellman, "Comments," spring 1963, box 40, folder 5, Lillian Hellman Collection, HRC. These were frivolous short pieces that smacked of selling one's soul for money.

55 Selma Wolfman to "Dear Mr. Lantz," October 28, 1963, box 72, folder 6, Lillian Hellman Collection, HRC.

56 LH to Robby Lantz, January 20, 1964, box 72, folder 6, Lillian Hellman Collection, HRC.

57 LH to Robby Lantz, February 12, 1964, box 72, folder 6, Lillian Hellman Collection, HRC.

58 LH to Robby Lantz, November 6, 1963, box 72, folder 6, Lillian Hellman Collection, HRC.

59 Robby Lantz to Caskie Stinnett, August 7, 1963, box 72, folder 6, Lillian Hellman Collection, HRC.

60 Don Congdon to LH, June 13, 1977, and LH to Don Congdon, June 15, 1977, box 3, "Feb-June, 1977" folder; Heather Hirson to Don Congdon, November 16, 1977, box 3, "July-Dec, 1977" folder, Harold Matson Company, Inc. Records, RBML.

61 LH to Don Congdon, June 16, 1971, box 51, folder 12, Lillian Hellman Collection. She used the phrase again in LH to Don Congdon, August 17, 1971, box 3, "June-Nov, 1971" folder, Harold Matson Company, Inc. Records, RBML.

62 Don Congdon to Viera Dinkova, October 29, 1971, box 48, "Lillian Hellman, '71" folder, Harold Matson Company, Inc. Records, RBML.

63 Patricia Naggiar to LH, July 19, 1977, box 3, "July-December" folder, Harold Matson Company, Inc. Records, RBML.

64 Rita Wade to Ephraim London, February 9, 1976, and Ephraim London to Rita Wade, February 10, 1976, box 77, folder 7, Lillian Hellman Collection, HRC.

65 Nancy Troland to LH, January 17, 1977, and Don Congdon to LH, November 23, 1976, box 52, folder 1, Lillian Hellman Collection, HRC.

66 Don Congdon to Nancy Troland, January 21, 1977, box 52, folder 1, Lillian Hellman Collection, HRC.

67 Don Congdon to Antonia Handler Chayes, March 4, 1977, uncatalogued papers, "Hellman: Hammett Estate, 1977" folder, Harold Matson Company, Inc. Records, RBML.

68 Don Congdon to Flora Roberts, December 4, 1973, box 48, "Hellman/Hammett Jan-June" folder, Harold Matson Company, Inc. Records, RBML.

69 Don Congdon to LH, with handwritten LH note, May 13, 1977, box 3, "Feb-June, 1977" folder, and Don Congdon to Ruzica Vlaskalin, June 14, 1977, uncatalogued papers, "Hellman: Hammett Estate, 1977" folder, Harold Matson Company, Inc. Records, RBML.

70 Don Congdon to Helen Harvey, September 15, 1976, box 49, unfiled papers, Harold Matson Company, Inc. Records, RBML.

71 This went on until her death. See Robby Lantz to LH, March 6, 1984, box 72, folder 7, Lillian Hellman Collection, HRC.

72 Don Congdon to LH, December 17, 1974, box 3, "Feb-Nov, 1974" folder, Harold Matson Company, Inc. Records, RBML.

73 Don Congdon to LH, October 26, 1977, box 3, "July-Dec, 1977" folder, Harold Matson Company, Inc. Records, RBML.

74 Exchange of letters with Vicky Wilson of Alfred Knopf, December 1980, box 72, folder 3, Lillian Hellman Collection, HRC.

75 LH to Don Congdon, April 5, 1977, and Don Congdon to LH, April 11, 1977, box 3, "Feb-June, 1977" folder, Harold Matson Company, Inc. Records, RBML.

76 LH to Don Congdon, January 19, 1976, Don Congdon to LH, January 26, 1976, box 3, "Jan-Dec, 1976" folder, Harold Matson Company, Inc. Records, RBML.

77 Robby Lantz to Lillian Hellman, June 29, 1971, box 72, folder 6, Lillian Hellman Collection, HRC.

78 LH to Robby Lantz, July 15, 1971, box 72, folder 6, Lillian Hellman Collection, HRC.

79 LH to Donald Oresman, July 16, 1974, box 3, "July to December, 1974" folder, Harold Matson Company, Inc. Records.

80 LH to Don Congdon, August 16, 1977. See also exchange of letters with Congdon over a contract with ICM, August 2, 1977, August 5, 1977, and August 12, 1977, box 3, "July-December, 1977" folder, Harold Matson Company, Inc. Records, RBML.

81 Don Congdon to LH, September 23, 1983, box 52, folder 2, Lillian Hellman Collection, HRC.

82 Robby Lantz to LH, January 9, 1984, and February 6, 1984, box 72, folder 7, Lillian Hellman Collection, HRC.

83 LH to Robby Lantz, July 7, 1969, box 72, folder 6, Lillian Hellman Collection, HRC.

84 For example, see LH to Lantz, July 15, 1971, box 72, folder 6, Lillian Hellman Collection, HRC.

85 LH to Robby Lantz, June 11, 1964, box 72, folder 6, Lillian Hellman Collection, HRC.

86 LH to Robby Lantz, February 8, 1966, box 72, folder 6, Lillian Hellman Collection, HRC.

87 LH to Herman Shumlin, August 13 and 15, 1969, box 73, folder 2, Lillian Hellman Collection, HRC.

88 Donald Oresman to Jack Klein, November 11, 1977, box 52, folder 1, Lillian Hellman Collection, HRC.

89 LH to Donald Oresman, December 28, 1978, box 52, folder 3, Lillian Hellman Collection, HRC.

90 Donald Oresman to Lillian Hellman, January 17, 1979, box 52, folder 4, Lillian Hellman Collection, HRC.

91 In New York lingo, that meant a twenty-four-hour doorman, an on-site superintendent, a handyman, elevator operators, and janitorial service.

92 The offer she turned down was from Douglas Elliman. She bought the house in 1944 for $48,000.

93 Theodore Zimmerman to LH, May 23, 1969, box 66, folder 8. See also letters and memos from LH to Zimmerman, May 29, 1969, September 17, 1969, November 6, 1969, box 66, folder 8, Lillian Hellman Collection, HRC.

94 LH to Joyce Hartman, August 20, 1969, box 66, folder 8, Lillian Hellman Collection, HRC.

95 LH to Joan Zimmerman, October 13, 1970, box 66, folder 7, Lillian Hellman Collection, HRC.

96 LH to Theodore Zimmerman, October 6, 1972, box 66, folder 5, Lillian Hellman Collection, HRC.

97 LH to Paul O'Dwyer, May 8, 1973; see also letters of October 3, 1973, October 12, 1973, October 17, 1973, January 14, 1974, box 66, folder 5, Lillian Hellman Collection, HRC.

98 Hellman closed on apartment 10A on June 23, 1970, and the move, supervised by Mrs. Loftus, took place on July 25–27. Hellman returned from the Vineyard to the completed apartment in September.

99 LH to William Michael, December 14, 1970, box 66, folder 8, Lillian Hellman Collection, HRC.

100 LH to Mildred Loftus, August 10, 1970, box 66, folder 8, Lillian Hellman Collection, HRC.

101 Ibid.

102 LH to Selma Wolfman, handwritten note, 1958, box 68, folder 4, and LH to Mr. Barton, November 8, 1961, box 68, folder 3, Lillian Hellman Collection, HRC.

103 Lillian Hellman, typescript, "Things to Do," April 10, 1973, box 67, folder 1, Lillian Hellman Collection, HRC.

104 LH to Miss Jovic, April 6, 1979, box 67, folder 1, Lillian Hellman Collection, HRC.

105 Rosemary Mahoney, *A Likely Story: One Summer with Lillian Hellman* (New York: Doubleday, 1998).

106 Per author conversation with Rose Styron, who tells of walking toward Hellman's Martha's Vineyard home one afternoon and turning back in embarrassment after she heard Hellman loudly berating her helper.

107 LH to "Dear Amy," June 8, 1980, box 67, folder 1, Lillian Hellman Collection, HRC.

108 Ming Hu to LH, September 29, 1980, November 25, 1980, December 25, 1980, box 67, folder 1, Lillian Hellman Collection, HRC.

109 LH to Mercedes Tello, December 31, 1980, box 67, folder 1, Lillian Hellman Collection, HRC.

110 LH to Nell Mohn, May 16, 1980, box 67, folder 1, Lillian Hellman Collection, HRC.

111 LH to "Whom it may concern," October 6, 1980, box 67, folder 1, Lillian Hellman Collection, HRC.

112 Typescript, untitled statements, April 8, 1981, and April 10, 1981, box 67, folder 1, Lillian Hellman Collection, HRC.

113 Letter (name changed to protect the writer) to Rita Wade, May 21, 1981, box 67, folder 1, Lillian Hellman Collection, HRC.

114 LH to "Linda," September 21, 1981, box 67, folder 1, Lillian Hellman Collection, HRC.

115 LH to Paul O'Dwyer, July 5, 1972, box 89, folder 7, Lillian Hellman Collection, HRC.

116 Nancy Bragdon to Stanley Isaacs, June 25, 1946, box 87, folder 6, Lillian Hellman Collection, HRC.

117 Arthur Cowan to LH, December 23, 1957, box 89, folder 6, Lillian Hellman Collection, HRC.

118 Florence Newhouse to LH, May 27, 1960, box 89, folder 7, Lillian Hellman Collection, HRC.

119 LH to Florence Newhouse, June 13, 1960, box 89, folder 7, Lillian Hellman Collection, HRC.

120 LH to Paul O'Dwyer, July 5, 1972, box 89, folder 7, Lillian Hellman Collection, HRC.

121 Morris and Lore Dickstein, interview by author, March 24, 2005.

122 Florence Newhouse to LH, c. 1968, box 89, folder 7, Lillian Hellman Collection, HRC.

123 LH to Paul O'Dwyer, December 6, 1973, box 90, folder 1, Lillian Hellman Collection, HRC.

124 LH to Paul O'Dwyer, July 5, 1972; see also O'Dwyer to LH, June 27, 1972, box 89, folder 7, Lillian Hellman Collection, HRC.

125 LH to Donald Oresman, May 1, 1979, box 52, folder 4, Lillian Hellman Collection.

126 Jack Klein, Lillian Hellman estate statements, box 29, folder 1, Lillian Hellman Collection, HRC.

8. A Known Communist

1 Winston Churchill, "The Sinews of Peace," March 5, 1946, Fulton, Missouri.

2 Harry Truman, "'Word Has Just Been Received': Truman Speaks on the Railroad Strike," May 24, 1946, http://historymatters.gmu.edu/d/5137/.

3 LH to John Melby, c. May 28, 1946, box 81, folder 7/8, Lillian Hellman Collection, Harry Ranson Center, University of Texas at Austin.

4 Studs Terkel, "The Wiretap This Time," New York *Times* (October 29, 2007): A19.

5 Lillian Hellman, "From America," in Daniel S. Gillmor, ed., *Speaking of Peace* (New York: National Council of the Arts, Sciences and Professions, 1949), 122; see also FBI case file, New York Section, April 9, 1951, file no: 100-2858 EXM, box 74, folder 5, 10, William Miller Abrahams Papers, M1125, Department of Special Collections, Stanford University Libraries, Stanford, CA. The FBI, keeping track of Harry Hopkins, thought Hellman, "an alleged communist," might have had an affair with Hopkins, whom it described as "very pro Russian and pro Communist."

6 The clearest exposition of this phenomenon is in Richard Pells, *The Liberal Mind in a Conservative Age: American Intellectuals in the 1940s and 1950s* (New York: Harper and Row, 1985), 284–85.

7 Ibid., 285.

8 Clifton Brock, *Americans for Democratic Action* (New York: Public Affairs Press, 1962), 52.

9 Pells, *Liberal Mind*, 285: the fundamental argument was between the belief of many liberals (including liberal intellectuals like Schlesinger, Hook, and Philip Rahv) in what Richard Pells calls "the continuing danger of traitors and spies in high places, the necessity of security checks and legislative restraints to safeguard democracy, the tendency of Communists on trial to dissemble and deceive, the definition of Communism itself as a foreign conspiracy, and the need for intellectuals to acknowledge their moral guilt and cast off their political innocence."

10 Marilyn Berger, "Profile, Lillian Hellman," in Jackson Bryer, ed., *Conversations with Lillian Hellman* (Jackson: University Press of Mississippi, 1986), 251–252.

11 Richard Parker, *John Kenneth Galbraith: His Life, His Politics, His Economics* (New York: Farrar, Straus and Giroux), 261.

12 Pells, *Liberal*, 265. Here Hellman is placed among a handful of intellectuals who refused to "serve the State." He includes among these Dwight MacDonald, Henry Steele Commager, I. F. Stone, Mary McCarthy, Arthur Miller, and Michael Harrington.

13 LH to Muriel Rukeyser, February 8, 1945, box 41, folder 7, Lillian Hellman Collection, HRC.

14 LH to John Melby, c. May 28, 1946, box 81, folder 7/8, Lillian Hellman Collection, HRC.

15 *Daily Worker*, "Women Ask for Peace" (March 8, 1946): 9. Other equally respectable signatories included Mrs. Henry Wallace, Mrs. J. Borden Harriman, Rep. Helen Gahagan Douglas (Richard Nixon's first political victim), Helen Hayes, Katherine Lenroot, chief of the U.S. Children's Bureau, Mrs. David de Sola Pool, and Mrs. La Fell Dickinson, president of the General Federation of Women's Clubs.

16 Lillian Hellman, "From America," 22.

17 Draft typescript, "Statement by Miss Lillian Hellman," April 14, 1952, and revised statement, April 28, 1952, box 72, folder 9, William Miller Abrahams Papers, SUL.

18 Sidney Hook, *Out of Step: An Unquiet Life in the 20th Century* (New York: Harper and Row, 1955), chapter 24.

19 FBI reports, October 26, 1947, and March 1948, box 119, folder 1, Lillian Hellman Collection, HRC.

20 Many conservative historians agree that communists did not run the campaign. See William L. O'Neill, *A Better World: The Great Schism, Stalinism and the American Intellectuals* (New York: Simon and Schuster, 1982), 147–48.

21 Reminiscences of Michael Straight (1982), on page 226 in the Columbia Center for Oral History.

22 Call for "Cultural and Scientific Conference for World Peace," *Daily Worker* (January 10, 1949).

23 Reminiscences of Thomas Emerson (1955), vol. 5, part I, on page 1889, CCOH.

24 Call for "Cultural and Scientific Conference for World Peace," box 10c, Harlow Shapley Papers, Harvard University Library.

25 John Rossi, "Farewell to Fellow Traveling: The Waldorf Peace Conference of March, 1949," *Continuity* 10 (Spring 1985): 1.

26 "From America" speech typescript, March 1949, box 42, folder 11, Lillian Hellman Collection, HRC.

27 Ralph Chapman, "Rally's Leaders Challenged by Counter-Group," *New York Herald Tribune* (March 24, 1949): 12.

28 Hellman, "From America."

29 Reminiscences of Thomas Emerson (1955), vol. 5, part I, on page 1889, CCOH. For an analysis of the event, see Neil Jumonville, *Critical Crossings: The New*

York Intellectuals in Postwar America (Berkeley: University of California Press, 1991), ch. 1.

30 See account of this in Michael Wreszin, *A Rebel in Defense of Tradition: The Life and Politics of Dwight MacDonald* (New York: Basic Books, 1994), 214–20; Rossi, "Farewell," 21.

31 Reminiscences of Virginia Durr (July 14, 1975), on pages 214–15, CCOH.

32 "Red Visitors Cause Rumpus," *Life* (April 4, 1949): 42–43. Thanks to Judith Friedlander for calling this to my attention.

33 Arthur Miller, *Timebends: A Life* (New York: Grove Press, 1987), 235.

34 John Patrick Diggins, "The -Ism that Failed," *American Prospect* (December 1, 2003): 78.

35 Arien Mack, conversation with author, June 2010.

36 The FBI took Hellman off its internal security index in 1945 after she returned from the Soviet Union but after the Waldorf conference decided once again to keep her under surveillance.

37 FBI case statement, New York Office, April 9, 1951, box 74, folder 5, 13, William Miller Abrahams Papers, SUL.

38 Robert Newman, *The Cold War Romance of Lillian Hellman and John Melby* (Chapel Hill: University of North Carolina Press, 1989), 329.

39 Christopher Lasch, *The Agony of the American Left* (New York: Vintage, 1969), 82.

40 Joseph Rauh, "Draft Statement," April 28, 1952, box 72, folder 9, 5, William Miller Abrahams Papers, SUL.

41 Freda Kirchwey, "How Free Is Free? *Nation* (June 28, 1952): 616.

42 Reminiscences of Leonard Boudin (1983), on page 199, CCOH.

43 Stefan Kanfer, *Journal of the Plague Years* (New York: Atheneum, 1973), 77. For the emergence of the Hollywood blacklist see Paul Buhle, Mari Jo Buhle, and Dan Georgakas, *Encyclopedia of the American Left* (New York: Oxford University Press, 1990), and Larry Ceplair and Stephen Englund, *The Inquisition in Hollywood: Politics in the Film Community, 1930–1960* (Chicago: University of Illinois Press, 2003).

44 Hellman "The Judas Goats," *Screen Writer* (December 1947): 7.

45 Hellman notes called "The Picture Finished," typescript in Harvard Lectures folder, box 44, folder 6, 7–8, Lillian Hellman Collection, and Ceplair and Englund, *The Inquisition in Hollywood*, suggest that Hellman was part of a group that tried to head off the blacklist.

46 LH to William and Talli Tyler, September 15, 1975, box 32, folder 4, Lillian Hellman Collection, HRC. Stefan Kanfer has a different account of this story in *Journal of the Plague Years*, 139.

47 Hellman, "The Picture Finished," 7–8.

48 Typescript, "Lillian Hellman, Playwright," box 28, folders 14–177, Counterattack Papers, Tamiment Library/Robert F. Wagner Labor Archives, New York University Libraries, New York, NY.

49 Reminiscences of Leonard Boudin (1983), on page 197, CCOH.

50 Walter Metzger, "The McCarthy Era," *Academe* 75 (May–June 1989): 27. See also Ellen Schrecker, *No Ivory Tower* (New York: Oxford University Press, 1986), 93–94, which describes the policy as effectively protecting only those who had never lied about Communist Party affiliation, thus leaving exposed those who had never been asked about or openly admitted such affiliation in the past.

51 Russell Porter, "Colleges Vote Freedom Code Banning Reds from Faculties," *New York Times* (March 31, 1953): 1.

52 Untitled typescript, box 28, folder 14–177, 11, 12, 22, 24, Counterattack Papers, TL.

53 FBI report, April 9, 1951, box 119, folder 1, 8, Lillian Hellman Collection, HRC.

54 Lillian Hellman, "Typescript: Statement by Miss Lillian Hellman, April 28, 1952 (Draft)," April 14, 1952, box 72, folder 9, William Miller Abrahams Papers, SUL.

55 Lillian Hellman, "Typescript: Harvard Lecture No. 2," spring 1961, box 44, folder 6, 7, Lillian Hellman Collection, HRC.

56 Oscar Hammerstein to LH, April 13, 1950; LH to Oscar Hammerstein, April 20, 1950, box 53, folder 1, Lillian Hellman Collection, HRC. The signed affidavit was later returned to her after the labor board decided that council members of the Authors' League need not sign them. See Louise Sillcox to LH, June 7, 1950, box 53, folder 1, Lillian Hellman Collection, HRC.

57 Lillian Hellman, "Typescript: Swarthmore," April 6, 1950, box 43, folder 1, Lillian Hellman Collection, HRC. She repeated that theme a few years later, telling students at Smith and MIT that "We have lived through a period of great economic security, great social fear in which many of the values we relied on seem to melt before us. Fears began to show: fear of other countries fear of ourselves and our neighbors, and the discomforts and shame that comes with fears and the displacement of ordinary middle class values." (Lillian Hellman, "Typescript: Smith/MIT," April 15 and 18, 1955, box 43, folder 1, 8, Lillian Hellman Collection, HRC.)

58 FBI memo, undated, box 132, folder 4, Lillian Hellman Collection, HRC.

59 Ring Lardner Jr., *I'd Hate Myself in the Morning: A Memoir* (New York: Nation Books, 2000), 140.

60 LH to Ruth Shipley, July 13, 1951, box 72, folder 9, William Miller Abrahams Papers, SUL.

61 LH to Henry Beeson, August 16, 1951, box 133, folder 1, Lillian Hellman Collection, HRC.

62 Charlie Schwartz to LH, telegraph, August 15, 15 1951, box 53, folder 2, Lillian Hellman Collection, HRC.

63 Katherine Brown to LH, August 23, 1951, box 53, folder 2, Lillian Hellman Collection, HRC.

64 Elia Kazan, *Elia Kazan: A Life* (New York: Knopf, 1988), 460.

65 Ted O. Thackrey, "Miss Hellman's Answer," *New York Compass* (May 1952): 10.

66 Lillian Hellman, "Typescript: Harvard Lecture No. 1," Spring 1961, box 44, folder 6, 9, Lillian Hellman Collection, HRC.

67 Ibid., 9–10.

68 Lillian Hellman, random notes found in box 43, folder 5, Lillian Hellman Collection, HRC.

69 Typescript: FBI document, February 23, 1966, box 132, folder 5, Lillian Hellman Collection, HRC.

70 Lillian Hellman, *Scoundrel Time* (Boston: Little, Brown, 1976), 53.

71 Joseph Rauh to Lillian Hellman, July 6, 1976, box 71, "Lillian Hellman, 1974–76" folder, Joseph Rauh Papers, Part I, Manuscript Division, Library of Congress.

72 Rauh to LH, April 30, 1952, box 71, "Lillian Hellman, 1974–76" folder, Joseph Rauh Papers.

73 Rauh to Andrew Caploe, December 2, 1977, box 71, "Lillian Hellman, 1974–76" folder, Joseph Rauh Papers, LOC.

74 Ibid.

75 Daniel Pollitt, interview by author, February 6, 2007.

76 Joseph Rauh, memo, box 72, folder 9, William Miller Abrahams Papers, SUL.

77 Rauh to LH, April 30, 1952, box 124, folder 2, Lillian Hellman Collection, HRC.

78 Lillian Hellman, Typescript, "Statement by Miss Lillian Hellman (Draft)," April 28, 1952, box 124, folder 5, Lillian Hellman Collection, HRC.

79 Don Irwin, "Lillian Hellman Refuses to Say if She Was Red," *New York Herald Tribune* (May 22, 1952): 1.

80 "Hearings Before the Committee on Un-American Activities, House of Representatives," 82nd Congress, 2nd session, May 21, 1952 (Washington, DC: GPO, 1952), 3545.

81 Daniel Pollitt, interview by author, February 6, 2007.

82 "Hearings Before the Committee on Un-American Activities, House of Representatives," 82nd Congress, 2nd session, May 21, 1952 (Washington, DC: GPO, 1952), 3546.

83 "Lillian Hellman Balks House Unit," *New York Times* (May 22, 1952): 15.

84 Murray Kempton, "Portrait of a Lady," *New York Post* (May 26, 1952): 17.

85 Brooks Atkinson to LH, May 27, 1952, box 72, folder 9, William Miller Abrahams Papers, SUL.

86 LH to Bill Alfred, May 23, 1952, box 20, Papers of William Alfred, Brooklyn College Archives & Special Collections, Brooklyn College Library.

87 LH to John Melby, c. May 26, 1952, box 81, folder 7, Lillian Hellman Collection, HRC.

88 LH to Joe Rauh, May 29, 1952, box 72, folder 9, William Miller Abrahams Papers, SUL.

89 LH to Melby, c. May 1952, box 81, folder 7, Lillian Hellman Collection, HRC.

90 Ibid.

91 LH to Melby, c. August 1952, box 81, folder 7, Lillian Hellman Collection, HRC.

92 Reminiscences of Helen Van dernoot Rosen (1994), CCOH.

93 Newman, *The Cold War Romance*, 181–82, 209.

9. The Most Dangerous Hours

1 Austin Pendleton, interview by author, December 12, 2009.

2 LH to McGeorge Bundy, June 7, 1960, box 65, folder 3, Lillian Hellman Collection, Harry Ransom Center, University of Texas at Austin.

3 Lillian Hellman, "Typescript: Harvard Lecture No. 1," Spring 1961, box 44, folder 6, Lillian Hellman Collection, HRC.

4 Irving Howe, *A Margin of Hope: An Intellectual Biography* (New York: Harcourt Brace Jovanovich, 1982), 309–11.

5 Alan M. Wald, *The New York Intellectuals: The Rise and Decline of the Anti-Stalinist Left from the 1930s to the 1980s* (Chapel Hill: University of North Carolina Press, 1987), 311.

6 LH, Typescript, "Madison Square Garden McCarthy Rally," box 42, folder 17, 2, Lillian Hellman Collection, HRC.

7 Hellman commencement address, Mount Holyoke College, May 30, 1976, box 42, folder 9, 6, Lillian Hellman Collection, HRC.

8 Typescript notes, no date, box 42, folder 3, Lillian Hellman Collection, HRC.

9 Notebook titled "Notes for Sophronia's Grandson," box 42, folder 2, 2, 4–5, Lillian Hellman Collection, HRC.

10 Lillian Hellman, "Sophronia's Grandson Goes to Washington," *Ladies' Home Journal* (December 1963): 80; "Complaint, Dewey P. Colvard v The Curtis Publishing Company . . . and Lillian Hellman," box 109, folder 3, Lillian Hellman Collection, HRC.

11 Roy McCord's letter of December 18, 1963, the journal's retraction, and Hellman's statement are all in *Ladies' Home Journal* (March 1964): 82.

12 "Mrs. Cabell Outlaw of Mobile Alabama to Dear Editor," *Ladies Home Journal* (February 24, 1964), clipping in box 72, folder 5, Lillian Hellman Collection, HRC.

13 Unknown lawyer to LH, March 13, 1964, box 109, folder 5, Lillian Hellman Collection, HRC. See also letter from Mrs. Mary Hartay of Austin, Texas, *Ladies' Home Journal* (December 5, 1963).

14 Notes of interview with Senator Sparkman, no date, box 42, folder 3, Lillian Hellman Collection, HRC.

15 Typescript notes, untitled, no date, box 42, folder 3, Lillian Hellman Collection, HRC.

16 Seeger interviewed on the *Tavis Smiley Show*, WNYC, February 19, 2010. Thanks to Shayna Kessler for calling this to my attention.

17 Fred Gardner, interview by author, May 27, 2010.

18 Typescript, "Madison Square Garden McCarthy Rally."

19 Hellman speech to the National Book Awards in 1970 for *An Unfinished Woman*. As quoted in *Publishers Weekly* (March 23, 1970): 1.

20 Typescript, "Madison Square Garden McCarthy Rally."

21 The notion of a "moral beacon" comes from Wald, *The New York Intellectuals*, 311.

22 Catherine Kober Zeller, interview by author, November 19, 2010.

23 Untitled typescript, c. May 1967, box 43, folder 3, Lillian Hellman Collection, HRC.

24 Martin Arnold, "Lillian Hellman Says She Found Ferment Among Soviet Writers," *New York Times* (May 31, 1967): 11.

25 Lillian Hellman, "The Baggage of a Political Exile," *New York Times* (August 23, 1969): 26.

26 "A Letter to Anatoly Kuznetsov," *Time* (December 5, 1969): 49; "Talk of the Town," *New Yorker* (September 13, 1969): 21.

27 LH to William Shawn, September 16, 1969, box 42, folder 6, Lillian Hellman Collection, HRC.

28 Robert Lantz to Andrew Heiskell, December 8, 1969, box 42, folder 6, Lillian Hellman Collection, HRC.

29 LH to Charles Friedman, August 23, 1969, box 42, folder 6, Lillian Hellman Collection, HRC.

30 Anne Peretz, conversation with author, June 25, 2010.

31 Christine Doudna, "A Still Unfinished Woman: A Conversation with Lillian Hellman," *Rolling Stone* (February 24, 1977): 54.

32 Lillian Hellman, Introduction to *The Big Knockover* (New York: Random House, 1966), 5.

33 Reminiscences of Donald Angus Cameron (1977), on page 534 in the Columbia University Center for Oral History Collection.

34 Doudna, "A Still Unfinished Woman," 53.

35 William Abrahams to Arthur Thornhill Sr., March 17, 1969, box 50, folder 30, William Miller Abrahams Papers, M1125, Department of Special Collections, Stanford University Libraries, Standford, CA.

36 Philip French, "A Difficult Woman," *New Statesman* (October 24, 1969): 580.

37 Dorothy Rabinowitz, "Experience as Drama," *Commentary* 48 (December 1969): 95.

38 Michaela Williams, "Miss Hellman's Personal Fragments Merge into Personality of Beauty," *National Observer* (July 14, 1969): 91.

39 Robert Kotlowitz, "The Rebel as Writer," *Harper's* (June 1969): 92.

40 Christopher Lehmann-Haupt, "The Incompleat Lillian Hellman," *New York Times* (June 30, 1969): 37.

41 Stanley Young, "An Unfinished Woman" *New York Times Book Review* (June 29, 1969): 8. V. S. Pritchett, "Stern Self-Portait of a Lady," *Life* (June 27, 1969): 12.

42 Peter Feibleman, interview by author, August 4, 2002.

43 Hellman made these comments in early 1947 on the note cards she prepared for a lecture. In her own hand, she expressed her disappointment at "what the emancipation of woman has done to women." 1947, box 43, folder 2, Lillian Hellman Collection, HRC.

44 Lillian Hellman, "An Address by Lillian Hellman to the Women of America," February 10, 1948, pamphlet printed and distributed by the Wallace Campaign for President, box 43, folder 4, 2, Lillian Hellman Collection, HRC.

45 Note cards, box 46, folder 2, 6, Lillian Hellman Collection, HRC.

46 Irving Wardle, "On Not Falling Sadly Apart," *The Times Saturday Review* (October 18, 1969): 4.

47 Nora Ephron, "Lillian Hellman Walking, Cooking, Writing, Talking," in Jackson Bryer, ed., *Conversations with Lillian Hellman* (Jackson: University Press of Mississippi, 1986), 136.

48 Katherine Brown, "Talking with Lillian Hellman," *Family Circle* (April 1976): 24.

49 Hiram Haydn to LH, April 27, 1972, box 46, folder 1, Lillian Hellman Collection. HRC. Other participants included Ann Birstein, Nancy Wilson Ross, Norma Rosen, Renata Adler, Carolyn Heilbrun, Alice Walker, and Elizabeth Janeway.

50 American Scholar Forum, *American Scholar* 41 (Autumn 1972): 600, 601, 612, 614. On race differences, she added, "The upper-class lady, or the middle-class lady, has made out very well as the weaker and the more fragile of the pair, husband and wife. The lower-class lady—particularly American blacks, had to earn a living," 603.

51 Ibid., 617.

52 Anthony Gornall to Don Congdon, June 13, 1977, box 52, folder 1; Congdon to LH, July 22, 1982, box 52, folder 2, Lillian Hellman Collection, HRC.

53 Mount Holyoke College commencement address, 14–15.

54 Lillian Hellman, "For Truth, Justice and the American Way," *New York Times* (June 4, 1975): 39.

55 Gloria Emerson, "Lillian Hellman: At 66, She's Still Restless," *New York Times* (September 7, 1973): 24.

56 Lillian Hellman, interview by Barbara Walters, "Not for Women Only," NBC, April 1, 1976 box 31, folder 1, 2–3, Lillian Hellman Collection, HRC.

57 Ibid., 10

58 Lillian Hellman, interview by National Educational Television, April 9, 1974, box 31, folder 2, 9, Lillian Hellman Collection, HRC.

59 Ibid., 9.

60 Brown, "Talking with Lillian Hellman," 24.

61 See, for example, Morris Dickstein, *Gates of Eden: American Culture in the Sixties* (New York: Basic Books, 1977); Maurice Isserman and Michael Kazin, *America Divided: The Cold War of the 1960s*, 2nd ed. (New York: Oxford University Press, 2004).

62 Robert Silvers, speech, October 22, 1978, box 42, folder 19, Lillian Hellman Collection, HRC.

63 LH to Telford Taylor, April 30, 1970, *Telford Taylor Papers*, Arthur W. Diamond Law Library, Columbia University, NY (TTP-CLS: 11-0-8-108).

64 Roger Wilkins, "To Fight for Freedom" *New York Times* (December 22, 1970): 33.

65 Burke Marshall to "Dear Friend," May 25, 1970, TTP-CLS: 11-0-8-108.

66 Typescript, "Statement of Purpose of Citizen Group," TTP-CLS: 11-0-8-108.

67 By the early 1970s, the letterhead carried such names as labor leaders Leonard Woodcock, Moe Foner, and Adam Yarmolinsky; social and natural scientists C. Vann Woodward, Robert Coles, Arthur Schlesinger Jr., Barry

Commoner, and James Watson; military experts General David Schoup and George Kistiaskowsky; businessman Harold Willens; Mrs. Marshall (Ruth) Field; and department-store heiress Elinor Gimbel.

68 Leon Friedman, interview by author, June 3, 2007.

69 Telford Taylor to Thomas Eliot, Dec 23, 1970, TTP- CLS: 11-0-8-108.

70 Stephen Gillers, interview by author, October 12, 2007.

71 Norman Dorsen and Roger Wilkins, "Memorandum," June 19, 1970, TTP-CLS: 11-0-8-108.

72 LH to Telford Taylor, June 23, 1970, TTP-CLS: 11-0-8-108.

73 Frances X. Clines, "F.B.I. Head Scored by Ramsey Clark," *New York Times* (November 18, 1970): 48. Clark had previously published a book in which he described FBI director J. Edgar Hoover as having "a self-centered concern for his own reputation."

74 Karl Meyer, "Clark Scores FBI Over 'Ideology,' Lack of Diversity," *Washington Post* (November 18, 1970): A3.

75 M.A. Jones to Mr. Bishop, FBI memorandum, "Members of the Committee for Public Justice," November 19, 1970, box 75, folder 2, William Miller Abrahams Papers, SUL. Guilt by association still remained a key tool in the FBI's arsenal. Jerome Wiesner, for example, was acknowledged to be an "internationally known scientist," but the file noted among other things that "Several of his associates at MIT were publicly identified as having been affiliated with the CP." Harold Willins was said to have signed a petition "appealing for executive clemency for Morris U. Schappes, Communist party member convicted of perjury." That all these people were associated with Hellman in the CPJ was, of course, another mark against them.

76 Ibid.

77 "Panel Announces Inquiry into FBI," *Chicago Tribune* (April 28, 1971): 6.

78 Robert M. Smith, "Hoover, in an Unusual Letter, Defends Operation of F.B.I.," *New York Times* (Oct 17, 1971): 1.

79 J. Edgar Hoover to Duane Lockard, October 7, 1971, as reproduced in Pat Watters and Stephen Gillers, eds., *Investigating the FBI: A Tough, Fair Look at the Powerful Bureau, Its Present and Its Future* (Garden City, NY: Doubleday, 1973), 466–67. The press summarized the FBI's stance as dismissive, repeating Hoover's position that "If the FBI responded every time it was attacked somewhere, it would not have time to go about its normal business." See "Hoover Defends FBI in a Letter," *Chicago Tribune* (October 17, 1971): 9.

80 Tom Wicker, Introduction to Watters and Gillers, eds., *Investigating the FBI*, xiv.

81 Watters and Gillers, *Investigating the FBI*, 477.

82 Allan C. Brownfield, "F.B.I. Under Increasing Attack," *Roll Call* (November

18, 1971). Brownfield suggested that the conference's bias was illustrated by its effort to disguise the true identities of participants. The executive council of the CPJ, he reported, consisted of people like Ramsey Clark, known for his long-standing hostility to Hoover, Lillian Hellman, "who has for years refused to answer questions about her involvement with the Communist Party," and Burke Marshall, "who was one of the first to rush to Chappaquiddick in an effort to assist his old friend, Edward Kennedy." Martin Peretz, Brownfield pointed out, was a member of the CPJ to be sure, but he had also served on the executive board of the National Conference for New Politics ... which collaborated with the Communist Party, U.S.A. (Peretz subsequently became owner of the *New Republic*, and much more conservative) in a 1967 Chicago convention. Brownfield sent the piece to Hoover, who consulted with advisers as to whether to respond. They advised against it after investigating his background. See G.E. Malmfeldt to Mr. Bishop, November 26, 1971, microfilm, FBI file on the CPJ (Wilmington, DE: Scholarly Resources, 1984). Thanks to Leon Friedman, for providing much of this information.

83 Jack Nelson and Bryce Nelson, "Zimbalist, Two Others Open Drive to Back FBI," *Los Angeles Times* (June 15, 1971): 17. See also Robert M. Smith, "Friends of FBI in a Fund Appeal," *New York Times* (July 21, 1971): 20.

84 This material provided by Leon Friedman and acknowledged with thanks.

85 Ken W. Clawson, "Monetary Support Is Abundant," *Washington Post and Times Herald* (October 30, 1971): A2.

86 "Speakers Hit Bureau's Power" *Washington Post and Times Herald* (October 30, 1971): A2.

87 Robert Smith, "The FBI Agrees to Hear Its Chief Critic," *New York Times* (June 7, 1972): 17.

88 Tom Wicker, "A Battle Congress Could Win," *New York Times* (April 5, 1973): 45.

89 Typescript, "Grand Jury Project," December 10, 1971, TTP-CLS: 11-0-8-108.

90 Lesley Oelsner, "Grand Jury System Is Assailed Here," *New York Times* (May 1, 1972): 23.

91 *New York* (October 22, 1973): 36–37.

92 "Lillian Hellman Keynotes CIA meeting," *CPJ Newsletter*, June 1975, box 51, folder 11, Lillian Hellman Collection, HRC. Early in 1975, Senator Frank Church launched a series of senatorial investigations into the domestic activities of the CIA. Arguable the CPJ catalyzed these.

93 Typescript of call for funds, February 8, 1978, courtesy of Leon Friedman, private collection.

94 "Bill to Bar FBI Wiretaps, Curb Probes Unveiled," *Los Angeles Times* (February 15, 1977): A2.

95 James Lardner, "Lillian Hellman, Writer," *Washington Post* (July 1, 1984): 67.

96 See for example, "Lillian Hellman—Above the Fuss," *San Francisco Chronicle* (November 14, 1975): 37.

97 Leon Friedman and Stephen Gillers, executive directors of the CPJ, agree on this point, as does chair of the Executive Council, Norman Dorsen. See interviews of Leon Friedman, Norman Dorsen, and Stephen Gillers by author.

98 William Wright, *Lillian Hellman: The Image, the Woman* (New York: Simon and Schuster, 1986), 339.

10. Liar, Liar

1 Lillian Hellman, *Pentimento* (Boston: Little, Brown, 1973), 23.

2 Lillian Hellman, "Typescript: Harvard Lecture No. 1, Spring 1961, box 44, folder 6, 4, Lillian Hellman Collection, Harry Ransom Center, University of Texas at Austin.

3 Typescript of reading, University of Michigan, April 1960, box 43, folder 2, 1, Lillian Hellman Collection, HRC.

4 Hellman, "Typescript: Harvard Lecture No. 1, Spring 1961, box 44, folder 6, 2–3, Lillian Hellman Collection, HRC.

5 Dan Rather, "An Interview with Lillian Hellman" in Jackson Breyer, ed., *Conversations with Lillian Hellman* (Jackson, MS: University Press of Mississippi, 1986), 298.

6 Christine Doudna, "A Still Unfinished Woman: A Conversation with Lillian Hellman," *Rolling Stone* (February 27, 1977): 55.

7 LH to Diane Johnson, October 11, 1978, box 72, folder 1, William Miller Abrahams Papers, M1125, Department of Special Collections, Stanford University Libraries, Stanford, CA.

8 Hellman, "Typescript, Harvard Lecture No. 1," box 44, folder 6, Lillian Hellman Collection, HRC.

9 Lillian Hellman, "The Time of the Foxes," *New York Times* (October 22, 1967): 117.

10 James Lardner, "Lillian Hellman, Writer," *Washington Post* (July 1, 1984): 67.

11 Doudna, "A Still Unfinished Woman," 55.

12 Doris Lessing, *Under My Skin: Volume One of My Autobiography, to 1949* (New York: Harper Collins, 1994).

13 Lillian Hellman to William Abrahams, June 30, 1971, box 51, folder 12, William Miller Abrahams Papers, SUL.

14 Hellman, *Pentimento*, 3.

15 LH to Donald Erickson, May 23, 1973, box 124, folder 1, Lillian Hellman Collection, HRC.

16 Hellman, *Pentimento*, 10

17 Lardner, "Lillian Hellman, Writer," 67.

18 Mark Schorer, "Pentimento," *New York Times Book Review* (September 23, 1973): 1. The word *honest* comes from James Walt, "An Honest Memoir," *New Republic* (October 20, 1973): 27.

19 John Leonard, "1973: An Apology and 38 Consolations," *New York Times Book Review* (December 2, 1973,): 2; Peter Prescott, "Leftover Life," *Newsweek* (October 1, 1973): 95.

20 Edward Grossman, "Pentimento by Lillian Hellman," *Commentary* 57 (1974): 88.

21 Martha Duffy, "Half-Told Tales," *Time* (October 1, 1973): 116.

22 Hellman, *Pentimento*, 153

23 Ibid., 225

24 Schorer, "Pentimento," 1.

25 Christopher Lehmann-Haupt, "Seeing Others to See Oneself," *New York Times* (September 17, 1973): 31L.

26 Muriel Haynes, "More on the Unfinished Woman," *Ms.* (January 1974): 33.

27 Louise Knight, "Sibling Rivalry: History and Memoir," *Women's Review of Books* 24 (July/August 2007): 12–13.

28 Richard Eder, "Down the Rabbit Hole in a Story Book Memoir," *New York Times* (December 12, 2006).

29 Joel Agee, "A Lie that Tells the Truth," *Harper's* (November 2007): 53, 57. Daniel Kornstein put it this way: "The facts could be lies, but the book could be true. Truth can emerge from a context of untruths, just as it does in fiction." Daniel J. Kornstein, "The Case Against Lillian Hellman: A Literary/Legal Defense," *Fordham Law Review* 57 (April 1989): 692.

30 John Simon, "Pentimental Journey," *Hudson Review* 26 (Winter 1974): 748. At the end of the piece, Simon reveals that he had an axe to grind, concerning a brief unpleasant encounter he had had with Hellman when he was still a student.

31 Lardner, "Lillian Hellman, Writer," 67.

32 Bill Moyers, "Lillian Hellman: The Great Playwright Candidly Reflects on a Long Rich Life," in Bryer, ed., *Conversations*, 154.

33 Hellman, *Pentimento*, 224–5.

34 Nora Ephron, "Walking, Cooking," Writing, Talking," *New York Times Book Review* (September 23, 1973): 2.

35 Hellman, *Pentimento*, 225.

36 Peter Feibleman, interview by author, August 4, 2002.

37 Lillian Hellman, *Scoundrel Time* (Boston: Little, Brown, 1976), 39.

38 Rex Reed, *Valentines and Vitriol* (New York: Delacorte Press, 1977), 104–05.

39 Mel Gussow, "For Lillian Hellman, More Honors and a New Book," *New York Times* (November 7, 1975): 28.

40 Hellman, *Pentimento*, 225.

41 Ephron, "Walking, Cooking," 2.

42 Hellman, *Scoundrel Time*, 35, 38, 39, 82, 149.

43 Paul Gray, "An Unfinished Woman," *Time* (May 10, 1976): 83.

44 Robert Coles, "The Literary Scene," *Washington Post Book World* (May 17, 1966): 32.

45 Typescript of BBC interview with Philip French, "Critics Forum," Radio 3, June 11, 1976, box 19, folder 2, William Miller Abrahams Papers, SUL.

46 Murray Kempton, "Witnesses," *New York Review of Books* (June 10, 1976): 22–25.

47 Exchange of letters, LH to Ephraim London, May 3, 1976; LH to Joseph Consolino, May 5, 1976, both in box 32, folder 6; Ephraim London to Joseph Consolino, May 10, 1976, box 32, folder 4, Lillian Hellman Collection, HRC.

48 William F. Buckley Jr., "Who Is the Ugliest of Them All?" *National Review* (January 21, 1977): 105

49 I am indebted to Bert Silverman for these insights. On the seventies, see also Judith Stein, *Pivotal Decade, How the U.S. Traded Factories for Finance in the Seventies* (New Haven, CT: Yale, 2010); Jefferson Cowie, *Stayin' Alive: The 1970s and the Last Days of the Working Class* (New York: New Press, 2010); Natasha Zaretsky, *No Direction Home: The American Family and the Fear of National Decline* (Chapel Hill: University of North Carolina Press, 2007).

50 Nathan Glazer, "An Answer to Lillian Hellman," *Commentary* (June 1976): 36–39.

51 Catherine Kober Zeller, interview by author, November 19, 2010.

52 Hellman, *Scoundrel Time*, 150.

53 Sidney Hook, "Lillian Hellman's Scoundrel Time," *Encounter* 48 (February 1977): 86, 82–91.

54 Ibid., 88.

55 William Appleman Williams, *The Shaping of American Diplomacy: Readings and Documents in American Foreign Relations* (New York: Rand McNally, 1956); Lloyd Gardner, *The Origins of the Cold War* (Waltham, MA: Ginn-Baisdell, 1970);

Gabriel Kolko, *The Roots of American Foreign Policy: An Analysis of Power and Purpose* (Boston: Beacon Press, 1969).

56 Nathan Glazer, "An Answer to Lillian Hellman," 36–39.

57 Richard A. Falk, "Comment: Scoundrel Time," *Performing Arts Journal* 1 (Winter 1977): 97.

58 Hilton Kramer, "The Blacklist and the Cold War," *New York Times* (October 3, 1976): 1, 16, 17. Kramer preceded this comment with one that declared *Scoundrel Time* "as much a part of this re-examination of the 1960s . . . as they are an attempt to redraw the history of an earlier era along lines—often alas, fictional lines—that are sympathetic to the present climate of liberal opinion."

59 Arthur M. Schlesinger's letter appeared among others from Alfred Kazin, Eric Foner, Bruce Cook, and Michael Meeropol, *New York Times* (October 17, 1977): 12.

60 LH to Arthur Schlesinger Jr., no date, Arthur Schlesinger Jr. Papers, Manuscripts and Archives Division, the New York Public Library, Astor, Lenox and Tilden Foundations. Schlesinger's reply, dated October 20, 1976, acknowledges their political differences and claims that they have never mattered because they are "such an inferior part of life that the more important things survive political disagreements." He continues, "Though you may now hate me, I will continue to regard you with unrelenting affection and admiration for your charm, wit, inexorable human dignity and the passion that has produced so much including, I suppose, your letter to me."

61 Arthur Schlesinger to Joseph Rauh, October 22, 1976, box 72, folder 10, William Miller Abrahams Papers, SUL.

62 These arguments were well captured and expressed by Melvin J. Lasky, "Left-Wing America's Martyr-in-Waiting," *Encounter* (June 11, 1976): 56.

63 Ibid.

64 Sidney Hook to Norman Podhoretz, May 5, 1976, box 78, folder 19, Sidney Hook Collection, Hoover Institution Archives, Stanford University.

65 Buckley, "Who Is the Ugliest of Them All?" 105.

66 William Phillips, *A Partisan View: Five Decades of the Literary Life* (New York: Stein and Day, 1983), 174–75.

67 Buckley, "Who Is the Ugliest of them All?" 104.

68 Walter Goodman, "Fair Game" *New Leader* 59 (May 24, 1976): 10. See also Walter Goodman, *The Committee* (New York: Farrar, Straus, 1968)

69 Kempton, "Witnesses," 22.

70 William F. Buckley Jr., "Night of the Cuckoo with Fonda, Hellman," *St. Louis Globe-Democrat* (April 4, 1977): 11.

71 Hellman, *Scoundrel Time*, 81. A lengthy correspondence between the

Trillings and Lillian extending from the mid-sixties to the mid-seventies testifies to the friendship. See also Lionel Trilling Papers, box 3, Rare Book and Manuscript Library, Columbia University, New York, NY.

72 Diana Trilling, *We Must March, My Darlings: A Critical Decade* (New York: Houghton Mifflin, 1977), 41.

73 Diana Trilling to LH, October 8, 1976, box 32, folder 7, Lillian Hellman Collection, HRC.

74 Robert McFadden, "Diana Trilling Book Is Canceled," *New York Times* (September 28, 1976): 1; Little, Brown's executive director, Arthur Thornhill, confirms the story—taking full responsibility for the decision to ask Trilling to withdraw the offending words. See Roger Donald to Lillian Hellman, December 10, 1976, box 32, folder 4, Lillian Hellman Collection, HRC.

75 Michiko Kakutani, "Diana Trilling: Pathfinder in Morality," *New York Times* (November 16, 1981): C13.

76 Rose Styron, interview by author, August 17, 2010; Annabel Davis-Goff, interview by author, September 2, 2010.

77 Greil Marcus, "Undercover: Remembering the Witch Hunts," *Rolling Stone* (May 20, 1976): 97.

78 Buckley, "Who Is the Ugliest of Them All?" 101.

79 Alfred Kazin, "The Legend of Lillian Hellman," *Esquire* 88 (August 1977): 28.

80 Buckley, "Who Is the Ugliest of Them All?" 101.

81 Lasky, "Left-Wing America's Martyr-in-Waiting."

82 Kempton, "Witnesses," 2.

83 Walter Goodman, "Fair Game," *New Leader* 59 (May 24, 1976): 10.

84 Kazin, *New York Jew* (New York: Knopf, 1978), 30.

85 Hellman, *Scoundrel Time*, 39

86 Mary Geisheker, "The Worst of Times," *Baltimore Sun* (April 25, 1976): D1.

87 LH to William Schmick Jr., May 7, 1976, box 124, folder 1, Lillian Hellman Collection, HRC.

88 LH to George Will, April 18, 1978, box 77, folder 7, Lillian Hellman Collection, HRC.

89 Lillian Hellman, "On Reading Again," in *Three: An Unfinished Woman, Pentimento, Scoundrel Time* (Boston: Little, Brown, 1978), 9.

90 Ibid., 9.

91 Lillian Hellman, *Maybe: A Story* (New York: Little, Brown, 1980), 51.

92 This story comes from Dick Cavett, "Lillian, Mary, and Me," *New Yorker* (December 16, 2002): 35.

93 Transcript of interview with Dick Cavett, October 17 and 18, 1979, box 258, 50, Mary McCarthy Collection, Vassar College Library.

94 Cavett, "Lillian, Mary, and Me," 36.

95 Ann Terry, typescript "notes and comments," October 16, 1979, box 258, Cavett folder, Mary McCarthy Collection, VCL. McCarthy, at her deposition, testified that she could, "not recall having agreed to respond to this question." Deposition of Defendant Mary McCarthy West, August 12, 1981, *Hellman v McCarthy et al.*, Supreme Court of the State of New York, Index # 16834/80, 12.

96 Nan Robertson, "McCarthy Mellows as an Expatriate in Paris," *New York Times* (July 31, 1979): C5.

97 Each also had a somewhat complicated relationship to their Jewish heritage. McCarthy's grandmother on her mother's side was born Jewish, a fact that McCarthy only belatedly and uncomfortably acknowledged. Note the number of references to Jews in McCarthy's *How I Grew* (New York: Harcourt Brace Jovanovich, 1987), 45; *On the Contrary* (New York: Farrar, Straus and Cudahy, 1951), 66–67; and *Intellectual Memoirs: New York, 1936–1938* (New York: Harcourt Brace, 1992), 60.

98 Mary McCarthy, *How I Grew*, 1; Nan Robertson, "McCarthy Mellows," C5.

99 Richard Poirier, interview by author, May 24, 2005.

100 Mary McCarthy on *North Star* in *Town and Country* (April 1944): 72, 12; Mary McCarthy, "The Reform of Dr. Pangloss," *New Republic* (December 17, 1956): 30–31.

101 Mary McCarthy review of O'Neill's *The Iceman Cometh* in *Partisan Review* (November/December 1946): 577.

102 Mary McCarthy, *Intellectual Memoirs*, 60; Typescript, "Lillian Hellman's Comments on Mary McCarthy's Answers to Plaintiff's First Interrogatories," December 8, 1980, box 78, folder 4/5, 7, Lillian Hellman Collection, HRC.

103 McCarthy's version of this story is in Joan Dupont, "Mary McCarthy: Portrait of a Lady," *Paris Metro* (February 15, 1978): 15–16.

104 Typescript, "Lillian Hellman's Comments on Mary McCarthy's Answers," 8.

105 Stephen Spender to LH, September 15, 1983, box 259, Spender file, Mary McCarthy Collection, VCL.

106 LH to William Alfred, August 19, 1963, The Papers of William Alfred, Brooklyn College Archives & Special Collections, Brooklyn College Library.

107 Dupont, "Mary McCarthy: Portrait of a Lady," 16.

108 LH to Ephraim London, December 10, 1980, box 78, folder 4/5, Lillian Hellman Collection, HRC.

109 Hellman never much liked Hardwick, referring to her as "Madam" in her letters to Lowell.

110 Arien Mack, interview by author, June 10, 2010.

111 Typescript, "Lillian Hellman's Comments on Mary McCarthy's Answers," 10.

112 This history is recounted by Javsicas in a letter to Mary McCarthy, October 28, 1979, just a few days after she taped the Cavett interview. It is one of a long series of letters, all of them in the Javsicas file, folder 203.7, Mary McCarthy Collection, VCL.

113 Gabriel Javsicas to Nancy MacDonald (punctuation and spelling corrected), November 10, 1978, Spanish Refugee Aid Collection, Tamiment Library/Robert F. Wagner Labor Archives, New York University Libraries, New York, NY. The reference to censorship concerns the Diana Trilling controversy.

114 Nancy MacDonald to Dearest Gabriel, November 4, 1978, Spanish Refugee Aid Collection, TL.

115 Mary McCarthy to Nancy MacDonald, Nov 28, 1978, Spanish Refugee Aid Collection, TL.

116 Gabriel Javsicas to Nancy MacDonald, June 26, 1979, Spanish Refugee Aid Collection, TL.

117 Mary McCarthy to Javsicas, October 10, 1979, Spanish Refugee Aid Collection, TL.

118 Mary McCarthy to Javsicas, December 18, 1979, Spanish Refugee Aid Collection, TL.

119 Mary McCarthy to Carol Gelderman, November 12, 1980, box 259, Gelderman file, Mary McCarthy Collection, VCL.

120 Lardner, "Lillian Hellman, Writer," 67.

121 Mary McCarthy to Ben O'Sullivan, August 23, 1980, box 259, O'Sullivan file, Mary McCarthy Collection, VCL.

122 Mary McCarthy to Carol Gelderman, November 12, 1980, box 259, Gelderman file, Mary McCarthy Collection, VCL.

123 These and more details in Carol Gelderman to Mary McCarthy, February 6, 1981, Box 259, Gelderman file, Mary McCarthy Collection, VCL.

124 Carol Gelderman to Mary McCarthy, February 6, 1981, box 259, Gelderman File, Mary McCarthy Collection, VCL.

125 Mary McCarthy, *Memories of a Catholic Girlhood* (New York: Harvest Books, 1972), 11

126 Mary McCarthy to Mrs. Hale, August 18, 1980, Hale file, box 259, Mary McCarthy Collection, VCL.

127 William F. Buckley Jr., "The Honor of Lillian Hellman and her pro-Stalin Past," *New York Post* (May 22, 1980).

128 Mary McCarthy to Cleo Paturis, June 19, 1981, box 259, Paturis file, Mary McCarthy Collection, VCL.

129 Lillian Hellman, "Baggage of a Political Exile," *New York Times* (August 23, 1969): 26.

130 Mary McCarthy to Walter Goldwater, August 7, 1980, Goldwater file, box 259, Mary McCarthy Collection, VCL. Mary McCarthy made inquiries to this effect to James Angleton, a former CIA agent. Angleton had no information that would confrm her suspicions. Mary McCarthy to Ben O'Sullivan, box 259, O'Sullivan file, Mary McCarthy Collection, VCL.

131 Robert M. Kaus, "The Plaintiff's Hour," *Harper's* (March 1983): 14.

132 Mary McCarthy to Ben O'Sullivan, August 23, 1980, box 259, O'Sullivan file, Mary McCarthy Collection, VCL.

133 Mary McCarthy to Ben O'Sullivan, November 29, 1980, box 259, O'Sullivan file, Mary McCarthy Collection, VCL.

134 Diana Trilling to Bill Jovanovich, November 16, 1980, box 259, O'Sullivan files, Mary McCarthy Collection, VCL.

135 Cleo Paturis to Mary McCarthy, c. June, 1981, and Mary McCarthy reply, June 19, 1981, box 259, Paturis file, Mary McCarthy Collection, VCL. Paturis was the wife of James Farrell.

136 Martha Gellhorn to Mary McCarthy, August 15, 1980, box 259, Gellhorn file, Mary McCarthy Collection, VCL.

137 Martha Gellhorn to Mary McCarthy, August 30, 1980, box 259, Gellhorn file, Mary McCarthy Collection, VCL.

138 Martha Gellhorn to Mary McCarthy, September 25, 1980, box 259, Gellhorn file, Mary McCarthy Collection, VCL.

139 Martha Gellhorn to Mary McCarthy, May 29, 1981, box 259, Gellhorn file, Mary McCarthy Collection, VCL.

140 Raisa Orlova, *Memoirs* (New York: Random House, 1983), 117.

141 Martha Gellhorn to Mary McCarthy, August 30, 1980, box 259, Gellhorn file, Mary McCarthy Collection, VCL.

142 Martha Gellhorn to Mary McCarthy, May 29, 1981, box 259, Gellhorn file, Mary McCarthy Collection, VCL.

143 Mary McCarthy to Robert Silvers, February 27, 1981, box 259, Silvers file, Mary McCarthy Collection, VCL.

144 Martha Gellhorn to Mary McCarthy, May 29, 1981, box 259, Gellhorn file, Mary McCarthy Collection, VCL.

145 Stephen Spender, "Stephen Spender Replies," *Paris Review* 79 (1981): 304-7.

146 Stephen Spender, *Journals 1939-1983*, ed. John Goldsmith (New York: Random House, 1986), 482-83. On the subject of both McCarthy and Hellman lying see Timothy Dow Adams, *Telling Lies in Modern American Autobiography* (Chapel Hill: University of North Carolina Press, 1990), chs. 5 and 6.

147 Mary McCarthy to Walter Goldwater, August 7, 1980, box 259, Goldwater file, Mary McCarthy Collection, VCL.

148 Mary McCarthy to Charles Collingwood, September 20, 1980, box 259, Collingwood file, Mary McCarthy Collection, VCL.

149 Martha Gellhorn to Mary McCarthy, May 29, 1981, box 259, Gellhorn file, Mary McCarthy Collection, VCL.

150 Doudna, "A Still Unfinished Woman," 55. In an odd coincidence, Gardiner was married for many years to Joseph Buttinger, a leader of the Austrian socialists and a generous funder of Irving Howe's *Dissent* magazine. Presumably, Howe did not need another reason to dislike Hellman, but his relationship with the Buttingers surely provided one. See Irving Howe, *Margin of Hope: An Intellectual Biography* (New York: Harcourt Brace Jovanovich, 1982), 235.

151 Marilyn Berger, "Profile: Lillian Hellman," in Breyer, ed., *Conversations*, 238.

152 Mary McCarthy to Walter Goldwater, August 7, 1980, box 259, Goldwater file, Mary McCarthy Collection, VCL.

153 Muriel Gardiner, *Code Name "Mary": Memoirs of an American Woman in the Austrian Underground* (New Haven, CT: Yale University Press, 1983), xv.

154 LH to George Gero, May 4, 1983, box 77, folder 7, Lillian Hellman Collection, HRC.

155 LH to George Gero, May 27, 1983, box 77, folder 7, Lillian Hellman Collection, HRC.

156 LH to Ephraim London, May 27, 1983, box 77, folder 77, 7, Lillian Hellman Collection, HRC. Anne Peretz, interview by author, August 31, 2010.

157 Alex Szogyi, "Lillian," *Hunter College Magazine* (July 1985): 27.

158 Sam Jaffe to LH, August 12, 1980, box 78, folder 5, Lillian Hellman Collection, HRC.

159 Norman Mailer to Richard Poirier, June 16, 1980; copied to McCarthy, Locke, William Phillips, Silvers, and Steven Marcus, among others, box 78, folder 5, Lillian Hellman Collection, HRC.

160 LH to Norman Mailer, July 5, 1980, box 78, folder 5, Lillian Hellman Collection, HRC.

161 Barbara Epstein to LH, December 1, 1980, box 78, folder 5, Lillian Hellman Collection, HRC.

162 LH to Mrs. Victor Pritchett, September 14, 1981, box 132, folder 2, Lillian Hellman Collection, HRC.

163 Robert Silvers to Mary McCarthy, March 10, 1981, box 259, Silvers File, Mary McCarthy Collection, VCL.

164 Elizabeth Hardwick to Mary McCarthy, September 5, 1980, box 259, Hardwick folder, Mary McCarthy Collection, VCL.

165 Bill Alfred to LH, October 8, 1980, box 78, folder 4/5, Lillian Hellman Collection, HRC.

166 LH to Bill Alfred, November 3, 1980, Papers of William Alfred, BCASC.

167 William Styron to LH, April 2, 1980; LH to William Styron, April 9, 1980, box 78, folder 4/5, Lillian Hellman Collection, HRC.

168 Cavett, "Lillian, Mary, and Me," 36.

169 LH to Bill Alfred, November 3, 1980, Papers of William Alfred, BCASC.

170 Mary McCarthy to Ben O'Sullivan, July 13, 1982, box 259, O'Sullivan file, Mary McCarthy Collection, VCL.

171 George Trow to "Dear Lillie pie," no date, box 78, folder 5, Lillian Hellman Collection, HRC.

172 LH to Ephraim London, November 5, 1981, box 77, folder 7, Lillian Hellman Collection, HRC.

173 Martha Gellhorn to Mary McCarthy, May 29, 1981, box 259, Gellhorn file, Mary McCarthy Collection, VCL.

174 LH to Stephen Spender, August 4, 1983, box 77, folder 7, Lillian Hellman Collection, HRC.

175 Stephen Spender to LH, August 19, 1983, and September 15, 1983, box 259, Spender file, Mary McCarthy Collection, VCL.

176 Charles Collingwood to Mary McCarthy, September 26, 1980, box 259, Collingwood file, Mary McCarthy Collection, VCL.

177 Burke Marshall to LH, August 18, 1983, box 77, folder 7, Lillian Hellman Collection, HRC.

178 Marcia Chambers, "Lillian Hellman Wins Round in Suit," *New York Times* (May 11, 1984): C3.

179 Deposition of Defendant Mary McCarthy West, 42–43.

180 Chambers, "Lillian Hellman Wins," C3.

11. Life After Death

1 Hellman diaries, box 115, "California, 1980, Feb 1–March" folder, Lillian Hellman Collection, Harry Ransom Center, University of Texas at Austin.

2 Kristin von Kreisler-Bomben, "Lillian Hellman: from Sickbed to Center Stage," *San Rafael Independent* (February 25, 1980): 1.

3 Lillian Hellman, *Three: An Unfinished Woman, Pentimento, Scoundrel Time* (Boston: Little, Brown, 1978), 724–26

4 Kay Boyle to Jessica Mitford, February 24, 1980; and Kay Boyle to William Abrahams, February 24, 1980, both in box 17:1, William Miller Abrahams

Papers, M1125, Department of Special Collections, Stanford University Libraries, Stanford, CA.

5 Annabel Davis-Goff, interview by author, September 2, 2010.

6 Robin to Rita Wade, January 27, 1982; Maryellen to Rita, January 14, 1983; box 47:10, Lillian Hellman Collection, HRC.

7 Robert Brustein, "Epilogue to Anger: Lillian Hellman's" (August 13, 1984): 23.

8 Peter Feibleman, funeral speech, "Lillian Hellman, 1905–1984," box 5, folder 12, Arthur Thornhill Collection, Seeley Mudd Library, Princeton University.

9 Robert Brustein, "Epilogue to Anger," 23.

10 John Hersey, funeral speech, "Lillian Hellman, 1905–1984," box 5, folder 12, Arthur Thornhill Collection, SML.

11 Rose Styron, interview by author, August 17, 2010.

12 William Styron, funeral speech, in "Lillian Hellman, 1905–1984," box 5, folder 12, Arthur Thornhill Collection, SML.

13 Ibid.

14 Alex Szogyi, "Lillian," *Hunter College Magazine* (July 1985): 27.

15 Helen Dudar, "Shaping a Portrait of a Playwright," *New York Times* (January 24, 1986): Arts Section, 1.

16 Zoe Caldwell, interview by author, September 24, 2010.

17 Undated and unnamed lists, box 47, folder 10; Maryellen to Rita Wade, January 14, 1983, box 47, folder 10, Lillian Hellman Collection, HRC.

18 Patricia Neal, funeral speech, "Lillian Hellman, 1905–1984," box 5, folder 12, Arthur Thornhill Collection, SML.

19 William Styron, funeral speech.

20 Peter Feibleman, funeral speech.

21 Leo O'Neill to William Abrahams, June 25, 1984, box 71, folder 6, William Miller Abrahams Papers, SUL.

22 Warren Fugitt to William Abrahams, June 27, 1984, box 71:6, William Miller Abrahams Papers, SUL.

23 Walter Sheldon to William Abrahams, June 25, 1984, box 71, folder 6, William Miller Abrahams Papers, SLU.

24 Samuel McCracken, "'Julia' and Other Fictions by Lillian Hellman," *Commentary* (June 1984): 35–43.

25 Christopher Hitchens, "American Notes," *Times Literary Suplement* (July 6, 1984): 754.

26 Richard Bernstein, "Critics Notebook: An Unfinished Reputation: Reassessing Lillian Hellman," *New York Times* (November 12, 1998): sec. E, 2.

27 Herbie French to Sidney Hook, July 1, 1984, box 174, folder 17, Sidney Hook Collection, Hoover Institution Archives, Stanford University.

28 See, for example, Ralph Melnick, *The Stolen Legacy of Anne Frank: Meyer Levin, Lillian Hellman and the Staging of the Diary* (New Haven, CT: Yale University Press, 1997), 34; Frances Kiernan, "New York Observed; In the Court of Memory," *New York Times* (November 24, 2002). See also George Shadroui, "Are the National Book Awards Biased in Favor of Liberals?" Front Page Mag .com (March 5, 2004), which simply attaches the adjective *communist* to Hellman's name.

29 A 2011 production of the story of Meyer Levin and *The Diary of Anne Frank* makes exactly this point. See Rinne Groff, *Compulsion*, mounted at the Public Theater, New York, February 17, 2011.

30 Carl Rollyson, "The Lives and Lies of Lillian Hellman," *New York Sun* (November 25, 2005): 5.

31 "Last Will and Testament of Lillian Hellman," 13, provided by Peter Stansky.

32 Michael Davies, "The Life and Lies of Lillian Hellman," *Observer* (October 26, 1986): 64.

33 William F. Buckley Jr., "Viewpoints," *Dallas Morning News* (October 19, 1992): 17A.

34 Elia Kazan, *Elia Kazan: A Life* (New York: Knopf, 1988), 460

35 William Wright, "Stage View," *New York Times* (November 3, 1996): sec H, 9.

36 Phyllis Jacobson, "Two Invented Lives: Hellman and Hammett by Joan Mellen," *New Politics* 6 (Summer 1997).

37 Kazan, *A Life*, 462.

38 Wright, "Stage View."

39 Kazan, *A Life*, 324–25.

40 Ibid., 382.

41 Stanley Hart, "Lillian Hellman and Others," *Sewanee Review* 107 (Summer 1999): 402.

42 William E. Sarmento, "'Lillian' Is a Tour de force," *Lowell Sun* (January 31, 1986): 4.

43 Kazan, *A Life*, 382.

44 Zoe Caldwell, interview by author, September 24, 2010.

45 Letters (October 29, 1985, November 11, 1985, February 19, 1986, October 30, 1986) from the private collection of Zoe Caldwell Whitehead; names withheld.

46 David Kaufman, "What Became a Legend Most?" *Chronicles* (April 1986): 46.

47 Sarmento, "'Lillian' Is a Tour De force," 4.

48 Kaufman, "What Became a Legend Most?" 46.

49 Richard Dodds, "Hellman Wrote All the Rules for 'Lillian,'" *New Orleans Times Picayune* (February 21, 1997): L21.

50 Gregory Speck, "Lillian Hellman's Notoriety Well Reflected in Play," *New York City Tribune* (January 28, 1986): 5.

51 Frank Rich, "The Stage: Zoe Caldwell as Hellman in 'Lillian,'" *New York Times* (January 17, 1986): sec. C, 3.

52 Davies, "The Life and Lies of Lillian Hellman," 64.

53 Gordon Osmond, "A *Curtain Up* California Review: *Imaginary Friends*," http://curtainup.com/imaginaryfriends.com.

54 Ben Brantley, "Literary Lions, Claws Bared," *New York Times* (December 13, 2002).

55 Bernstein, "Critics Notebook."

56 Rollyson, "The Lives and Lies of Lillian Hellman," 5.

Bibliographical Guide

Archival Sources

The main source for this book has been the marvelous Lillian Hellman Collection at the Harry Ransom Center, University of Texas at Austin. The papers there are rich in manuscript materials and contain as well a plethora of records having to do with Hellman's business and financial interests, and some very good correspondence from Dashiell Hammett and to John Melby. To supplement these papers I have drawn extensively on a variety of other archival collections. The most important of these is the William M. Abrahams Collection in the Cecil Green Library at Stanford University. Hellman designated Abrahams, her friend and editor for many years, her official biographer. To fill this mandate, he collected a great deal of information that has now been made available to researchers. I made good use as well of additional collections, which in alphabetical order include the papers of:

William Alfred, Brooklyn College Archives and Special Collections

Leonard Bernstein, Library of Congress

Millen Brand, Columbia University Rare Book & Manuscript Library

Blair Clark, Seeley Mudd Library, Princeton University

Samuel Goldwyn, Margaret Herrick Library of the American Motion Picture Academy

Sidney Hook, Hoover Institution Archives

Arthur Kober, Wisconsin Historical Society, Madison, Wisconsin

Dwight MacDonald, Beinecke Library, Yale University

Mary McCarthy, Vassar College

Eve Merriam, Arthur and Elizabeth Schlesinger Library, Radcliffe College

Joseph Rauh, Library of Congress

Arthur Schlesinger, New York Public Library

Harlow Shapley, Houghton Library, Harvard University

Herman Shumlin, Wisconsin Historical Society, Madison, Wisconsin

Telford Taylor, Columbia University Rare Book & Manuscript Library

Arthur Thornhill, Seeley Mudd Library, Princeton University

Lionel Trilling, Columbia Rare Book and Manuscript Library

Additional papers include:

Counterattack Collection, Tamiment Library, New York University

House of Representatives, Committee on Un-American Activities (HUAC), Name Files, National Archives

Little, Brown papers, Widener Library, Harvard University

Harold Matson Papers, Columbia University Rare Book & Manuscript Library

Spanish Refugee Aid Collection, Tamiment Library, New York University

Veterans of the Abraham Lincoln Brigade, Tamiment Library, New York University

Interviews and Conversations

Hellman had an enormous number of friends and acquaintances. I benefited from speaking with a few, some at length and others more briefly. Crucial insights and information came from:

Robert Brustein

Zoe Caldwell-Whitehead

Annabel Davis-Goff

Morris and Lore Dickstein

Norman Dorsen

Peter Feibleman

Leon Friedman

Fred Gardner

Stephen Gillers

Bobbie Handman

Maureen Howard

Catherine (Shirah) Kober Zeller

Richard Locke

Peter London

Arien Mack

Victor Navasky

Patricia Neal

Wendy Nicholson

Austin Pendleton

Maurice Peress

Martin Peretz

Anne Peretz

Richard Poirier

Daniel Pollitt

Robert Silvers

Rose Styron

Susan Styron

Nancy Wechsler

The transcribed oral histories conducted over the years with Hellman's friends and acquaintances have supplied additional stores of memory. Among those I found most useful are those on deposit in the Columbia Center for Oral History, Columbia University Library:

Leonard Boudin

Donald Angus Cameron

Harold Clurman

Virginia Durr

Thomas Emerson

Albert Hackett

Helen Van dernoot Rosen

Michael Straight

Academy of Motion Picture Arts and Sciences, Margaret Herrick Library:
Phillip Dunne

Sam Jaffe

Regenstein Library, University of Chicago:
Richard Stern

New York Public Library, Berg Collection:
Joan Mellen tapes

General Bibliography

There is no shortage of commentaries on Lillian Hellman as a dramatist, a memoirist, a celebrity, and a litigious person. I've noted many of these in the endnotes that accompany each chapter. Here I focus on some of the sources that illuminate various phases of her life story and help us to understand how she participated in, and shaped, the twentieth century. What follows is not an attempt at a comprehensive list, but a few of the volumes that I found most helpful as I tried to unravel the many choices that Hellman made throughout her life.

On the question of writing the biography of a difficult woman, several volumes stirred my imagination. These included the essays in Sara Alpern et al., *The Challenge of Feminist Biography: Writing the Lives of Modern American Women* (Urbana, IL: University of Illinois Press, 1992); Catherine N. Parke, *Biography: Writing Lives* (New York: Routledge, 2002); and Teresa Iles, *All Sides of the Subject: Women and Biography* (New York: Teachers College Press, 1992). Linda Wagner-Martin, *Telling Women's Lives: The New Biography* (New Brunswick, NJ: Rutgers University Press, 1994), remains among the most stimulating of such sources. Timothy Dow Adams, *Telling Lies in Modern American Autobiography* (Chapel Hill: University of North Carolina Press, 1990) provoked much thought into the question of whether lying is inevitably part of the presentation of self. Alan Ackerman, *Just Words: Lillian Hellman, Mary McCarthy, and the Failure of Public Conversation in America* (New Haven, CT: Yale University Press, 2011) came out while this book was in press, but its thoughtful analysis of Hellman's language sheds light on the culture that nurtured her.

The best way into Hellman's life is through her own work. *The Collected Plays* (Boston: Little, Brown, 1972) provides an essential beginning point and a view of thirty years of her dramatic imagination. Three memoirs: *An Unfinished Woman: A Memoir* (Boston: Little, Brown, 1969), *Pentimento* (Boston: Little, Brown, 1973), and *Scoundrel Time* (Boston: Little, Brown, 1976) elucidate Hellman's sense of herself and her stance toward the world she lived in. *Maybe: A Story* (Boston: Little, Brown, 1980) offers a sometimes painful view from the end of her life. And some of Hellman's unique perspectives can be garnered from the extraordinary collection of interviews assembled by Jackson Bryer in *Conversations with Lillian Hellman* (Jackson, MS: University Press of Mississippi, 1986).

Hellman's life has been examined by many people, but by far the most valuable single source is Peter S. Feibleman. *Lilly: Reminiscences of Lillian Hellman* (New York: Morrow, 1988) presents a not uncritical but loving assessment of a forty-five-year relationship. Of the several biographies, the most informative are those by Carl E. Rollyson, *Lillian Hellman: Her Legend and Her Legacy* (New York: St. Martin's Press, 1988) and Deborah Martinson, *Lillian Hellman: Life with Foxes and Scoundrels* (New York: Counterpoint, 2005). The former provides a comprehensive account of her daily life and a stern view of the political Lillian; Martinson provides a more empathetic perspective. On the major relationships in Hellman's life, see Richard Layman, *Shadow Man: The Life of Dashiell Hammett* (New York: Harcourt Brace Jovanovich, 1981); Diane Johnson, *Hammett: A Life* (New York: Random House, 1983); and Robert P. Newman, *The Cold War Romance of Lillian Hellman and John Melby* (Chapel Hill: University of North Carolina Press, 1989).

I gained insight into Hellman's identification as a southerner and thought about the impact of her New Orleans Jewish childhood after reading the classic W. J. Cash, *The Mind of the South* (New York: Vintage, 1991). To find out more about growing up as a white woman in the South I turned to Anne Firor Scott, *The Southern Lady: From Pedestal to Politics, 1830–1930* (Chicago: University of Chicago Press, 1972), and to Susan K. Cahn, *Sexual Reckonings: Southern Girls in a Troubling Age* (Cambridge, MA: Harvard University Press, 2007). For a sense of Jewish life in the extended South, I drew on Eli N. Evans, *The Provincials: A Personal History of Jews in the South* (New York: Atheneum, 1980), and Ronald Lawrence Bern, *The Legacy: A Novel* (New York: Mason/Charter, 1975). Several essays in Leonard Dinnerstein and Mary Dale Palsson, eds., *Jews in the South* (Baton Rouge: Louisiana State University Press, 1973) proved useful as well.

Hellman's Jewish identity and her relationship to the Jewish community formed a continuing piece of her struggle with the American left. On issues of cultural connections see David A. Hollinger, *Cosmopolitanism and Solidarity: Studies in Ethnoracial, Religious, and Professional Affiliation in the United States*, Studies in American Thought and Culture (Madison, WI: University of Wisconsin Press, 2006) and Judith E. Smith, *Visions of Belonging: Family Stories, Popular Culture, and Postwar Democracy, 1940–1960* (New York: Columbia University Press, 2004). For the specifically contentious relationships of Jews to each other, see Stephen J. Whitfield, *In Search of American Jewish Culture* (Hanover, NH: Brandeis University Press/University Press of New England, 1999). On Hellman's relationship to the Anne Frank case, it is worth beginning with the accusations made by Meyer Levin, *The Obsession* (New York: Simon and Schuster, 1973). A more measured account of Levin's obsession can be found in Lawrence Graver, *An Obsession with Anne Frank: Meyer Levin and the Diary* (Berkeley: University of California Press, 1990). Hellman was roundly condemned for failing to acknowledge Stalin's persecution of Jews. This issue is illuminated by Joshua Rubenstein and

Vladimir P. Naumov, eds., *Stalin's Secret Pogrom: The Postwar Inquisition of the Jewish Anti-Fascist Committee* (New Haven, CT: Yale University Press, 2001).

The culture that Hellman entered in the early twentieth century and the 1930s, especially as it relates to women, is explored in Christine Stansell, *American Moderns: Bohemian New York and the Creation of a New Century* (New York: Metropolitan Books, 2000). The world of literary culture is the subject of Ann Douglas, *Terrible Honesty: Mongrel Manhattan in the 1920s* (New York: Farrar, Straus and Giroux, 1995). Morris Dickstein, *Dancing in the Dark: A Cultural History of the Great Depression* (New York: Norton, 2009) is the essential source on the impact of the depression on 1930s popular and highbrow culture. For the relationship of popular culture to the labor movement see Michael Denning, *The Cultural Front: The Laboring of American Culture in the Twentieth Century* (London: Verso, 1996). For the rise of the Screenwriters' Guild see Nancy Lynn Schwartz and Sheila Schwartz, *The Hollywood Writers' Wars* (New York: Knopf, 1982). Larry Ceplair, *The Inquisition in Hollywood: Politics in the Film Community, 1930–1960* (Garden City, NY: Doubleday Anchor Books, 1980) carries the story into the 1950s. Dan Georgakas and Lenny Rubenstein, *The Cineaste Interviews: On the Art and Politics of the Cinema* (Chicago: Lake View Press, 1983) provides a fount of insider information.

Personal accounts of the years from the 1930s into the postwar period are numerous, as are biographies of some of the participants in the causes that Hellman cared about. Illuminating and helpful recollections that touch on Hellman's experiences include Edmund Wilson and Leon Edel, *The Thirties: From Notebooks and Diaries of the Period* (New York: Farrar, Straus and Giroux, 1980). Among the biographies, Marion Meade, *Lonelyhearts: The Screwball World of Nathanael West and Eileen McKenney* (Boston: Houghton Mifflin, 2010) and A. Scott Berg, *Goldwyn: A Biography* (New York: Knopf, 1989) are most useful for the 1930s. Other biographies in which Hellman makes more than a casual appearance include Martin B. Duberman, *Paul Robeson* (New York: Knopf, 1988); Dorothy Herrman, *S. J. Perelman: A Life* (New York: Simon and Schuster, 1986); and Marion Meade, *Dorothy Parker: What Fresh Hell Is This?* (New York: Penguin Books, 1987). Hellman also enters into the stories told by Elia Kazan, *Elia Kazan: A Life* (New York: Knopf, 1988), and Arthur Miller, *Timebends: A Life* (New York: Grove Press, 1987).

The most useful assessment of Hellman's life in the theater and in the world of entertainment is still Jacob H. Adler, *Lillian Hellman* (Austin, TX: Steck-Vaughn Company, 1969), though it is worth examining as well Richard Moody, *Lillian Hellman, Playwright* (Indianapolis: Bobbs-Merrill Co., 1972). More general assessments of Hellman as a playwright in context can be found in Joseph Wood Krutch, *The American Drama Since 1918* (New York: George Braziller, 1957) and John Gassner, *The Theatre in Our Times: A Survey of the Men, Materials and Movements in the Modern Theatre* (New York: Crown, 1954).

Hellman spent much of her political life on the fringes of New York's powerful intellectual culture. On this subject there are many good volumes in which Hellman scarcely appears but which illuminate the world that she confronted on a daily basis. Readers might want to begin with Richard H. Pells, *The Liberal Mind in a Conservative Age: American Intellectuals in the 1940s and 1950s* (New York: Harper & Row, 1985) and then move to Terry A. Cooney, *The Rise of the New York Intellectuals: Partisan Review and Its Circle, 1934–45* (Madison, WI: University of Wisconsin Press, 1986); Alexander Bloom, *Prodigal Sons: The New York Intellectuals and Their World* (New York: Oxford University Press, 1986); Alan M. Wald, *The New York Intellectuals: The Rise and Decline of the Anti-Stalinist Left from the 1930s to the 1980s* (Chapel Hill: University of North Carolina Press, 1987); and Neil Jumonville, *Critical Crossings: The New York Intellectuals in Postwar America* (Berkeley: University of California Press, 1991). Several memoirs come from individuals who crossed swords with Hellman over political issues. They include Irving Howe, *A Margin of Hope: An Intellectual Autobiography* (New York: Harcourt Brace Jovanovich, 1982), and William Phillips, *A Partisan View: Five Decades of the Literary Life* (New York: Stein and Day, 1983). Michael Wreszin, *A Rebel in Defense of Tradition: The Life and Politics of Dwight MacDonald* (New York: Basic Books, 1994), is a masterful account of one individual who intersected with Hellman's life from the late 1930s until her death.

The spirit of American communists and the divided attitudes toward Joseph Stalin make painful reading. A contemporary view of the communist threat in the 1930s can be found in Eugene Lyons, *The Red Decade* (New York: Arlington House, 1941). William O'Neill, *A Better World: The Great Schism: Stalinism and the American Intellectuals* (New York: Simon and Schuster, 1982) provides a more measured sense of the meaning of Stalinism to communist partisans, and Joseph Starobin, *American Communism in Crisis, 1943–1957* (Berkeley: University of California Press, 1972) suggests some of the internal struggles of the CPUSA. Maurice Isserman, *If I Had a Hammer: The Death of the Old Left and the Birth of the New Left* (New York: Basic Books, 1987) explores the transition from the old left to the new. European perspectives on the political struggle can be found in Michael Scammell, *Koestler: The Literary and Political Odyssey of a Twentieth-Century Skeptic* (New York: Random House, 2009) and Jonathan Miles, *The Dangerous Otto Katz: The Many Lives of a Soviet Spy* (New York: Bloomsbury, 2009). Katz's life overlapped with Hellman's in intriguing ways.

The McCarthyism of the late forties and early fifties is well captured by three books: David Caute, *The Great Fear: The Anti-Communist Purge under Truman and Eisenhower* (New York: Simon and Schuster, 1979); Stanley Kutler, *The American Inquisition: Justice and Injustice in the Cold War* (New York: Hill and Wang, 1982); and David Oshinsky, *A Conspiracy So Immense: The World of Joe McCarthy* (New York: Free Press, 1983). For the evolution of HUAC, see Walter Goodman, *The Committee: The Extraordinary Career of the House*

Committee on Un-American Activities (New York: Farrar, Straus and Giroux, 1968). Stefan Kanfer, *A Journal of the Plague Years* (New York: Atheneum, 1973) provides a sense of the tangled web in which Hellman was caught and Victor Navasky, *Naming Names* (New York: Viking Books, 1980) suggests the price of conscience. Some of the most remarkable accounts of those years come from memoirs. See especially Ring Lardner, *I'd Hate Myself in the Morning: A Memoir* (New York: Nation Books, 2000); Dalton Trumbo, *The Time of the Toad: A Study of Inquisition in America by One of the Hollywood Ten* (New York: Harper and Row, 1972); and the revelatory discussion by Bud Schultz and Ruth Schultz, *It Did Happen Here: Recollections of Political Repression in America* (Berkeley: University of California Press, 1989).

For the impact of the Cold War on families during the McCarthy period, Elaine Tyler May, *Homeward Bound: American Families in the Cold War Era* (New York: Basic Books, 1988) provides a great introduction. Carl Bernstein, *Loyalties: A Son's Memoir* (New York: Simon and Schuster, 1989), is a moving account of the long-lasting effects of the Cold War mentality. Lary May, ed., *Recasting America: Culture and Politics in the Age of Cold War* (Chicago: University of Chicago Press, 1989) suggests some of the permanent change that resulted from McCarthyism.

Culture and politics in the sixties fuse with one another as they did in Hellman's experience. Edmund Wilson, *The Sixties*, ed. Lewis M. Dabney (New York: Farrar, Straus and Giroux, 1990) provides some sense of the tension implicit in this experience. Morris Dickstein, *Gates of Eden: American Culture in the Sixties* (New York: Basic Books, 1977) suggests the changes in popular and highbrow culture that resulted. Norman Podhoretz, *Making It* (New York: Random House, 1967) characterizes some of the opportunities the decade provided. The relationship between cultural tensions and politics is well captured in Maurice Isserman and Michael Kazin, *America Divided: The Civil War of the 1960s*, 2nd ed. (New York: Oxford University Press, 2004). There is a huge and exciting literature on race relations in the 1960s, but for a glimpse of how the Cold War impacted on activists like Hellman, see Martin Bauml Duberman, *Paul Robeson* (New York: Knopf, 1988). Thomas Borstelman, *The Cold War and the Color Line: American Race Relations in the Global Arena* (Cambridge, MA: Harvard University Press, 2001) provides a broad overview. For the student movement in the same period, James Miller, *Democracy Is in the Streets: From Port Huron to the Siege of Chicago* (New York: Simon and Schuster, 1987) is a good start.

By the 1970s, politics had begun to take a new form. David Harvey, *A Brief History of Neoliberalism* (New York: Oxford University Press, 2005) is perhaps the best summary of the ideas that began to take shape and David Greenberg's *Nixon's Shadow* (New York: Norton, 2003) an intriguing look at the political consequences that haunted Hellman in the 1970s. The impact of deindustrialization is evident in Judith Stein, *Pivotal Decade: How the United States Traded Factories for Finance in the Seventies* (New Haven, CT: Yale

University Press, 2010) as it is in Jefferson Cowie, *Stayin' Alive: The 1970s and the Last Days of the Working Class* (New York: New Press, 2010). Natasha Zaretsky, *No Direction Home: The American Family and the Fear of National Decline, 1968–1980* (Chapel Hill: University of North Carolina Press, 2007) offers an incisive interpretation of the spirit of the times as it affected personal life.

Lillian Hellman, caught up in accusations of lying and Stalinism during her last years, faced the venom of opponents. It would be remiss to avoid mentioning some of the literature in which she was attacked implicitly and explicitly, and yet such a list would be lengthy. Good beginnings can be made by perusing Sidney Hook, *Out of Step: An Unquiet Life in the 20th Century* (New York: Harper and Row, 1987); Alfred Kazin, *New York Jew* (New York: Knopf, 1978); Diana Trilling, *We Must March, My Darlings: A Critical Decade* (New York: Harcourt Brace Jovanovich, 1978); Norman Podhoretz, *Ex-Friends: Falling Out with Allen Ginsberg, Lionel and Diana Trilling, Lillian Hellman, Hannah Arendt, and Norman Mailer* (New York, NY: Free Press, 1999); and Muriel Gardiner, *Code Name "Mary": Memoirs of an American Woman in the Austrian Underground* (New Haven, CT: Yale University Press, 1983).

Index

A Note on the Author

Alice Kessler-Harris is the R. Gordon Hoxie Professor of American History at Columbia University. She is one of America's most renowned scholars, known for her work on labor and gender history. She is the author of the classic history of working women *Out to Work*. Her *In Pursuit of Equity: Women, Men, and the Quest for Economic Citizenship in Twentieth-Century America* won the Joan Kelly, Philip Taft, Herbert Hoover, and Bancroft prizes. In 2011–2012, she served as president of the Organization of American Historians.